Perceptual Modification

ADAPTING TO ALTERED
SENSORY ENVIRONMENTS

**ACADEMIC PRESS
SERIES IN COGNITION AND PERCEPTION**

SERIES EDITORS:
**Edward C. Carterette
Morton P. Friedman**
*Department of Psychology
University of California, Los Angeles
Los Angeles, California*

Stephen K. Reed: *Psychological Processes in Pattern Recognition*

Earl B. Hunt: *Artificial Intelligence*

James P. Egan: *Signal Detection Theory and ROC Analysis*

Martin F. Kaplan and Steven Schwartz (Eds.): *Human Judgment and Decision Processes*

Myron L. Braunstein: *Depth Perception Through Motion*

R. Plomp: *Aspects of Tone Sensation*

Martin F. Kaplan and Steven Schwartz (Eds.): *Human Judgment and Decision Processes in Applied Settings*

Bikkar S. Randhawa and William E. Coffman: *Visual Learning, Thinking, and Communication*

Robert B. Welch: *Perceptual Modification: Adapting to Altered Sensory Environments*

IN PREPARATION

Lawrence E. Marks: *The Unity of the Senses*

Perceptual Modification

ADAPTING TO ALTERED SENSORY ENVIRONMENTS

Robert B. Welch
Department of Psychology
University of Kansas
Lawrence, Kansas

ACADEMIC PRESS   New York   San Francisco   London   1978
A Subsidiary of Harcourt Brace Jovanovich, Publishers

ACADEMIC PRESS, INC.
111 Fifth Avenue, New York, New York 10003

United Kingdom Edition published by
ACADEMIC PRESS, INC. (LONDON) LTD.
24/28 Oval Road, London NW1 7DX

Library of Congress Cataloging in Publication Data

Welch, Robert B   Date
    Perceptual modification.

    (Series in cognition and perception)
    Bibliography: p.
    Includes indexes.
    1. Perception. 2. Perceptual motor learning.
3. Optical illusions. I. Title.
BF311.W42   153.7'4   78–6475
ISBN 0–12–741850–4

To Renate

Contents

Contents

Preface

This is a book about the study of human perception using a particular research strategy: the systematic alteration of vision or audition. It is assumed that by observing how the sensory apparatus copes with this disturbance it will be possible to formulate valuable hypotheses about the structure and development of "normal" perception and perceptual–motor coordination.

The specific goals of this book are, first, to organize the vast and confusing literature on adaptation to perceptual rearrangement and, second, to assess its contribution to our understanding of "normal" perception and perceptual learning.

The organization is described at the end of the introductory chapter. In brief, I have begun by discussing the research on prismatic displacement—the most popular form of visual rearrangement—and then dealt with each of the various other distortions investigators have used. I have also included a chapter on a relatively new area—adaptation to the optical distortions that confront the underwater diver. Even though I have discussed, or at least cited, in these chapters a large number of studies, there have inevitably been a few omissions. Some of these were, of course, inadvertent, while others were due simply to an inability to find an appropriate place to mention the studies in question or to the fact that they appeared too late to be included. The final chapter deals specifically with the contribution of this area to our understanding of human perception, perceptual learning, and perceptual–motor capacity. A portion of this chapter is devoted to my formulation of a general model of adaptation. My hope is that this model summarizes the essence of adaptation to all of the various forms of sensory distortion to which human subjects have been exposed.

The book is written for researchers and graduate students in experimental psychology. I trust it will be of value and interest whether the reader is a specialist in the area of perceptual modification, or indeed a generalist.

ACKNOWLEDGMENTS

A great many people have contributed, directly or indirectly, to this book. First, I am most grateful to David H. and Lynda W. Warren for their kind hospitality to my family and me during my sabbatical year (1974–1975) in the Department of Psychology at the University of California, Riverside, where the book got its start. I must also thank Ivo Kohler, whose presence at the University of Kansas in Fall, 1973 ultimately inspired this work. A number of individuals read and criticized preliminary drafts of selected chapters. I wish to thank for this service Malcolm M. Cohen, Sheldon M. Ebenholtz, Charles R. Hamilton, Charles S. Harris, Ian P. Howard, Jo Ann S. Kinney, James R. Lackner, Harutune H. Mikaelian, Bruce B. Platt, Gordon M. Redding, Irvin Rock, Helen E. Ross, Wayne L. Shebilske, Chong Choe Suh, Edward Taub, John J. Uhlarik, Benjamin Wallace, and David H. Warren. I would like to single out for special recognition Sheldon M. Ebenholtz, Charles S. Harris, and Irvin Rock, not only for reading significant portions of the preliminary manuscript but also for their extensive discussions with me. I wish also to thank some of my colleagues at the University of Kansas: Margaret Schadler and Edward L. Wike for their suggestions about wording in several sections of the book and James F. Juola for assistance in devising the flow diagram used to depict my proposed model of adaptation. Many of my ideas have come from or been stimulated by my students, both undergraduate and graduate, particularly Merilyn R. Abel, Robert J. Bermant, Richard J. Bleam, Janice Harrington, Daniel R. Heinrich, Maria E. Motta, Michael Nardie, Sherry A. Needham, Katherine Poindexter, Robert W. Rhoades, Thomas Sawin, Carolyn H. Shelly, Chong Choe Suh, Sally E. Wells, and Mel H. Widawski.

I am indebted to the National Eye Institute and the Biomedical Sciences Support Grant Subcommittee (through the University of

Kansas) for grants that supported the published and unpublished research of mine described in this book. Numerous grants from the University of Kansas General Research Fund have also supported these efforts. The University of Kansas was also responsible for my sabbatical leave of absence in 1974–1975, during which the major organization of this book was accomplished, and for financial aid for some of the book's preparation costs. For all of this assistance from my university, I am most grateful.

Typing of the book and its many drafts was done by Terry Bair, Susan Brewer, and Joyce Yocum. The figures were drawn by Kathe Koch and inked by Susan Waldorf. I am most appreciative of the professional care with which these people carried out these all-important tasks.

One must possess certain personality characteristics if he is to accomplish an undertaking of the present sort. For these qualities—a capacity for hard work, a perfectionistic nature, and a lot of compulsivity—I thank my father and mother, Ronald B. and Margaret H. Welch. Finally, I wish to express my heart-felt gratitude to my wife, Renate, soon to be a psychologist herself, for her editorial assistance and, most of all, her moral support in this endeavor. To her I dedicate this book.

Perceptual Modification

ADAPTING TO ALTERED
SENSORY ENVIRONMENTS

1

Introduction

It is a fact of life that we often learn how something works only when it fails. For example, many people's understanding of their automobile is based *entirely* on this principle. Science, including psychology, is replete with discoveries that occurred because the normal state of affairs had gone awry. The field of geology, for instance, has been advanced significantly by the incidence of unusual and disruptive events such as volcanoes and severe earthquakes. In psychology, it is the study of perception that has probably benefited most from this principle. Like a perfectly running automobile, human perception is both taken for granted and poorly understood; it has often required a severe malfunction or obstruction of its performance to reveal its workings. Anomalies such as color blindness and congenital cataracts, for example, have taught us things not likely to have emerged from the study of "normal" perception. Of course, natural events of this sort occur infrequently. For the most part, everyday perception is fully developed, very accurate, and served by a redundancy of cues. Consequently, in order to increase our understanding of this capacity it has become a common strategy to interfere with its operation. The aim of this book is to examine one variety of this procedure.

The physiologist Weiss (1941) was the first to distinguish among three classes of "interference experiment" and, although this distinction was made in the context of investigating the nervous system, it is equally applicable to perceptual research. These three classes were

1

termed by Weiss the *defect, isolation,* and *recombination* experiments. In the defect experiment a given component is removed or otherwise incapacitated and the effect of this operation upon the behavior of the system is observed. Any change is usually assumed to reflect the properties and functions of the part that was tampered with. An example of this method as used to investigate perception would be the elmination of one of the many potential depth cues present in a normal visual environment. For instance, it might be demonstrated that by excluding the cue of "interposition" (i.e., one object obstructing the view of another) accuracy of depth perception is significantly impaired. Such a result would suggest that under normal circumstances interposition is an important cue for the perception of depth.

In the isolation experiment all of the components of a system are made inoperative, save one. Thus, it is the complement of the defect experiment. The resulting behavior is assumed to indicate the role normally played by this isolated part. An example, again with reference to visual depth perception, would be an experiment in which the observer is forced to make depth judgments when provided with only one of the normally occurring cues. Epstein (1963), for example, eliminated all cues but that of familiar size (he used mounted photographs of a dime, quarter, and half-dollar) and found that this cue sufficed to produce reasonably accurate depth judgments.

As Weiss noted, the defect and isolation experiments have certain disadvantages. The most important of these is that the validity of both techniques rests upon the assumption that an individual part operates in the same fashion in isolation as it does when united with the rest of the system. This assumption is probably incorrect in many instances. With visual depth perception, for example, it is likely that even if under normal circumstances a particular cue (e.g., interposition) is heavily "weighted," its elimination would not lead to a large decrement in accuracy or precision of depth estimates. Rather, the remaining cues will probably "take up the slack." Conversely, even if a potential cue for depth perception is ignored when it is one of many redundant cues, it might prove quite effective if it is the only one available. Thus, in each case the investigator will draw an incorrect conclusion about the role normally played by the individual facet of the system.

It was because both the defect and isolation experiments involved the functional elimination of either one part or all but one part of the system that Weiss urged investigators to consider the merits of the third type of experiment—the recombination procedure. In this case, the system is left intact, while the normal *relationship* among the parts is altered. An example from the type of research with which Weiss was concerned is a study by Sperry (1947b), in which the efferent connections to the extensor and flexor muscles of the limbs of monkeys were reversed. The question here was whether the animal would be capable of overcoming its initial drastic errors in limb movement. The answer was that monkeys eventually compensated quite well to this disruption. In the study of human perception, Wallach, Moore, and Davidson (1963) implemented a recombination experiment in which subjects wore a "telestereoscope," which by means of mirrors functionally increases the distance between the eyes, resulting in altered retinal disparity, one of the cues for visual depth perception. Subjects were required to observe a rotating three-dimensional wire form while wearing this device. The changing retinal projection from a rotating solid object is known as the "kinetic depth effect" (KDE) and, like retinal disparity, it represents a cue for the visual appearance of solidity. Thus, the telestereoscope induced a conflict between retinal disparity and the KDE. The initial experience was one of a form whose third dimension appeared longer than it actually was. The investigators were interested in whether or not this discrepancy would ever be resolved perceptually and, if so, in favor of which of the conflicting cues. It is reasonable to argue, as these investigators did, that the cue which "dominates" in a situation of intersensory discordance is the one which is the more heavily "weighted" during everyday perception. Wallach et al. (1963b) found that after a relatively short period of exposure to the conflict the distortion in apparent depth was partially overcome. This result indicates that the retinal disparity cue had become recalibrated in the direction of conformance with the KDE, suggesting that under normal circumstances the latter is the more powerful depth cue.

The great advantage of the recombination procedure is that it leaves the perceptual system intact, albeit rearranged in some manner. Therefore, rather than potentially leading to a *deficit* in behavior, it produces a *malfunction,* the response to which is likely to provide important clues about the normal operation of the system. Weiss argued that investigators ought to make greater use of the recombination procedure for questions that might be amenable to this line of attack. It would seem that perceptual psychologists have heeded his suggestion. In the last two decades, a wide variety of perceptual capacities have been examined by means of the recombination procedure, although investigators, with a few exceptions (e.g., Taub,

1968), have failed to acknowledge Weiss's early recognition of its advantages. The result has been the accumulation of a vast body of data, shedding light on the perceptual and perceptual–motor abilities involved as well as on their capacity for modification. The type of recombination procedure most often used by the perceptual psychologist involves placing before the observer a device that displaces, transposes, or otherwise alters visual or auditory space and then noting his perceptual or perceptual–motor response to this confrontation. If the subject demonstrates a persistent change in perception or perceptual–motor behavior that serves to reduce the sensory discordance, it may be said that he has *adapted*. It is specifically this type of recombination experiment to which the present book is devoted.

The earliest experiments on adaptation to perceptual rearrangement reveal the basic paradigm used in this research area as well as some of the questions it was hoped would be answered.

THE EARLY EXPERIMENTS

Helmholtz (1925) was apparently the first to record the behavioral response of an observer actively exposed to perceptual rearrangement.[1] In this "experiment" a wedge prism was placed before each eye, causing the visual field to be displaced laterally by about 17°. This device and some of its optical effects are depicted in Figure 1.1. Naturally, when the subject first attempted to reach quickly for objects he erred significantly in the direction of the displacement. With further practice, however, these initial errors were overcome. Even more interesting was the fact that, upon removing the prisms, reaching errors again occurred, but this time they were to the side opposite the direction of the prismatic displacement. In short, error-corrective behavior continued even when it was no longer appropriate. Thus, the subject had become adapted to the visual rearrangement, as seen in both the elimination of his pointing errors during exposure to the prism and his subsequent visuomotor "negative aftereffect."

The classic and most often cited study of adaptation to visual rearrangement was performed by Stratton (1896, 1897a,b), who served as his own subject in two long-term studies in which he wore a device

[1] As Rock (1966, p. 111) pointed out, this observation has, on occasion, been attributed incorrectly to Czermak (1855).

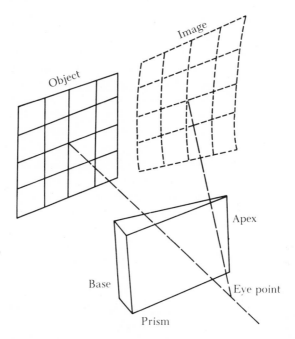

Figure 1.1. A wedge prism and its optical properties. (After K. N. Ogle, *Optics: An Introduction for Opthalmologists,* 2nd ed., 1968. Courtesy of Charles C Thomas, Publisher, Springfield, Illinois.)

that rotated the visual field by 180°. His concern was the old philosophical question of why it is that the world does not appear upside down despite the fact that the retinal image is inverted. Several then-current theories about this apparent anomaly held that upright spatial vision actually *requires* an inverted retinal image. Stratton felt that if while wearing his inverting goggles he eventually came to see the world as upright again, he would thereby have disconfirmed these theories.

In the longer of the two studies, Stratton wore the monocular inverting goggles for 8 days, blindfolding himself immediately after removing the device at night before going to bed. Upon first donning the goggles his experience was of a drastic disturbance in visuomotor coordination, nauseating illusory motion of the visual field when he moved his head, and an inverted picture of the world. However, after several days of more-or-less normal activities, both the visuomotor disturbance and the apparent field motion had disappeared. Unfortunately, the crucial question of whether or not the optically inverted world could ever come to look right side up again was never satisfactorily answered. In brief, Stratton reported that during the latter stages of the experiment the visual field occasionally appeared upright, but primarily when he was engrossed in some activity or otherwise not critically comparing his visual experience to his memory of the preexperimental appearance of things. After removing the goggles at the end of the exposure period Stratton underwent negative aftereffects in visuomotor coordination and in the "swinging of the scene" with head movements. However, the visual field was experienced in its normal upright orientation. Several investigators (Ewert, 1930; Kohler, 1964; Peterson & Peterson, 1938; Snyder & Pronko, 1952) attempted to replicate Stratton's classic observations, with varying success. The details of these and other studies of adaptation to inverted and mirror-reversed vision are presented in Chapter 5.

THE EXPERIMENTAL PARADIGM

Research on adaptation to perceptual rearrangement has relied on one experimental paradigm. In its basic form it entails (a) a preexposure measure of perception or perceptual–motor performance; (b) a period of exposure to the rearrangement; and (c) a postexposure measure. A compensatory shift in perception or perceptual–motor coordination over the course of the experiment is considered evidence of adaptation. The pre- and postexposure measures are usually taken in the absence of feedback to the subject regarding his accuracy. During the exposure period the subject is confronted with the effects of the distorting device, typically by means of visuomotor behavior, such as moving the head, reaching for objects, or actively moving about in the environment. In some studies compensation for the distortion is assessed periodically during this exposure period, while in others it is not measured until afterward. In either case, however, adaptation is seen in the difference between the pre- and postexposure measures. If the two tests occur while the device is being worn (but with visual feedback precluded), the shift may be referred to as the *reduction of effect*, since it serves to reduce the error initially produced by the optical device. A perceptual or perceptual–motor shift measured after the device has been removed is termed the *negative aftereffect*, since it represents an error in the direction opposite that of the distortion. The distinction between these two indexes of adaptation may be clarified by an examination of Figure 1.2. It will be argued subsequently that the negative aftereffect

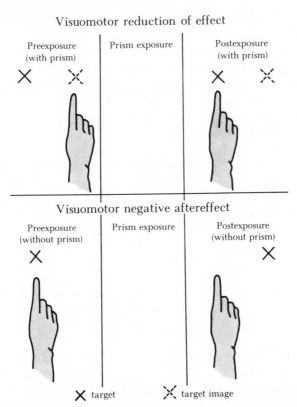

Figure 1.2. A schematic representation of the distinction between the visuomotor reduction of effect and the negative aftereffect, as manifested in target-pointing accuracy with and without rightward prismatic displacement.

is often a more convincing form of evidence for perceptual–motor adaptation than is the reduction of effect.

It is of great theoretical importance to differentiate between perceptual adaptation and perceptual–motor adaptation. As Stratton's experiment clearly demonstrated, the presence of visuomotor adaptation does not necessarily indicate that visual adaptation has occurred. Though Stratton was able to overcome completely and consistently his visuomotor errors (and revealed a subsequent visuomotor negative aftereffect), he rarely if ever saw the world as right side up. On the other hand, it is not conceivable that a change in vision could exist in the absence of a change in visuomotor behavior since the former is automatically reflected in the latter.

It may be argued that the acquisition of accurate reaching and locomotory behavior *during* exposure to rearrangement (i.e., the reduction of effect) should not be considered trustworthy evidence that the
field has come to appear normal. There are two reasons for this conclusion. First, it is quite possible for a subject to deliberately compensate for the distortion by means of a conscious strategy. It is for
this reason that many investigators have argued that the proof of
adaptation is the presence of a negative aftereffect, since a conscious
correction would not be expected to continue if it is apparent to the
subject that the rearranging device has been removed. Second, even if
visuomotor behavior becomes adapted, such an effect might be based
not on a change in apparent visual location but on the acquisition of a
corrective eye–hand response that has become "automatic" or on the
recalibration of the felt position of the limb. These two possibilities
are examined in Chapter 3.

THE DEFINITION OF ADAPTATION
TO PERCEPTUAL REARRANGEMENT

Before continuing, it is important to define clearly the term *adaptation* as it will be used in this book, since this word has come to be
applied to a wide variety of perceptual and other phenomena.
Adaptation can be used either as a verb, to indicate a *process*, or as a
noun, referring to the *end state* to which the process leads. Typically,
the context makes it clear which of these is the referent. For now it
will be sufficient to provide the definition of adaptation as it applies to
the end state. It is proposed here that adaptation to perceptual rearrangement be defined as a *semipermanent change of perception or
perceptual–motor coordination that serves to reduce or eliminate a
registered discrepancy between or within sensory modalities or the
errors in behavior induced by this discrepancy.* Note that this definition specifies neither the necessary or sufficient conditions for
producing adaptation nor its *locus.* As will become apparent in subsequent chapters, a number of rather different conditions of exposure
have proven capable of inducing adaptation and in a variety of forms.

An important aspect of the present definition is the term *semipermanent.* It is used to indicate that "true" adaptation to perceptual rearrangement represents a change that *persists* for some
period of time after the termination of the exposure period. Clearly,
adaptation implies a change in perception or perceptual–motor
behavior that has become automatic, unthinking, or assimilated into

the observer's perceptual or behavioral repertoire. Consequently, the change should last for a while in the absence of any further exposure to the perceptual rearrangement and resulting feedback. Of course, it can be argued that an adaptive change could occur during exposure, yet fail to appear in the postexposure test measures, as a result of extremely rapid spontaneous decay or the change in stimulus conditions. While this is certainly possible, it is advisable to adhere to the present, more conservative, definition, since the requirement that the change be persistent helps to rule out deliberate corrective strategies that the subject may acquire during the exposure period. In fact, when the measure of adaptation involves eye–hand coordination, it may be argued that the negative aftereffect is a more convincing index of adaptation than is the reduction of effect, since the former is taken without the distorting device present and therefore is less likely to be confounded with such a strategy. With *perceptual* measures of adaptation, such as a shift in the apparent location of a visual target, it is less important whether or not the distorting device is present during the postexposure tests. That is, even when the subject knows that his perception contines to be rearranged, it is not possible for him to deliberately perceive differently than he does at the time and it is unlikely that he would respond as if his perception were becoming normal once again when it is not, since this would represent a blatant disregard of the experimenter's instructions.

The phrase *registered discrepancy* may need some clarification. Clearly, the *sensory* discrepancy, such as exists between vision and proprioception when one looks at the hand through displacing prisms, will remain as long as the rearranging device is worn. However, if the discrepancy, *as registered at some central locus*, is lessened after a period of exposure, and this resolution persists, perceptual adaptation may be said to have occurred. This is not to say that the observer will necessarily be aware of the initially registered discrepancy. In one type of exposure condition commonly used in studies of adaptation to prismatic displacement the subject merely swings his arm from side to side in front of his eyes (e.g., Held & Gottlieb, 1958) and it is rarely the case that he is able to verbalize the presence of the visual–proprioceptive discordance. However, it is likely that while awareness of the discrepancy is not necessary for adaptation, its presence will affect the level achieved. It is important to observe that the present definition does not specify the *direction* in which the intersensory discordance is resolved; that is, regardless of whether exposure to visual rearrangement induces a shift of vision to an alignment with the felt position of the hand or vice versa, adaptation, according to the present definition, may be said to have occurred, even though in the latter case the result is nonveridical. In fact, as will be seen in Chapter 3, it is the initially accurate body position sense that is most often the modality to be altered as a result of exposure to visual rearrangement.

LATER STUDIES

A variety of perceptual rearrangements were examined in the experiments that followed Stratton's pioneering efforts. Besides inversion, these included optically induced tilt and curvature, visual depth distortion, right/left reversal and lateral displacement of auditory space by means of "pseudophones," prismatic displacement, and, with lower organisms, the anatomical rearrangement of eyes or head. Much of this "older" literature was reviewed by Smith and Smith (1962, Chapters 4 and 5). In brief, this research has provided overwhelming evidence that adult human subjects are capable of adapting their perceptual–motor coordination quite well to almost any conceivable form of stable rearrangement. However, the evidence for adaptive changes in vision, in terms of the egocentric significance of retinal loci, is relatively sparse or equivocal. Only with minor distortions such as optically induced curvature or tilt is it clear that visual adaptation of this sort can occur, and such adaptation is typically far less than complete.

In the last two decades the number of studies on adaptation to perceptual rearrangement has increased remarkably.[2] There are two sources of this rekindled interest: (a) the publication in English of the extensive program of research undertaken at the University of Innsbruck by Erismann (1947) and Kohler (1955, 1962, 1964) and (b) the research and theorizing of Richard Held (e.g., 1961). While the Innsbruck studies involved a wide variety of visual distortions, including inversion, Held and his colleagues typically used small prism-induced lateral displacements of the visual field, in the tradition of Helmholtz's experiment. Other investigators have followed suit, making prismatic displacement the most commonly investigated form of perceptual rearrangement. There are several reasons for its popularity. Probably most

[2] Reviews of some of this "modern" literature have been presented by Epstein (1967, Chapter 9), E. J. Gibson (1969, Chapter 10), Harris (1965), Hochberg (1971, pp. 532–546), Howard and Templeton (1966, Chapter 15), Kornheiser (1976), Rock (1966), and Welch (1974a).

important is the fact that "prism adaptation" can be observed after even very brief exposure periods. Thus, extended experiments, like those of Stratton, are unnecessary, making it possible to test many subjects in a short period of time and to have better control over the nature of the experimental conditions. Related to this is the fact that with prismatic displacement it is possible to measure *partial* adaptation. In contrast, adaptation to inverted vision would be expected to be an "all-or-none" affair. It has been assumed that the outcomes of studies on prism adaptation can be generalized validly to other forms of rearrangement; however, as will become apparent in later chapters, the evidence has not always supported this belief.

THE SPECIFIC AIMS OF REARRANGEMENT RESEARCH

The original and continuing goal of research involving adaptation to rearranged perception is to elucidate the capacities of perceptual–motor coordination and perception, particularly spatial vision. There are three major questions which it has been hoped this research would answer.

First, it has been argued that the results of rearrangement studies have implications for the origin and development of spatial perception. A number of investigators (e.g., Kohler, 1964; Weiss, 1941) have proposed that if a perceptual or perceptual–motor capacity proves to be modifiable in adult human subjects when exposed to perceptual rearrangement, this capacity must have been acquired by the neonate as a result of experience. This argument is based on the long-held belief that if a system can be changed by experience, it must therefore have been acquired from experience. Likewise, the failure of adaptation has been used as evidence for the innateness of the capacity in question. A judgment about the validity of both of these arguments will be deferred to a later chapter.

A second aim of the rearrangement studies is to reveal the nature of perception and perceptual–motor coordination in adult subjects, regardless of the origin of these capacities. An example is the study by Wallach et al. (1963b), described earlier, in which a telestereoscope pitted retinal disparity against the KDE to assess the relative weighting of these two cues in depth perception.

Finally, the rearrangement study may serve to assess the adaptability of the perceptual or perceptual–motor system. This, in turn, has implications for the "real-life" situations in which organisms are confronted with discrepant sensory inputs. One example is the atypical perceptual environments to which the astronaut and under-water explorer are exposed. A second involves the changes in visual and auditory localization that result from the increase in interocular and interaural distances of the rapidly growing human infant.

THE ORGANIZATION OF THE BOOK

Inspired by the research of Held and his colleagues, a tremendous literature on adaptation to small prism-induced displacements of the visual field has accumulated. It is necessary here to devote two chapters to this topic. Chapter 2 presents those studies that have delineated the necessary and sufficient conditions for prism adaptation, while Chapter 3 describes what is known about the nature of the adapted state. Chapter 4 examines the proposition that adaptation to prismatic displacement and other forms of rearrangement is actually a form of learning. Other chapters deal with adaptation to inverted and reversed vision (Chapter 5), optical tilt (Chapter 6), illusory motions of the visual field (Chapter 7), size–depth distortions (Chapter 8), and distortions of form (Chapter 9). Chapter 10 treats the relatively few studies of auditory rearrangement. Chapter 11 examines individual and interspecies differences in adaptability, while Chapter 12 is devoted to a very recent and rapidly growing area—the study of adaptation to the visual distortions encountered by the underwater observer.

Finally, Chapter 13 deals with the all-important question: What has this research told us about "normal" perception? In sum, the aim of this book is to organize the vast and diverse literature on adaptation to perceptual rearrangement and to assess its impact on our current understanding of perception and perceptual–motor coordination.

2

Adaptation to
Prismatic Displacement:
Necessary and Sufficient Conditions

THE VISUAL EFFECTS OF A WEDGE PRISM

The typical study of adaptation to prismatically displaced vision entails placing before one or both of the subject's eyes a base-right or base-left 20-diopter wedge prism, housed in a pair of goggles. The result is a lateral rotation of the visual field by approximately 11° in the direction of the prism's apex.[1] However, the effects of a wedge prism are not limited to displacement. As can be seen in Figure 1.1 (p. 5), the prismatic visual field appears compressed on the base side and expanded on the apex side because light rays are deflected differently according to their angle of incidence and the varying thickness of the prism. For the same reason, vertical contours appear curved, an effect which increases toward the apex of the prism. This distortion and the capacity of subjects to adapt to it have been the subject of numerous experiments, many of which are described in Chapter 9. In addition, vertical brightness contours may appear to have attached to them a fringe of red and blue. The latter effect is referred to as *chromatic aberration* and results from the fact that a prism displaces by different amounts the various frequencies of white light, just as falling rain may create a rainbow from sunlight. A final effect of the stationary prism is

---

[1] One prism diopter corresponds to a deviation of 1 cm at a 1-m distance from the eye. This represents .57° of visual angle.

to cause horizontal lines above and below eye level to appear converged to one side.

Prismatic *displacement* is confounded by a variety of visual "side effects." There are, however, ways of dealing with these unwanted distortions. Chromatic aberration, for example, is cancelled by the use of a narrow-pass filter (e.g., Held, 1955a), while the compression and expansion effects can be eliminated by means of an appropriately curved prism (Ogle, 1968, p. 75). Apparent curvature of contours can also be avoided by eliminating all edges from the subject's visual field. Actually, the simplest way to produce optical displacement in the absence of extraneous visual effects is to use two parallel mirrors. The details of this procedure are described by Warren and Cleaves (1971). Furthermore, it is interesting to note that in work by Weinstein, Richlin, Weisinger, and Fisher (1967), the visuomotor negative aftereffect was found to be nearly twice as great after exposure to prismatic displacement than after exposure to mirror-induced displacement of the same magnitude. Although there are some advantages to the use of mirrors, investigators of adaptation to laterally displaced vision have generally chosen to use 20- to 30-diopter wedge prisms, with all of their side effects.

Since in most studies of prism adaptation the wedge prism is affixed to goggles worn on the subject's head, movements of the eyes alone have no effect on the perceived distortion. The apparent egocentric direction of a prismatically displaced target remains the same whether the observer is fixating it or looking elsewhere. However, if the head is moved, a number of visual effects are experienced, due to the fact that the prism is now also moving relative to the environment. Movements in the direction of the apex lead to an alternating expansion of that side of the field, followed by compression. If head movements are perpendicular to the line of displacement (e.g., up and down while wearing base–right prisms), the field appears to rock in a see-saw fashion. Thus, a prism-wearing subject who is free to move his head is confronted with a visual field that looks "rubbery." In a few studies, a miniature wedge prism was attached to the subject's eye by means of a contact lens (Festinger, Burnham, Ono, & Bamber, 1967; Slotnick, 1969; Taylor, 1962, pp. 222–231). In contrast to the case in which the prism is attached to goggles, movements of the eyes now result in visual effects. Thus, a subject's attempt to fixate an object is likely to be in error, since the magnitude of the displacement varies as a function of eye position relative to the object. One final logical possibility is the situation in which the prism is independent of the subject's body. For example, the prism may be rigidly attached to a holder, while the subject peers through it (Hamilton, 1964a). In this case, head and eye movements, if permitted, will have little effect on the apparent position of targets, although they will lead to a "rubbery" appearance of the field if the prism is rather close by.

COMMON VARIETIES OF PRISM EXPOSURE

The many possible ways of exposing a subject to prismatic displacement can be divided into two procedures. The *unconstrained* procedure allows the prism-wearing subject to move about in a natural indoor or outdoor environment, usually with freedom of head movement. However, partly because this form of exposure introduces the entire gamut of prism effects described previously, most investigators have used some sort of *constrained* procedure. In the typical study of prism adaptation the subject sits at a table with his head immobile and views only his hand and perhaps part of his arm through the prism. Such an arrangement is depicted in Figure 2.1. A

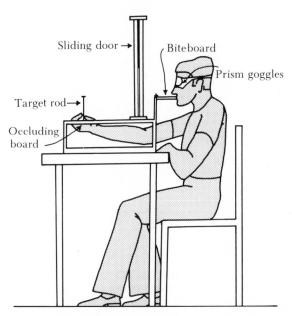

Figure 2.1. Side view of a representative apparatus used in prism adaptation research. (After R. B. Welch & R. W. Rhoades. The manipulation of informational feedback and its effects upon prism adaptation. *Canadian Journal of Psychology*, 1969, *23*, 415–428. Copyright 1969, Canadian Psychological Association. Reprinted by permission.)

more sophisticated version of this device was created by Uhlarik (1972).

There are two major varieties of constrained prism exposure that involve a view of the manual limb. In the first, the subject repeatedly reaches out in front of his body and views his hand or finger only after each response (depicted in Figure 2.1). Howard (1968) referred to this as *terminal display* and it can occur with or without the opportunity to point at a target. A second type of constrained exposure entails an uninterrupted view of the moving hand and, again, a target may or may not be present. This is termed *concurrent display*. Typically, when a target is provided the arm movement is sagittal (in–out), whereas when no target is present the arm is moved from side to side, in a transverse arc. One of the most popular types of prismatic exposure, devised by Held and Gottlieb (1958), is concurrent display without a target, where the subject views his hand and arm against a homogeneous background as the limb moves from side to side.

Another variety of constrained prismatic exposure, which has been used primarily by Craske and his colleagues (e.g., Craske & Templeton, 1968), involves having the subject stand erect with head held by a biteboard in a position that allows him to view the prismatically displaced image of his feet and lower legs. These most commonly used prism-exposure conditions are summarized in Table 2.1.

Several investigators have directly compared the various types of prismatic exposure and, not surprisingly, found them to differ in their effectiveness. Freedman (1968a) observed that the Held/Gottlieb procedure led to markedly less visuomotor adaptation than did either concurrent or terminal display of the hand as it was directed by the subject to a target. Unfortunately, it is difficult to interpret this result,

Table 2.1

Common Varieties of Prism Exposure

   I. Unconstrained (e.g., Held & Bossom, 1961)
  II. Constrained
      A. Observing the moving hand
          1. Terminal display (and sagittal arm movement)
             a. With target (e.g., Wooster, 1923)
             b. Without target (e.g., Welch, 1969)
          2. Concurrent display
             a. With target (and sagittal arm movement) (e.g., Harris, 1963)
             b. Without target (and transverse arm movement) (e.g., Held & Gottlieb, 1958)
      B. Observing the stationary legs (e.g., Craske & Templeton, 1968)

---

due to a confounded factor. In the two target-pointing conditions, exposure and test arm movements are both sagittal, whereas with the procedure of Held and Gottlieb the exposure movements are transverse, while the posttest movements are sagittal.

Let us now turn to the question of the necessary and sufficient conditions for prism adaptation.

THE NECESSITY OF A STABLE REARRANGEMENT

It seems self-evident that adaptation should be impossible if the perceptual rearrangement were to change randomly from moment to moment. An inter- or intrasensory discordance must be *stable* in some sense if adaptation is to occur. It is less obvious, however, whether adaptation could occur for an optical rearrangement that varies in a *systematic* manner from moment to moment. Cohen and Held (1960) created this condition by having subjects view the actively or passively moving hand through prisms whose strength was varied continuously from 22° leftward displacement through no displacement to 22° rightward displacement and the reverse, at a rate of one cycle every 2 min. This condition of "disarrangement" failed to lead to measurable visuomotor adaptation, although it did produce an increase in the *variability* of target-reaching accuracy along the right/left dimension when limb movement was active.[2] Thus, even when changes in visual distortion are cyclical, and therefore potentially predictable, adaptation will not occur.

A seeming exception to the conclusion that adaptation requires an unchanging rearrangement is the report by Kohler (1964, pp. 34–42) and others of partial adaptation to the "rubbery" appearance of the prismatically distorted visual field during head movements. However, a form of perceptual stability does exist here, namely, the constancy of the *relationship* between each placement of the head and the particular degree of optical displacement or tilt with which it is associated. As will be seen in Chapter 4, it is likely that adaptation can become conditioned to the cues of head or eye position. It may be concluded that one of the necessary conditions for adaptation is that

---

[2] Similar results were reported by Efstathiou (1963) and Abplanalp and Held (1965). In these studies the subject viewed his prismatically displaced hand as it was caused to move in a fashion that was poorly correlated with the subject's efferent commands to the limb. Contrary to the Cohen and Held study, the disarrangement here was essentially random.

the rearrangement be constant or that if changes in the distortion occur they be consistently tied to specific bodily or other cues.

ASSUMPTIONS ABOUT AND AWARENESS OF THE PERCEPTUAL SITUATION

Assumptions about the Source of the Discrepant Inputs

When a single distal object is providing sensory information that, under normal circumstances, would indicate the presence of separate spatial referents, a discrepancy is said to exist between the modalities involved. Such an intersensory discordance is *registered* as such by the observer only if he is under the impression that his different inputs are referring to the same event. Several studies (Miller, 1971, 1972; Welch, 1972) have examined the effects of experimentally manipulating this assumption.

In the experiment by Welch (1972), subjects were exposed to *simulated* lateral prismatic displacement. In a darkened room the experimenter placed his luminous finger to one side of the subject's nonvisible finger. One group was misinformed that the discrepancy between the felt position of the finger and the visual image was due to the prism goggles they were wearing. (In fact, the goggles contained only clear glass.) A second group was correctly informed that the finger they saw was not their own. Both groups were instructed to attempt to correct for their "errors" in pointing at a luminous target. That is, the experimenter maintained a fixed distance between his finger and the subject's and the task of the subject was to place his (unseen) finger in such a manner that the finger he saw was in line with the visible target. This, of course, was precisely what would have been required of him if he were seeing his own finger through a wedge prism. After 25 target-pointing trials, subjects in both groups demonstrated significant "adaptation" in terms of both the negative aftereffect of target pointing and a shift in the felt position of the hand. The shift was measured by having the subject move a motor-driven visual pointer laterally until it appeared to be located directly above his nonvisible right index finger. The most important finding was that the misinformed subjects adapted, on both measures, significantly more than the informed group. This result indicates that magnitude of prism adaptation can be influenced by the belief that visual and proprioceptive inputs emanate from the same distal object. Thus, a mere sensory discrepancy between motor movements and their visual consequences is not sufficient for maximal adaptation. The fact that some adaptation occurred even when the subject was told that his vision and proprioception were not in conflict suggests that it is difficult, if not impossible, to destroy by instructions alone the inherent or overlearned assumption of identity between felt and seen limb position.

Awareness of the Prism

A related issue concerns whether the subject is or becomes aware of the presence and nature of the prismatic distortion. In most experiments the subject is not told of the properties of the prism goggles. When exposure conditions are designed to preclude error-corrective feedback or other obvious clues about the rearrangement, as in the case of the concurrent, no-target exposure condition used by the Held group, the subject typically remains unaware that his vision has been tampered with. On the other hand, when the subject is allowed to point at targets during the exposure period it is very likely that he will quickly become aware of the fact and precise nature of the rearrangement. Unfortunately, very few studies have included a measure, such as postexperiment interrogation, to assess the subject's degree of awareness about the distortion and what effect this awareness might have had on the results. Complicating matters is the fact that in some studies the subject who has become aware of the distortion during the exposure period may not know that it has been eliminated prior to the postexposure period, a likely occurrence when a "variable prism" is used, since this prism can be changed to zero displacement without removing the goggles. Since measures of adaptation are taken without feedback, the subject in this situation has little or no way of knowing that his vision is now normal, unless the experimenter informs him. The false assumption that his vision continues to be displaced could lead the subject to maintain a deliberate corrective response acquired during exposure, thereby causing the experimenter to overestimate the magnitude of the true adaptation.

Although it may seem obvious that the subject's awareness of the perceptual rearrangement could be a very important variable in adaptation research, it has virtually been ignored. Indeed, there appears to be only one published experiment examining this factor. This study, carried out by Uhlarik (1973), deserves a detailed description. In one condition, which Uhlarik termed "complete prism awareness," the subject was told about and shown the effects of the 20-diopter prismatic displacement as it was being instituted prior to the exposure period and again when it was eliminated for the posttests. In a second condition ("partial prism awareness") the subject was not informed of the prism until immediately after the exposure period, but prior to the posttests. In a third condition ("no prism awareness") the subject was never purposefully made aware of the optical displacement. A second variable was type of prism exposure: (a) concurrent with no target and transverse arm movements (the Held/Gottlieb method); (b) terminal with target and sagittal arm movements; and (c) verbal feedback about accuracy after each (sagittal) target-pointing response. The effects of this manipulation are discussed in a later section entitled The Effect of "Cognitive" Feedback.

Adaptation was measured in terms of the negative aftereffect of target pointing, shift in the felt position of the unseen hand when trying to place it in the midline of the body, and shift in the apparent straight ahead of a dot of light. There was a significant effect due to the degree of prism awareness, primarily for the visuomotor negative aftereffect, in that being unaware of the prism at all times led to a larger adaptive postexposure shift in target pointing than did partial or complete awareness, the latter two being about equally effective. This difference was quite large for the terminal display and verbal feedback conditions but relatively small for concurrent display. Unfortunately, it seems possible to attribute these results, at least in part, to the persistence of a conscious correction, rather than to differences in adaptation. It may be proposed that those groups in the terminal display or verbal feedback condition that were not informed of the prism effects prior and subsequent to the exposure period may have become aware of them as soon as they experienced their initial errors.[3] This awareness of the displacement during exposure may have led many of these subjects to adopt a conscious correction strategy. Since at the end of the exposure period a subject in the no prism awareness group was not notified that the visual displacement was being removed, it is possible that this conscious correction persisted and added to the true (i.e., assimilated) adaptive shift in target pointing. As was argued in Chapter 1, such a conscious correction would not be expected to influence to any great extent *perceptual* adaptation (i.e., changes in vision or felt limb position), and Uhlarik's results bear this out.

[3] This is probably one reason for the failure of Beckett, Melamed, and Halay (1975) to obtain a difference in adaptation between a target-pointing prism exposure group that was informed of the presence and nature of the prism and one that was not. A replication of this experiment using a no-target exposure condition might lead to a different result.

It appears that the presence or absence of awareness about the nature of the optical distortion has an effect on measured adaptation, particularly in terms of the visuomotor negative aftereffect. It remains to be seen whether this effect involves genuine adaptation or merely conscious correction. In any event, future investigators of prism adaptation should take heed of the potential effects of subject awareness.

THE ROLE OF BODILY MOVEMENT

Held's "Reafference Hypothesis"

Clearly, the adaptive process cannot be instigated unless the observer is provided with some form of information concerning the presence and nature of the perceptual rearrangement. An issue first raised by Held and his colleagues (e.g., Held & Hein, 1958), and one that has stimulated a great deal of research and controversy, concerns whether or not this information must be derived from active bodily movement. Held was inspired by a theory, proposed by Helmholtz (1925) and elaborated by Holst and Mittelstädt (1950), that attempts to explain the constancy of visual position experienced by organisms as they move about in a stationary visual environment. According to this theory, when body, head, or eyes are moved, a neural copy of the motor outflow is "compared" with the resulting retinal image motion, the latter referred to as visual "reafference" (Holst, 1954). As long as these two neural events "match," the visual field will appear stationary; a mismatch, as occurs when the environment is physically moved, will result in apparent visual motion. This model and its implications for visual position constancy are discussed in Chapter 7. Held proposed that this hypothetical construct, modified by the addition of a memory component, could explain the process of adaptation to perceptual rearrangement. According to Held's model, which is shown in Figure 2.2, when a particular motor act (e.g., a movement of the hand) is initiated, a neural copy of the efferent signal is emitted and held in the "correlation storage." With normal experience, a correlation is established and strengthened between this "efference copy" and the copy of the visual reafference to which it leads. For example, the motor command to move the hand in a certain direction and by a particular amount becomes linked to a specific motion of the hand's image across the retina.

When a distorting device is placed before the eye, the normal efferent–reafferent correlation is no longer obtained. The initiation of

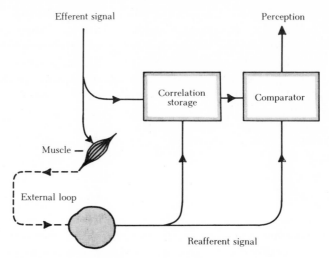

Figure 2.2. Schematic representation of the reafference hypothesis model. (After A. Hein & R. Held. A neural model for labile sensorimotor coordinations. In *Biological Prototypes and Synthetic Systems.* Vol. 1. New York: Plenum Press, 1962.)

a motor response revives a copy of the "expected" reafference, which is now discrepant with the reafferent signal from the retina. According to Held's model, it is this initial mismatch between the typical reafference resulting from a given motor response and that caused by the optical rearrangement that represents the necessary condition for the adaptive process, making the end product of adaptation a recorrelation of efferent outputs with the new reafferent inputs. If Held's "reafference hypothesis" is correct, and assuming that there are no other usable forms of information, adaptation should be limited to situations in which bodily movement is actively initiated. Thus, only if efferent impulses are generated can there be copies elicited of the predisplacement reafference to be compared with the "new" (i.e., prism-displaced) reafference.

Held and his collaborators have performed a variety of studies that support the reafference hypothesis, many of which are reviewed by Held and Freedman (1963). A representative experiment from Held's laboratory is by Held and Hein (1958), who compared three conditions of prismatic exposure: active arm movement, passive arm movement, and no arm movement. For the movement conditions the subject either swung his arm back and forth in the frontal plane (active movement) or had it transported in the same manner by means of a moving "cradle" to which it was strapped (passive movement). During this exposure period the subject could view only his limb, as it moved before a visually homogeneous background. Adaptation was measured in terms of the visuomotor negative aftereffect. The investigators found that active movement produced adaptation, whereas the passive and no-movement conditions did not.[4] This general result from a comparison of active and passive prism exposure has been replicated in several experiments from Held's laboratory for both visuomotor negative aftereffects (Held & Gottlieb, 1958; Held & Schlank, 1964) and adaptive shifts in the apparent visual locus of a target (e.g., Held & Bossom, 1961).

Passively Induced Adaptation

Unfortunately for proponents of the reafference hypothesis, subsequent experiments by other investigators have generally failed to replicate the absence of adaptation with passive body movement. An example is an experiment by Singer and Day (1966), who proposed that the active–passive difference in adaptation may be an artifact of the way it is measured. Since the pre- and posttests of adaptation used by the Held group required active bodily movement, it is possible that these measures were insensitive to adaptation acquired in a passive fashion. Accordingly, Singer and Day designed two studies that replicated Held's paradigm and exposure conditions, but also included conditions in which test and exposure involved the same form of bodily activity (either both passive or both active). However, the results failed to demonstrate a relation between test and exposure activities. That is, the visuomotor negative aftereffect was just as large when the two activities were the same as when they were different. More important, the investigators found no difference in adaptation between active and passive exposure, contrary to the reafference hypothesis. The fact that it was possible to measure adaptation by means of a passive test, regardless of how the adaptation was produced, also seems to contradict Held's model.

Other investigators (Baily, 1972b; Fishkin, 1969; Foley & Maynes, 1969; Pick & Hay, 1965; Weinstein, Sersen, & Weinstein, 1964) also failed to replicate the original active–passive difference reported by Held and his colleagues, although occasionally passive exposure was found to produce a smaller amount of adaptation. Thus, these studies have provided support only for a "weak" form of the reafference

---

[4] A paper by McCarter (1975) suggests that the crucial aspect of the prism exposure activity is the information emanating from the change in speed and/or direction of the actively moving hand at the end of each lateral excursion.

hypothesis. A potentially important difference between these studies and those of Held and his colleagues is the fact that, in the former, visible objects or contours were present during the exposure periods, although only in the studies by Baily (1972b) did the subject actually attempt to reach for them (this point will be discussed later).

It would seem that active movement is not a *necessary* condition for adaptation, although in some instances its presence may facilitate the adaptive process. Indeed, Held has maintained only that active visuomotor behavior is the best and "most natural" condition for adaptation, not that it is the only one (e.g., Held & Mikaelian, 1964). It may be possible to clarify the role of active movement if the various kinds of information that can be used in the prism-adaptive process are described.

INFORMATIONAL SOURCES OF PRISM ADAPTATION

The "Information Hypothesis"

Many different forms of information about the optical effects of the prism are available as potential sources of adaptation. In the constrained exposure condition, for example, this information might be found in a registered discrepancy between (a) "old" and "new" reafference (the reafference hypothesis); (b) vision and the body position sense[5]; (c) the present appearance of the visual field and the memory of how it looked before; and (d) the apparent location of an object and the errors that occur when attempting to reach for it. A number of studies have investigated which of these types of information actually lead to adaptation.

Several investigators (e.g., Freedman, 1968b; Rock, 1966; Uhlarik & Canon, 1971; Wallach, 1968; Wohlwill, 1966) have argued that adaptation will occur when *any* form of sufficiently salient information concerning the presence and nature of the optical rearrangement is available. This is the "information hypothesis." On the basis of this very general notion, it has been argued that the superiority of active visuomotor behavior in producing adaptation is due largely to the fact that it provides the subject with a great deal of salient information

---

[5] The more general phrase "body position sense" is used here and will continue to be used, rather than "proprioception" or "kinesthesis," because the latter terms generally refer to *afferent* input, thereby excluding the very real possibility that the felt position and motion of body parts are subserved, at least in part, by efferent outflow (cf. Lester, 1968).

about the prismatic displacement. One important form of information stems from the conflict between felt and seen limb position, which may become particularly intense or salient during active movement.

The Discrepancy between Vision and the Body Position Sense

An examination of the concurrent display, no-target prism exposure situation used by the Held group reveals at least two important forms of information concerning the distortion. The first is the discrepancy between neural copies of the "old" and "new" reafference, which could only be present in the active movement condition. The second is the discrepancy between felt and seen position of the prism-exposed limb.[6] This latter form of information is available during either active or passive movement and presumably even when the hand is not moving at all.

Since in their original studies adaptation was found only for the active movement condition, Held and his colleagues quite reasonably drew the conclusion that it is the reafference-induced conflict that serves as the primary condition for prism adaptation. Adherents to the information hypothesis, however, have maintained that while the reafference conflict might serve as one source of prism adaptation, the discrepancy between body position sense and vision also represents usable information for this purpose. Indeed, it has been proposed that the typical superiority of active movement in producing adaptation may derive primarily from its effect on this intermodal discrepancy. It is likely that when the arm is moved actively its felt position is more intense and precise than during passive movement. This would certainly be the case if efferent outflow contributes to felt limb position. In addition, muscle spindle input, one of the bases of body position

---

[6] This is not to say that vision and proprioception are in *direct* conflict. It is more likely, as Berkeley (1910) argued, that different sensory modalities are, in the final analysis, incommensurate. Thus, it is inappropriate to say that an observer with normal vision can literally see the hand where he feels it. Nevertheless, it may be argued that, at least for the adult subject, the visual input from a part of the body, when placed in a particular position, is *correlated* with a particular complex of neural activity subserving position sense of the body part in that position. Consequently, the registered intersensory discrepancy that arises when the hand is viewed through a wedge prism is the result of a mismatch between (a) the "expected" visual input, given the (unchanged) position sense information, and (b) the actual visual input or between (a) the "expected" position sense information, given the (altered) visual input, and (b) the actual position sense information. It is a separate issue whether this correlation between vision and position sense derives from experience or is given innately.

sense, is particularly intense during active movement (e.g., Paillard & Brouchon, 1968).

The passive movement condition, too, may contribute to the active–passive difference in adaptation. Since the implementation of this condition by Held and his colleagues entailed intensive "relaxation training," it may have served to reduce or eliminate the salience of proprioceptive input. Melamed, Halay, and Gildow (1973) drew this conclusion and then proposed that the introduction of visible contours into the background upon which the subject views the prismatically displaced image of his limb will facilitate adaptation by allowing him to assess more accurately the conflict between felt and seen limb position. Thus, while active movement probably enhances the vision–position sense discrepancy, passive exposure may result in the subject losing track of or ignoring the felt position of the arm unless he receives the "assistance" of contours in the background with which to align the limb. Melamed et al. replicated the Held active–passive design, but included as a second factor the presence or absence of numbered vertical black lines in the exposure background. In the target line conditions the subject called out the associated number as the index finger passed each line. As predicted, when the background was homogenous, 10 min of passive exposure to 20-diopter prisms failed to induce a visuomotor negative aftereffect, whereas active exposure led to a large shift, replicating the original results of the Held group. When the background was heterogeneous, no active–passive difference was found, just as Singer and Day (1966) and Fishkin (1969) had reported.[7]

Kravitz and Wallach (1966) demonstrated that even when the prism-exposed limb is immobile, adaptation is possible if the salience of the discrepancy between felt and seen position is enhanced by means of vibration. A significant negative aftereffect of target pointing was obtained after 10 min of viewing the stationary, vibrated hand through 30-diopter prisms, although no consistent adaptive shifts in the apparent locus of a visual target were found.

In a more recent study, Moulden (1971) produced results that clearly support the importance of a discrepancy between vision and position sense as a source of prism adaptation and, at the same time, seriously weaken the reafference hypothesis. In the crucial condition

---

[7] A recent study by Wallace (1975) essentially replicated the results of Melamed et al. (1973) and found that if the background contours are *moving*, the adaptation for the passively moved limb is attenuated, although still greater than zero. Presumably, it is more difficult to compare the felt position of the limb to a contour when the position of the latter is unstable.

of this experiment the subject actively moved his arm back and forth but received only one brief glimpse of it on each swing, a view too short to allow the experience of movement. The position of the arm when it was seen was the same on every cycle. According to the reafference hypothesis, adaptation would not be expected to take place under this condition because an integral part of this hypothesis is exposure to the visibly *moving* limb. On the other hand, if it is maintained that a discordance between seen and felt limb position can serve to produce adaptation, exposure to a "visually stopped" limb could lead to adaptation, particularly if it is assumed that body position sense is especially intense, precise, or salient during active movement. In short, Moulden's results revealed significant, *equal* visuomotor negative aftereffects after 3 min of 20-diopter prism exposure for both "stopped" viewing and full viewing, the latter replicating Held's active exposure condition. Moulden (1971) concluded that "Held's admirably seminal 'reafference' principle should be replaced by an 'efference-enhanced afference' principle [p. 117]."

Further support for Moulden's conclusion comes from a study by Mather and Lackner (1975), who obtained a very large target-pointing negative aftereffect for subjects exposed to the prismatically displaced arm as it was caused to move *involuntarily* by means of 100-Hz vibration of the skeletal muscle. In fact, the adaptive shift was greater than that found after an equal amount of prismatic exposure to the voluntarily moved limb. These results clearly contradict the reafference hypothesis, which would not predict adaptation when bodily movement is involuntary, since no "efference copies" are involved. Instead, the fact that the muscle spindles were being stimulated indicates that it was again a discrepancy between seen and felt limb position that led to the adaptation.

Finally, if a passive exposure condition can result in adaptation when the position sense is experimentally enhanced, it should be possible to reduce or eliminate the adaptation from active exposure if the position sense can be attenuated. Wallace and Garrett (1973) were able to create the latter condition by means of hypnotically induced anesthesia. They found that prism adaptation, as measured by the visuomotor negative aftereffect, could be completely precluded when subjects were given the hypnotic suggestion that they had lost the sense of position of the arm and hand.[8] From these results we may conclude that the discrepancy between "old" and "new" reafference is both unnecessary and insufficient as a condition for adaptation. The

---

[8] An unpublished study by Welch and Snyder found similar results.

hypnotized subjects in this experiment, although presumably insensitive to the position of their arms, were still able to move them about,
and therefore the crucial elements of Held's theory—efference and
visual reafference—were present, but no adaptation resulted.

A Critique of the Reafference Hypothesis

The evidence presented in the preceding section makes it clear that
active bodily movement per se does not represent a sufficient condition for visuomotor prism adaptation. Thus, there are empirical
grounds for questioning the validity of the reafference hypothesis as
an explanation of this form of adaptation. In addition, several writers
(Howard, 1970, 1971; Lackner, 1974a; Rock, 1966, pp. 116–119) have
expressed strong doubts that this theory should ever have been
applied to prism adaptation in the first place.

First, while there is face validity to Holst and Mittelstädt's notion
that the constancy of visual position is subserved by the cancelling of
efference copies and reafferent inputs, it is not clear what this model
has to do with situations in which an observer views his moving limbs.
It is obvious that when a visible portion of the body is moved,
whether actively or by means of an external force, it is seen to move.
There is no visual position constancy here, so why should a model
originally devised to explain this constancy be appropriate? Indeed,
the hypothesis of Holst and Mittelstädt was designed to explain visual
perception, while the reafference hypothesis has been applied primarily as an explanation of *visuomotor* adaptation.

Second, it has never been clear how the efferent–reafferent recorrelation, which is the postulated end product of adaptation according
to the reafference hypothesis, was supposed to lead to prism-adapted
eye–hand coordination. The problem is that the subject in the no-
target prism-exposure condition used by Held and his colleagues is
never actually allowed to acquire new responses during the exposure
period. Rock (1966, p. 117) has suggested one mechanism by which
the recorrelation might lead to an adaptive visuomotor shift. He
proposed that the sight of a visual target elicits the visual memory of
the reafference that occurs when the observer places his limb at the
locus of the target, which in turn arouses the appropriate efference
copy, which finally evokes the appropriate motor movement. Otherwise, as Rock notes, Held's theory merely seems to predict that initially the observer will be surprised to see his hand where he does
(i.e., a mismatch between expected and actual reafference) and later

he will cease to be surprised (i.e., expected and actual reafference are the same).

Finally, it has been noted (e.g., Howard, 1971) that efferent outflow is known to determine amplitude, direction, and speed of limb movement, but not limb *position*. Therefore, since the only relevant effect of prismatic *displacement* is to disrupt the normal relation between seen and felt limb position, a model of prism adaptation stressing efference is inappropriate. Of course, as the previous results indicate, it is likely that active motor movement enhances the discrepancy between vision and felt limb position, thereby leading to greater adaptation. However, the latter process does not derive from the reafference hypothesis.

In conclusion, it must be emphasized that, regardless of the ultimate judgment concerning its validity, the reafference hypothesis proposed by Held and his colleagues has had a very significant and positive impact on the field of adaptation and perception as a whole. Furthermore, the logical objections raised here probably do not apply to visual rearrangements that involve a loss of visual position constancy. Indeed, as will be seen in Chapter 7, it is here that the reafference model has found clear support.

The Importance of Error-Corrective Feedback

In the concurrent display, no-target adaptation procedure the subject is deliberately deprived of the opportunity to reach for visual targets and perhaps even to match the image of the limb with background contours. Presumably, one of the ultimate goals of prism adaptation research is a better understanding of the normal perception of radial direction and sensorimotor coordination. Therefore, since an organism's visual field in the "real world" is rarely devoid of contours or target objects, there is some justification for their inclusion during exposure to visual rearrangement.

Studies that have provided the subject with visual targets clearly indicate that their presence enhances prism adaptation. This facilitation will be referred to as the *target-pointing effect*. There appear to be several possible bases for this phenomenon. The first of these is that the discordance between seen and felt limb position may be made more precise and/or salient when the subject can compare the visual image of the limb to that of the target. However, Melamed et al. (1973) showed that this may be important only with passive limb movement. Templeton, Howard, and Lowman (1966) also examined prism adaptation when targets were present and limb movement was passive. However, they provided subjects with an opportunity to experience directly the placement of the limb at the objective location of the target. The subject's right arm was tied into a "cradle" that could be moved about by means of a motor controlled by the experimenter. The subject instructed the experimenter in moving the cradle until he felt that his index finger was in line with the prismatically displaced target. A screen was raised when he was satisfied with the position of his limb, allowing him to see the displaced image of his pointing finger and its relation to the target. On subsequent trials the subject was expected to correct for his errors, although not while the finger was in view. Significant adaptation was measured after an exposure period of about 16 trials. The investigators concluded that when a subject is allowed to practice the error-corrective response the absence of movement-produced reafference does not preclude adaptation.[9]

Baily (1972b) found essentially the same results as Templeton et al. (1966). However, in neither case is it certain that anything more was occurring than the enhancement of position sense. To demonstrate that error-corrective practice during exposure is a source of prismatic adaptation, independently of the enhancement of felt position sense, one can compare (a) a condition in which subjects are allowed to make errors and then correct them with (b) a condition in which subjects are provided with a target but either never make an error or are precluded from correcting their errors. One of the few published studies to make this comparison was by Coren (1966), who exposed subjects to 12° prismatic displacement in the presence of a target. One group was kept from making target-pointing errors by having the pointing finger placed in a "cart" that moved along a track leading directly to the target. The subjects in the other group were not restricted and, as a result, made target-pointing errors that were subsequently corrected. The error-correction group adapted by twice the amount of the no-error group, which confirms the importance for prism adaptation of error-corrective feedback and the substitution of a correct visuomotor response for an initially incorrect one. Coren's results were essentially replicated by Welch (1969, 1971a) and Welch

[9] In a similar study, Weinstein, Sersen, Fisher, and Weisinger (1964) demonstrated that prism adaptation could be produced in the form of a shift in the apparent locus of a visual target. During the exposure period the subject rotated his entire body until a vertical luminous line in an otherwise dark room appeared to bisect it. After each trial his body was rotated by the experimenter until it was directly in line with the true position of the target, thereby providing the subject with information about his initial error.

and Rhoades (1969). The Welch and Rhoades study suggested that the presence of both error-correction and discordance between vision and limb position sense leads to more adaptation than if only one of these conditions is present. This shows that the greater the amount of information about the distortion, the greater the adaptation.

Foley and Maynes (1969) suggested that the target-pointing effect is merely an artifact of using a postexposure measure that also involves pointing at a target. To examine this possibility, Welch and Abel (1970) compared target and no-target prism exposure conditions and measured adaptation on two pre- and postexposure tasks: (a) reaching for a target with an in-and-out motion of the hand along the sagittal plane and (b) moving the hand laterally from an extended far-right or far-left starting position until reaching the apparent location of the target. The exposure period for both target and no-target conditions involved the in-and-out motion. It was found that target-pointing experience greatly enhanced adaptation over that resulting from no-target experience, whether the pre–post shift in target-pointing accuracy was measured with the in–out response or the lateral movement response. In fact, the adaptive shift was statistically identical for the two types of target-localizing movements. Thus, target-pointing prism exposure leads to an augmentation of visuomotor adaptation regardless of how this adaptation is measured.

Practicing the Error-Corrective Response

In the studies cited so far the presence of error-corrective feedback has been confounded with practice of the adaptive visuomotor response. It would seem difficult if not impossible to separate these two factors. However, Howard (1968) has devised an ingenious technique whereby the subject may acquire the prism-corrective response without ever experiencing a significant error. This procedure involves the stepwise displacement of the optical array from zero to full displacement by such small trial-to-trial increments that the subject never makes a large enough target-pointing error to suspect that his vision has been rearranged. The naiveté of the subject if further preserved by physically transporting the target in the direction opposite that of the prismatic displacement so that it always appears straight ahead. Howard aptly termed this procedure *prismatic shaping*. If target-pointing responses are continued after full displacement has been reached, the effect of practicing the prism-corrective response can be assessed apart from the influence of error information. Howard and his colleagues made use of the shaping technique in several studies (Howard, 1967, 1968; Howard, Anstis, & Lucia, 1974; Templeton, Howard, & Wilkinson, 1974) and found significant adaptation in terms of visuomotor negative aftereffect, shift in felt limb position, and change in apparent visual direction.

Dewar (1971) has provided evidence that making errors facilitates adaptation independently of practicing the corrective response by comparing conditions of gradual increments in optical displacement with ones in which displacement was increased suddenly, thereby producing large initial errors. He found that the more abrupt the introduction of the distortion, the greater the subsequent adaptation.

It may be concluded that the facilitating effect of target-pointing experience during prism exposure involves at least three factors. First, the target serves as a "landmark" with which the felt position of the limb can be compared, thereby lending salience to the discrepancy between vision and the limb position sense, which in turn vigorously activates the adaptive process. Second, if attempts to localize the target are made, the initial errors represent a potent source of information that vision has been distorted and thus provide an additional stimulus for adaptation. Finally, deliberately substituting a correct reaching response for an initially incorrect one and having the subject subsequently practice the correct response hasten its assimilation, resulting in a significant level of adaptation as measured by the visuomotor negative aftereffect or reduction of effect. Unfortunately, in most experiments in which exposure targets are provided, these three potential causes of the target-pointing effect have been confounded.

The Effect of "Cognitive" Feedback

The information hypothesis implies that any form of information about a subject's rearranged perception can lead to adaptation. If this is true, then it ought to be possible to produce adaptation merely by providing the subject with a symbolic representation of his errors in visuomotor behavior. Such "cognitive" feedback has been provided in several experiments.

In an unpublished experiment by Dewar (1970c) subjects were provided with visual, verbal, or visual and verbal feedback about their errors in target-pointing accuracy during 20-diopter prism exposure. The three types of information led to equivalent amounts of adaptation, as measured by the visuomotor negative aftereffect and reduction of effect. Unfortunately, the procedure of introducing and removing the prismatic displacement made it difficult for the subject to know that during the postexposure period his vision was once again normal. Thus, it is possible that during the target-pointing prism exposure period he acquired a conscious correction that was maintained during the postexposure tests. It will be recalled that tests of adaptation involving target pointing are particularly likely to be confounded by a conscious correction, assuming that the exposure period also involves reaching for visual targets.

In a study by Uhlarik (1973), introduced earlier in reference to the issue of "prism awareness," the subject was exposed to 20-diopter prismatic displacement and provided with one of three types of exposure feedback; concurrent display with no target, terminal display with target, and verbal error-corrective feedback (no visual display). The most important result in the present context was the finding of adaptation for both the shift in visual straight ahead and the visuomotor negative aftereffect when information about the prism effects was limited to verbal feedback. The largest adaptive shift was for the negative aftereffect in a condition described earlier in which the subject was never deliberately informed of the nature of the rearrangement. As argued previously, it is possible that a conscious corrective response confounded these results. On the other hand, the occurrence of an adaptive shift in visual straight ahead in this condition when the only source of information was verbal feedback represents convincing evidence that this form of information is sufficient to produce a certain amount of genuine adaptation. That is, as indicated in Chapter 1, it is unlikely that a conscious correction would be used when a purely perceptual measure of adaptation is being taken.

"Tactual" Feedback

Wooster (1923) was the first to implement a systematic replication of Helmholtz's classic observation of prism adaptation. She compared different types of feedback as sources of adaptation to 21° displacement, using terminal display with a target. The visuomotor reduction of effect over the 15-day period of her experiment was most rapid when exposure to the prism involved pointing under the horizontal occluding board with the right hand at the prismatically displaced left hand, all but the index finger of which was visible. However, Howard and Templeton (1966, p. 383) have argued that since the subject could literally have felt the target to which he was pointing, and could therefore have pointed accurately with his eyes shut, it is unclear that the rapid reduction in pointing error was indicative of genuine adaptation. Auditory feedback (even when the source was visibly vibrating) proved no more conducive of adaptive changes in pointing than did a no-feedback control condition. On the other hand, when the subject was allowed to touch the lower, unseen portion of a peg, the top of which was visible through the prism, adaptation appeared to be just as rapid and complete as that found when the subject could directly observe his finger. Wooster concluded that tactual feedback was nearly as effective a source of prism adaptation as visual feedback.

Unfortunately, Wooster's use of the reduction of effect measure of adaptation can be criticized on the grounds that it could have been confounded by conscious correction. The use of the visuomotor negative aftereffect would have provided more convincing evidence of adaptation and of the relative effectiveness of the types of feedback she examined. Thus, Wooster's conclusion regarding the efficacy of tactual feedback may have been based on an inappropriate measure of adaptation.[10]

Lackner (1974a, 1977) has carried out a series of studies evaluating tactual feedback as a source of prism adaptation, using measures of adaptation less subject to criticism than Wooster's. He reported significant visuomotor negative aftereffect and change in felt position of the "exposed" limb after the subject had repeatedly touched the unseen lower portion of a peg, the top of which was displaced optically or physically from the lower portion. He demonstrated further that passive exposure to the tactual targets failed to produce adaptation (Lackner, 1977).

Thus, Lackner's data convincingly support Wooster's conclusion that tactual feedback can lead to prism adaptation. Left unanswered, however, is how tactual feedback compares in effectiveness with visual feedback. To make this comparison, and to examine some other related sources of information about the prismatic displacement, a series of experiments was carried out by the present author in collaboration with Sherry A. Needham and Sally E. Wells. As these experiments have not previously been published, a relatively detailed description is provided in the addendum to this chapter. The results indicated, quite consistently, that tactual information about 20-diopter

---

[10] The same criticism applies to an experiment by Mandell and Auerbach (unpublished manuscript), who found a reduction in target-pointing error with prisms still on after 3 min of "tactual" feedback. Significantly, the felt position of the "exposed" hand remained unchanged and there was little evidence of visual adaptation.

prismatic displacement is a relatively ineffectual condition for producing prism adaptation. In terms of both the visuomotor negative aftereffect and shift in the felt position of the prism-exposed hand, tactual feedback led to significantly less adaptation than that resulting from direct visual feedback.

SUMMARY AND CONCLUSIONS

Prism adaptation occurs when an observer is exposed for a period of time to a stable perceptual rearrangement, provided that the discrepant sensory inputs are experienced as emanating from a single distal object. Information concerning the rearrangement can come from a number of different sources. However, it appears that, contrary to the reafference hypothesis of Held and his colleagues, the discrepancy between "old" and "new" reafference is not one of them. That adaptation can be instigated upon the receipt of a variety of different types of information is congruent with the fact that perceptual capacities are typically subserved by many cues, no one of which is indispensible. Visual distance perception is a good example of such a multiply determined capacity. However, a mere listing of the types of information that lead to prism adaptation is not very enlightening; it is more important to ascertain their relative weighting in the adaptive process. This is what Wooster (1923) attempted to do in one of the pioneering studies of adaptation to perceptual rearrangement. The evidence now clearly indicates that the discrepancy between vision and position sense has a greater impact on adaptation than any of the other types of information examined. When limb movement is active this discrepancy becomes more salient, which explains why active movement facilitates adaptation. Error-corrective feedback (together with practice of the adaptive visuomotor response) also facilitates adaptation. Tactual feedback is another, although relatively poor, source of prism adaptation.

Finally, it is possible that a certain amount of adaptation can be induced by means of verbal or other types of "cognitive" feedback. However, further studies are needed here that eliminate the possibility of conscious corrective strategies on the part of the subject.

In the course of this chapter it has been seen that exposure to prismatic displacement results in more than one type of adaptive end state. The next chapter examines in detail these various components of prism adaptation.

ADDENDUM: A COMPARISON OF VISUAL AND
TACTUAL FEEDBACK AS SOURCES OF
PRISM ADAPTATION

Six experiments attempted to compare directly the effectiveness of visual and tactual information concerning the presence and nature of the subject's prismatically displaced visual field.

The basic testing apparatus was similar to that in Figure 2.1. Monocular prism goggles displaced the subject's visual field approximately 11° to the left. Adaptation was measured in terms of pre–post shifts in (a) target-pointing accuracy ("negative aftereffect"); (b) the apparent straight-ahead position of a visual target ("visual shift"); and (c) the felt position of the previously prism-exposed but now unseen hand ("position sense shift"). The last of these was measured by having the subject manipulate a motor switch, causing a luminous target to move to a position perceived to be directly above his unseen right index finger. Naturally, error-corrective feedback was precluded for all three pre- and postexposure measures. To control for potential differential decay of adaptation, the order of the three postexposure tests was counterbalanced across subjects in those studies in which the subject was measured on only one type of adaptation. The nature of the exposure period varied among different conditions and experiments but typically entailed feedback at the terminus of each of a number of target-pointing responses. Aside from the luminous target, the testing room was in darkness throughout all phases of testing.

Experiment 1 involved five groups of 18 subjects each. In four of the conditions the subject's vision was displaced by the prism; the fifth condition was a no-prism control. Immediately prior to the exposure period, the subject was informed as to the nature of the goggles he was to wear. In all conditions his task during this period was to reach under the horizontal occluding board with the right hand for the luminous target, which was located at the middle of the far edge of the board. The subject made 200 of these responses at a rate of approximately one response every 5 sec. If the subject did not immediately feel the lower half of the target, he was to move the finger laterally (usually to the right because of the leftward visual displacement) until he made contact with it. Upon touching the unseen portion of the target a subject in the Vision Group brought the finger up until he could directly view its prismatically displaced image as it protruded above the far edge of the board. In the Moving-Target Group the subject pushed up on the bottom of the target, which caused it to move vertically a few inches. Thus, although not able to see his finger, he could view an indirect visual result of his actions in the form of the optically displaced, moving target. In the Prolonged-Touch Group the subject, after making contact with the target, slid his finger along it, thus receiving relatively prolonged tactual–kinesthetic feedback but no visual information. This is similar to the type of touch feedback provided in the studies by Lackner (1974a, 1977). In the Touch Group the subject merely touched the lower half of the target and then retracted his hand. The latter situation closely approximates the tactual feedback condition of Wooster's experiment (pp. 33–34). Finally, a subject in the Control Group engaged in the same response as one in the Vision Group, but wore prismless goggles.

Table 2.2 summarizes the kinds of informational feedback provided in each of the four experimental conditions. It will be noted that all conditions entailed "kinesthetic corrective feedback"; that is, in each case the subject would initially err in pointing by reaching to the left of the target and then move the finger laterally to the right to make contact with the target. This form of feedback was thus confounded with the specific type(s) of information provided by a given condition, as was also true in Wooster's and Lackner's experiments.

Before examining the results of this study it should be noted that it is probably misleading to speak of "tactual feedback," since this suggests that the source of information about the rearrangement was a discrepancy between vision and touch; it was not, of course, since touch alone cannot specify the radial direction of a target. The real discrepancy in each of the experimental conditions of Experiment 1 was between vision and the felt position of the hand. What varied was the degree to which visual and limb position sense information were "tied" to each other. When a view of the finger was allowed, the association was, of course, very strong, based presumably on either a lifetime of experiencing the felt and seen limb simultaneously or perhaps an innate correlation between the two inputs. It would seem

Table 2.2
Types of Feedback Provided to Each of the Experimental Groups in Experiment 1

Group	Type of feedback
Touch	Kinesthetic corrective and momentary tactual
Prolonged-Touch	Kinesthetic corrective and prolonged tactual
Moving-Target	Kinesthetic corrective, prolonged tactual, and indirect visual
Vision	Kinesthetic corrective, prolonged tactual, and direct visual

reasonable to conclude that the greater the tendency to experience two sensory events as arising from a single distal source, the more impact an imposed discordance between them will have on the adaptive mechanism. If the subject were allowed to move a visual target, as in the Moving-Target Group, the connection between the seen and felt position of the limb would be expected to be somewhat less than when actually seeing the finger. That is, it would seem necessary that the subject take the intermediary step of "assuming" that it was the movement of the hand that led to the movement of the rod. Finally, in the two tactual feedback conditions the link between vision and body position sense should have been even more tenuous, since it was based on the subject's belief that what he was touching was the same object he was viewing.

The results of this experiment are shown in Figure 2.3. As expected, the Control Group failed to manifest adaptation on any of the three measures. Furthermore, none of the experimental groups revealed a visual shift significantly different from that of the Control Group, but

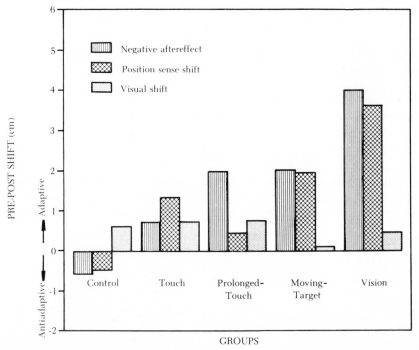

Figure 2.3. Negative aftereffect, position sense shift, and visual shift for the Control, Touch, Prolonged-Touch, Moving-Target, and Vision Groups of Experiment 1.

both negative aftereffect and position sense shift were produced in some of the conditions. With respect to the negative aftereffect, it was found that the Prolonged-Touch, Moving-Target, and Vision Groups all differed (.05) from the Control Group, the Prolonged-Touch and Moving-Target Groups did not differ from each other, and both differed from the Vision Group. The Touch Group did not differ from the Control Group, indicating that a brief touch of the target (along with kinesthetic correction) was insufficient to produce adaptation in terms of negative aftereffect, even after 200 exposure trials. The latter result contradicts Wooster's conclusion that tactual feedback is an important source of prism adaptation. Prolonged touch and movement-induced visual target motion both led to some adaptation, but direct visual feedback from the finger was clearly the most influential form of information. The position sense shift measure led to somewhat different results. Although the Vision Group appeared to experience a greater shift than the Moving-Target Group, this difference did not prove statistically significant. Both, however, differed from the Control Group. Neither the Prolonged-Touch nor Touch Group differed significantly from the Control Group. Once again, tactual feedback, even when prolonged, did not prove conducive to prism adaptation.

Since Experiment 1 confounded a number of different types of information (see Table 2.2), further experiments were undertaken. Experiments 2, 3, and 4 each involved conditions of visual feedback alone (Vision Group), tactual feedback alone (Touch Group), or visual and tactual feedback combined (Vision–Touch Group). The experiments differed only in terms of the adaptive measure used: negative aftereffect, position sense shift, and visual shift for Experiments 2, 3, and 4, respectively. In each exposure condition of a given experiment the subject's reaching hand was led to the true position of the prismatically displaced target by means of a "guide rail" attached to the underside of the horizontal occluding board. This kept the subject from misreaching for the target, thereby obviating the kinesthetic correction.[11] In the Touch Group the subject felt a target located directly behind the visible one, but could not see his finger. Finally, a subject in the Vision–Touch Group simultaneously saw his finger and felt the

[11] Lackner (personal communication, 1975) has pointed out that this procedure may not have succeeded in its goal. That is, it is reasonable to suppose that as the subject's hand traversed the guide rail he could feel that it was moving in a different direction than that of the target. To solve this problem, he proposes (and has used in his 1977 study) the technique of gradually incrementing the visual–tactual discrepancy, a variation of Howard's prismatic shaping procedure.

target. The exposure period entailed 100 reaching responses. Seventy-two subjects were tested in each of the three experiments. Half of the subjects wore base–left prisms during the exposure period and half wore base–right prisms.

The results of these three experiments are seen in Figure 2.4. It is clear that for both negative aftereffect and position sense shift visual and visual–tactual feedback were equally productive of prism adaptation. This conclusion was verified statistically. Touch alone produced a small, but statistically significant, negative aftereffect and a marginally significant position sense shift. Visual shift was not found for any of the conditions in the third experiment. Thus, the results of the original study were confirmed: Tactual feedback is a relatively poor source of prism adaptation. Furthermore, the addition of touch input to vision appears to have added nothing to the effect of vision alone.

In two final studies, Experiments 5 and 6, an attempt was made to provide the subject with visual feedback in the absence of visual reaference, by presenting the feedback only after the finger was stationary. Seventy-two subjects were tested in the first study and 108 in the second. When the subject curled his finger around the far edge of

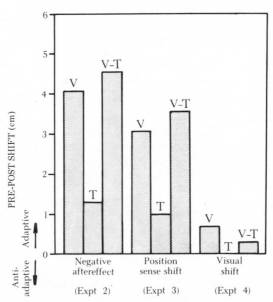

Figure 2.4. Adaptation for Vision (V), Touch (T), and Vision-and-Touch (V–T) Groups in terms of negative aftereffect (Experiment 2), position sense shift (Experiment 3), and visual shift (Experiment 4).

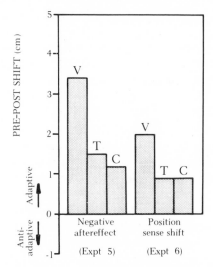

Figure 2.5. Adaptation for Vision (V), Touch (T), and Control (C) Groups in terms of negative aftereffect (Experiment 5) and position sense shift (Experiment 6).

the board a light came on, allowing him to see the now-motionless finger. A tactual feedback condition was included, as well as a control condition in which the subject moved the finger along the guide rail in the same manner as subjects in the other two groups, but merely curled the finger around the far edge of the board without seeing it or touching the target. This condition served to assess the possible effects on adaptation of moving the finger along a guide rail and feeling the edge of the board while viewing an optically displaced target. The two studies differed only in terms of the adaptive measure—negative aftereffect in Experiment 5 and felt position sense shift in Experiment 6. Contrary to the previous experiments, position sense shift was measured by having the subject point straight ahead of his nose in the dark. Visual shift was not examined since this had proved fruitless in the preceding experiments.[12] The exposure period entailed 100 reaching responses. Prismatic displacement was to the left for half of the subjects and to the right for the remainder.

The results of the two studies are shown in Figure 2.5. Again, visual feedback appeared to have produced significantly more adaptation, in

---

[12] It is not clear why a prism-adaptive change in visual localization was not obtained in these experiments, since other investigators (e.g., Uhlarik & Canon, 1971) have succeeded. Nevertheless, its absence suggests that the visual pointer method of assessing position sense shift in Experiments 1 and 3 was not confounded by visual shift.

terms of negative aftereffect, than did tactual feedback or the more general tactual feedback received by the Control Group. The shifts found for these latter two groups, although small, were statistically significant in both experiments. Unfortunately, although an analysis of variance produced a significant effect, $F(2,69) = 4.92$, $p < .01$, a Neuman–Keuls test failed to demonstrate that any group differed from any other.

Taken as a whole, the results of this series of experiments strongly suggest that although tactual feedback is capable of leading to prism adaptation, it is markedly inferior in this respect to direct visual feedback from the hand. Thus, Wooster's conclusion that this form of information could serve as an *important* source of prism adaptation was not supported when adaptation was measured in ways that precluded the conscious correction that may have confounded the reduction of effect measure used in her experiment.

3

Adaptation to Prismatic Displacement: End Products

The previous chapter dealt with the *causes* of prism adaptation; here the issue will be, "What is it that adapts?" Before attempting to answer this question, it is necessary to take note of several perceptual and behavioral events that occur almost immediately after the prism is placed before the eye, but do not represent genuine adaptation. It is important to be familiar with these phenomena, first, because they have often been confused with adaptation, and, second, because some of them may represent precursors or correlates of subsequent adaptation.

THE IMMEDIATE EFFECTS OF PRISM EXPOSURE

The "Dominance" of Vision over Other Sensory Modalities

When a person looks at his stationary or moving hand through a 20-diopter prism he rarely experiences a significant intersensory discrepancy, but rather reports that the limb feels as if it is located pretty much where it is seen. This has been referred to as *visual capture* (Hay, Pick, & Ikeda, 1965; Tastevin, 1937). Although this phenomenon was noted quite early (J. J. Gibson, 1933; Stratton, 1896; Tastevin, 1937), not until a relatively recent study by Hay et al. (1965) was it subjected to systematic investigation. Hay et al. observed nearly complete visual dominance of proprioception for an 11° optical displacement, an effect which declined markedly if tested 3 sec after vision was precluded. The procedure for measuring visual capture in this and in most subsequent investigations (e.g., Pick, Warren, & Hay, 1969; Welch, Widawski, & Matthews, 1975) involves having the subject attempt to point beneath a horizontal occluding board to the *felt* position of the index finger of the other hand, which is seen through the prism as it lies on top of the board. Typically, the subject will indicate by his pointing response that he feels his prism-exposed finger to be located in a position only slightly short of its optically displaced image.

Vision has been shown to dominate other modalities as well. For example, a discrepancy between the visual and auditory location of a sound is resolved strongly in the direction of vision (Jackson, 1953; Weerts & Thurlow, 1971). This "ventriloquism" effect, as Howard and Templeton (1966, p. 361) have referred to it, is discussed in Chapter 9 in the context of adaptation to auditory rearrangement. The dominance of vision has also been observed for conflicts between seen and "felt" size (Miller, 1972; Rock & Victor, 1964), shape (Rock & Victor, 1964), and orientation (Over, 1966). Thus, in a prism-adaptation study entailing a no-target, concurrent display condition, the resulting visual capture typically prevents the subject from experiencing a discrepancy between seen and felt limb position. Clearly, then, awareness of the rearrangement is not a necessary condition for prism adaptation.

Although visual capture is too rapidly acquired and lost to qualify as adaptation, it may be a precursor of the prism-adaptive response. It has been suggested that prolonged, active prism exposure leads to a "consolidation" of the visual capture in the form of a change in the felt position of the exposed arm, an effect that remains for some period of time after the prism has been removed and serves as the basis of the visuomotor negative aftereffect. According to this notion, visual capture and adaptation of the hand differ only in terms of their longevity. If this analysis is correct, it would seem likely that a variable having a particular effect on adaptation will have a similar effect on visual capture, a hypothesis recently examined by Welch et al. (1975). The variable chosen for manipulation in this experiment was whether the subject actively moved his limb or had it moved for him by the experimenter. The results of this experiment were that active movement led to greater adaptation than did passive movement (the traditional "active–passive difference," as described in Chapter 2), while this variable had exactly the opposite effect on visual capture. This would appear to contradict the assumption that the two phenomena differ only in degree. The explanation offered by Welch et al. for this finding involves the so-called "modality precision hypothesis." The argument is that both visual capture and prism adaptation are dependent on the relative precision of the subject's senses of seen and felt limb position. According to this hypothesis, vision will "dominate" the less precise felt body position sense when the two are discrepant. However, as was argued in Chapter 2, an actively moving limb is more precisely localized in terms of position sense than is a passively moving limb. Therefore, one would predict less visual capture for active than for passive movement, as Welch et al. found. Conversely, since the maximal activation of the prism-adaptive process would seem to require a sharp discrepancy between felt and seen bodily position, one should expect that any procedure that serves to increase the precision of felt position sense, such as active movement, would facilitate adaptation. Evidence from the study by Welch et al. (1975), in terms of standard deviations of seen and felt localization in the active and passive conditions, tended to support this explanation of the results for visual capture, although it did not for prism adaptation.

The "Immediate Correction Effect"

Rock, Goldberg, and Mack (1966) were the first to investigate a phenomenon that appears to represent another example of an immediate, partial reduction of the perceived prismatic displacement. When subjects in this experiment viewed a *well-structured* field through a prism they reported that an object within this field apppeared to be shifted by only about 40% of the 11° prismatic displacement. This occurred even though the subject had remained stationary and had neither seen his body nor been provided with any of the other sources of information usually assumed to be sufficient for prism adaptation. In addition, continuous exposure to this so-called "immediate correction effect" for periods ranging from 1 to 10 min resulted in a postexposure adaptive shift in the reported radial direction of a point of light. The magnitude of this apparent visual aftereffect varied from 2 to 4° in different experiments and was subject to rapid, although incomplete, spontaneous decay.

Rock et al. demonstrated that the immediate correction effect could not be explained in terms of conscious correction or the "Roelofs effect"[1] and that the visual aftereffect was not the result of the maintenance of a deviated eye position.

[1] This is the phenomenon in which an object that is located in the center of a visual framework appears to be straight ahead of the observer even when the framework and the object are presented off to one side.

Other investigators (Melamed & Wallace, 1971; Wallace, Melamed, & Cohen, 1973; Wallace, Melamed, & Kaplan, 1973; Wilkinson, 1971, Experiment 1) also obtained the immediate correction effect, although not always the subsequent visual aftereffect that Rock *et al.* observed. Thus, the immediate correction effect appears to be a well-established phenomenon. However, the proposal that a very brief period of stationary prism exposure can result in significant visual adaptation is rather improbable, given the arguments and evidence presented in Chapter 2 in support of the importance of informational feedback for adaptation. Furthermore, the reported shifts in visual straight ahead in the Rock *et al.* experiment and in other experiments have often exceeded those found in studies involving active movement for much longer periods of exposure (e.g., Held & Bossom, 1961); consequently, it is likely that this phenomenon does not represent adaptation at all, but rather some form of artifact.

The "Straight-Ahead Shift"

Harris (1974) has amassed a convincing array of arguments and data to support the hypothesis that a number of anomalous or contradictory "prism effects," including the immediate correction effect, are the result of the subject's *interpretation* of the concept of "straight ahead." His argument is that when a subject is confronted with a prismatically displaced, structured visual field and asked to make a perceptual judgment of the apparent straight ahead in terms of the midsagittal plane, he may be influenced in his response by the apparent orientation of the major axes of the visual framework. To the extent that this occurs, he will set the spot of light off in the same direction as the visual field is displaced, leading the experimenter to conclude incorrectly that the subject has undergone partial visual adaptation to the prism.

Not only can this "straight-ahead shift" account for the correction effect, it may also lead to an aftereffect. That is, it might be expected that the subject's postexposure setting of a point of light to the apparent straight ahead in the dark will be influenced by his recent memory of the appearance of the room during the preceding exposure period.

The straight-ahead shift should operate for any task involving the concept of straight ahead. For example, it might confound the adaptation test in which the subject is required to place his extended arm in the straight-ahead position in the dark (e.g., Uhlarik, 1973). A prism-adaptive shift in the felt position of this limb is one that causes it to feel located off in the direction of the previously displaced image (as may be seen in Figure 3.1). However, if the prism-exposure condition has induced a straight-ahead shift (but no adaptation) and the posttest measure of felt straight-ahead limb position is taken with the memory of the structured visual field still vividly in the subject's mind, the response might be swayed in terms of the straight-ahead defined by that visual framework. Instead of his pointing response conforming to his midsagittal plane, it would be shifted in the *same* direction as the previous prismatic displacement. However, this shift is in the direction opposite to the shift that represents compensation for the displacement. Consequently, it is possible to imagine the straight-ahead shift leading to what would be interpreted as a "counteradaptive" shift of felt limb position. Several investigators (e.g., Bauer & Efstathiou, 1965) have reported just such an effect, and Harris, Harris, and Karsch (1966) demonstrated that this was likely to have been the result of the straight-ahead shift. In the latter experiment it was found that merely viewing a prismatically displaced structured visual field led to subsequent counteradaptive shifts in pointing straight ahead with eyes shut. If the field was less structured, the maladaptive shift in pointing straight ahead was reduced. Bauer and Vandeventer (1967) reported similar results. Finally, in a set of elegantly simple experiments, Harris and Gilchrist (1976) demonstrated that when a visual framework is placed on a 10° slant, subjects (with undistorted vision) erred by 4° in setting a rod to the median plane, whereas pointing at the rod, with hand unseen, remained accurate. The only reasonable conclusion to draw from this is that the errors in straight-ahead setting were not errors in visual perception but in the subjective median plane.

Thus, the straight-ahead shift hypothesized by Harris (1974) is a cognitive, rather than a perceptual, effect, although it does not appear to be due to a failure of the experimenter to indicate clearly that the subject's referent for "straight ahead" should be his median plane. Furthermore, the straight-ahead shift appears to resist any attempts at modification by means of instructions or conscious effort (Harris, 1974). There are, however, several ways in which this artifact may be avoided. First, if prism exposure takes place in the absence of a visual framework, no straight-ahead shift should occur. Second, even if the shift has been produced, a measure of adaptation not involving judgments of straight ahead will be unaffected. The latter point means that the straight-ahead shift will not affect such tasks as pointing at visual targets, aligning a visual and auditory target, pointing at auditory targets, and pointing the eyes or nose at some other part of the body.

It would seem that the concept of straight-ahead shift proposed by

Harris may be the correct explanation for the immediate correction effect and "adaptation" first noted by Rock et al., as well as for many other anomalies in the prism-adaptation literature. To quote Harris (1974):

> A straight-ahead shift may be the culprit when one encounters failures to replicate, inequality of adaptation and aftereffects, negative intermanual transfer, absence of expected correlations and presence of peculiar ones, unduly rapid or evanescent adaptation, disagreement among related measures (converging operations), departures from additivity of components and their variances, nonmonotonic growth or decay curves, uninterpretable individual differences, and other suchlike perplexities [p. 474].

Altered Visuomotor Behavior during Prism Exposure

When exposure to the prism involves pointing at an object, initial reaching attempts are in error by a significant amount. However, the resulting visual feedback concerning errors usually leads to a complete correction of pointing behavior after only a few trials. Although this very rapid reduction or elimination of misreaching is the most obvious indication that the subject is adjusting to the prismatic displacement, it is both trivial and potentially misleading. As discussed in the preceding chapters, it is quite possible for the subject to deliberately redirect his perceptual–motor behavior without having adapted in any way. This is especially apparent in the initial stages of exposure to the most dramatic forms of rearrangement, such as visual inversion or right/left reversal (Chapter 5). It is conceivable, of course, that a prism-corrective visuomotor response could become so automatic as to persist subsequent to the removal of the distorting medium independently of any perceptual changes. Such an aftereffect, although not based on altered vision or limb position sense, would qualify as adaptation according to the present definition. This potential component of prism adaptation is discussed in a later section (The "Assimilated Corrective Response"). On the other hand, if the error-corrective behavior disappears as soon as the distorting medium is removed, then it is quite likely to have represented a deliberate correction and therefore should not be considered an example of adaptation. In short, the present definition of adaptation to perceptual rearrangement requires that effects be manifested for some period of time subsequent to prism exposure. An evaluation of the nature of the long-term effects that may legitimately be called prism adaptation comprises the remainder of this chapter.

THE LONG-TERM EFFECTS OF PRISM EXPOSURE

Potential Adaptive End States

THE VISUOMOTOR NEGATIVE AFTEREFFECT
AND ITS POSSIBLE BASES

The most common measure of prism adaptation is the pre–post shift in target-reaching accuracy, referred to here as the visuomotor negative aftereffect. It is important to note that the presence of this effect does not necessarily mean that *perception* has been modified or, if it has, whether the resolution of the intersensory discordance has been in favor of the eye or the arm (or something else). Before examining the studies relevant to these questions, it will be useful to delineate the possible loci of the visuomotor negative aftereffect and how they may be indexed. Then it may be seen to what extent the existing data support the occurrence of these potential end states.

Although a number of possible loci for the effects of prism exposure may be proposed (e.g., Harris, 1965), there are three that are of particular importance: (a) the body position sense; (b) the egocentric values of retinal points; and (c) visuomotor coordination. These three possibilities will be dealt with in turn.

Changes in felt position of body parts

a. The arm. Presumably, a prism-induced modification of position sense could involve any or all of the points of bodily articulation. As indicated in Chapter 2 (footnote 5), both efference and afference might be involved in such a recalibration. The obvious place to begin looking for prism-induced changes in position sense is in the exposed arm. As shown in Figure 3.1, a shift in the felt position of the arm in the direction of its optically displaced image would cause target pointing to become more accurate with the prism in place and produce a visuomotor negative aftereffect when the prism is removed. In the example depicted in Figure 3.1 it is assumed that the prism-adaptive shift in eye–hand coordination is complete and is based entirely upon a recalibration of the felt position of the prism-exposed arm. The steps in the figure are as follows.

1. During the preexposure period, the arm is felt to be where it is and the subject is relatively accurate in reaching for the target. The arm is not seen at this time, since visual feedback is precluded.

1	2	3	4
Preexposure	Beginning of prism exposure	End of prism exposure	Postexposure

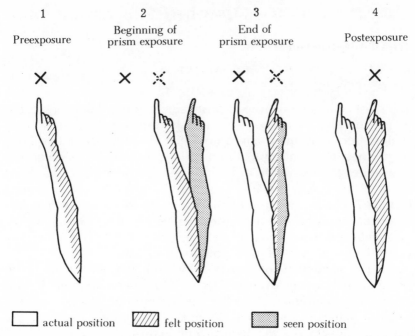

☐ actual position   ▨ felt position   ▓ seen position

Figure 3.1.   A recalibration of the felt position of the prism-exposed arm as the basis for the visuomotor reduction of effect and negative aftereffect (see the text for details).

2. At the beginning of the prism-exposure period, the subject sees the target in a position that is displaced to the right of its true position. The subject reaches for the apparent locus of the target and, of course, errs to the right. The arm is felt to be where it is (the possibility of visual capture is ignored in this example). Because of the prism, the arm, like the target, is seen to be to the right of its actual location.

3. By the end of the prism-exposure period, the subject is reaching accurately, but is still seeing both target and arm off to the right of their true positions. The felt position of the arm, however, now coincides with its seen position, a resolution of the intersensory discordance that accounts for the accuracy in reaching.

4. Finally, with the prism removed and visual feedback precluded, the subject errs to the left of the target because only when he places his arm in this way does it feel as if it is in line with the target.

The appropriate test for a shift in felt arm position is one in which the subject attempts to align this limb with some nonvisual target, such as a sound, an unseen point located straight ahead of the nose (provided, of course, that no straight-ahead shift has occurred), or an unadapted (and unseen) part of the body, such as the big toe of the right foot. Given that an adaptive position sense change in the arm is detected, it would be possible to examine each of the points of articulation of the limb for its contribution to the overall shift. Potential changes with respect to the hand–forearm articulation (i.e., the wrist) could be assessed by requiring the subject, with eyes covered, to align hand with forearm. Likewise, a position sense change involving the articulation at the elbow would be seen as a misalignment of forearm to upper arm. Finally, a test for changes at the shoulder might involve having the subject keep his entire arm and hand in a straight line while he attempts to place the limb in the straight-ahead position, with eyes shut.

b. The head. The next potential site for recalibrated position sense is the neck, the point of articulation for the head relative to the trunk. It is possible to imagine as an end result of exposure to prismatic displacement a change in the felt position of the head, such that when it is off to one side it is felt to be in line with the rest of the body. The hypothesized sequence of events for this form of adaptation is depicted in Figure 3.2. In this example, it is assumed that the eyes remain pointing straight ahead of the nose at all times. The sequence is as follows.

1. During the preexposure period, the head is felt to be where it is and the subject is relatively accurate in aiming his nose at the target, which is located straight ahead.
2. At the beginning of the prism-exposure period, the subject sees the target in a position which is optically displaced to the right. Consequently, in order to look directly at the target, the subject must turn his head to the right. Initially, the subject correctly perceives that his head is turned.
3. By the end of the prism-exposure period, the subject's head must still be turned to the right to point his nose at the apparent target, but now the head feels as if it is pointing straight ahead.
4. Finally, with the prism removed, the subject holds his head straight ahead when aiming it at the objectively straight-ahead target. However, because of the change in felt head position that occurred during the prism-exposure period, the head now feels as if it is turned to the left. It is crucial that during the post-exposure (and preexposure) measures the observer be kept from viewing any part of his body. Such a view would allow him to

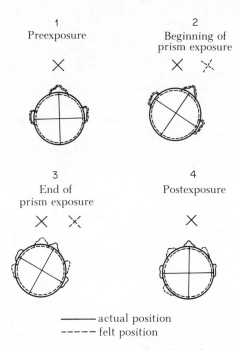

————— actual position
– – – – felt position

Figure 3.2. A recalibration of the felt position of the head during prismatic exposure as the basis for various forms of adaptation (see the text for details).

assess correctly the position of head relative to trunk independently of proprioceptive–kinesthetic information.

A change in the felt position of the head would account for both the visuomotor reduction of effect and the negative aftereffect. Take, for example, the subject who, after removing the prism goggles, feels that his head is turned to the left when it is actually pointing straight ahead (Figure 3.2, Step 4). When he is looking at a visual target that is in fact directly in front of his *nose* he will perceive it as such (since he is no longer wearing the goggles), but because his head feels turned to the left he will experience the target to be to the left of his *trunk* and that is where he will point. The result, of course, is an error—the visuomotor negative aftereffect. It is important to note, then, that a change in the felt position of the head could be the basis for a change in visual perception, even though the egocentric values of retinal loci remain unchanged.[2]

[2] Of course, if the observer uses his *head*, rather than his trunk, as the standard of reference for visual and auditory direction, his judgments will remain veridical.

The recalibration of the felt relation of head to trunk has implications for a number of different tasks. For example, such a change would affect equally the pointing of either limb—a form of intermanual transfer. Furthermore, because the ears are attached rigidly to the head, the subject would misperceive the location of *auditory* targets relative to his body and, of course, err in pointing at them, with either hand. The best evidence for a change in the felt relation of head to trunk would appear to be the presence of a constant error when attempting to align these two body parts without vision.

c. *The eye.* The final bodily articulation at which a position sense change might take place is the eye–head relation, as proposed by Helmholtz (1925) and Harris (1965). Such a modification would lead to many of the same behavioral manifestations produced by a change in felt head position: the visuomotor negative aftereffect and reduction of effect, complete intermanual transfer of this eye–hand coordination shift, and a change in the apparent direction of visual objects with respect to the trunk. A shift in visual direction relative to the *head* would also occur, but no change in auditory localization is expected since the head's felt relation to trunk remains unchanged in this situation. One possible test of a shift in the felt direction of gaze would be to have the subject attempt to direct the eyes straight ahead of the nose in the dark, which, however, would be invalidated if a straight-ahead shift has occurred. Less equivocal tests would involve looking at an unseen auditory source (on the assumption that no auditory adaptation has taken place) or at an unadapted (and unseen) part of the body.

Although the prism-induced shift in felt head position discussed in the previous section could be explained in terms of a recalibration of proprioceptive input (from the neck muscles), such an explanation may not be sufficient for the "oculomotor shift." There is convincing evidence that motor commands to the eyes play an important role in determining their felt position. In fact, until recently, it had been thought that the felt direction of gaze is *entirely* the result of neural outflow. Brindley and Merton (1960), for example, demonstrated that when the human eye is passively turned (by as much as 40°) no change in felt ocular position is reported. However, a variety of recent studies (e.g., Skavenski, 1972) have produced evidence that neural inflow from the extraocular muscles may play some role in the felt position of the eye, although it can be overridden by outflow. This research is discussed in Chapter 7.

Thus, perhaps a prism-induced oculomotor shift represents a recalibration of the efferent outflow and/or inflow for eye position that in turn leads to a change in apparent visual direction relative to head and trunk. Again, one should note that a change in position sense could alter apparent visual location without modifying the relation between retina and cortex.

Changes in retinal values

The second possible major form of prism adaptation is a change in the egocentric significance of retinal loci. The proposal here is that as a result of exposure to prismatic displacement, and in the absence of a change in the felt direction of gaze, stimulation of a given set of retinal elements comes to elicit a different apparent visual direction than was the case prior to exposure. Such a purely visual effect would produce a visuomotor negative aftereffect and reduction of effect, together with complete intermanual transfer. One means of demonstrating the presence of "retinal" adaptation would be to find a change in apparent straight ahead while simultaneously failing to obtain a shift in the felt direction of gaze. A second form of evidence would be the presence of an adaptive shift in visual direction that is confined to a limited portion of the visual field. Thus, if a visual target is incorrectly localized when exposed to one area of the retina but not to another, this would be clear evidence of visual adaptation not explainable in terms of a shift in felt position of the eyes. On the other hand, the failure to obtain such a difference would not rule out the possibility of retinal adaptation.

Changes in visuomotor coordination

The third possible prism-adaptive end state is not perceptual, but rather a highly overlearned visuomotor corrective response that persists as an aftereffect in the absence of a change in position sense or retinal values. If the prism-exposure period includes target-pointing experience, the subject might simply learn how to point correctly and then continue to make this correction after the prism has been removed, even when he has been made aware that his vision is normal again. This proposed adaptive end state would therefore represent a case of motor learning. The most appropriate test for its existence would appear to the demonstration of (a) the visuomotor negative aftereffect in the absence of a concomitant change in position sense or retinal values or (b) a negative aftereffect that exceeds the measured positional and/or visual recalibration.

These are the three most important and likely "simple sites" for the prism-induced visuomotor negative aftereffect. Table 3.1 summarizes the preceding discussion and includes two potential "complex sites" of adaptation, which are discussed in a later section entitled A Resolution: Higher Order Position Sense Recalibration. It remains now to determine which of these potential end states of prism adaptation have actually been observed.

Evidence for the Proposed Adaptive End States

ALTERED RETINAL VALUES

The evidence for changes in the egocentric significance of retinal loci as the result of prismatic displacement is both sparse and conflicting. Cohen (1966) is often cited as having obtained this kind of adaptation on the basis of his report that adaptation for prism-exposed peripheral areas of the retina failed to generalize to the fovea. This experiment has been criticized on methodological grounds by Crawshaw and Craske (1974), who failed to replicate Cohen's findings, but corroborated by Howard (1970), who claimed to have obtained retinal prism adaptation when prismatic exposure was limited to the periphery of the eye. Howard argued that such oculocentric adaptation should be expected in this area of the retina since it does not include the clear "landmark" that the fovea represents. Clearly, there is a need for further research on the difference between foveal and parafoveal prism exposure. In the meantime, the occurrence of oculocentric adaptation to prismatic displacement remains uncertain; however, there are other forms of optical rearrangement for which it is clear that such an alteration of retinal spatial values can be produced. These are optically induced tilt and curvature (Chapters 6 and 9, respectively).

The great bulk of the remaining research on the end products of prism adaptation has been concerned with potential positional changes and, to a lesser extent, motor learning. This research will be organized in terms of (a) effects limited to the arm and (b) effects involving positional changes in the head–shoulder or eye–head articulations (and the concomitant shifts in apparent visual direction).

PRISM-INDUCED CHANGES IN THE ARM

Altered position sense

In the early 1960s, Harris (1963, 1965) and Hamilton (1964a) independently came to the conclusion that, in many instances, prism-

Table 3.1

Potential End States of Adaptation to Prismatic Displacement: Some Direct Tests and Other Manifestations

Recalibration site	Test[a]	Evidence of recalibration	Other manifestations[b]
Simple sites			
Wrist	Align hand with forearm.	Misalignment—hand turned to side opposite the displacement.	Misreaching, with the hand only, at targets in any sensory modality, as well as to the straight-ahead position.
Elbow	Align forearm with upper arm.	Misalignment—forearm turned (if possible) to side opposite the displacement.	Same as above—for the forearm.
Shoulder	Point straight ahead of the nose. Point at unadapted part of body (e.g., big toe).	Misalignment—arm placed off to side opposite the displacement.	Same as above—for the entire arm.
Neck	Align head with trunk.	Misalignment—head turned to the same side as the displacement.	Misreaching, with any limb, at either visual or auditory targets and possibly the straight-ahead position. Shift in apparent visual and auditory straight ahead in the direction opposite the displacement. (All effects assume that the trunk is used as the standard of reference.)

Eyes	Place eyes in felt straight-ahead position. Direct eyes to unadapted part of body (e.g., big toe).	Misalignment—eyes turned to the same side as the displacement.	Misreaching, with any limb, at visual targets. Shift in apparent visual straight ahead in the direction opposite the displacement.
Retina	Indicate when a visual target appears straight ahead. Place eyes in felt straight-ahead position.	A shift in apparent visual straight ahead in the absence of a shift in the felt position of the eyes.	Misreaching, with any limb, at visual targets.
Complex sites			
Assimilated corrective response	Point at visual target, together with separate measures of recalibration for arm, head, eyes, head–arm, and eye–arm sites.	Error in pointing—in the direction opposite the displacement. Either no other shifts or algebraic sum of shifts is less than target-pointing error.	No other manifestations.
Head–arm	Point head toward hand, together with separate measures of felt arm and head position.	Misalignment—head turned in the same direction as the displacement. No shift in felt arm or head position.	Misreaching for visual or auditory targets in the direction opposite the displacement.
Eye–arm	Direct eyes toward hand, together with separate measures of felt arm position and of the felt direction of gaze.	Misalignment—eyes turned in the same direction as the displacement. No shift in felt arm position or direction of gaze.	Misreaching for visual targets in the direction opposite the displacement.

[a] Unless otherwise indicated, test occurs in the absence of vision.
[b] Assumes that the prism has been removed.

adaptive shifts in eye–hand coordination are explainable in terms of a recalibration of position sense, such that the exposed limb comes to feel as if it is located off in the direction in which it was seen through the prism.[3] Harris (1965) reported that after several minutes of constrained prism exposure *equal* prism-adaptive shifts in pointing at visual and unseen auditory targets and to the unseen straight-ahead position were obtained. These results were replicated independently by Pick, Hay, and Pabst (1963). Furthermore, Harris (1963) and Hamilton (1964b) both reported little or no transfer of the eye–hand correction to the nonexposed hand, at least when the subject's head was immobilized. The absence of intermanual transfer and the generalization of reaching errors to nonvisual targets clearly indicate that the prism adaptation produced under these conditions of constrained exposure did not include a visual component. In a later test, Harris (1965) showed that if a subject with eyes closed pointed to his previously prism-exposed hand with the unexposed hand, he erred in the direction of the visual displacement, presumably indicating that he felt his exposed hand to be located to that side of its true position. This result was replicated by Welch (1969). Harris (1965) also reported that prism exposure caused the subject to estimate incorrectly the distance between his unseen hands.

Several studies have examined more closely the locus of the shift in felt arm position. Craske (1966a) found that after exposure to a 20-diopter prism the felt position of the hand was displaced more than that of the elbow and the elbow more than the shoulder, the latter not feeling displaced at all. In short, there was a linear shift in felt limb position as a function of distance from the shoulder. This result does not necessarily indicate that adaptation occurred in each of the three joints; rather, it is possible that the entire position sense recalibration was in the shoulder and, because this involves a change in the perceived *angle* of the entire arm, led to increasingly larger absolute errors in felt limb position at the various loci from shoulder to finger tip. Very few studies have actually attempted to confine an adaptive position sense change to a specific joint. One of these was by Putterman, Robert, and Bregman (1969), who required their subjects to point to prismatically displaced targets with the hand, while the arm remained immobilized. Although they suggested that the result of this

---

[3] Much earlier, Walls (1951) had argued cogently that if an optically induced discordance between vision and felt body position were to be resolved, it would be in terms only of the latter modality. However, Wall's discussion was directed primarily at adaptation to inverted vision (e.g., Stratton, 1897b), and he was not certain that such a change in felt body position had actually occurred.

was a shift in the felt relation of hand to forearm, they failed to substantiate this statement. Craske (personal communication, 1977) has reported that one of his students was unable to obtain evidence of wrist adaptation in a replication of the Putterman et al. experiment. Furthermore, in a series of experiments, Craske and Kenney (1977) consistently failed to produce adaptation involving the elbow joint (even though reaching behavior became adapted). Their subjects wore base–up (downward-displacing) prisms and attempted to reach for targets, using forearm movements only. Instead of evidencing elbow adaptation, the subjects revealed that their arms had come to feel *shorter* then they actually were! Thus, it may be tentatively concluded that in the typical study of lateral prismatic displacement the change in felt limb position comes from a recalibration of the neural centers involved specifically with the shoulder joint.

In general, it would appear warranted to conclude from the studies described in this section that at least one component of the adaptation induced by the typical constrained prism-exposure condition is a recalibration of the felt position of the exposed arm. An alternative interpretation, proposed by a number of investigators from Held's laboratory, is that it is not limb position sense that is recalibrated as a result of prism exposure but the *relationship* between vision and motor behavior. In other words, it has been argued that prism-induced shifts in target-reaching behavior are based on a change in sensorimotor coordination.

Prism adaptation as a new sensorimotor coordination

Although the "reafference hypothesis" of the Held group has proven inadequate as an explanation of the *process* of adaptation to prismatic displacement (see Chapter 2, pp. 28–29), it might provide an accurate specification of its *end product*. As theorized by Efstathiou, Bauer, Greene, and Held (1967), Greene (1967), and Hardt, Held, and Steinbach (1971), prism adaptation in a no-target, concurrent display condition results in a change in the relationship between hand and head or between hand and eye so that when vision is normal, target-reaching responses coincide with the actual or potential orientation of the head or eyes when aimed at the target. However, exposure to the prism eventually results in a mismatch between head or eyes and the exposed limb, which serves to compensate for the effects of the optical displacement. It is important to note that this effect entails the relationship between *nonadjacent* body parts (e.g., head and arm) and that the changes in reaching behavior occur with respect to any target to which the subject can potentially orient his head or eyes. Thus, prism exposure will lead to modified pointing not only at visual targets but at sounds, other parts of the body, and the straight-ahead position in the dark; the head or eyes will also be in error when the subject attempts to direct them to these nonvisual targets. In short, it is maintained that although the observer will perceive veridically the positions of the head (or eyes) and the exposed hand, his *coordination* of the two systems after exposure to the prism will serve to compensate for the optical displacement or lead to the visuomotor negative aftereffect if the prism has been removed.

Since the present hypothesis incorporates the observation that prism exposure causes misreaching for nonvisual targets, it is difficult to see how it may be differentiated from the position sense hypothesis, which predicts equal shifts for visual and nonvisual targets, assuming that only the arm's position has been recalibrated. One observation supporting a distinction is the finding by Efestathiou et al. (1967) of significantly less aftereffect for pointing at the felt position of the nonexposed hand than at visual targets. Unfortunately for the sensorimotor coordination hypothesis, this finding is subject to several plausible alternate interpretations (Craske, 1966b; Hillyard & Hamilton, 1971), and Craske and Gregg (1966) failed to replicate it.[4] It should be pointed out, however, that Craske's exposure period involved target pointing and terminal exposure, while the Held group limited its theory to the no-target, concurrent display condition. In any event, the controversy between the sensorimotor coordination and position sense hypotheses has centered upon another finding by Efstathiou et al., that no adaptation was revealed for "remembered hand positions." The latter involves training the subject to remember several different placements of the arm, effected without vision, and then having him attempt to duplicate these positions during the postexposure period. According to the position sense hypothesis, this measure should reveal an adaptive shift. If, on the other hand, remembered positions of the arm are independent of the felt position of other parts of the body, as Efstathiou et al. assumed, then the sensorimotor coordination hypothesis predicts no change, which is what they found. The investigators trained the subject to place his unseen hand in four different spatial positions until he reached a high degree of accuracy. Then, after taking pretest measures of both visual target-pointing accuracy and remembered positions, the subject was exposed to 3 min of no-target, concurrent prism exposure. The pre-post difference revealed a significant visuomotor negative aftereffect,

---

[4] Although dated earlier than the paper by Efstathiou et al., Craske's study was actually in response to it.

but no change in the relocated hand position measure. This result was replicated by Greene (1967) and by Hardt et al. (1971), who ruled out the possibility that a change had actually occurred in the felt position of the subject's exposed limb but had been canceled by an equal but counteradaptive change in his internalized visual framework or by a straight-ahead shift.

Several studies (Hamilton, Sullivan, & Hillyard, 1971; Kennedy, 1969) have failed to replicate the finding of no shift of remembered arm positions using various prism-exposure conditions, including the no-target concurrent display favored by the Held group. One possible explanation for this contradiction, suggested by Hamilton et al. (1971), is that if the subject is overtrained on the repositioning task (as appears to have been the case in the studies by the Held group), his arm movements may become insensitive to or independent of a change in felt limb position. This hypothesis assumes that a prism-induced shift in the felt position of the arm does not operate when the limb is in its starting position. If it does, then it should not matter how stereotyped or ballistic the arm movement is, since it would be incorrectly placed or aimed even before the reaching response was initiated. A study is needed to assess the effect of amount of training upon the degree to which position sense input is used in directing arm reaching.

There are two important problems with the sensorimotor coordination hypothesis and the use of the remembered positions task as a test of it. First, it appears as if the Held group assumes that when replicating a hand position it is possible for the subject to divorce the felt position of his limb from its relationship with the rest of the body, which seems improbable since felt position sense must involve the joints and these are points of articulation between two body parts. The second problem is that if adaptation results in a change in sensorimotor coordination but not in felt limb position, it becomes necessary to explain why the subject does not feel as if he has erred in his reaching for an object after the response has been completed. Harris (1965) has argued that this point is sufficient to support the likelihood that the primary end product of prism adaptation is altered limb position sense.[5]

---

[5] There are, however, at least two ways in which one might explain the apparent anomaly of misreaching even though proprioceptive input remains veridical. One possibility is that the afferent position sense is not sufficiently precise to signal the relatively minor misreaching errors involved. Second, the activation and implementation of instructions to reach for a given location may provide an efferent source of felt limb position, one which overrides, at least partially, the proprioceptive input.

A resolution: Higher order position sense recalibration

It is possible that the conflict between the position sense and sensorimotor coordination hypothesis is more apparent than real. As proposed independently by Hamilton et al. (1971) and Howard (1971), *both* hypotheses might be correct and, given a liberal conception of position sense, both may be considered position sense hypotheses. It may be suggested that changes in position sense need not be limited to adjacent body segments, such as the arm–shoulder relation (a "simple site"), but can occur as well for the neural centers associated with *nonadjacent* parts, such as arm–head (a "complex site"), as seen in the lower portion of Table 3.1. This reformulation assumes that the remembered hand position results of the Held group tentatively indicate that felt arm position had not changed in their experiments but that the felt relation between arm and head (or eyes) was recalibrated. In other experiments, presumably using somewhat different conditions of prism exposure, changes in the felt position of arm to shoulder have occurred. An important corollary of this general hypothesis is that adaptation at several simple sites will combine additively in a response involving these two joints. Evidence for this "additivity hypothesis" is examined in a later section (Direct Tests of the "Additivity" Hypothesis). On the other hand, if the locus of adaptation is at a complex site, the separate simple sites, if tested in isolation, will fail to manifest a change. It is suggested that the absence of a shift in remembered hand positions, assuming that this actually occurred in the experiments by the Held group, resulted because the prism-exposure conditions had led to a sensed position change that was limited to the relation between head (or eyes) and hand and thus was not revealed when the arm alone was tested. Unfortunately, it is unclear which conditions of exposure are necessary and sufficient to elicit changes at the various proposed simple and complex sites, and it remains a mystery why the conditions used by the Held group appear to have failed to alter felt arm position while those of Hamilton et al. and Kennedy succeeded.

The "assimilated corrective response"

Based on the results of several studies, Welch (1974b) and Welch, Choe, and Heinrich (1974) argued that under certain circumstances prism exposure may induce a change in eye–hand coordination that is relatively independent of any perceptual changes that might also occur. It was proposed that when the prism-exposure period entails pointing at targets, particularly with spaced trials and terminal exposure, the subject may quickly acquire a "rule" for correct pointing, which, if practiced for a period of time, should become automatic and therefore persist for a while after the prism is removed, even if the subject is aware that a corrective response is no longer necessary. This, then, is a form of motor learning. Unfortunately, the evidence by Welch and his colleagues for this so-called "assimilated corrective response" was indirect: the difference between the negative aftereffect and the algebraic sum of the changes in (a) felt limb position (point straight ahead in the dark) and (b) visual direction (set a point of light in the straight-ahead position). Templeton et al. (1974) also observed, for some of their subjects at least, an "excess" of adaptation over that accounted for by the sum of the shifts in limb position sense and apparent visual direction (as measured by the position of the eyes when attempting to fixate the unseen big toe). A similar result was also reported by Beckett, Melamed, and Halay (1975).

Clearly, there is some support for the existence of an assimilated corrective response, a form of adaptation found in certain prism-exposure conditions, although it may account for only a relatively small portion of the total visuomotor negative aftereffect. On the other hand, this form of motor learning may contribute quite importantly to the adaptive response to more drastic distortions such as inversion and right/left reversal. This possibility is considered in Chapter 5.

PRISM-INDUCED CHANGES IN VISUAL DIRECTION BASED ON ALTERED POSITION SENSE

Changes in the felt position of the head

Although several investigators (e.g., M. M. Cohen, 1967; Hamilton, 1964b; Harris, 1965) speculated that exposure to prismatic displacement might result in a change in the felt position of head to shoulders, most of the evidence for such a positional recalibration is indirect. For example, Bossom and Held (1959) and Hamilton (1964b) showed that if the subject's head was immobilized during the prism-exposure period, adaptation was limited to the exposed arm, whereas unconstrained head movement led to a significant amount of adaptation for the unexposed arm as well. It is plausible, as Hamilton argued, that this intermanual transfer resulted from a change in apparent visual direction due to the recalibration of felt head position.

Further indirect evidence of a prism-induced shift in felt head position was produced in an experiment by M. M. Cohen (1974), who obtained a large postexposure error in pointing with either hand at *auditory* targets as a result of terminal prism exposure. Cohen concluded, in line with the previous analysis (see Table 3.1), that this finding represented evidence for a change in felt head position, since a change in felt direction of gaze would not have led to a shift in auditory localization. Direct evidence for a shift in felt head position was obtained by Kohler (1964, p. 38), who reported that prism-wearing subjects eventually became unaware of the fact that they were walking around with their heads turned in the direction of the displacement.

Changes in the felt direction of gaze:
The "oculomotor shift"

Kohler (1964, pp. 75–104) was apparently the first investigator to measure the effects of prismatic exposure on oculomotor behavior. In one of his many experiments with Erismann, subjects were exposed to "split-field" prism spectacles, which involve a prismatic displacement of only the upper (or lower) half of the visual field. After wearing this device for a period of time, a scan of an objectively vertical line led to a steplike eye movement of which the subject was unaware. This observation was later replicated by Pick, Hay, and Martin (1969).

A number of more recent experiments have been carried out in which the subject is exposed to full prismatic displacement, usually about 11°, bracketed by measures of his ability to direct the eyes straight ahead of his nose in the dark. Measurement of eye position has usually been obtained by means of infrared photography. The first experiment of this sort was by Kalil and Freedman (1966b), who photographed the subject's eyes in the dark before and after 4 min of terminal target-pointing exposure to a 20-diopter prism. Instead of looking straight ahead of the nose when asked to do so during the postexposure period, the subject placed his eyes off in the direction of the previous prismatic displacement, indicating the presence of an "oculomotor shift." Craske (1967), McLaughlin and Webster (1967), and Webster (1969) have also obtained evidence of this form of adaptation.

It would appear that prism-adaptive changes in the apparent location of visual objects can be the result of a misperception of eyes relative to head. However, Rock (1966, pp. 134–135) has suggested that perhaps it is the other way around; that is, the egocentric direction of the prismatically displaced objects becomes altered and this leads to a misperception of felt eye position. If this were true, however, it is a little difficult to understand why there is a prism-induced change in the felt direction of gaze *in the dark*. To handle this, Rock proposed that the act of looking straight ahead in the dark involves *visualizing* a position to look at and then doing so, and that perhaps this visualized position has also been shifted by the prism exposure. The validity of Rock's interpretation remains uncertain.

Still another interpretation of the oculomotor shift was proposed by Kornheiser (1976), who noted that in none of the studies that purport to have obtained this effect were subjects also measured on the felt position of the *head*. If these prism-exposure conditions produce a shift in felt head position, it is possible that the subject will place his eyes incorrectly when asked to set them straight ahead, even though their felt position remains veridical. For example, if a subject were to feel that his objectively straight-ahead head were turned to the right, then, when asked to turn his eyes to the straight-ahead position, he would set them off to his left, assuming that he were using his *trunk* as the standard of reference. Such a change in eye positioning is not indicative of a shift in felt direction of gaze, but merely a "symptom" of recalibrated felt head position. Some support for this proposal comes from a study by Lackner (1973b), who found that a prismatically induced change in felt head position led to an equal and opposite shift in eye positioning when subjects were asked to set the eyes straight ahead. It will be necessary to include measures of felt head position in prism-adaptation studies to interpret properly a measured oculomotor shift, unless it is clear that the subject is using his head as the standard of reference. In the latter case, the felt position of head relative to trunk is irrelevant to the act of setting the eyes straight ahead.

Interocular transfer of the visual shift

In many previous prism-adaptation experiments vision was limited to one eye. It may be asked if in those instances of monocular prism exposure in which there occurred an adaptive shift in visual direction based on an oculomotor shift one would find a shift for the unexposed eye as well. The answer is that not only should such changes be expected to occur for the previously occluded eye, but this interocular transfer should be *complete*. This prediction is based on Hering's Law of Equal Innervation (Hering, 1868), which states that it should not be possible to innervate the muscles of one eye independently of the other. In line with this prediction, several studies (Crawshaw & Craske, 1976; Foley & Miyanshi, 1969) have revealed 100% interocular transfer of a prism-induced shift in visual direction. Unfortunately, as Ebenholtz (1970) pointed out, tests for the interocular transfer of visual prism adaptation have not always been appropriate. One problem is the failure of investigators to take into account the potential decay of adaptation after the exposure period has been terminated. Thus, if the unexposed eye is tested after the exposed eye, adaptation may decay, thereby leading to what appears to be less than 100% transfer. Ebenholtz argued that such differential decay may account for a number of instances in which interocular transfer was not found to be complete, as in one of his studies of adaptation to optical tilt (Ebenholtz, 1967). A second problem is the fact that the observation of visual adaptation for the unexposed eye might, in some instances, be due not to an oculomotor shift but to a change in the felt position of other parts of the body, such as the head or hand. For example, a prism-adaptive shift in the felt position of the hand would be manifested equally when tested with either the exposed or the unexposed eye. This observation has been reported in several studies (e.g., Pick et al., 1963), but clearly does not represent genuine interocular transfer.

In several studies (Craske & Crawshaw, 1974; Foley, 1970; Foley & McChesney, 1976; Foley & Miyanshi, 1969; Hajos, 1968) subjects have been exposed to prismatic displacements of different amounts or directions in the two eyes. An example is a 9-day study by Hajos (1968) in which subjects wore prism spectacles that simultaneously displaced vision by about 5° to the right for the right eye and 5° to the left for the left eye. In this kind of optical situation, the Law of Equal Innervation requires that if an oculomotor shift is induced it should be in the same direction for both eyes; therefore, it would be counteradaptive for one of the eyes. However, in several of these experiments, eye-specific changes in apparent visual direction were noted. In an attempt to explain this apparent violation of Hering's law, Ebenholtz (1970) suggested that in these instances the "fusional reflex" had had an overriding influence on the principle of equal innervation. However, if the difference in optical displacement between the eyes is too large, Hering's law would be expected to reassert itself. Foley (1974), for example, found that when each eye was exposed to a 10-diopter base-out prism, equal adaptation in opposite directions was obtained, whereas when 20-diopter prisms were used, one eye "dominated" the other.

There is a very important difference between Ebenholtz's and Foley's interpretations of these results. Foley assumed that the visual shifts measured for each eye represent evidence of genuine adaptation to the eye-specific prismatic displacements. In contrast, Ebenholtz argued that the fusional reflex merely caused the subject to maintain an atypical eye convergence position that persisted subsequent to the removal of the prisms and resulted in the visual effects. Ebenholtz (1974, 1976) has extended this interpretation to the observed visual or oculomotor effects in all studies of prismatic displacement and to other forms of optical distortion as well. It is important to note that to accept this interpretation is to conclude that changes in apparent visual location and the oculomotor shift are *artifacts* of prism exposure, rather than adaptive responses to an intersensory discordance. Such a radical suggestion warrants careful examination.

"Eye muscle potentiation" as an alternative to oculomotor recalibration

a. *The hypothesis.* It is well known that a muscle system subjected to sustained innervation will continue to contract reflexively for some time after the voluntary signal to relax (Kohnstamm, 1915; Matthaei, 1924). This phenomenon, which at a physiological level may be the result of "post-tetanic potentiation" (Hughes, 1958), is easily demonstrated if one forcefully presses the back of the hand against a wall for about a minute and then moves away while relaxing the arm. The result is the unusual experience of the limb lifting away from the body, as if controlled by some mysterious force.

Since this phenomenon has been observed for a variety of muscle systems (Matthaei, 1924), under both isotonic and isometric conditions, it is plausible that it would occur for the eye muscles as well. This means that holding the eyes to one side (asymmetrical convergence) for a period of time would lead to a reflexive tendency to maintain this ocular position after attempting to relax the eyes.

Ebenholtz and his colleagues (Ebenholtz, 1974, 1976; Ebenholtz & Paap, 1976; Ebenholtz & Wolfson, 1975; Paap & Ebenholtz, 1976, 1977) have argued that such "eye muscle potentiation" (EMP) would result in some important oculomotor and visual–spatial effects. These effects are predicted because, like other forms of muscle potentiation, EMP would be involuntary. It would be as if a hidden load had been placed upon the eyes, causing the voluntary eye movement commands to be abnormal. This atypical efference, in turn, leads to the misperception of the position of the eyes directly and/or on the basis of altered inflow.

As an example, assume that a subject has held his eyes off to the right for a while. After he gives the command to relax, the persisting innervation will cause his eyes to remain off to the right of the normal position of "physiological rest." If the subject is asked to look straight ahead (in the dark), he will emit the normal instructions to the eyes for this placement but, because of the EMP, will fail to achieve his goal and will feel as if his eyes are straight ahead when they are actually off to the right. This has direct implications for apparent visual direction as well. That is, if a visual target is placed directly in front of the subject's eyes, which are deviated to the right but registered straight ahead, he should incorrectly perceive the object to be straight ahead. Finally, if the subject were to look at a visual target placed straight ahead of the head and trunk, he would feel as if he were looking off to the left when he is actually looking straight ahead, and the visual target would also appear to be to his left.

These proposed changes in the felt direction of gaze and apparent visual location are precisely those that have served previously as indexes of prism adaptation. Since the exposure conditions used in studies of prismatic displacement (and some other visual rearrangements as well) almost invariably force the subject to maintain a deviated position of the eyes, it is reasonable to ask if the observed oculomotor and visual effects are not merely the result of EMP, rather than evidence for *recalibration*. Thus, there are two questions:

1. Does deviated eye position lead to EMP, with its predicted oculomotor and visual effects?
2. If so, should it be concluded that these effects account for some or perhaps all of what have been assumed to be the end products of a prism-adaptive (i.e., recalibrative) process?

b. Evidence of EMP effects. There is evidence to support an affirmative answer to the first question. MacDougall (1903) reported shifts in the apparent level of the visual horizon in the direction (up or down) in which the subject had previously held his eyes, while Park (1969) found a small change in apparent visual straight ahead as the result of a 30-sec period of lateral eye turn. Paap and Ebenholtz (1976) demonstrated that the shift in apparent straight-ahead position of a visual target increased as monotonic functions of eye turn duration (30, 60, or 120 sec) and magnitude (12, 22, 32, or 42° for 2 min). These effects compare favorably with those of previous prism-adaptation studies (e.g., Redding, 1973b, 1975b). In a second study, EMP effects were obtained when eye position varied from trial to trial, although the *average* eye turn was 32° to one side of the median plane. The fact that these effects occurred for unrestrained eyes is important, since in most prism-adaptation studies the eyes are free to move about.

c. EMP effects as a result of prismatic exposure. There is clear support for the contention that a shift in apparent straight ahead can be produced merely by holding the eyes to one side, either continuously or on the average, but it must be determined if these

EMP effects can account for the oculomotor and visual effects obtained in prism-adaptation studies. One way in which this possibility can be tested is to compare a prism-exposed group with one provided with undistorted vision but required to maintain the same ocular posture as the first group. If the normal-vision condition resulted in effects comparable to those produced by prismatic exposure, it would seem unnecessary to argue in the latter case that adaptive recalibration had taken place. Very few studies of this sort have been done, and the results are mixed. Craske (1967), for example, failed to find a change in felt direction of gaze for subjects who held the eyes off to one side for a period of time. On the other hand, Craske and Crawshaw (1974) found adaptive shifts in apparent *distance* as a result of having the subject view his feet through goggles containing a 10-diopter base-out prism in each eyepiece or, with normal vision, a disk that was located in a position that required for fixation the same degree of convergence necessary for the experimental group.[6] Since in the nonprism situation there was no possibility of adaptation occurring, the shift must have been due to the atypical convergence of the eyes. Perhaps the most convincing evidence that prism-induced changes in apparent visual direction are largely, if not completely, the result of EMP comes from one of the experiments by Paap and Ebenholtz (1976, Experiment 3), who pitted the EMP and recalibration hypotheses against each other by examining the impact of various kinds of postexposure activity upon prism-induced shifts in apparent visual straight ahead. Of the five conditions examined by Paap and Ebenholtz, two are of particular interest. In the Exercise Group, the subject spent his time during the postexposure period moving his eyes back and forth between visual targets in an otherwise dark room. In the Induction Group, he held his eyes off in the same direction and by the same amount as the prismatic displacement. Since in neither case was the subject provided with any visual feedback, the recalibration hypothesis would predict equal adaptation decay rates. According to the EMP hypothesis, however, a very significant difference should appear, since in the first condition the EMP is presumably being eradicated by the vigorous eye movements, while in the second condition the deviated position of the eyes is main-

---

[6] Actually, they concluded that the shift for the control condition was not significantly different from zero. However, Ebenholtz and Wolfson (1975) reanalyzed their data and found that (a) the shift for the control group was significant if analyzed by means of a one-tailed statistical test; and (b) there was no difference in shift between the experimental and control groups.

tained. The results clearly confirmed this prediction. The prism-induced shift in apparent visual direction had completely disappeared for the Exercise Group by the 3-min posttest measure, whereas there was no evidence of decay for the Induction Group, even by the end of the 15-min postexposure period. A third condition entailing active exposure to the visual environment with the prisms removed did not lead to as rapid dissipation of the visual effect as had occurred for the Exercise Group. This result clearly contradicts the recalibration hypothesis, since here the subject was provided with informational feedback about his now-normal vision and therefore should have "readapted" most rapidly of all.

Ebenholtz (1976) has extended the theory of prism-induced muscle potentiation effects to include changes in the felt direction of the head. A much earlier study by Hein (1965) had demonstrated that a shift in eye–hand coordination could be induced merely by having the subject (with eyes shut) hold his head to one side for 10 min. The maintenance of this deviated head position presumably resulted in a change in felt direction of the head, thereby affecting the apparent locus of visual targets relative to the trunk. In the experiment by Ebenholtz, subjects were exposed to various combinations of left and right head and eye rotations for a 10-min period. The results, in terms of eye–hand coordination, indicated that a prolonged turn of the eyes and head leads to shifts in visual localization and that these changes summate algebraically.

In a study by Craske and Crawshaw (1978), every attempt was made to produce a prism-adaptive shift in visual direction when an explanation in terms of muscle potentiation would not be viable. The subject stood and looked down at his prismatically shifted right foot, which was placed off in the direction opposite the visual displacement, thereby necessitating a straight-ahead eye position to view it. Likewise, the head and trunk were positioned symmetrically around the sagittal midline. Five minutes of such exposure was found to produce a 2° shift in visual straight ahead and thus appears to demonstrate that it is possible to obtain a genuine visual recalibration as the result of exposure to prismatic displacement. This finding does not rule out the likely possibility that in most previous research genuine visual prism adaptation was augmented (or perhaps occasionally attenuated) by eye or head muscle potentiation effects.

d. Conclusions. The preceding evidence has demonstrated quite convincingly that at least some of the effects found in studies of prism adaptation are the result of the prolonged eye and/or head turn that is the nearly inevitable concomitant of prism exposure. Future studies of prism adaptation must include means of excluding this possibility before it can be legitimately claimed that prism-induced shifts in visual straight ahead (and the resulting modification of eye–hand coordination) represent a recalibrative reaction to the inter-sensory discordance. One precaution would be to include a control condition in which a subject with undistorted vision is required to place his eyes in the same position as a subject in the prism-wearing group, as Craske (1967) has done.[7] Another is to force the subject to keep his eyes straight ahead at all times during the exposure period, as in the study by Craske and Crawshaw (1978) described previously. At first glance, the prismatic shaping procedure, devised by Howard (1968) and described in Chapter 2, would seem to represent a means of precluding all possible eye or neck potentiation effects. However, even though with this procedure the visual target is made to appear straight ahead at all times, the subject's pointing errors, small as they are, will nearly always be to the side of the displacement. Since the subject will naturally fixate his finger as it comes into view at the ter-minus of each target-pointing response, the average placement of the eyes will be asymmetrical, the necessary condition for the induction of EMP. Therefore, it remains uncertain if the changes in oculomotor and visual direction noted by Templeton et al. (1974) and Howard et al. (1974) when using the prismatic shaping procedure represent recalibration or merely another case of EMP.

DIRECT TESTS OF THE "ADDITIVITY" HYPOTHESIS

It is evident that prismatic exposure can lead to recalibrations at any one (or more) of several different points of bodily articulation. Furthermore, it has been proposed (e.g., Hamilton, 1964b; Harris, 1965) that when changes occur at more than one "simple site" the magnitude of the visuomotor negative aftereffect is the algebraic sum of the magnitudes of the individual components. Finally, it is argued that recalibration of a "higher" articulation (e.g., the neck) will over-ride any changes that may have occurred at "lower" articulations (e.g., the arm). This is the "additivity" hypothesis mentioned previously. Experiments to test this notion have involved independent tests of

[7] Rock et al. (1966) also included a condition of this sort and found that it had no effect on the magnitude of the adaptive visual shift resulting from continued exposure to the "immediate correction effect." However, in light of Harris's reinterpretation of this effect in terms of the "straight-ahead shift," it is not clear that this experiment is relevant to the present issue.

changes at specific loci and a comparison of the sum of these effects with the magnitude of the visuomotor negative aftereffect and, in general, support the additivity model. The only controversy concerns the number of components entering into the equation.

Several studies have provided good evidence that the size of the visuomotor negative aftereffect equals the sum of the shifts in (a) the felt position of the prism-exposed arm and (b) visual direction (presumably based on a change in felt head and/or eye position). Hay and Pick (1966a) were the first investigators to test this two-component model, and their experiment has become a classic. During 6- or 42-day periods, subjects were exposed to 20-diopter prismatic displacement while engaging in everyday activities. In both cases a large adaptive shift in felt limb position, as measured by pointing straight ahead with eyes shut, was observed during the first day, followed and superseded by a shift in visual straight ahead. More important, it was demonstrated (in the 6-day experiment) that the sum of the position sense and visual shifts equaled the prism-adaptive change in visual target-pointing accuracy—evidence for an additive, two-component model of prism adaptation. Subsequent studies by McLaughlin, Rifkin, and Webster (1966), McLaughlin and Webster (1967), and Wilkinson (1971) have confirmed this result.

Several papers (Beckett, Melamed, & Halay, 1975; Templeton et al., 1974; Welch, 1974b; Welch et al., 1973) have provided evidence for the existence of an adaptive component that is apparently not based on the recalibration of either arm or eye. This evidence, which was discussed under The Assimilated Corrective Response (pp. 62–63), suggests that under certain circumstances the visuomotor negative aftereffect can be explained as the linear sum of shifts in the felt position of the arm and the eye, together with a third component, variously referred to as a "superordinate site" (Templeton et al., 1974) or an "assimilated corrective response" (Welch, 1974b).

It appears that prism exposure can lead to two, and sometimes three, major adaptive components and that they sum algebraically to produce the adaptive change in eye–hand coordination. As we have seen, while the "arm" and "eye" shifts can be measured independently of each other and of the negative aftereffect, evidence for other components has so far taken the form of an "excess" after these two components have been accounted for. Left unanswered is the question of how one can know in advance what the end products of prism exposure will be. That is, what are the necessary conditions for the various adaptive components? The next section attempts to answer this question.

Which Conditions Lead to Which End Products?

For the sake of simplicity, it will be assumed that there are only two components of prism adaptation: (a) a shift in the felt position of the exposed limb and (b) a shift in visual direction (based on a change in felt eye and/or head position).

SHIFT IN FELT LIMB POSITION

With respect to the felt arm position shift, the optimal condition would appear to be concurrent display to the actively moving limb. Harris (1963), for instance, found that after a continuous view of the target-pointing arm, which the subject moved ballistically in the sagittal plane, the magnitudes of the visuomotor negative aftereffect and shift in pointing straight ahead with eyes shut were nearly equal in size, implying that the recalibration was limited entirely to the prism-exposed arm. Hay and Pick (1966a) obtained a much greater felt arm position shift when the subject was allowed to see only this actively moving limb than when exposed to his body from the chest down. Finally, a number of studies (H. B. Cohen, 1966; M. M. Cohen, 1967; Greene, 1967; Hamilton, 1964a; Mikaelian, 1963, 1966; Mikaelian & Malatesta, 1974) have demonstrated that when exposure is in the form of concurrent display, little or no intermanual transfer of adaptive eye–hand coordination occurs, suggesting that the adaptive shift for the exposed hand was primarily the result of altered position sense in that limb.

What is it about the condition of continuous prismatic exposure to the moving limb that makes it conducive to a shift in the felt position of that limb? One possibility is derived from the fact that an uninterrupted view of the body is the ideal condition for producing visual capture (Hay et al., 1965). It may be that when bodily movement is active, or the visual–proprioceptive discrepancy otherwise made salient, this capture becomes "consolidated" into the semipermanent change measured as a postexposure shift in felt limb position. This point is an important one because when the sense of felt limb position is degraded or attenuated in some fashion, as when the hand is moved passively, visual capture is quite extensive but fails to result in a long-lasting recalibration (Welch et al., 1975).

VISUAL SHIFT

The conditions that lead to a prism-adaptive shift in visual direction (measured either directly or in terms of the oculomotor or head shift) are quite varied. They include walking about in everyday environ-

ments (Hay & Pick, 1966a; Held & Mikaelian, 1964; Kohler, 1964), viewing the stationary or moving legs and feet (Craske & Templeton, 1968;
Mikaelian, 1970a; Wallach, Kravitz, & Landauer, 1963), and viewing the
target-pointing hand only at the terminus of each response (e.g., Kalil
& Freedman, 1966b). Concurrent exposure to the prismatically displaced hand does not appear to be sufficient to produce the visual
shift (Held & Mikaelian, 1964). To understand why these conditions
are more conducive to a change in felt relation of eye to head or head
to shoulder than to altered position sense of the arm, it will first be
necessary to determine if these visual effects are evidence of adaptive
recalibration or merely the results of prolonged eye and/or head rotation, as Ebenholtz (e.g., 1974) has proposed; it will be assumed
initially that prism-induced visual or oculomotor effects represent
adaptive recalibration.

One possible explanation for some of the findings is that the locus
of adaptation resides in the bodily articulation whose behavior has
been caused to change during exposure to the rearrangement
(Hamilton, 1964a; Howard & Templeton, 1966, p. 380). This general
hypothesis might explain, for example, why adaptive visual effects are
found when the subject views his prismatically displaced, but stationary, feet, since it is the eyes that are forced to change their cus-
tomary behavior.[8] In a similar manner, the finding that the terminal
display condition of prismatic exposure is conducive to visual and
oculomotor shifts might be explainable by the fact that here the subject's eyes are forced to make a rather large "jump" (at least initially)
from the expected to the observed location of the finger as it emerges
from behind the far edge of the occluding board.

Further evidence in support of this notion comes from an experiment by Hamilton (1964a), who found intermanual transfer of eye–
hand shifts when the head was free to move but none when it was
constrained. On the other hand, an experiment by Howard et al.
(1974) failed to confirm the present hypothesis by finding greater
intermanual transfer (visual shift?) when the adaptation period entailed
pointing with the right index finger at a stationary nose extension than
when the nose extension was pointed, by means of a head movement,
to the stationary finger. Since a change in felt head position relative to

[8] Another possibility, suggested by Harris (personal communication, 1977), is that
when most of the body is visible through the prism its felt position is altered in the
direction of the optical displacement. Perhaps the trunk and legs are accepted as the
standard of reference and, hence, although the felt position of the head and eyes has
not been altered, they are now perceived to be turned to the side opposite the
displacement.

torso will lead to visual shift, larger intermanual transfer had been expected when the head was the actively moving body part. However, the results were exactly the opposite of this. The post hoc explanation given was that when the head is stationary its position becomes less precisely known (e.g., Paillard & Brouchon, 1968) and therefore presumably more susceptible to adaptation.

A second proposal concerning the nature of the exposure conditions necessary for the end products of prism adaptation is the "directed attention hypothesis" of Canon and Uhlarik (Canon, 1966, 1970, 1971; Uhlarik & Canon, 1971), which states that when two spatial modalities are providing discrepant information about the distal object it is the *non*attended modality that becomes recalibrated. The initial test of this hypothesis was provided by Canon (1966, 1970, 1971) in studies in which the subject was confronted with spatially discrepant visual and auditory inputs from an object that moved erratically in an arc around his head. Canon demonstrated that when the subject was instructed to pay close attention to the visual stimulus, auditory localization, as measured by a pointing task, came to be shifted in the direction of the visual stimulus. On the other hand, instructions to attend to the auditory source led to visual adaptation, as well as to a small auditory shift. The latter was presumed to have been a result of the subject's inability to ignore completely the visual source. Canon explained his effects in terms of the "efferent readiness theory" of adaptation to perceptual rearrangement (e.g., Festinger et al., 1967), a theory that is discussed in Chapter 9. Canon proposed that when behavior is being initiated by an attended stimulus, it is the other stimulus that is "out of line." According to the efferent readiness theory, if and when motor behavior in the presence of an intersensory discrepancy becomes accurate and has been well practiced, the discrepancy will no longer be perceived. Canon's hypothesis has the advantage of providing a means of predicting the *direction* of this resolution.

The directed attention hypothesis leads to certain expectations concerning the nature of the end products measured in the typical prism-adaptation study. Uhlarik and Canon (1971), for example, predicted that the condition of terminal display should lead to a large amount of visual shift and little or no change in felt limb position, since the subject's attention is directed primarily to the proprioceptive cues of the arm during its unseen excursion beneath the horizontal occluding board. Alternatively, with concurrent display, where the hand is visible at all times, attention is concentrated on the visual input, leading to the expectation of a large shift in felt limb position and little, if any, visual shift. These were precisely the results of the experiment by Uhlarik and Canon, in which the subject reached for targets with terminal or concurrent 11° prismatically shifted display of the hand. Actually, terminal exposure also led to a small, marginally significant felt limb position shift but, as in Canon's (1970) experiment, this may have been due to the impossibility of ignoring the brief visual input that was provided.[9] Similar to the results of Uhlarik and Canon are those reported by Redding and Wallace (1976), who found that concurrent exposure to the actively moving hand led to a greater shift in felt limb position than did active exploration of a hallway, with no part of the body visible. Conversely, visual adaptation (shift in apparent straight ahead) was greater for the hall-exposure condition than for exposure to the hand.

These results and their interpretation would seem to make sense of a number of previous findings. M. M. Cohen (1967, 1973, 1974), for example, found that terminal display leads to intermanual transfer of the visuomotor negative aftereffect, whereas continuous display does not. If intermanual transfer is assumed to be evidence for visual shift, then these results are identical to those of Uhlarik and Canon. A number of other investigators (e.g., Baily, 1972a; Howard et al., 1974) have also found intermanual transfer of the visuomotor negative aftereffect as the result of terminal display.

Taub and Goldberg (1973) have argued that the terminal–concurrent difference in prism adaptation should be reinterpreted as a difference between "distributed" and "massed" practice. They demonstrated that when concurrent display, with transverse arm movements, was interrupted by 30-sec rest periods, intermanual transfer (visual shift?) was the result, whereas when no rest periods were provided, transfer failed to occur. They concluded that prism adaptation is another example of learning, a possibility that is considered in Chapter 4. However, this conclusion does not explain why distribution of practice apparently leads to recalibration specific to the eye–head (or

[9] An alternate explanation of the advantage of terminal over concurrent exposure with respect to the production of visual adaptation was proposed by C. Smith (1973). She suggested that the crucial difference is that with terminal exposure the eye movements used by the subject to fixate the hand as it emerges from behind the occluding screen are, at least initially, saccadic in nature, whereas concurrent exposure requires only tracking movements. Festinger and Canon (1965) showed that saccades provide much better information about visual direction than do tracking movements. Therefore, the visual/position sense discrepancy should be greater when the limb is fixated saccadically, thereby eliciting a more vigorous adaptive response, presumably involving the visual system.

head–trunk) articulation, while the effects of massed practice are limited to the arm. One possibility, again arguing on the basis of Canon and Uhlarik's hypothesis, is that, when practice is distributed, the subject inevitably pays more attention to proprioceptive cues than during massed practice, since in the former case the hand is out of view periodically.

The directed attention hypothesis was subjected to its most direct test in an experiment by Kelso, Cook, Olson, and Epstein (1975), where the subject viewed a prismatically displaced light located above his unseen left hand and was specifically informed that the two objects were physically coincident; consequently, this situation was presumably experienced as one of intersensory conflict. During the exposure period the subject reached with his right hand either for his unseen left hand (proprioceptive attention) or for the visual target (visual attention). As predicted from the directed attention hypothesis, adaptation of the pointed-to hand was entirely in the form of arm position sense in the visual attention condition and entirely visual in the proprioceptive attention condition. Kelso et al. argued, contrary to Canon's explanation, that the effects of selective attention on prism adaptation result from the intersensory dominance relation thereby effected. That is, recalibration will be in the modality that is being dominated. Under normal circumstances, vision dominates proprioception and so the latter becomes recalibrated. However, if attention is forced onto the proprioceptive modality at the expense of vision, the normal dominance relationship can be reversed, resulting in an adaptive shift in vision.

It is important to remember that prism-induced visual shifts and altered felt direction of gaze or head position might turn out to be entirely the result of muscle potentiation. Only by the use of appropriate control conditions, as discussed previously, can the validity of this alternative be determined. Thus, it would be worthwhile to evaluate the various conditions of prismatic exposure to see to what extent they are likely to lead to muscle potentiation. For example, it is possible that the terminal–concurrent display difference is due to the differential production of EMP. That is, it could be argued that terminal exposure to the finger quickly leads the subject to maintain a static deviated eye position and therefore an EMP-based shift in visual straight ahead, whereas continuous exposure (especially in conjunction with lateral arm movements) involves a moving eye that is only deviated on the average from the straight-ahead position. The finding of a visual shift for a stationary observer looking down at his optically displaced feet (e.g., Craske, 1967) is also parsimoniously explained as the result of prolonged deviated eye position rather than a recalibration process.

Although it remains quite unclear to what extent the visual effects of prismatic exposure are the outcome of muscle potentiation, it should be pointed out that the findings of some studies appear not to be amenable to this interpretation. It would seem, for example, that the results of the experiment by Kelso et al. (1975) cannot be attributed to differential opportunity for the development of muscle potentiation, since a control condition involving the same eye (and head) placement as occurred during the intersensory discordance conditions failed to result in adaptive shifts of any sort. Likewise, the study by Craske and Crawshaw (1978), which was mentioned previously, appears to have demonstrated a discrepancy-induced visual shift in the absence of EMP.

SUMMARY AND CONCLUSIONS

Although prismatic exposure leads to a number of immediate and short-lived perceptual, perceptual–motor, and cognitive effects, such as "visual capture" and the "straight-ahead shift," it is the persistent effects that are of primary concern. These changes qualify as adaptation, according to the present definition, and the most commonly used of these is the pre–post shift in eye–hand coordination, referred to as the visuomotor negative aftereffect. Logically, the possible bases for the negative aftereffect include (a) a recalibration of the felt position of the exposed arm (or segments of this limb); (b) a recalibration of visual direction; and (c) the acquisition of a new mode of target-pointing behavior that becomes assimilated into the subject's behavioral repertoire. There is little evidence that adaptive shifts in vision could occur at a retinal level. Instead, such changes would appear to be based on a recalibration of the felt position of eye to head and/or head to trunk. The evidence supports the existence of each of the three proposed end products of prism adaptation. However, it is conceivable that under some as yet unspecified conditions recalibration may also occur at "complex sites," such as the relation between eye and hand. Furthermore, it has been shown that when recalibration at several "simple sites" occurs, the adaptive shift for a response subserved by these points of articulation is the algebraic sum of their individual magnitudes.

Although prism-adaptive visual shifts have been observed and are clearly based on altered felt position of eye and/or head, it is possible that these visual and oculomotor effects are evidence of "muscle potentiation," rather than a recalibrative process. Future research on prism adaptation must include means of assessing or precluding this possibility.

With respect to the specification of the necessary exposure conditions for the various end products of prism adaptation, it may be concluded that shifts in the felt position sense of the arm are maximally effected by active, concurrent exposure to that limb, while changes in vision result from a variety of conditions. The most satisfactory theory for specifying the necessary exposure conditions for the various prism-adaptive components is the directed attention hypothesis of Canon and Uhlarik, which holds that recalibration will occur for the less-attended modality involved in the intersensory discordance. The most likely explanation for this is that an attended modality is taken as the standard of veridicality by the perceiver, causing the other modality to become congruent with it.

4

Adaptation as Learning

An issue of potential theoretical importance is whether adaptation to perceptual rearrangement is a unique event or merely another form of learning. The evidence in support of the nonlearning position includes the observations that (a) complete adaptation can take place in the absence of error-corrective feedback (e.g., Held & Bossom, 1961); (b) adaptation does not appear to require any of the traditional forms of motivation or reinforcement; (c) intermanual transfer has not generally been observed in the continuous exposure, no-target conditions used by Held and his colleagues (e.g., Mikaelian, 1963); and (d) very brief delays of visual feedback are sufficient to preclude adaptation (Held, Efstathiou, & Greene, 1966). On the other hand, a number of investigators (e.g., Snyder & Pronko, 1952; Taub, 1968; Taylor, 1962) have argued that adaptation to perceptual rearrangement is indeed an example of learning. Taub and his associates (Goldberg, Taub, & Berman, 1967; Taub, 1968; Taub & Goldberg, 1973, 1974) have been the most vigorous defenders of this viewpoint. Taub (1968) cited as indirect evidence for the learning position the fact that capacity to learn and adaptability to perceptual rearrangement covary with phylogenetic level. Thus, salamanders are apparently incapable of adapting to visual rearrangement (e.g., Sperry, 1947a), baby chicks adapt only under special conditions (Rossi, 1968), and monkeys adapt quite easily (e.g., Bossom, 1964) (see Chapter 11).

The present chapter will systematically evaluate the claim that adaptation to perceptual rearrangement is a form of learning as it has traditionally been defined. The experiments are organized in terms of their bearing on the following questions.

1. Do adaptation and learning have characteristics in common?
2. Do the so-called "learning variables" affect adaptation in the same way as they do learning?
3. Do adaptation and learning require the same conditions of motivation and reward for their occurrence?

CHARACTERISTICS OF LEARNING AND ADAPTATION

Acquisition and Postacquisition Functions

ACQUISITION FUNCTIONS

Adaptation measured by the visuomotor negative aftereffect or reduction of effect has been found to increase as a negatively accelerated function of exposure time or trials (e.g., Dewar, 1970b; Efstathiou, 1969; Redding, 1975a). Figure 4.1 depicts the typical acquisition function, which can be seen to resemble the "learning curve" for perceptual–motor tasks, such as the pursuit rotor (e.g., Ammons, 1947; Reynolds & Adams, 1953). When prism exposure involves error-corrective feedback the acquisition function for shifts in eye-hand coordination is especially steep and reaches a relatively high asymptote (e.g., Welch, 1971a; Wertheimer & Arena, 1959), but only rarely (Hay & Pick, 1966a; Hein, 1972) has 100% adaptation been achieved. The fact that adaptation is typically much less than complete would appear to represent an embarrassment for the hard-line empiricist, an issue dealt with in Chapter 13.

The few experiments examining the acquisition curves for the "simple" components of prism adaptation have reported negatively accelerated acquisition curves for both the changes in visual direction or oculomotor shift (Hay & Pick, 1966a; McLaughlin & Webster, 1967; Redding, 1973b, 1975b; Rekosh & Freedman, 1967) and the shift in felt position of the prism-exposed limb (Hay & Pick, 1966a). Asymptotic acquisition curves have also been reported for adaptation to optical tilt (e.g., Ebenholtz, 1966; Redding, 1973b; Rierdan & Wapner, 1966), altered visual position constancy (e.g., Wallach & Floor, 1970), optically induced curvature (e.g., Hay & Pick, 1966a), prism-induced "optical stretching" (e.g., Pick, Hay, & Willoughby, 1966), and prismatic color fringes (e.g., Hay & Pick, 1966b).

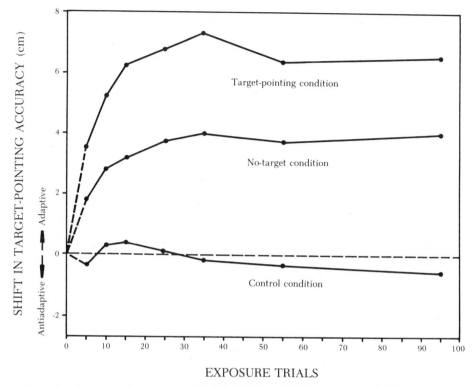

EXPOSURE TRIALS

Figure 4.1. Visuomotor negative aftereffect (in centimeters) as a function of prism-exposure trials for target-pointing, no-target, and control (no prism) conditions. (From R. B. Welch. Prism adaptation: The "target-pointing effect" as a function of exposure trials. *Perception & Psychophysics,* 1971, 9, 102–104.)

POSTACQUISITION FUNCTIONS

After a perceptual–motor task has been learned, there are at least three different events that can take place. First, the subject might be prevented from practicing the acquired response, a condition that represents a test of spontaneous decay. Second, he might be un-rewarded or "punished" for the practiced response, which is a test of extinction, or "unlearning." Finally, the subject might be forced to acquire a response quite different from the original one, a condition referred to as "relearning," and any interference noted for this new task (when compared to a control condition) represents "negative transfer." The decay of adaptation to perceptual rearrangement may be measured by having the adapted subject sit quietly in the dark, while unlearning involves providing him with undistorted visuomotor experience and relearning involves exposure to a different rearrangement. The literature pertaining to each of these three postacquisition situations will now be examined.

Decay

Adaptation to rearrangement can be quite a forgettable experience. The visuomotor negative aftereffect and reduction of effect show that spontaneous decay is a negatively accelerated function of post-exposure time (Fishkin, 1969; Hamilton & Bossom, 1964; Taub & Goldberg, 1973), although the rate of decay is typically more gradual than that of acquisition (e.g., Dewar, 1971, Klapp, Nordell, Hoekenga, & Patton, 1974). The short-term "forgetting curve" for visuomotor tasks in traditional learning studies (e.g., Adams & Dijkstra, 1966) is even more gradual and less complete than the adaptation decay curve and a complex motor act may be retained over many years of non-practice. However, it is probably more appropriate to compare the adaptive response, particularly shifts in eye–hand coordination, with such motor acts as reaching on cue to levers located in specific positions in space (e.g., Mengelkoch, Adams, & Gainer, 1958) or turning an unseen lever by a particular amount (e.g., Bilodeau & Levy, 1964), responses which are more likely to be forgotten than are complex everyday motor behaviors. Nevertheless, some retention for discrete motor tasks is often measured after several months (e.g., Ammons, Farr, Block, Newmann, Dey, Marion, & Ammons, 1958), an unlikely observation in the case of adaptation.

Complete decay of visuomotor prism adaptation has been noted by Goldberg et al. (1967), Taub and Goldberg (1973), and Redding (1975b) for postexposure periods of an hour or more, but the time course probably depends upon the length of the exposure period. If exposure is terminal, adaptation is more resistant to decay than if it is continuous (Dewar, 1970b; Goldberg et al., 1967; Welch, 1971a), while the presence of a target during exposure does not appear to have an effect on the rate of decay, at least over a 15-min postexposure period (Welch, 1971a).

Few investigations have measured the decay of recalibrated arm position sense or of changes in apparent visual direction. Choe and Welch (1974) found significant partial decay of position sense adaptation during a 15-min postexposure period, as did Templeton et al. (1974) for an 18-min period, while visual (or oculomotor) shift *increased* (nonsignificantly) in both studies. With 32- and 56-min periods, Redding (1973b, 1975b) found generally linear drops in visual shift, which in one study reached the baseline level.

A number of experiments have examined the decay of adaptation to optical tilt (see Chapter 6) and found that the curve declines sharply at first, reaching asymptote at a level significantly above baseline (e.g., Ebenholtz, 1967; Redding, 1973b). The rate of decay does not seem to be affected by the size of the tilt (up to 30°, at least) to which the subject has adapted (Redding, 1975b). Compensation for altered visual position constancy (Wallach & Frey, 1969, 1972a; Wallach and Floor, 1970) and adaptation to image magnification (Ross, Franklin, Weltman, & Lennie, 1970) also show negatively accelerated decay functions.

In general, the spontaneous decay of adaptation appears to be relatively slow and/or incomplete, although the rate varies with the type of rearrangement. Redding (1973b), for example, reported that while the decay of prism-induced visual shift is slow, but ultimately complete, decay of visual adaptation to tilt is quite rapid but reaches asymptote at a level significantly greater than zero.

In nearly all of the studies on decay of adaptation, the subject has served as his own control during the postexposure period. The results might be different if this phenomenon were examined by means of a between-groups design, in which the subject is measured only once during the postexposure period, the delay between the end of exposure and this measure varying among groups. This alternate design is suggested because it is likely that the relatively slow adaptation decay rate is, at least in part, an artifact of situationally induced adaptation; that is, if the presence of adaptation is tested under conditions similar to those in which it was originally acquired, it may persist even after long periods of normal visuomotor experience. Klapp et al. (1974) reported a small visuomotor negative aftereffect after 2–4 weeks of normal experience, which would seem more likely to have been due to the "situational effect" than resistance to decay. A related possibility is that a subject who has been repeatedly tested will become stereotyped in his responding, which gives the impression that adaptation is still present. Using a different group of subjects at each retention interval would eliminate both of these artifactual sources of resistance to decay.

It appears that visual shift decays rather slowly and even appears to increase during the initial portion of the postexposure period (Choe & Welch, 1974; Templeton et al., 1974). It was seen in Chapter 3 that terminal prismatic exposure produces visual shift and, if it is true that it is relatively resistant to decay, the finding that the visuomotor negative aftereffect induced by terminal exposure decays relatively slowly could be explained as the result of that portion of the negative aftereffect that is based on a change in apparent visual direction (Choe & Welch, 1974).

It is well known that memory for verbal material is subject to interference when the learning period is preceded by the acquisition of similar material, a process referred to as *proactive inhibition*(e.g., Underwood, 1948). It has been suggested that adaptation decay is the result of a similar process (Day & Singer, 1967; Devane, 1968; Wallach & Floor, 1970; Wallach & Frey, 1972a), that during the postexposure period memory traces for the normal visual arrangement replace the more recently acquired changes induced by the visual distortion. Perhaps the most direct test of the proactive inhibition hypothesis was by Devane (1968), who found that if the subject was adapted first to a 9° prismatic displacement in one direction and then switched immediately to a 9° displacement in the opposite direction, the decay curve for the visuomotor negative aftereffect following adaptation to the second displacement was affected by the adaptation to the first. The curve was quite steep and reached complete "recovery" after adaptation to the two successive displacements, but was negatively accelerated and asymptotic well above zero after exposure to only one displacement. The steep decay curve for the first group may be explained by proactive inhibition due to adaptation to the previous displacement, which presumably counteracted the latter.

Thus, proactive inhibition may operate to produce prism adaptation decay. Another possibility has been proposed by Hamilton (1964a), however, who suggested that one source of decay of adaptation is inadvertent contact between the adapted limb and unadapted parts of the body. Evidently, Harris (cited by Hamilton, 1964a) has carried out some unpublished research which supports this hypothesis.

Unlearning

Very few experiments have examined adaptation during a postexposure period that provides normal visual and visuomotor experience. Hamilton and Bossom (1964) found no difference between the rates of unlearning and decay for the visuomotor negative aftereffect. However, their data suggest that unlearning was actually more rapid and that with less intersubject variability (only eight subjects were tested) the two curves would have been statistically different. Welch, Bleam, and Needham (1970) replicated this experiment and found that unlearning was rapid over a 10-min postexposure period, while spontaneous decay was nonexistent.

Epstein (1972a) reported a negatively accelerated "unlearning curve" for adaptation to uniocular image magnification (see Chapter

8), as did Ebenholtz (1968b) for adaptation to optical tilt. In both studies the rate of unlearning exceeded that of decay.

Relearning

Ebenholtz (1967) and Welch et al. (1970) have compared the rate of adaptation to the rate at which adapted subjects "readapt" to the opposite rearrangement. Using optical tilt, Ebenholtz (1967) found no evidence of negative transfer when the subject was forced to adapt to the opposite tilt, but Welch et al. did observe it when acquisition and "relearning" curves for visuomotor adaptation to lateral prismatic displacement were compared. Thus, there appears to be a qualitative difference between the processes of visual and visuomotor adaptation and between tilt and displacement adaptation (see also Redding, 1973a,b, 1975a,b).

The functions for acquisition, decay, unlearning, and relearning of adaptation to optical rearrangement are generally of the same form (i.e., a negatively accelerated function of time or trials). Epstein (1972a) has suggested that this similarity implies that the underlying processes responsible for the acquisition of adaptation are the same as those involved in its subsequent dissolution.

Prism-Aftereffect Reminiscence

Ballard (1913) was the first to report that the performance of a verbal task is often better a day or two after the learning than it is at the end of the original practice period. He referred to this phenomenon as *reminiscence,* the opposite of forgetting, and later research appears to have ruled out rehearsal during the delay period as its primary source. Reminiscence has also been observed for the learning of perceptual–motor tasks (e.g., Kimble, 1949) and the intermanual transfer of this learning (e.g., Grice & Reynolds, 1952).

Taub, Goldberg, Bossom, and Berman (1966) have reported an analogous effect for prism adaptation, using normal and forelimb-deafferented monkeys adapted to 20-diopter prismatic displacement and then measured periodically on visuomotor negative aftereffect over a 51-min postexposure period. Adaptation was much greater for the deafferents than for the normals and, more importantly, it *increased* during the first few minutes for both groups, a phenomenon the investigators referred to as "prism-aftereffect reminiscence." Using human subjects and terminal target-pointing prismatic exposure, Goldberg et al. (1967) again demonstrated reminiscence for both the group decay curves and, more strikingly, the curves for individual subjects, which revealed large intersubject differences for the "peak minute" of reminiscence. Adaptation of the nonexposed hand (intermanual transfer) occurred for a separate group of subjects and also manifested reminiscence. As the investigators pointed out, the presence of reminiscence for prism adaptation is rendered more striking by the fact that it is presumably in conflict with a strong tendency for visuomotor behavior to return to "normal" (proactive inhibition?).

While several other studies have produced results suggestive of reminiscence (Baily, 1972b; Choe & Welch, 1974; Fishkin, 1969; Templeton et al., 1974), many have failed to obtain this effect. Dewar (1971), for example, measured visuomotor negative aftereffect during a 10-min postexposure period for several different experimental conditions and found only a continuous decline in the level of adaptation. Taub and Goldberg (1973) and Choe and Welch (1974) compared massed and distributed prism exposure and found no evidence of reminiscence during the decay periods. These two failures are particularly detrimental to the learning position since the traditional learning literature (e.g., Kimble, 1949) suggests that reminiscence is differentially affected by the distribution of trials. Specifically, reminiscence seems to be enhanced by massed practice.

Thus, prism-aftereffect reminiscence does not appear to be a reliable phenomenon, a state of affairs that also exists for reminiscence in verbal memory (cf. Postman, 1971). On the other hand, it is possible that this effect has actually occurred in many studies of adaptation but was masked by the use of decay curves based on group means. Examining individual curves, as did Goldberg et al. (1967), might reveal the presence of reminiscence that, because it takes place at different rates, is "smoothed out" when averaged across subjects. Another possibility is that reminiscence is limited to repeated-measure conditions and will not be observed if each subject is measured after only one of the postexposure intervals.

Generalization of Adaptation

Another well-known characteristic of learning is its tendency to generalize to new stimuli and/or new responses, properties having obvious adaptive significance. Studies of *stimulus generalization* (e.g., Hovland, 1937a,b; Guttman & Kalish, 1956) have shown that if a subject is repeatedly rewarded for a response to a specific stimulus, it will continue, although to a somewhat lesser degree, in the presence of stimuli that differ on some dimension from the original stimulus. The drop in rate and amplitude and the increase in latency of the response as a function of the difference between learning and generalization test stimuli represent the *stimulus generalization gradient,* which varies in steepness as a function of such factors as the level of drive and number of training trials (cf. Blough & Lipsitt, 1971). *Response generalization* generally refers to the manifestation of a *range* of responses to a particular conditional stimulus (e.g., Wolf & Kellogg, 1940).

Nearly all studies of adaptation to rearranged vision have demonstrated both stimulus and response generalization. These tests of adaptation typically occur under conditions that differ to a significant degree from the exposure situation in terms of both the stimulus situation and response requirements. Response generalization occurs whenever exposure to rearrangement induces more than one component of adaptation. To measure the generalization *decrement* it is necessary to compare at least two conditions in which (a) the stimulus situation is relatively constant while the response demands vary (to measure response generalization) or (b) the required response is constant while the stimulus conditions vary (to measure stimulus generalization).

To examine the two types of generalization as they apply to adaptation, the response that the subject acquires during the exposure period must be known. This is not always easy. When a target is provided, the task is clear—to reach accurately despite the displacement of the visual stimulus. This response can be viewed as an operant, in which target-pointing errors serve as punishment and their elimination as reward. On the other hand, when exposure is concurrent and without a target (e.g., Held & Gottlieb, 1958), the nature of the subject's response is uncertain since he is not confronted with a specific task. Taub (1968) suggested that the presence of the intersensory discordance elicits "automatic" responses (e.g., a shift in felt limb position) aimed at reducing the discrepancy. Such "elicited" responses are probably also included among the adaptive components induced in the target-pointing situation. The issue of generalization of adaptation will now be examined, with the phenomena of stimulus and response generalization receiving separate consideration.

STIMULUS GENERALIZATION AND DECREMENT

The "ideal" test of stimulus generalization of adaptation to rearranged vision would involve measures of adaptation obtained in situations whose stimulus characteristics differ from those of the exposure period in increments along a particular stimulus dimension, while the response demands remain constant throughout the experiment. Such a study has not yet been performed and may not be possible. Clearly, the requirement of using the same task in the generalization test as during exposure cannot be met in the concurrent exposure, no-target situation. In this case, it would be necessary to introduce a specific response (e.g., target pointing) for the postexposure generalization tests and then compare the amount of adaptation for that response under different postexposure stimulus conditions. Because spontaneous decay of adaptation over time might occur, it is mandatory that the order of generalization tests taken during one postexposure session be counterbalanced.

The clearest example of stimulus generalization of prism adaptation can be seen when both exposure and test entail pointing at a target because the response remains essentially unchanged, while the stimulus conditions are varied in a number of ways. If the posttest of adaptation involves only the exclusion of visual feedback, then the stimulus situation has been changed very little, this measure being the visuomotor reduction of effect. The fact that this measure tends to be smaller in magnitude than the target-pointing correction occurrring during exposure and with feedback may be attributable in part to stimulus generalization decrement, although one cannot rule out the possibility of spontaneous decay. When the posttest of adaptation after target-pointing exposure involves both elimination of visual feedback and removal of the prism (but not necessarily the spectacle or goggle frame), the measure is referred to as the visuomotor negative aftereffect and the stimulus situation has been changed even more. Removing the prism eliminates the apparent curvature of vertical contours, chromatic aberration, expansion and contraction of various parts of the visual field, and apparent slanting of the frontoparallel plane. As previously indicated, the visuomotor negative aftereffect tends to be reduced in size from the reduction of effect, which may represent another instance of stimulus generalization decrement. Unfortunately, spontaneous decay and the discontinuance of a "conscious correction" after removing the prism represent further potential sources of decrement, which could be avoided by using the prism-shaping technique of Howard (e.g., 1968). Regardless of the alternate explanations for the decrements found in the two previous instances, it is clear that stimulus generalization does occur for prism adaptation when exposure and the subsequent test both involve a visual target-pointing response.

When the exposure period does not involve a specific task, a test for stimulus generalization must use a comparison between two or more posttests (for the same subjects or separate groups) where the response is constant while the nature of the stimulus is changed. Of course, this procedure could also be used with studies involving target-pointing exposure.

It appears that Kohler (1964, p. 85) was the first to notice stimulus generalization of adaptation to rearrangement. In studies involving exposure to 10° prismatic displacement of the upper half of the visual field only, he found a greater aftereffect when the postexposure measures were taken while the subject was wearing empty spectacle frames containing a horizontal dividing wire than when wearing no spectacles. Similar results were obtained for chromatic adaptation to spectacles whose right halves contained a blue filter and the left halves yellow. These studies of adaptation to "split-field" spectacles are discussed in a later section (The Conditioning of Adaptation).

A variety of subsequent experiments were designed specifically to measure stimulus generalization and generalization decrement. Uhlarik and Canon (1970) tested two groups who were exposed to 30-diopter prismatic displacement while actively moving the hand from side to side. In the pre- and posttests the subjects in both groups were measured on no-feedback target-pointing accuracy while wearing the prism goggles to obtain a measure of the visuomotor reduction of effect. The groups differed in terms of how the no-prism (negative aftereffect) measures were taken: One group wore prismless goggles while the other wore no goggles. The investigators found that the ratio of negative aftereffect to reduction of effect was essentially 1.0 for the "goggles-on" condition, but only .60 for "goggles-off." Thus, adaptation as measured with the prism on (reduction of effect) generalized fully to the negative aftereffect measure when only the prisms were removed, but revealed a decrement when the goggles were also absent.[1] In another experiment, Graybiel and Held (1970) found that prism adaptation acquired under dim light generalizes equally to dim and bright light test conditions, while adaptation acquired under bright light reveals a significant generalization decrement when tested under dim light.

The results of the preceding studies have often been considered to be evidence of *conditioned* adaptation, but this interpretation is incorrect. The concept of conditioned adaptation should be limited to stimuli that *elicit* an adaptive response in a subject who is initially either nonadapted or adapted in some other manner. What was

[1] Using a similar paradigm, Mikaelian (1974b) was unable to obtain a generalization decrement for "goggles-off" measures of visual or proprioceptive vertical after 2 hr of exposure to 20° optical tilt.

shown in the experiments discussed above was simply that the act of removing some of the cues that had been present at the time of adaptation leads to a decrement in the adaptation manifested by the subject on the postexposure test. This distinction between stimulus generalization and conditioned adaptation is reexamined in the section entitled Conclusions.

It might be argued that stimulus generalization has occurred whenever prism adaptation is manifested in tests involving nonvisual targets, such as a sound source or proprioceptive straight ahead (e.g., Harris, 1963). However, the preceding chapter made it quite clear that these observations are best interpreted as evidence that prism exposure has led to a shift in felt limb position, affecting any response made by that limb. Thus, the position sense hypothesis predicts *complete* generalization to nonvisual targets (assuming that differential decay has not occurred). Nevertheless, a variety of studies have revealed a certain amount of decrement in the adaptive shift when reaching for nonvisual targets. Hillyard and Hamilton (1971) calculated this generalization decrement for each of 20 studies and found that the median level of adaptation for the nonvisual target was 72% of that obtained with the visual target. But they pointed out that part of the apparent generalization decrement might have been the result of a visual shift, which of course would affect only pointing at the visual target. When visual shift was subtracted from the adaptation found for the visual target, they noted that the proportion of nonvisual target adaptation to visual target adaptation was raised to .83, still suggesting a generalization decrement.

RESPONSE GENERALIZATION AND DECREMENT

In the "ideal" study of response generalization of adaptation the subject would be led to acquire a specific adaptive response during the exposure period and then, in the presence of the same stimuli, be tested for adaptation by means of other motoric responses.[2] Unfortunately, since the postexposure tests of adaptation are always taken without feedback and usually in the absence of the distorting optical medium (with all of its "side effects"), the stimulus conditions between the exposure period and later generalization tests are probably not kept constant. As with the stimulus generalization studies described in the preceding section, one alternative is to compare several different postexposure conditions, in this case keeping

---

[2] Although intermanual (or bilateral) transfer of prism adaptation would fit this description, this topic will be dealt with separately in the following section.

the stimulus characteristics constant while varying the response measure. In practice, the studies of adaptation to rearrangement relevant to the issue of response generalization have been of two varieties. In the first, the subject is adapted by means of a particular exposure activity and then tested on the basis of responses that differ by varying degrees from the exposure activity and/or from each other, while keeping the stimulus conditions as similar as possible. In the second, the subject is required to practice one of several different visuomotor responses during exposure and is then tested for adaptation by means of a response that is either the same as or different from the practiced response. The results of both of these paradigms clearly support the conclusion that adaptation to visual rearrangement is subject to response generalization.

A clear example of a study of the first type is one by Harris (described in Harris, 1965), who adapted subjects by having them point at a target located in the median plane during prism exposure and then tested for the presence of adaptation with targets in other spatial positions (necessitating new muscular movements). He observed generalization of the visuomotor negative aftereffect with little decrement to the new arm positions, a finding later replicated by Baily (1972a,b).

The second category includes a variety of experiments. In one of these, Freedman, Hall, and Rekosh (1965) used a 20-diopter prismatic displacement exposure period in which the subject was required to reach for a target by means of either a sagittal or a transverse arm movement. Error-corrective feedback was provided in both cases. During the postexposure period the subject was tested by pointing either sagittally or transversely at a target, without feedback. "Asymmetrical response generalization" was found. That is, sagittal prismatic exposure movement led to visuomotor negative aftereffects of equal magnitude for the two types of postexposure response, whereas transverse prismatic exposure movement induced adaptation that generalized significantly to the transverse postexposure measure but only with marked decrement to the sagittal response measure.

In experiments cited in Chapter 2, Baily (1972b), Pick and Hay (1965), and Singer and Day (1966) combined active and passive prismatic exposure with active and passive postexposure tests, finding generalization with little or no decrement even when exposure and test movements were of opposite types. Using a similar paradigm, Baily (1972a) reported that after prismatic exposure in which the subject engaged in ballistic target-pointing responses, equally large visuomotor negative aftereffects were observed for ballistic and slow ("zeroing-in") target-pointing motions during the postexposure tests. If prismatic exposure entailed the slow localization response, a test for adaptation using this same movement revealed much more adaptation than one involving the ballistic motion, another example of asymmetrical generalization.

Finally, several experiments (Mikaelin, 1967, 1970a; Kinney, McKay, Luria, & Gratto, 1970b) have deliberately varied both the stimulus conditions and the response demands between exposure and test. A good example is the experiment by Kinney et al. (1970b), who examined stimulus and response generalization of adaptation to 20-diopter prismatic displacement by combining three exposure activities with the same three tasks used as pre- and posttests. The tasks were (a) placing a small chess piece marker on a square within a checkerboard grid; (b) reaching under a transparent table for a target; and (c) rapidly spearing a bullseye with a wooden dowel. When these tasks were used as exposure activities the subject was provided with continuous visual feedback from his moving limb; when employed as pre- and posttests no view of the limb was allowed. Every subject was measured on all three tasks (in counterbalanced order) during the pre- and postexposure periods, but engaged in only one of the tasks during 5 min of prismatic exposure. The greatest amount of adaptation (about 65% of the total possible compensation) occurred for the trained task, regardless of the order of testing. The nontrained tasks for a given exposure condition revealed generalized adaptation with decrement.

The research presented in this section indicates that adaptation to rearranged vision, like learning, is subject to both stimulus and response generalization, usually with small to moderate decrements.

Intermanual Transfer of Adaptation

A thoroughly examined "learning phenomena," as it applies to adaptation to perceptual rearrangement, is intermanual (or bilateral) transfer. In traditional learning studies the presence of intermanual transfer of visuomotor performance for such tasks as mirror drawing (e.g., Cook, 1933) and the pursuit rotor (e.g., Kimble, 1952) has usually been viewed as evidence for a "central" component such as a rule or strategy. The same has been true in research on adaptation, with the proposed components usually being changes in felt direction of gaze (e.g., Kalil & Freedman, 1966a) or of head position (e.g., M. M. Cohen, 1974; Hamilton, 1964b). Other possibilities are a change in "pointing instructions" or a "conscious correction," which would probably be limited to exposure conditions involving target pointing.

It has been demonstrated repeatedly that terminal exposure to prismatic displacement leads to intermanual transfer of the visuomotor negative aftereffect and reduction of effect and to a large ipsilateral shift, whereas continuous exposure does not (e.g., M. M. Cohen, 1967). It was concluded that this is because terminal prismatic exposure is conducive to changes in visual localization.

The possibility of intermanual transfer of a shift in the felt position of the arm has been *directly* examined in only two published studies. McLaughlin and Bower (1965) reported no intermanual transfer of pointing straight ahead in the absence of vision, while at the same time an adaptive shift in pointing at a visual target revealed 100% transfer (probably due to a "conscious correction" on the part of the subject). Choe and Welch (1974) found that when exposure trials were "massed" an adaptive shift in pointing straight ahead with eyes shut was subject to intermanual transfer equal to approximately 45% of the ipsilateral shift. The interpretation of such transfer is unclear, although one possibility is that the act of pointing straight ahead of the nose without vision is governed not only by felt limb position but also by a response tendency for pointing to an imagined ("visualized") position in space. Presumably, it is only the latter component that transfers to the contralateral limb. A second alternative is that as a result of prismatic exposure the head came to feel as if it were turned to one side, leading to an error in reaching, with either hand, when attempting to follow the instruction to point straight ahead.

Learning Sets

Harlow (e.g., 1959) and others have demonstrated that higher organisms (most notably, primates) are capable of acquiring strategies for quickly mastering those learning tasks with which they have had a great deal of experience. These so-called "learning sets" thus transform a trial-and-error learner into one capable of "insight" or one-trial learning. With respect to adaptation to perceptual rearrangement, the best evidence for the presence of a learning set would be the demonstration of an increase in the rate and/or extent of adaptation as a function of repeated exposure periods, excluding any "conditioned adaptation" that might also occur. The latter phenomenon is discussed in the following section.

Lazar and Van Laer (1968) appear to have carried out the only published experiment on adaptation learning sets. They compared three conditions where the subject was exposed successively to three prismatic displacements for 10 min each but without intervening "unlearning" periods. For one group the displacements were 10, 20, and 30 diopters; for the second they were 20, 20, and 30 diopters; and for the third the displacement remained at 30 diopters for all three sessions. Adaptation, in terms of the visuomotor reduction of effect, was measured periodically throughout each exposure period. The investigators did not find evidence of a learning set since no change in the rate of adaptation was observed in the third exposure period (30 diopters) for either the "10–20–30" or "20–20–30" groups, in comparison to that of the "30–30–30" group.

Further research is needed before it can be concluded that adaptation to visual rearrangement is not subject to learning sets, especially since a number of less-controlled studies or casual observations, which are discussed later, suggest that it is.

THE EFFECT OF "LEARNING VARIABLES"

In the following section, discriminative conditioning of adaptation and the effects of massed (versus distributed) practice and delayed feedback will be examined for their relevance to adaptation to visual rearrangement.

The Conditioning of Adaptation

THE RESEARCH FINDINGS

Traditional learning studies have shown that organisms can learn to discriminate the stimuli that indicate when a certain response will be rewarded. This is *discriminative conditioning* and it appears that adaptation to rearranged vision is also subject to it. In most of the adaptation studies that are relevant here a procedure known as the "alternation technique" has been used. The most common variety of this procedure involves alternately exposing the subject to visual rearrangement while wearing goggles and normal vision without goggles and examining the *initial* response when the goggles (with or without the distorting medium) are placed upon the subject's head. Ideally, it should be ascertained that all vestiges of adaptation have disappeared by the end of each normal-vision period. The occurrence of conditioned adaptation is based on the assumption that during exposure to rearrangement the primary stimulus for adaptation is the presence of the intersensory discrepancy but that other, "neutral" stimuli that are present will become associated with the adaptive process. The feel of the goggles, reduced size of the visual field, and possibly the "side effects" or other nonadapted visual effects of the distorting medium could all serve as cues that an adaptive perceptual or perceptual–motor response on the part of the subject will be "rewarded" by the reduction of the intermodal discordance. Conversely, the absence of these cues could become associated with normal (nonadapted) or even counteradaptive behavior.

The most common observation of discriminative conditioning comes from a number of studies in which the subject has been adapted and tested on two or more occasions (as part of a within-subjects design), separated by a relatively long period of time. In these studies partial adaptive shifts were found in the *preexposure* measures of the experimental conditions that occurred subsequent to the first. Although some investigators (e.g., Held, 1968b; Klapp et al., 1974) have assumed that this effect represents the persistence of adaptation (i.e., incomplete decay), this seems quite unlikely, since there is typically fully sufficient interpolated normal visuomotor experience to completely abolish ("unlearn") the adaptive shift. Because many potential discriminative cues are present in these situations (e.g., feel of the goggles and size of the visual field), this example of conditioned adaptation may be referred to as the *situational effect*. It has been reported for the prismatically induced visuomotor negative aftereffect and reduction of effect (Hein, 1972; Klapp et al., 1974; Lackner & Lobovitz, 1977; Welch et al., 1974; Wooster, 1923), the visual shift (Welch et al., 1974), and the oculomotor shift (McLaughlin & Webster, 1967), as well as for visual adaptation to optical curvature (Festinger et al., 1967; Slotnick, 1969). An important finding reported by both Welch et al. (1974) and Lackner and Lobovitz (1976) is that the situational effect appears to reduce the total pre–post adaptive shift found in the second (and subsequent) testing sessions, suggesting the existence of a "ceiling" on adaptation. Researchers using a repeated-condition design should take heed of this potential source of within-group variance.

A more deliberate use of the alternation technique as a means of investigating conditioned adaptation involves switching back and forth between exposure to rearrangement and exposure to normal vision, with approximately the same time period for each condition. Taylor (1962, pp. 198–207) introduced this procedure in a long-term experiment using one subject who was exposed for half of each day to a right/left-reversed visual field and for the remainder of the day to normal vision. Eventually, the subject was able to remove or replace the distorting goggles with apparently little or no disturbance to his behavior or vision. The potential stimuli that could function as discriminative cues in this situation are limited to those associated with wearing the distorting goggles. Taylor carried out further tests of discriminative conditioning of adaptation, apparently succeeding with adaptation to prismatically induced slant of horizontal contours but failing with adaptation to lateral displacement. Unfortunately, Taylor's observations were rather uncontrolled and nonquantitative. In particular, he failed to withhold feedback from the subject in either the rearranged or normal-vision condition, so it is impossible to distinguish the occurrence of conditioned adaptation from a learning set in which the subject merely acquired the ability to more quickly overcome the rearrangement after its presence became known to him from his initial responses.[3]

Subsequent studies using Taylor's paradigm have produced mixed results. Foley (1967) and Foley and Abel (1967) failed to obtain evidence of conditioned adaptation, while Welch (1971b) succeeded. In the latter study the subject repeatedly alternated between prismatic exposure while wearing goggles, and normal vision without goggles. It was found that the shift in felt arm position was greater for test measures taken when the subject wore the goggles (now prismless) than for measures taken without the goggles. No such conditioning was found for adaptive shifts in visual direction. Kravitz (1972) independently replicated Welch's observations of conditioned felt limb position adaptation, but proposed that this result might be reinterpreted as a deliberate error-corrective response signaled by the feel of the goggles. Kravitz and Yaffe (1972) used an auditory tone as the conditional stimulus to test this possibility, on the assumption that since such a stimulus is not inherently associated with prismatic displacement, a conscious correction interpretation of any apparent conditioned adaptation would be untenable. The experimental group alternated between prismatic exposure in the presence of the auditory tone and normal vision with no tone, but wearing the prismless goggles. The visuomotor negative aftereffect was found to be significantly greater for tests taken with the tone than without, regardless of the additional presence of the goggles during the test. The shift in felt arm position gave evidence of discriminative conditioning only for the combined cues of tone and prismless goggles. Kravitz and Yaffe concluded that these data support the existence of genuine conditioned adaptation. However, this experiment did not completely rule out the

[3] In fact, it is not altogether clear what the nature of the adaptation was here. Although visuomotor behavior evidently became accurate and unaffected by a switch between the two optical situations, it is uncertain that the visual field had likewise come to appear normal (see Chapter 5).

possibility that the subject had merely learned to make a deliberate compensatory response at the sound of the tone. To rule out this possibility the subject should be clearly informed at the outset of the postexposure period that the prism has been removed. This procedure, used by Welch (1971b), would almost guarantee that the subject would not engage in a deliberate correction. Another way to avoid this problem is to use an exposure condition unlikely to lead to subject awareness of the distortion. A no-target, concurrent display condition using transverse arm movements (Held & Gottlieb, 1958) would be ideal for this purpose.

Kohler (1951) introduced a third variety of the alternation technique, using the split-field prism and color spectacles described in an earlier section. Continuous exposure for many days led to a state where eye movements in one direction or the other caused immediate, although partial, reduction of the effects originally associated with the respective directions of gaze. The same eye movements in the absence of the distorting medium led to conditioned aftereffects. The conditional stimulus in this situation was self-generated, rather than externally presented.[4] Unfortunately, the gaze-contingent color adaptation effect could not be replicated in later attempts (Harrington, 1965; McCollough, 1965b). In the case of the split-field prism spectacles, Kohler found contingent adaptation to the visual displacement of the upper half of a vertical contour relative to the lower half, as well as to the prism-induced effects of curvature, "stretching," and "shearing" with head movements. These findings were subsequently replicated and elaborated upon by Giannitrapani (1957) and Pick, Hay, and Martin (1969).

In other studies by Pick and his associates, gaze-contingent adaptation was observed with respect to "full" prisms, in terms of their shearing and stretching effects (Hay & Pick, 1966b; Pick & Hay, 1966a; Pick et al., 1966), confirming observations made by Kohler (1964, pp. 34–42). In the Pick et al. (1966) study the two gaze-contingent effects were subject to complete or nearly complete interocular transfer, implying central involvement for these types of adaptation. The investigators also observed moderate interocular transfer of curvature adaptation, but little or none for adaptation to color fringes. The latter results confirm those of Hajos and Ritter (1965).

---

[4] Rock (1966, p. 206) has argued that this form of adaptation is actually conditional on the *phenomenal position* of the stimulus relative to the subject's head, rather than to felt direction of gaze. However, experiments to test this alternative have not yet been done.

CONCLUSIONS

The evidence clearly indicates that adaptation to visual rearrangement is affected by the alternation technique. The conditional stimulus (CS) may lead to partial adaptive shifts for a nonadapted subject (as in the "situational effect") or for a subject who is already adapted to the "opposite" distortion (as with split-field prism spectacles).

It is important to note that, depending upon how adaptation occurs during exposure, these situations may be cases of classical conditioning or of instrumental discriminative conditioning. Thus, if adaptation is elicited "automatically" by exposure to the visual distortion, the situation is operationally the same as the classical conditioning paradigm. Take, for example, a subject who after wearing split-field or full prism spectacles reveals adaptation of one sort with eyes placed in a particular position and another sort (or none at all) with eyes placed differently. In this instance the felt direction of gaze (the CS), after repeated pairing with the intersensory discordance (the unconditioned stimulus, or UCS), elicits an adaptive shift (the conditioned response, or CR). If, on the other hand, adaptation is a matter of perceptual–motor learning, involving rewards and punishments, the situation is more like one of discriminative instrumental conditioning.

In a number of the experiments described in the present section (e.g., Welch, 1971b) subjects were repeatedly alternated between rearranged and normal vision, and it was usually found that adaptation was measurable both with and without the CS, although to a greater extent when the CS was present. However, the fact that adaptation is measurable even in the absence of the discriminative cue makes the resulting conditioning different from that found in traditional learning experiments, where there is usually no response at all without the CS. Thus, conditioned adaptation might be merely an example of stimulus generalization, although the use of the alternation procedure distinguishes this paradigm from that of the typical stimulus generalization study. With a very prolonged period of alternation between rearranged and normal vision, the subject might come to reveal an adaptive change to the CS and no adaptation (or even a counteradaptive shift) in its absence. In this case, the distinction from stimulus generalization would be clear. However, only in the study by Taylor (1962, pp. 198–207) with right/left reversal has such "all-or-none" conditioning been reported. The clearest distinction between the two learning phenomena is that, in a test for stimulus generalization, an already-adapted subject is measured for adaptation in one or more conditions varying in their stimulus characteristics, while in a test of conditioned adaptation the CS is presented to the subject when he is either totally "unadapted" (e.g., Klapp et al., 1974) or adapted to a distortion in the opposite direction (e.g., Taylor, 1962).

The distinction between conditioned adaptation and learning set should also be made. The most important difference between the two is that conditioned adaptation is ideally measured at the onset of the CS and without any feedback, while a learning set is measured in terms of the subject's "recovery rate" with feedback as he is alternated between rearranged and normal vision or between two different rearrangements. A progressively faster rate of adaptation or unlearning is best interpreted as evidence for a learning set. Thus, analogous to the results of Harlow's (e.g., 1959) studies of problem-solving behavior in monkeys, the subject may become quite adept at invoking (not necessarily consciously) the necessary perceptual or perceptual–motor correction after only the one or two responses required to identify the nature of the rearrangement. As seen earlier, however, the one published attempt to measure "learning to learn" in prism adaptation (Lazar & Van Laer, 1968) was unsuccessful.

It should be obvious that conditioned adaptation and learning sets are very closely related and that in some experiments their effects have probably been confounded. Peterson and Peterson (1938) and Snyder and Snyder (1957), examining optical inversion, and Kinney, Luria, Weitzman, and Markowitz (1970a), measuring underwater perceptions of divers, reported that repeated, unrestricted exposure to rearrangement with relatively long intervening periods of normal vision led to very rapid or even "immediate" adaptation. Because of the relatively uncontrolled nature of the exposure periods used, probably both conditioned adaptation and a learning set (and possibly "conscious correction" as well) contributed to the large "savings" reported.

The existence of conditioned adaptation has implications for the use of an aftereffect measure, particularly for those designs where the subject is used as his own control. Thus, with repeated adaptation sessions separated by periods of normal visuomotor experience, the subject should come to reveal progressively smaller aftereffects. However, this will be the case only if the rearranged and normal-vision conditions are differentiated by at least one salient stimulus characteristic (e.g., feel of the goggles) and if this difference also exists between exposure and posttest. If the pre- and posttest measures are taken with prismless goggles and most of the other cues are left unchanged from the exposure period, aftereffects can be accepted as good estimates of adaptation even in repeated-condition studies.

Massed versus Distributed Practice

It is well known that distributed (or "spaced") practice of a perceptual–motor task, such as the pursuit rotor, leads to more rapid learning and/or better performance of that task than does massed practice (e.g., Kimble & Shattel, 1952). Several investigators have examined the potential effect of this variable upon prism adaptation and have found contradictory results.

Using 20-diopter, concurrent prismatic exposure without a target, Hein (1972) observed that the optimal condition for the production of complete adaptation was a 3-min exposure period administered every half hour. No details were given about the nature of the less optimal conditions of spacing. On the other hand, Van Laer (1968) failed to find the "distribution effect" with respect to the visuomotor negative aftereffect and reduction of effect resulting from 15 50-sec exposures to 20-diopter prisms while engaging in the pursuit rotor task. Dewar (1970a) also failed to observe an effect of practice distribution, using Howard's (1968) prismatic shaping technique in conjunction with terminal target-pointing exposure.

However, Taub and Goldberg (1973) found significantly greater adaptation to concurrent, no-target exposure to 20-diopter prisms when practice was spaced than when it was massed and also observed that only distributed practice led to intermanual transfer. The investigators argued that the differential effects of terminal and concurrent display on prism adaptation and the concomitant transfer to the nonexposed hand result from the fact that terminal exposure is actually a form of distributed practice, while concurrent exposure represents massed practice. Using a very similar design, procedure, and type of exposure, Goldberg, Gordon, and Taub (cited by Taub & Goldberg, 1974) replicated the results of Taub and Goldberg (1973) and showed that only when practice is massed does passive movement of the arm fail to result in adaptation.

In response to Taub and Goldberg, Cohen (1973) carried out two experiments manipulating both type of exposure (terminal/continuous) to 30-diopter prismatic displacement and the distribution of trials and found no relationship between the degree of spacing of target-pointing prism-exposure trials and the magnitude of visuomotor negative aftereffect for the exposed hand in either terminal or concurrent display conditions. When exposure was continuous, no intermanual transfer was observed, regardless of the extent to which the trials were spaced, which appears to contradict Taub and

Goldberg's findings.[5] However, with terminal exposure, intermanual transfer was observed for highly spaced exposure trials and declined in magnitude to zero with a decrease in intertrial interval. Cohen concluded that type of exposure has an effect on adaptation that is independent of the effect of practice distribution.

Finally, Choe and Welch (1974) found, in contradiction to Cohen (1973), that distributed practice (with either concurrent or terminal exposure) induced significantly greater visuomotor negative aftereffect than did massed practice. The distribution of trials did not affect the felt arm position shift. All conditions revealed intermanual transfer of visuomotor negative aftereffect and the massed conditions also led to intermanual transfer of the shift in felt arm position.

Clearly, the studies of practice distribution and prism adaptation have produced mixed results. It may be concluded that whether or not the distribution of practice has an effect upon prism adaptation depends upon a number of factors, probably the most important of which is the operational definition given to "spaced" and "massed" in a given experiment.

The Effects of Delayed Feedback

A variable that has received a great deal of attention in the learning literature is the length of the time interval between the response and its result. Two general paradigms have been used. In the first, the subject's behavior and the delayed feedback occur simultaneously, as when playing a musical instrument while exposed to delayed auditory feedback. In this situation an already-mastered task often suffers disruption (e.g., Smith, 1966) and little or no learning of a new task occurs. In experiments concerned with delay of *reward* (e.g., Grice, 1948) the behavior may also continue during the delay interval, and the typical result is a relatively steep performance decrement gradient as a function of delay. In the second paradigm, separate trials occur, a new trial not beginning until some time after the receipt of feedback from the response on the previous trial. Delays, even relatively long ones, tend to produce only small decrements in performance (e.g., Bilodeau, 1966). Thus, in assessing the effects of a delay of

---

[5] Taub (personal communication, 1975) has suggested that in none of Cohen's continuous exposure conditions was practice actually distributed, since the subject was allowed to view his immobile right hand between trials. If this argument is correct, Cohen's failure to find intermanual transfer with continuous exposure, whatever the trial spacing was, is not in conflict with the results of Taub and Goldberg (1973).

feedback, it is important to distinguish between the continuous- and separate-trials situations, which in the present context represent the difference between concurrent and terminal display.

The first published experiment to examine the effect of delayed feedback on adaptation was by Held et al. (1966). During the exposure period, the subject wore 20-diopter prisms and viewed a luminous oscilloscope trace that substituted for his unseen hand. In the experimental conditions a lag of .3, .5, .9, 1.7, or 3.3 sec was imposed between the hand's motion and movement of the oscilloscope trace. A control condition entailed no lag. The exposure task involved transverse arm movements with concurrent exposure and no target. Pre- and posttest measures of no-feedback target-pointing accuracy were taken. The results showed that adapation occurred only when there was no delay. It was concluded that unless feedback is immediate (disregarding the transmission time of light), the correlator is unable to make the adjustments necessary for adaptation to occur. Thus, a "simple correlator" is implied.

Hay and Goldsmith (1973) found that adaptation to altered visual position constancy (see Chapter 7) could occur to the same extent with a .15-sec delay as with essentially no delay, but only when the delay used during the pre- and posttests matched that of the exposure period. Delays of .3 or .6 sec failed to produce adaptation, confirming the results of Held et al. (1966). In a second experiment the investigators found that if the exposure period involved a .23-sec delay, position constancy adaptation occurred in the posttest only if essentially the same delay was instituted. Hay and Goldsmith argued, contrary to the conclusions of Held et al. (1966), that the adaptive mechanism serves as a "cross-correlator," since it is capable (within limits) of finding the particular lag of time between motor movement and visual feedback for which the maximum correlation holds.

Hay (1974) exposed the subject to variable time delays and found that position constancy adaptation could be measured only when the posttest stimulus was provided with a delay equal to the average of the delays used during the exposure period. It was argued that this result provides added evidence for the existence of a cross-correlator.

It appears that the preceding studies, in finding complete abolition of adaptation for delays greater than a certain amount, support the results of previous learning studies of delayed feedback with ongoing behavior (the first paradigm). A more specific interpretation is that when behavior and feedback reach a certain critical degree of asynchrony the condition becomes essentially one of "disarrangement" (e.g., Cohen & Held, 1960), whereby a given motor response is associated over time with a wide variety of visual inputs, making adaptation unlikely or impossible (see Chapter 2, p. 17).

Apparently, no published experiments of the effect of delayed feedback on adaptation have been done using the separate-trials paradigm. However, for procedural reasons, a number of investigators have instituted a short delay between response and feedback and all of them reported significant adaptation (Baily, 1972a; Dewar, 1970a; Gyr, Willey, & Gordon, 1972; Templeton et al., 1966, 1974; Welch, 1972). The only systematic examination of the effect of feedback delay in a separate-trials paradigm is found in an unpublished study by Rhoades (1968). In one condition, a target was provided and error correction was encouraged; in the other, the subject merely brought the finger around the far edge of the horizontal occluding board in "random" positions, without reference to a specific target. Delays of 0, 4, and 8 sec occurred between the end of each response and the visual feedback. Significantly greater visuomotor negative aftereffect was obtained when the target was present, confirming the results of studies described in Chapter 2 (e.g., Coren, 1966; Welch, 1969). It was found that adaptation (visuomotor negative aftereffect and felt hand position shift) occurred with a 4-sec delay, although it was significantly less than when no delay was instituted. A small but significant negative aftereffect was also obtained in the 8-sec delay condition, but only when a target had been provided during exposure.

Thus, it appears that when relatively short delays of feedback occur in conjunction with the separate-trials paradigm, prismatic adaptation, like learning, may be retarded but not eliminated.

NECESSARY CONDITIONS: THE MOTIVATION FOR ADAPTATION

The proposal that adaptation to visual rearrangement is a form of learning, particularly if it is thought to be instrumental conditioning, leads one to look for some form of motivating force or drive that is reduced by the act of adapting. When exposure to rearrangement involves a specific visuomotor task, potentially motivating conditions are easy to find. One can reasonably argue that the experiences of bumping into objects or misreaching for targets are sufficiently unpleasant as to provide the basis for an aversive drive. Consequently, the reacquisition of the ability to avoid obstacles and accurately localize objects should be rewarding as the result of the diminution of this drive. It is also possible that successful visuomotor behavior is intrinsically rewarding independently of any previous difficulty. Kohler (e.g., 1964), Taylor (1962), and Festinger et al. (1967) have all proposed such a reinforcement model of adaptation. They argue not only that visuomotor adaptation is acquired by the action of rewards and punishments but that *visual* adaptation occurs only after visuomotor adaptation is highly "overlearned." That is, correct viewing awaits correct behavior. This theory is evaluated in later chapters.

The preceding analysis becomes difficult to maintain for situations where the subject does not engage in a specific visuomotor act, for example, the concurrent exposure, no-target condition. Because such a condition produces a certain amount of adaptation, some investigators have suggested that prismatic adaptation is not an example of learning. However, Taub (e.g., 1968) has proposed a motivational model designed to handle the "no-task" situation. He points out that although the subject experiences neither punishment nor reward for his actions, he is exposed to an intersensory discordance (e.g., between felt and seen limb position), which both informs him (although not necessarily at a conscious level) of the existence and nature of the optical rearrangement and induces an aversive drive. The latter is either innately determined or the result of previous punishing experiences. Adapting serves to reduce this drive and, thus, according to Taub, prism adaptation is an example of learning to avoid a situation that might lead to behavioral difficulties. Thus, adaptation is not necessarily escape learning since it can occur even where there is no target present and thus no errors in behavior. Learning can occur for a paralyzed organism (e.g., Black, Carlson, & Solomon, 1962), and Taub likens this to an adaptive response occurring without a response being practiced.

In a direct test of one aspect of Taub's avoidance learning hypothesis, Taub and Goldberg (1974) caused the amount of optical displacement of a variable prism to be contingent upon the rate at which the subject moved his arm back and forth. The subject reduced (or increased) his responding rate when this change led to a decrease in displacement. It is important to note that the subject was apparently unaware of the reward contingency and, for that matter, of the existence of the prism. Thus, it appears that intersensory discordance is aversive and that responses leading to its attentuation are reinforcing.

SUMMARY AND CONCLUSIONS

What conclusions can now be drawn about the relationship between adaptation to rearranged vision and learning? First, both phenomena increase in magnitude as a negatively accelerated function of time or trials, although the acquisition rate for adaptation is generally much greater than that found for the typical learning task. However, the negatively accelerated acquisition function is observed so often in psychology that this similarity between adaptation and learning should not be considered convincing evidence for the identity of the two phenomena. The decay functions of learning and adaptation are also similar in form, although the forgetting of adaptation appears to be more rapid than that observed for traditional perceptual–motor tasks, presumably because proactive inhibition is much stronger for eye–hand localization responses than for many of the complex motor skills used in learning studies. As indicated previously, proactive inhibition appears to be involved in the decay of adaptation, which clearly supports the learning view. The finding of "prism aftereffect reminiscence" in some studies has been countered by failures in others, and until the necessary conditions for inducing this effect are known it will represent only tenuous support for the learning position. It is clear that adaptation to rearrangement is subject to both stimulus and response generalization, together with some decrement. Under certain conditions, intermanual transfer occurs for adaptation to prism-displaced vision and other types of rearrangement, which, although appearing to support the learning position, may be due simply to an adaptive change in apparent visual direction (presumably based on recalibrated felt head or eye position). No evidence for learning sets in adaptation has been found, although this is clearly an area deserving greater attention than it has received so far.

Adaptation can be discriminatively conditioned in much the same manner as are traditional learning tasks. This represents one of the most convincing forms of support for the claim that adaptation is learning. The evidence for the effect of distribution of practice on adaptation is mixed and, as with prism aftereffect reminiscence, it remains to be seen what the import of research on this factor will be for the learning position. Experiments on the effect of delays of feedback on adaptation have produced results that seem quite similar to those obtained in traditional learning studies. That is, for both learning and adaptation, delays of feedback are devastating for ongoing behavior and only moderately detrimental when separate responses are being performed. This represents another form of evidence in favor of the learning position. Finally, Taub (e.g., 1968) has shown that it is possible to propose a tenable motivational–reward system for adaptation comparable to systems assumed to operate in some traditional learning situations.

The question of whether or not adaptation to rearranged vision is a form of learning has led to a number of interesting experiments that have produced useful data. For this reason alone, the issue has proved fruitful. On the other hand, the hypothesis that adaptation is (or is like) learning may be oversimplified, since it implies that adaptation consists of a *unitary* process and end state, whereas the evidence contradicts this notion (Chapter 3). For example, it seems quite clear now that prismatic adaptation can involve up to three operationally distinct components: recalibration of felt arm position, shift in felt direction of gaze or felt head position, and an assimilated error-corrective response. Furthermore, it is possible that some prism-adaptive end states are like learning and others are not. It was proposed in Chapter 3 that the error-corrective response is most similar (if not identical) to traditional perceptual–motor learning. There is also evidence for the existence of qualitative differences between adaptation to different types of rearrangement, such as between lateral displacement and tilt (e.g., Redding, 1973b). Ebenholtz (1967) found no negative transfer for adaptation to optical tilt immediately following adaptation to the opposite tilt, whereas Welch *et al.* (1970) did observe such interference for visuomotor adaptation to lateral prismatic displacement. Thus, the "laws" of learning may apply to some forms of adaptation but not to others.

While it is true that adaptation to visual rearrangement sometimes looks like learning, this does not automatically indicate a similarity in underlying process. The latter possibility is quite attractive, since it would link two areas of psychological research considered to be qualitatively different, but there is evidence against such an assumption of identity. The point is that, although it is useful in the interest of parsimony to see how well the adaptation findings fit into a learning framework, one should beware of terminating the investigation prematurely. Once it has been shown that adaptation is similar in some respect to learning, one should examine further the underlying basis for this similarity. If future research shows that adaptation to perceptual rearrangement is an example of learning, then since we already know a lot about learning (behaviorally, physiologically, and pharmacologically), we will thereby know a lot about adaptation.

5

Adaptation to
Visual Transposition

THE "PROBLEM" OF THE INVERTED RETINAL IMAGE

In 1604 and 1611 Kepler showed that the retinal image must be inverted relative to the physical world. This, together with Sheiner's direct observation of the inverted image in 1625, led philosophers and others to wonder how it is that we perceive an upright visual field. To explain this seeming paradox, Descartes proposed that the neural representation of the image is *reinverted* before it reaches the pineal gland, which he believed to be the seat of perception. Some early psychologists were also concerned with the relationship between the orientation of the retinal image and the perceived orientation of the visual field, and the philosophical and psychological histories of this issue have been reviewed by Walls (1951, pp. 55–83).

The problem actually involves two questions:

1. Why does the world look right side up when the retinal image is upside down?
2. Is it necessary for the retinal image to be inverted to see an upright world?

The next section shows why it is now generally agreed that the first of these is actually a pseudo problem and should not be confused with the second.

Why a Right Side Up World When the Retinal Image Is Upside Down?

This question is nonsensical because it assumes that the anatomical structure and physiological events underlying perception are, or should be, identical to the resulting phenomenal events. The problem is obvious when it is considered that, contrary to Descartes's conception, the representation of the retinal image remains inverted after it reaches the visual area of the cortex. To be consistent, if the inverted image on the retina is an enigma, then the fact that an inverted "image" in the brain can lead to the experience of uprightness is also an enigma. However, the argument that stimulation of the upper part of the visual cortex (or retina) should denote "up" and the lower part "down" is fallacious, which is apparent if the same logic is applied to other sensory modalities. For the "body image" (somesthesis), for example, the assumption of "anatomical isomorphism" leads one to conclude that the cortical area receiving this input should be the same shape and size as the body. This, quite obviously, is nonsense.

Thus, it may be concluded that, in principle, the orientation of the retinal image (or cortical representation) is irrelevant to visual spatial orientation. However, the fact that there is no *necessary* relationship between the retinal image and phenomenal orientation does not contradict the now well-known fact that there is a relatively fixed point-for-point mapping of input from the retina onto the visual cortical projection area. Rock (1966, p. 27) and others have suggested that this fact indicates that the perceived *relation* among visual points, which is the basis of the perception of relative size, distance, angle, and orientation of one object to another, is probably given innately. Even if this were true, however, it does not follow that perceived orientation of the *field as a whole thereby requires* an inverted retinal image, as some investigators (e.g., Walls, 1951) have concluded. Perceiving that objects are located in different positions relative to each other does not imply that the visual field will look upright, since this relationship is independent of and unaffected by any change in the orientation of the field.

Is an Upside Down Retinal Image Necessary for Right Side Up Vision?

When it became apparent to psychologists that the inverted retinal image does not pose a problem for spatial vision, a different question was raised: Is there an innate (and possibly unmodifiable) connection between the inverted image and right side up vision? In other words, is it necessary that the human infant's retinal image be inverted for him to see an upright world? Several early theories of space perception, the "eye movement theory" and the "projection theory," said that it was. To test these notions, George Stratton (1896, 1897a,b) carried out several pioneering experiments in which he wore spectacles that reerected the retinal image and noted his initial and subsequent responses to this novel situation.[1] In the ensuing years, similar experiments appeared periodically. Although the majority of these involved 180° rotation of the visual field, a few entailed reversal of the right/left but not the up/down dimension, or vice versa. These three types of optical rearrangement are examples of *visual transposition*. Smith and Smith (1962, Chapters 4 and 5) have described the studies of transposed vision in detail and only a brief summary will be presented here, the emphasis continuing to be on inversion. Unfortunately, these experiments failed to provide an unequivocal answer to Stratton's original question.

STUDIES OF TRANSPOSED VISION

For 3 and then later 8 days (87 waking hours) Stratton wore a monocular device that rotated the visual field 180° by means of two pairs of double-convex lenses placed at the appropriate distance from each other within a tube. During the exposure periods, Stratton engaged in more or less normal activities and later wrote a long and fascinating report of his experiences. Subsequent studies were carried out by Ewert (1930) and Peterson and Peterson (1938), using 14 days of exposure to binocular inversion, and Snyder and Pronko (1952), using 30 days of binocular inversion. The most extensive investigations were undertaken by Erismann and Kohler, at the University of Innsbruck (Erismann, 1947; Kohler, 1951, 1955, 1962, 1964), and by some of their colleagues (Kottenhoff, 1957; Krüger, 1939; Taylor, 1962). Other organisms have also been used—houseflies (Holst, 1954), amphibia

---

[1] Actually, Ardigo (1886; cited by Giannitrapani, 1958) may have been the first to do an experiment of this sort. According to Giannitrapani (personal communication, 1976), Ardigo used a right-angle prism to produce the inversion and eventually not only came to experience the world as right side up, but also saw things as upside down immediately after the prism was removed. Unfortunately, further details about this early experiment were not available.

(e.g., Sperry, 1948), fish (Mittelstädt, 1944), chickens (Pfister, 1955), rats (Albert, 1966), cats (Bishop, 1959; Robinson, 1975a,b), and a monkey (Foley, 1940)—but adaptation, as measured by visuomotor performance, has been observed only for mammals. The research with animals is described in detail in Chapter 11; the present discussion will be limited to the relatively few experiments involving human subjects.

The theoretical bases of these experiments varied and influenced the investigators' choices of exposure conditions and adaptation measures. Stratton engaged in everyday activities during exposure and was concerned primarily with how the world looked to him. He found nearly complete visuomotor adaptation and occasionally stated that the visual field looked upright, or at least "normal," an occurrence which was more frequent toward the end of the longer exposure period. After removing the spectacles the world looked upright, even though a visuomotor negative aftereffect and compensatory head movement-induced change in visual position constancy (see Chapter 7) were observed. This suggests that visual adaptation to perceived orientation had failed to occur. In contrast to Stratton, Ewert (1930) used objective laboratory tests in his attempt to measure perceptual and perceptual–motor adaptation to binocular inversion. These tests included card sorting, reaching for visual, tactual, or auditory targets, and indicating where things appeared to be located. He found a very significant visuomotor reduction of effect and negative aftereffect, but did not find even fleeting experiences of upright vision. Peterson and Peterson's (1938) experiment is similar to Stratton's, in that it involved wearing inverting spectacles (binocular) under everyday circumstances and relied heavily on phenomenological reports of both perceptual experience and behavioral effects. The one subject acquired visuomotor adaptation but, like Ewert's subjects, failed to experience even a temporary righting of the phenomenal field. Snyder and Pronko (1952) used the longest exposure period (30 days), but were concerned with the development of visuomotor coordination and only incidentally reported how the world looked by the end of the exposure period. Snyder (serving as subject) reported that, while the orientation of the field had come to look *familiar* to him, it remained apparently inverted. As usual, the removal of the distorting spectacles led to visuomotor negative aftereffects.

Smith and Smith (1962) did an extensive series of experiments in which subjects viewed their hands via closed circuit TV while engaging in various eye–hand coordination tasks. In some experiments the video feedback was 180° rotated, up/down reversed, or right/left reversed. Since the visual transposition device was not attached to the subject's head, a number of the visual effects produced by distorting spectacles were absent. For this and other reasons it is quite unlikely that visual adaptation occurred in these experiments; in fact, the investigators did not look for this form of adaptation or even test for the visuomotor negative aftereffect. Some of these same limitations also characterize other experiments using video feedback to transpose the visual field (Hershberger & Carpenter, 1972; Smothergill, Martin, & Pick, 1971); consequently, this line of research will not be discussed further in the present context.

Erismann and Kohler (e.g., Kohler, 1964) based their conclusions almost entirely upon verbal reports of overall impressions. More important, their subjects engaged in very demanding interactions with the environment, such as skiing and mountain climbing, while wearing up/down or right/left-reversing goggles. The inclusion of such activities may be important to the issue of whether or not subjects with transposed vision can ever come to see the world right side up again, since these Innsbruck studies produced some of the most convincing evidence of perceptual righting of the visual field. Typically, these latter observations occurred only after visuomotor adaptation was well established. Some interesting instances in which some parts of the field looked correctly oriented while others did not were also reported and are examined in more detail later.

Only the Innsbruck studies, and perhaps Stratton, produced evidence to suggest that the world can eventually come to look normally oriented and, even then, the experiences were often transitory or inconsistent. Notwithstanding this rather equivocal state of affairs, many writers have concluded either (a) that the subjects in the experiments of Stratton and his successors had undergone a very definite and stable righting of the visual field or (b) that they continued to experience the world as visually transposed to the very end of the exposure period. Such diametrically opposed conclusions undoubtedly stem from the fact that the question "Does the world look upright?" is quite ambiguous. "Up" and "down" (and "right" and "left") have more than one meaning. In an attempt to clarify this matter, the initial and subsequent responses of an *imaginary* subject when confronted with a transposed visual field will be examined (based primarily on the detailed accounts of Stratton and Kohler). For simplicity, and in deference to the historical issue concerning the orientation of the retinal image, this discussion is limited to the case of upside down vision.

A HYPOTHETICAL SUBJECT'S INITIAL EXPERIENCE
WITH OPTICAL INVERSION

When a subject first peers through inverting spectacles at a familiar world, he reports that the scene looks "strange and unreal." And, of course, it looks upside down. At the same time, unseen parts are *visualized* as being in their normal, upright orientation. Another initial effect is a large error when reaching for an object because its apparent and actual loci are quite different. A highly disturbing illusion of visual motion of the field during head (but not eye) movements also occurs, which may lead to severe nausea—a case of motion sickness. The visual scene appears to move in the *same* direction as the head, but by twice the angle. Likewise, if the optical device transposes only one of the two dimensions (right/left or up/down), a *tilt* of the head causes the visual field to rotate twice as much.[2] The many disturbing effects and the novelty of the visually transposed field might also cause the subject to experience loss of control and a variety of other generally unpleasant affective states (Cegalis & Murdza, 1975; Cegalis & Young, 1974; Nielsen, 1963). Finally, the subject experiences a discrepancy between vision and other spatial modalities. A limb is felt to be located in one place but is seen in another, and the visual and auditory loci of sound-emitting objects are discrepant.

But what about gravity? Berkeley (1910) and Rock (1966, pp. 18–19) have argued that the gravitational sense boils down to the feeling that the feet are closer to the earth than the head, an experience that is independent of the apparent orientation of the visual field. If a subject wearing inverting spectacles were to look down at his legs, they would be seen in a position different from where they are felt to be (with reference to the felt position of the head and shoulders), but the perceived direction of gravity would still be from head to feet and the visible feet would continue to appear to be in contact with the visible ground. Therefore, vision and gravitational sense neither conflict nor agree, since gravitational sense is not affected by the optical rearrangement. Nevertheless, the sense of gravity can lead, in an *indirect* manner, to the experience that visual objects are inverted or otherwise disoriented. If it is assumed that human beings are capable

[2] These losses of "visual position constancy" are discussed in detail in Chapter 7. Only if the inverting lenses are directly attached to the eye (e.g., by means of a contact lens) will eye movements also lead to illusory visual motion, as seen in an experiment by Smith (1966). On the other hand, if the subject were exposed to the inversion by means of a TV monitor (e.g., Smith & Smith, 1962), neither head nor eye movements will result in apparent motion.

of perceiving the orientation of the retinal image relative to the coordinates of the retina (and therefore the head), then the veridical perception of the orientation of the body (or at least of the head) with respect to gravity should make it possible to assess the orientation of a visual object relative to gravity. For example, an arrow aimed at the physical ground will be perceived as pointing away from the ground when viewed through inverting spectacles because the subject senses that he is standing upright and that the direction of the retinal image is that signifying the direction of chin to forehead.

THREE ASPECTS OF SPATIAL VISION

The most salient initial effect of wearing inverting spectacles is the upside down appearance of the visual scene. That the world should look inverted for an adult when the retinal image has been optically righted would seem quite predictable and easily explained. However, a critical analysis of this and the entire question of visual orientation makes it clear that we are dealing with one of the most conceptually difficult problems in all of psychology! To understand why the optically inverted visual field appears to be upside down and, for that matter, why the normally viewed scene looks upright, it is necessary to differentiate among several aspects of spatial vision: (a) environmental orientation; (b) egocentric orientation; and (c) egocentric direction.[3]

Environmental Orientation

If one observes with normal vision a typical scene, objects are experienced as being oriented in some fashion with respect to their physical environment, appearing to be in line with or at some degree of variance from the vertical and horizontal dimensions of the world. There are two sources of this experience of environmental orientation: (a) the visual framework and (b) the perceived direction of gravity. For the upright observer viewing objects on the frontoparallel plane these two factors are confounded. For example, a picture hanging on a wall may appear to need straightening because its sides are misaligned with respect to both the coordinates of the room and the felt direction of gravity (the latter operating in the indirect manner discussed previously). It is possible to separate these two factors in the

---

[3] The distinction between (a) and (b) has been made previously by Rock (1975, Chapter 10).

laboratory. The visual framework may be eliminated by placing a luminous object in an otherwise dark room; only gravitational information is present, and observers are capable of perceiving rather accurately the orientation of objects on the basis of this cue alone. This is true even when the subject's head is tilted, which reaffirms the conclusion that the orientation of the retinal image does not determine perceived environmental orientation, but rather is "interpreted" by means of cues concerning the body's (or head's) relation to gravity. It is also possible to change the direction of gravity by means of the human centrifuge, which results in a concomitant change in the apparent gravitational orientation of a luminous line, an effect termed the *oculogravic illusion* (e.g., Graybiel, 1952). The term *illusion* is unwarranted though, since the subject's experienced shift in gravitational upright is completely congruent with his changed sense of gravitational direction (Howard & Templeton, 1966, p. 199).

Isolating the role of visual framework from that of gravitational sense is a more difficult matter, since typically it is impossible to eliminate gravitational force. However, the two cues may be pitted against each other by confronting the observer with a tilted visual framework and requiring him to set an object located within the framework to the gravitational vertical (e.g., Asch & Witkin, 1948a,b). These experiments indicate that the framework exerts a sizable effect on apparent orientation even though it conflicts with gravitational information. This framework effect is not germane to the present question, however, because it does not involve the entire visual field; on the other hand, the gravitational aspect of environmental orientation is relevant to the issue of adaptation to inverted vision and will be discussed further.

Egocentric Orientation

Even when gravitational cues for orientation are irrelevant, as when lying on one's back (Hafter, cited by Rock, 1975, p. 493), inverting spectacles lead to the experience of an upside down visual field because of the perceived relation of the visual environment to the observer—egocentric orientation. Rock (1966, pp. 28-34) has argued convincingly that the perception of egocentric orientation involves attributing egocentric significance to the orientation of the retinal image. He proposes that this occurs on the basis of information concerning the relation of retinal image orientation to the *visualized* head. For example, a line coincident with the vertical meridian of the eye is perceived as egocentrically vertical because such a retinal direction is in line with the sides of the head. Rock's theory is discussed more fully in a later section.

For the upright observer with normal vision the visual field appears both environmentally and egocentrically upright. However, the two perceptual modes can be pitted against each other simply by looking at the world from between one's legs, which causes the visual field to appear egocentrically inverted while remaining environmentally upright because gravitational cues allow the rotated retinal image to be attributed to the fact that the head is upside down.

When the retinal image is made upright, the visual field will appear egocentrically inverted, which does not mean that the observer will necessarily be *aware* of the inversion. For example, a subject wearing inverting spectacles and viewing a downward-pointing luminous arrow in an otherwise unlighted setting will misperceive the direction of the arrow but will not necessarily label it "upside down." This distinction is clear in the case of viewing a familiar object that has a normal up and down orientation. The observer will not only see the physically topmost part of the object as being "down" and the bottom as "up," he will also have the very definite experience that the object has been rotated 180°. Rock (1966, p. 31) has argued that the "righted" retinal image of the object leads to the memory of its normal orientation, which is at odds with the current experience, thereby leading to the impression that it is upside down.

Before going on to the third and last aspect of spatial vision it should be noted that when familiar, "monooriented" objects are egocentrically (or environmentally) disoriented they look strange or perhaps unrecognizable. This is easily demonstrated by rotating this book 180° and examining the print. Another good example is that inverted pictures of human faces look very odd and their expressions are difficult to interpret. However, continued exposure to inverted objects eventually causes them to look more familiar. Subjects who are exposed to inverted print for long periods of time are eventually able to read it as rapidly as they read upright print (Kolers, 1975). Thus, it is quite possible for an object or the entire visual field to continue to look inverted while simultaneously becoming more familiar and recognizable to the subject. Stratton describes such a familiarization toward the end of his experiment and, when he removed the spectacles, although the world looked upright once again, it had an "odd" appearance.

Egocentric Direction

Not only are extended objects in visual space perceived as having a particular orientation, but any point of an object (or the object as a whole) will be seen to be located in a particular radial direction relative to the observer. For example, a chair can be seen as right side up *and* located off to the left. In a field composed entirely of separate points of light only the perception of radial direction would be possible, since the perception of orientation requires *extended* objects, lines, or directions of movement. As seen in Chapter 3, directional perception involves the locus of the retinal image of a point, assessed in terms of the registered position of eye relative to head and/or head relative to trunk. If the felt positions of these loci of articulation were to be precluded or made unreliable in some fashion, the veridical perception of egocentric direction would not seem possible. It is likely that the standard of reference for directional perception is typically the trunk, rather than the head (Harris, 1965). For example, a visual position to the left of the trunk would be perceived by most observers to be to the left, regardless of the position of the head relative to the trunk.

It may be concluded that when a subject first dons inverting spectacles and walks about in an everyday environment, his experience of an upside down world is the result of three factors:

1. The field looks inverted with respect to gravity (environmental orientation).
2. The field looks inverted in comparison to the preexperimental orientation of the field relative to the head (egocentric orientation).
3. The apparent location of objects (egocentric direction) has been up/down (and right/left) reversed.

Thus, it is apparent that complete adaptation to transposed vision requires the alteration of several different components of spatial vision. However, even if the observer fails to adapt in any of these three major ways, it is safe to say that the disoriented visual field will eventually become quite familiar to him.

Let us now return to our hypothetical subject, who is still wearing his inverting spectacles, and see if and how he comes to terms with his new visual world.

THE RESPONSE OF A HYPOTHETICAL SUBJECT TO OPTICAL INVERSION

At first, the subject may avoid moving around very much because of the nauseating visual field motion. Fortunately, this illusion soon diminishes and may eventually disappear, whether or not any other form of adaptation occurs. If the spectacles are then removed, visual motion as the result of head movement will again be experienced, indicating that the subject has truly adapted to this effect. For reasons that are presented in Chapter 7, the *direction* of the visual motion aftereffect depends on whether or not the visual field has come to appear normal in terms of egocentric orientation. If this has not occurred, then the aftereffect of apparent motion will be in the direction opposite the head motion; if it has, the direction of apparent motion and head movement will be the same.

As exposure continues, the visual field comes to look increasingly less strange and nonseen portions are imagined to be inverted, in agreement with the visual field. The subject's upside down world has now become familiar to him and congruent with his visualization of unseen parts. Deliberate and slow reaching and locomotory movements give way to automatic and rapid responding. Conscious strategies for accurate visuomotor behavior may be used initially, although they require great concentration, are sometimes incorrect, and may be lost temporarily if the subject is forced to make a sudden and unexpected response. Ultimately, though, visuomotor behavior becomes virtually errorless. This is true visuomotor adaptation, since upon removal of the spectacles a strong behavioral negative aftereffect is revealed. The discrepancies between vision, on the one hand, and felt body position and audition, on the other, become resolved— in favor of vision. Thus, the subject may report that his limbs have come to feel as if they are located where he sees them and that sounds seem to emanate from their seen, rather than objective, sources. However, the resolution of the visual–auditory discrepancy does not appear to carry over to unseen sound sources, and auditory localization is not subject to aftereffect errors when the spectacles are removed.

Most important, of course, is the question of how the visual world appears to be oriented. As exposure to the visual inversion continues, the subject may report occasional, often contradictory, experiences of the scene appearing to be the right way around, particularly when he is actively engaged in everyday behaviors. Rarely, however, do these experiences withstand the subject's critical introspection. Further-more, he is unlikely to observe an aftereffect of visual orientation when the spectacles are removed.

REPORTS FROM ACTUAL SUBJECTS

Let us now examine the evidence from actual subjects concerning the crucial question of how the world looks after continued exposure to 180°-rotated or right/left-reversed vision. However, we must be very careful here in our choice of indicator responses. It should be clear by now that even if a subject demonstrates errorless visuomotor behavior, reports that the world looks familiar or "normal," and uses correctly labels such as "up" and "down," the visual scene might continue to appear to be the wrong way around. Nor should the reso-lution of the discrepancy between seen and felt body position necessarily be equated with visual adaptation, since this might mean only that parts of the body are felt to be where they appear to be. With these cautions in mind, let us look at the introspective reports that suggest the occurrence of true adaptive changes in the apparent orientation of a transposed visual field.

Stratton (1897b) reported on the fourth day of his 8-day experiment:

> The feeling of the inversion or uprightness of things was found to vary considerably with the strength and character of the representation of my body. When I looked at my legs and arms, or even when I reinforced by effort of attention their new visual representation, then what I saw seemed rather upright than inverted [p. 354].

After further exposure, several observations confirmed that only when he was paying attention to the current visual representation of his body or was engrossed in some activity did the world appear normally oriented.[4] Upon removing the spectacles after 8 days, Stratton (1897b) said:

> The scene had a strange familiarity. The visual arrangement was immediately recognized as the old one of preexperimental days; yet the reversal of everything from the order to which I had grown accustomed during the past week gave the scene a surprising, bewildering air which lasted for several hours. It was hardly the feeling, though, that things were upside down [pp. 470–471].

---

[4] Ewert (1930) concluded from this and the results of his own experiment that Strat-ton's reports of occasionally seeing the world right side up could be dismissed merely as lapses of attention that gave him an illusory "feeling of normalcy." This, in turn, might have been the result of either disattending the apparent orientation of the field or sup-pressing its remembered former orientation.

This failure to note a visual aftereffect indicates that a stable change in the apparent orientation of the field had not occurred for Stratton, although one cannot dismiss the possibility that there were fleeting instances of such adaptation at various times during the exposure period.

As indicated previously, some of the most clear-cut experiences of visual adaptation to transposition are found in the Innsbruck studies. In one experiment that lasted 9 days (Kohler, 1964, p. 32), the subject reported seeing more and more objects as right side up and, after removing the inverting device, had the striking experience of an upside down world. In addition, one subject misperceived "W"'s as "M"'s and vice versa (Kohler, 1964, p. 34).[5]

In two experiments subjects were exposed for very long periods to right/left reversal of the visual field by means of right-angle prisms. In one instance (Kohler, 1964, pp. 140–161), the subject wore the prism goggles for 37 days and reported that after several weeks the direction of objects was correctly perceived. Immediately after the goggles were removed, the subject described the room in which he was standing as being reversed. Kottenhoff (1957) and Taylor (1962), both of whom spent some time at the Innsbruck laboratory, also examined adaptation to this form of transposition. Taylor found that after his subject had been trained vigorously on a number of complex visuomotor tasks a visually right/left-reversed field came to appear normally oriented. More surprising was the fact that after repeated alternation between wearing the reversing goggles for half a day and going without them for the remainder of the day the subject was reportedly able to make the transition between the two visual situations while experiencing neither visuomotor disruption nor a change in the apparent orientation of the field.

Although Taylor's description implies that stable and consistent reorientation of the field was experienced by his subject, the Innsbruck studies indicate a more contradictory and inconsistent state of affairs. For example, one subject reported seeing a car driving on the correct side of the road while the numbers on the license plate continued to appear right/left reversed. In another case, a subject wearing inverting spectacles was confronted with two faces, one

[5] Kohler (1964, p. 31) also briefly described an interesting observation by an unnamed Russian investigator in a paper published in 1950, who reported that patients suffering from cataracts regained their vision when their corneas were used to focus real images on the retina. However, these images were right side up by the time they reached the retina. Despite this righting of the image, the patients were said to have soon come to see the visual world as right side up.

inverted relative to the other, and said that *both* of them looked upright! Seeing some objects the right way around while others remained reversed was frequently reported. These rather bizarre experiences have been termed *piecemeal adaptation* (e.g., Harris, 1965) and it is reasonable to suppose that such observations represent important clues concerning the nature of adaptation to transposed vision.

WHY SO LITTLE EVIDENCE OF VISUAL ADAPTATION?

A number of explanations have been proposed for the fact that subjects have rarely experienced consistent visual adaptation to inverted or right/left-reversed vision. The first possibility is that the human perceptual system is simply incapable of such compensation, a conclusion that assumes that, for adults at least, the inverted retinal image is necessary for upright and normal right/left vision (e.g., Walls, 1951, pp. 55–83). Rock (1966, p. 43), however, pointed out that in nearly all studies of inversion the visual field has been quite small, typically about 35°.[6] The only exception to this is the large (40–80°) fields that Kohler was able to achieve by the use of mirrors. Rock argued that a small visual field might inhibit adaptation to the transposed appearance of the world, since such a large part of the remaining field would be visualized in its preexposure orientation and little of the observer's own body would be visible. In addition, *binocular* inversion leads to a reversal of the stereoscopic and convergence cues for depth, a type of visual distortion that may be especially resistant to adaptation. As we have seen, what little evidence there is of true visual adaptation comes from the experiments by Stratton and Kohler, in which the optical reversal did not include the depth dimension. Ewert (1930) and Peterson and Peterson (1938), using a binocular arrangement, failed to observe even momentary signs of visual adaptation.

Another, rather obvious, explanation for the failure of the optically transposed visual field to come to look the right way around is that the exposure periods were simply not long enough to overcome a lifetime of experience with normal visual orientation. In fact, the length of exposure may be critical since, contrary to the situation with

---

[6] Actually, Stratton reported his visual field to be 45°. Subsequent investigators have uniformly been unable to exceed about 35° (except with mirrors), and it has been suggested (e.g., Rock, 1966, p. 43) that Stratton's measurements were incorrect.

many other forms of rearrangement, *partial* adaptation to inversion or right/left reversal is not possible (e.g., the world looks either right side up or upside down). Finally, if complete adaptation to all aspects of visual inversion is to occur, it is probably necessary for the subject to interact with the environment much more vigorously than has typically been the case. The subjects in Ewert's study engaged in relatively restricted activities, spending much of their time in the laboratory. Kohler (1964) and Taylor (1962), on the other hand, had subjects perform such demanding activities as fencing, mountain climbing, skiing, and bicycle riding in heavy traffic! It is plausible that the convincing reports of visual adaptation in these studies resulted from the fact that the subjects were highly motivated, were forced to acquire rapid and automatic visuomotor responses, and were provided with very good information about the nature of the rearrangement.

THEORIES OF VISUAL ADAPTATION TO OPTICAL TRANSPOSITION

Although the evidence is mixed, it can be concluded from Stratton's and Kohler's reports that, under certain conditions of exposure to transposed vision, some sort of adaptive change in the spatial appearance of the visual field takes place. Consequently, let us now turn to the various theories that have been proposed concerning the conditions necessary for such adaptation and exactly what is is that adapts.

Necessary Conditions

THE EFFERENT READINESS THEORY

There is general acceptance of the fact that changes in the apparent orientation of the optically transposed visual field appear only after *visuomotor* adaptation has been well established. According to some theories (e.g., Taylor, 1962), the acquisition of correct behavior is a necessary condition for such adaptation; others (e.g., Rock, 1966) say that it is merely helpful.

Taylor (1962), Kohler (1964), and Festinger et al. (1967) have argued that visual adaptation to transposed vision will be complete only when visuomotor adaptation is so ingrained that it is elicited automatically. They contend that the orientation of the visual world will once again be perceived correctly only when the subject reaches a state in which he is *ready* to make the correct visuomotor responses, a notion termed the *efferent readiness theory*. For example, an object is seen as "up" when the stimulation from the visually inverted object induces a readiness to engage in an upward limb (or eye) movement. Taylor has been the most explicit about this theory. In contrast to Kohler and Festinger *et al.*, he argues that for adult human subjects the *verbal*, as well as visuomotor, habits acquired from normal experience must be replaced if the optically transposed visual field is to look the right way around. This will occur, according to Taylor, as the result of punishments and rewards encountered during the course of the subject's interaction with his new visual environment. The theory suggests that "real-life" situations, where accurate and rapid responding is demanded, are ideal for the induction of complete visual adaptation. Perhaps the best possible condition for the production of adaptation is one in which eye movements are subject to disruption, along with the other muscle systems, which can be effected by attaching the inverting prism to a contact lens (see footnote 2). The visual field not only looks inverted with this device, but eye movements are grossly in error. It appears that the only study to make use of such an optical arrangement was by Smith (1966), and he found no adaptation of any sort. However, since the exposure period was only 45 min long, adaptation might have eventually occurred. Presumably, the efferent readiness theory would predict that if the subject ultimately acquired the ability to make the correct eye (and hand) movements accurately and easily while wearing the contact-lens prism, visual adaptation to the inversion would be in evidence.

Unfortunately, the validity of the efferent readiness theory remains very much in doubt. Although the data are certainly congruent with the expectation that visual adaptation (when it occurs) is preceded by visuomotor adaptation, there are a number of ways to interpret this. Clearly, no one has adequately tested the theory as it pertains to adaptation to transposed vision.[7] Demonstrating adaptation in the absence of active interaction with the optically transposed environment would represent a fatal blow to this theory. Of course, such passive exposure would need to entail adequate information regarding the nature of the rearrangement; Rock (1966, Chapter 2) has sug-

[7] A number of investigators (Burnham, 1968; Burnham & Aertker, 1970; Coren & Porac, 1974; Festinger *et al.*, 1967; Festinger, White, & Allyn, 1968) have examined the efferent readiness theory by means of lesser forms of visual rearrangement, such as prismatic curvature, as well as other tasks. In general, they have reported changes in perception to be concomitant with learning new visuomotor behavior. There is still some doubt, however, that these results are best interpreted as support for the theory. We will return to this theory in Chapter 9 and again in Chapter 13.

gested the conditions of looking at the stationary body or examining a scene filled with familiar objects.

THE REAFFERENCE THEORY

Although Held's reafference theory also makes active interaction with the environment a necessary condition for adaptation (Chapter 2), it is unclear if this theory has anything to say about *visual* experience. The theory attempts to explain how eye–hand coordination may adjust itself to visual rearrangement, but it does not formally address itself to the question of how the world *looks*. Thus, Held's theory is not relevant to the issue of visual adaptation to optical transposition and will not be discussed further in this context.[8]

End Products

It is perhaps of greater theoretical importance to determine what is actually changed by exposure to transposed vision than it is to specify the conditions under which such changes occur. The two most prominent theories concerning the end products of adaptation to visual transposition are those of Rock (1966) and Harris (1965).

ROCK'S THEORY

Rock points out that the crucial question is whether or not exposure to inverted vision leads to a modification of *egocentric* orientation. Changes with respect to other effects of the rearrangement are irrelevant to the theoretical question Stratton was attempting to answer. Rock also says that while it is *possible* that the inverted retinal image is necessary for upright vision and that human subjects are incapable of adapting to its optical righting, there are good reasons for maintaining that this is not the case. He proposes that the perception of egocentric upright is based on the acquisition of *memory traces* that are elicited by retinal stimulation, such that the normal (inverted) retinal image signifies that the visual field is oriented with the head. For example, an image of a point moving upward on the retina signifies a point moving egocentrically downward. When inverting spectacles are placed before the eyes, the reinverted image of external objects or direction

---

[8] It should be pointed out that although the reafference theory does not deal explicitly with visual experience, Held and his colleagues (e.g., Mikaelian & Held, 1964) have tested for visual adaptation in the case of optical *tilt* and have demonstrated, as they have for visuomotor adaptation to prismatic displacement, that active bodily movement is necessary for adaptation. The details of this and other experiments on the response to optical tilt are discussed in Chapter 6.

of movement elicits a memory trace for an inverted egocentric orientation, since until the time the spectacles were donned this was the relationship that had existed. If the subject learns that a new relationship exists between retinal image and head orientation, the reinverted image should thereby elicit a memory trace for upright egocentric orientation; thus, the world would once again look upright. According to this theory, it is crucial that the observer receive information concerning the nature of the optical rearrangement. Rock argues that, in principle, this information could be obtained by a passively moving or stationary observer, particularly if provided with a good view of his body. Active interaction in a real-life environment, with a view of the body, would probably be the most efficient and effective condition for replacing the old stimulus–memory trace relationship with the new one.

There have been very few reports that can be taken as good evidence for the occurrence of egocentric adaptation to transposed vision. Stratton occasionally said that the visual field looked upright, especially when he was involved in some activity, but failed to reveal a visual orientation aftereffect upon removing the spectacles. Kohler reported for at least one subject what seemed to be much more stable egocentric adaptation and, even more impressive, a clear-cut aftereffect. However, Rock argues that subjects who reported that the world looked upright once again were, in most instances, actually referring to *environmental* orientation. Stratton (1897b) reported on the eighth day of his longer experiment:

> As long as the new localization of my body was vivid, the general experience was harmonious, and everything was right side up. But when, for any of the reasons already given—an involuntary lapse into the older memory-materials, or a willful recall of these older forms—the pre-experimental localization of my body was prominently in mind, then as I looked out on the scene before me the scene was involuntarily taken as the standard of right directions, and my body was felt to be in an inharmonious position with reference to the rest. I seemed to be viewing the scene from an inverted body [p. 469].

Rock concludes that eventually Stratton's visual field came to be perceived as environmentally upright while remaining egocentrically inverted, but he is not completely clear on this matter. He appears to assume that reacquisition of the environmental upright was the result of increased familiarity with the inverted visual field, as well as an increased tendency to visualize unseen parts as being inverted. This is similar to what often occurs when a subject is placed in a physically tilted room. The room appears to be upright in the environment but, because it is egocentrically tilted with respect to the observer, he perceives that he is tilted. With 180° rotation of the room it is only the *familiar contents* that serve as information that the up and down in the environment have been altered. This might explain why an observer would not *immediately* perceive the room as environmentally upright and himself as inverted.

HARRIS'S THEORY

Harris, too, maintains that it is how the visual field *looks*, independently of gravitational cues, that represents the critical aspect of spatial perception in studies of transposed vision. However, contrary to Rock's theory, he is not referring to egocentric orientation (as defined here) but to a closely related concept that he has termed *pictorial perception*, which involves no reference to the felt or visualized head. Rather, it appears to represent how the brain "interprets" the orientation of the retinal image. Harris suggests that perhaps the most obvious test of this aspect of spatial vision involves a successive comparison, such as asking the subject if the words of an egocentrically upright book appear to be oriented in the same way as before. If "genuine" visual adaptation has occurred, the optically inverted words would be indistinguishable from their preinversion appearance. Rock agrees that such a result would represent unequivocal evidence of visual adaptation, but explains it in terms of a reinterpretation of the relationship between the orientation of the retinal image and the perceived coordinates of the head.

Rock and Harris most clearly depart on their prognosis for the eventual adaptation of egocentric orientation/pictorial perception. Rock argues that after a sufficiently long and active exposure period the visual world would be experienced precisely as it had before. Harris says that it is the felt position of the body that becomes congruent with vision (see Chapter 3). Thus, reaching for an object that appears to be in the upper portion of the visual field but is actually in the lower position will once again be accurate if the body has come to feel up/down reversed as well. Such a shift in felt body position would not only explain visuomotor adaptation to transposed vision but, more important, the reported changes in the way the visual field looks. Harris suggests that after continued viewing of the body (from the chest down) through the inverting spectacles its felt position will come to agree with its seen position and, since the pressure on the feet signals the direction of gravity, the subject should feel that his body (or most of it) is upright. Because the felt position of the unseen portions of the body (eyes, head, and shoulders) may remain unaltered, the observer might feel that his head is on upside down![9] Stratton reported this experience for both inversion (1896, p. 615) and a situation where a mirror apparatus projected the image of his body out in front of him (1899, p. 463). Harris agrees with Rock that it was environmental orientation that changed in Stratton's experiment and that this was accompanied by the acquisition of veridical egocentric direction, but he argues that this change was based on a shift in felt body position. This difference suggests a possible critical comparison of Rock's and Harris's views concerning the basis of environmental reorientation. A subject reporting that the visual field now looks environmentally upright should be tested on his perception of egocentric *direction* while lying on his back and viewing a display of luminous dots at right angles to his line of sight through the inverting spectacles. According to Rock, and assuming that no adaptation of egocentric orientation has occurred, the subject's perception of the radial direction of the visual objects would be in error, since environmental orientation is no longer relevant in this position (and the visual display is devoid of familiar, extended objects). However, if, as Harris proposes, the body is felt to be inverted relative to the head and shoulders, direction perception should continue to be veridical, since this position sense change would persist whether the subject is standing or reclining.

Harris also argues that since both environmental orientation and egocentric direction undergo modification, while egocentric orientation (or pictorial perception) remains nonveridical, this may explain some of the examples of "piecemeal adaptation." For example, the report by one of Kohler's subjects of an upright and an inverted face both looking right side up is actually quite reasonable, given that what the subject meant was that one face appeared egocentrically upright and the other environmentally upright (but egocentrically upside down). The same explanation would apply to another subject's report that a single face looked both upright and inverted at the same time.

Harris extended his theory to the case of right/left reversal of the visual field, a form of visual transposition examined by Kohler (1964, pp. 140–161) and Taylor (1962, pp. 198–207), by suggesting that a progressive right/left interchange of the felt position of the hands, arms, chest, and perhaps shoulders occurs with continued exposure. Ultimately, the subject may feel as if the right and left halves of his

---

[9] It is crucial for Harris's theory that the head (or, at the very least, the eyes) continue to feel inverted relative to the remainder of the body, since felt body position must involve the *relation* between body parts. That is, it is difficult to imagine how it would be possible for the *entire body*, eyes included, to feel inverted, and even gravity cues would not be a source of comparison.

body are reversed (see Figure 5.1), which was reported in the Innsbruck studies (Kohler, 1964, p. 153) and in an experiment by Charles S.
Harris and Judith R. Harris (described by Rock & Harris, 1967). In the
Harris and Harris study, subjects viewed their actively moving hands
through a right/left-reversing prism for 15 min on each of four
consecutive days. Not only did the right and left sides of the body
occasionally feel as if they had switched places during exposure, but
this shift appeared to persist for a short while after the removal of the
distorting device.[10] Subjects with eyes shut would often draw letters
and numbers mirror-reversed or draw them normally but feel as if the
hand were moving in a mirror-reversed manner. These aftereffects
dissipated very rapidly during the no-vision postexposure test period.

Clearly, a shift in the felt position of the arms and sides of the body
will lead to a change in egocentric direction if the trunk serves as the
standard of reference. The observer will see objects that are objectively
to his left as being closer to where he incorrectly feels the left half of
his body is located and hence will localize them correctly. Pictorial
perception, however, remains unaltered. The world continues to look
right/left reversed, even though the directions of objects from the
observer are perceived veridically. Harris points out that this explains
the paradoxical observation in which a subject saw an automobile
driving on the correct side of the road although the license number
appeared mirror-reversed (Kohler, 1964, p. 155). Harris's analysis of
how a right/left switch in the felt position of the body could lead to
an adaptive shift in visual egocentric direction while leaving pictorial
perception unaffected is shown in Figure 5.1. The hypothetical subject
is confronted with the letter "R" objectively on his right and the letter
"L" on his left (A). When the right/left-reversing spectacles are placed
on his head he reports seeing a mirror-reversed "L" on his right and a
mirror-reversed "R" on his left (B). During the course of the exposure
period the felt positions of his right and left arms become reversed
(C). Ultimately, the left half of his body (except perhaps the head)
comes to feel closer to the still mirror-reversed "L" and the right half
feels closer to the mirror-reversed "R" (D). His perception of the
egocentric location of the two letters is once again veridical, even
though they continue to appear right/left reversed.

This analysis may also apply to Taylor's observation of instanta-

[10] Harris (personal communication, 1975) reports that these experiences were quite
paradoxical. At first, the hands and part of the forearms might feel as if they had
switched places, but the remaining portions of the limbs continued to feel appropriately
attached to the trunk. With further exposure to the right/left reversal, more of the arm,
and perhaps the shoulders, came to feel reversed.

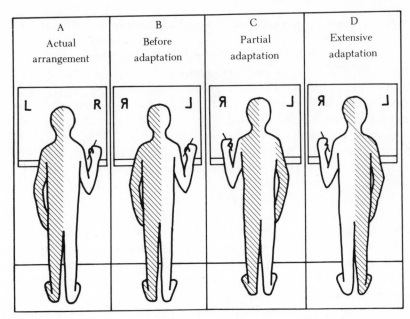

Figure 5.1. A subject's perceptions during the course of adaptation to reversed vision, according to Harris's position sense-change hypothesis (see text for details). (From C. S. Harris. Perceptual adaptation to inverted, reversed, and displaced vision. *Psychological Review*, 1965, *72*, 419–444. Copyright 1965 by the American Psychological Association. Reprinted by permission.)

neous adaptation and "readaptation" for the subject who alternated between right/left-reversed and normal vision. The subject's felt right/left orientation of the body may have become conditioned to cues associated with the goggles (or their absence). Since only directional perception would be affected by this change in felt body orientation, the subject should have continued to see objects as right/ left reversed whenever the goggles were in place. Unfortunately, Taylor (1962) does not say exactly how the field looked to the subject, other than that the "objects that he perceived as being on his left while wearing the spectacles were still on his left when he took them off [p. 204]." It is possible that only directional perception had changed, and if, for example, the subject had viewed a printed page he would have seen a drastic change in the appearance of the words as he took the spectacles from his eyes or replaced them.[11]

[11] Papert (personal communication, 1977) appears, in general, to agree with this analysis. He indicates that although the apparent *direction* of things was the same with or without the goggles, the *appearance* (pictorial perception?) of the visual field was not identical; however, as a subject, he found it difficult to specify or communicate the nature of this difference.

A COMPARISON OF THE THEORIES OF
ROCK AND HARRIS

Rock and Harris agree that the crucial issue is whether or not a visually transposed field can become indistinguishable from its preexposure appearance. They also agree that such visual adaptation may not actually have occurred for Stratton or most other subjects and conclude, instead, that, at best, the inverted visual field came to look *environmentally* upright. However, the two investigators differ regarding the basis of this environmental reorientation: Rock suggests that it is due to increased attention to familiar, monooriented aspects of the visual field, while Harris argues that it is the result of a drastic modification of the felt position of most of the body relative to the head (or perhaps to the eyes). Harris believes that visual adaptation will never occur, while Rock contends that such a perceptual change is possible, in principle. However, Rock points out that perhaps research aimed at Stratton's question should focus on optical *tilt* (rather than transposition) where there is a greater likelihood of obtaining measurable adaptation in a reasonable period of time.

Harris has handled more adequately the *existing* evidence from the introspective reports of the relatively few subjects confronted with transposed vision for extended periods of time. He has provided plausible explanations of the reports of "piecemeal adaptation," and he has dealt effectively with adaptation to right/left reversal, which Rock has not attempted to explain.

Perhaps it is unfair to pit Rock's and Harris's theories against each other, since they may apply to different stages in the adaptation process. Harris focused his attention on what was actually reported by the subjects during their exposure periods and, since they reported significant changes in the felt position of body parts, he concluded that this was all that would ever occur. Rock, too, is well aware that such alterations in position sense occurred for Stratton and others (Rock, 1966, pp. 238–243), but he concludes that this represents only an initial (and perhaps obstructive) stage in adaptation that is ultimately replaced by a genuine change in visual egocentric orientation. By means of a much more extended period of exposure, it might be possible to produce genuine changes in visual egocentric orientation/ pictorial perception, as Rock has argued. One wonders, for example, what the visual experience might ultimately be for some brave person willing to wear inverting spectacles for, say, 5 years, while engaged as a professional basketball player! However, as Harris (personal communication, 1977) has noted, the critical test of visual adaptation in this hypothetical experiment would require the use of monooriented stimulus materials to which the subject had never been exposed during the period of optical inversion so that he would not become accustomed to and able to deal effectively with the inverted objects. For example, we might wish to note how the print of an upright book appeared to the subject at the end of his exposure period and the degree to which his reading speed approximated normal. However, if this test were used, it would be necessary to keep our unfortunate basketball player from reading anything during his 5-year exposure period. Some of these problems could presumably be avoided by using an infant as subject, given some means of assessing his experience of egocentric orientation.

An even more serious problem that has become apparent in recent discussions between Harris and Rock (Harris, personal communication, 1977) is that there is no way of knowing how long the exposure period would have to be before one could conclude with confidence that adult subjects are not able to adapt egocentrically to inverted vision. Unless such a time limit could be specified, *and in a manner that is clearly independent of the visual adaptation itself,* the hypothesis that true visual adaptation to transposed vision will occur if one only waits long enough is irrefutable. Again, if a lesser distortion were examined (i.e., optical tilt), the required time period would presumably be much reduced.

THE "POLARITY HABIT" THEORY

Howard and Templeton (1966, pp. 406–408) argue that exposure to inverted vision leads to neither egocentric nor environmental adaptation. Instead, the observer merely becomes so familiar with the disoriented visual field that it no longer appears strange or unrecognizable, which is referred to as the acquisition of new *polarity habits.*[12] Clearly, such changes did occur for Stratton and the subjects in the Innsbruck studies and can also be produced by exposure to *physically* inverted, familiar stimulus objects, such as print (e.g., Kolers, 1975). Furthermore, it is reasonable to assume that old polarity habits may be maintained at the same time that new ones are being acquired. This might represent an alternative to Harris's suggested explanation for the subject's report of seeing both an upright and an inverted face as upright. Other examples of "piecemeal adaptation" might result from the fact that new polarity habits are acquired piecemeal as a function

[12] The term *polarity habit* may be somewhat misleading, since it implies that the habits of orientation must inevitably involve "poles," such as up and down (Harris, personal communication, 1975). In principle, a person could acquire habits regarding any habitual orientation of an object, not just those involving the primary axes.

of the amount of experience the subject has with the various parts of his environment.

Howard and Templeton correctly conclude that one of the major effects of continued exposure to inverted or right/left-reversed vision is learning to recognize and operate effectively with the new orientation of objects. The insistence that the perceptual system is not susceptible to adaptation of egocentric orientation is clearly in accord with most of the existing evidence. However, this view does not seem to incorporate the experiences of altered body position sense, which, as Harris proposes, may lead to changes in perceived environmental orientation and egocentric direction. More important, however, the polarity habit theory argues that *unfamiliar* objects will continue to appear inverted, even environmentally. For example, if an arrow with no associated polarity habit is physically pointing toward the earth, it should continue to appear to be pointing toward the sky for as long as the inverting spectacles are worn. In contrast, both Rock and Harris argue convincingly that eventually the subject will at least perceive veridically the arrow's orientation relative to gravity. Thus, we are led to the conclusion that adaptation to visual rearrangement involves more than the acquisition of new polarity habits.

SUMMARY AND CONCLUSIONS

The real issue concerning the orientation of the retinal image is not the fact that it is inverted with respect to the physical (and perceived) world, but whether or not this inversion is necessary for upright vision. This question instigated a number of experiments in which a few human subjects were exposed for varying periods of time to optically inverted or right/left-reversed vision. Unfortunately, since the subjects were often the experimenters themselves or otherwise quite experimentally sophisticated, "experimenter bias" might have affected their reports. Nevertheless, these studies show that subjects can overcome the visuomotor effects of transposed vision, although it is much less certain that the visual field ever came to look normally oriented. Harris proposed, for inverted vision, that eventually the world was seen as environmentally upright while it continued to appear egocentrically inverted because the subject felt as if his visible body were located where he saw it. Harris's theory also deals effectively with the case of right/left reversal, where the subject comes to feel as if the sides of his body have switched places. In both instances, the changes in felt body position are accompanied by a shift in egocentric direction, which accounts for some of the reports of "piecemeal adaptation." In addition, the inverted visual field comes to look familiar and recognizable, a phenomenon which Howard and Templeton have referred to as the acquisition of new polarity habits. In the absence of convincing evidence to the contrary, it appears that an inverted retinal image is indeed required for upright vision in adult human beings, but it does not follow from this tentative conclusion that egocentric visual orientation is innately determined. That is, contrary to a common belief, the unmodifiability of a perceptual capacity in adult human beings cannot be taken as evidence that this capacity is inborn. Thus, the nature–nuture issue must be investigated by observing the behavior of neonatal organisms. The only experiment of this sort that is relevant to the present discussion was by Bishop (1959), who exposed dark-reared kittens to optically inverted vision. The results, which are described in detail in Chapter 11, suggest that although adaptation occurs for the "visually naive" kitten, there is an innate *bias* in favor of upright vision (i.e., an inverted retinal image). Evidence that the perception of radial direction is innate for human beings has been provided by Schlodtmann (1902). He found that several people who had been blind from birth as the result of congenital cataracts, but whose optic nerves remained functional, pointed appropriately at the apparent direction of "pressure phosphenes" induced by physical stimulation of the retina in various places. Finally, Ganz (1975) has reviewed many experiments whose results argue convincingly for an innate basis of the perception of direction, if not orientation, in a wide range of organisms. Some of this research is discussed in Chapter 13. Thus, it may be concluded that visual direction is innately given for most or all animals, including human beings, but is nevertheless modifiable (at least for humans) in the face of optical rearrangement. On the other hand, egocentric orientation appears to be unmodifiable, based on the studies of visual transposition, although the ultimate test of this assertion of the null hypothesis may require an extremely long exposure period.

It might be that the perceptual system cannot undergo the complete "flip-flop" of egocentric orientation necessary to adapt to transposed vision. Perhaps, as Rock has suggested, Stratton's question could be investigated without having to alter so drastically the subject's visual experience. Instead of "righting" the retinal image, why not merely place it on a moderate *tilt*? If human observers are capable of adapting visually to this kind of optical distortion, it would seem that visual spatial orientation is not an inevitable consequence of a particular retinal image orientation. The evidence relevant to this possibility is examined in the next chapter.

6

Adaptation to Optically Induced Tilt

There are two important and related advantages of tilting the visual field, rather than subjecting it to inversion or right/left reversal. First, *partial* adaptation is at least possible for optical tilt and might be demonstrated after a relatively short period of exposure. Second, tilt adaptation, given that it occurs, may be *quantified,* because the subject can indicate when an object appears to be vertical and his error (if any) may then be recorded. For these and other reasons, the capacity of human subjects to adapt to optically induced tilt has received significant attention.

Brown (1928) was the first to do an experiment of this sort. He used a pair of Dove prisms in tandem within a brass tube and then rotated one prism of each pair to effect a 75° visual tilt. The second of the two prisms eliminated the right/left reversal produced by the first (Figure 6.1). Brown was interested primarily in whether or not subjects could adapt to the reduction in apparent depth that results from a large *binocular* tilt, and therefore his tests involved visual and visuomotor estimates of depth. Brown's subjects wore the tilting goggles for a half-hour period each day for 16 days and showed little or no adaptation of visual depth perception, although significant visuomotor adaptation occurred. However, Brown, himself, evidenced visual adaptation after wearing the goggles continuously for 7 days; he reported that by the second day the field had come to appear much less tilted. This could mean, though, that he had merely come to

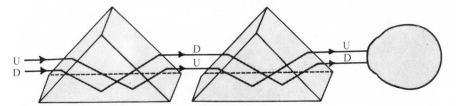

Figure 6.1. Two Dove prisms in tandem arrangement. Light rays U and D are up/down reversed by the first prism and normalized by the second before entering the eye. To produce optical tilt, one of the prisms is rotated by the desired amount.

accept his tilted field as normal and had stopped paying attention to its orientation. In any event, he took no quantitative measures of tilt adaptation, either during or subsequent to the exposure period.

Later studies of optical tilt adaptation were similar to Brown's pioneering experiment in their use of relatively unrestricted exposure periods in real-life environments, but there were a few significant differences as well. First, the optical tilts rarely exceeded 40°. Second, exposure was almost always monocular (to avoid the depth distortion) which resulted in a small visual field—between 10 and 30°. Third, exposure periods were relatively short, ranging from 15 min to 4 hr. Finally, Brown's introspective reports were replaced by more objective measures.

A representative study of adaptation to optical tilt was done by Ebenholtz (1966). The subject wore a monocular Dove prism that tilted the visual field by 10, 20, or 32° (either clockwise or counterclockwise) while he engaged for 4 hr in such activities as walking through corridors and throwing darts. Prior to and at hourly intervals during the exposure period, the prism was removed and the subject was asked to set a tilted luminous line in a dark room to apparent vertical with respect to gravity (and to the subject's upright body). Tilt adaptation increased rapidly during the exposure period, reaching asymptote after 1–2 hr at approximately 30% of the imposed optical tilt.

This experiment and others have demonstrated conclusively that exposure to optical tilt causes a reduction in apparent tilt and a negative aftereffect. However, in many cases this change in apparent visual orientation was probably based not only on adaptation to the rearrangement but on other effects as well. To isolate "genuine" optical tilt adaptation, it is necessary to determine why objects appear vertical or tilted in the first place.

ENVIRONMENTAL VERSUS EGOCENTRIC ORIENTATION

As discussed in the previous chapter, the perception of an object's orientation relative to gravity and the perception of its orientation relative to the perceiver are distinguishable events, referred to as environmental and egocentric orientation, respectively. Only when the observer is in an upright position do the two forms of orientation coincide. It is presumably because of this redundancy that the physical orientation of objects for the upright observer is very accurately and precisely discerned. The perception of spatial orientation is even better when the objects are located within a visual framework containing vertical objects or contours. However, a number of experiments (e.g., Neal, 1926; Witkin & Asch, 1948) have shown that even when the only visible object is the one whose orientation is being judged, upright subjects who attempt to set the object to gravitational vertical make errors (unsigned) of only .5 to 1.5°.

Environmental and egocentric orientation are no longer confounded as soon as the subject's head (or entire body) is placed on a tilt relative to gravity, because gravitationally vertical objects become egocentrically tilted in the opposite direction. A number of experiments have determined to what extent (if any) this situation leads to a change in the subject's perception of gravitational orientation. These studies are carried out in a dark room using a luminous line that is viewed by a subject whose head or entire body is tilted. In general, subjects' judgments in such a situation indicate that the perception of gravitational vertical remains reasonably constant, even with large body tilts. This perceptual constancy is made possible by the presence of gravitational and other postural cues, which allow the rotation of the retinal image to be "discounted." This is not to say that the constancy of gravitational vertical is perfect. For example, with body tilts of up to about 60° a physically vertical line will often appear to be tilted slightly (e.g., 2–3° for a 30° body tilt) in the same direction as the body. Müller (1916; cited by Howard & Templeton, 1966) was apparently the first to note this error and dubbed it the "E-effect." If body tilts exceed 60° (up to about 150°), the luminous line will appear to be tilted significantly in the opposite direction, a phenomenon first observed by Aubert (1861) and subsequently called the "A-effect." This error is generally larger than the E-effect. Both the E- and A-effects are departures from perfect orientation constancy, indicating that when only gravitational cues are present, perception of visual–

gravitational vertical is less accurate and less precise than when a visual framework is also provided.

When a luminous line is placed within a visual framework, its apparent gravitational and egocentric orientations are markedly affected by the orientation of the framework. If the framework is placed on a tilt, the line will appear vertical only when it has been rotated a certain amount in the same direction as the frame's tilt, and there are large individual differences in this tendency (e.g., Witkin, Dyk, Faterson, Goodenough, & Karp, 1962). Subjects who are markedly influenced by the tilted frame are referred to as "field dependent," whereas those whose judgments of vertical are relatively unimpaired are called "field independent."

Rock (1966, p. 68) has made the plausible suggestion that even when a subject reports that a tilted object looks vertical when located within a tilted frame, he might continue to perceive the frame as tilted. On the other hand, if the observer is placed *within* a tilted environment, particularly one filled with familiar objects, this environment may soon come to appear upright. The first observation of this latter phenomenon is usually attributed to Wertheimer (1912; cited by Howard & Templeton, 1966). He reported that after looking for a short while at the tilted mirror reflection of a room in which he was standing, the room and its contents came to appear normally oriented once again. This rapid apparent righting of the visual field has been termed the *Wertheimer effect* and similar observations were made by Gibson and Mowrer (1938) and Asch and Witkin (1948a,b). It seems likely, as Rock (1966, p. 73) has argued, that these experiences occur because the visual environment comes to dominate perceived body orientation. For example, when surrounded by a visual field apparently tilted to the left the observer may come to experience himself as tilted to the right, and the field should once again appear environmentally (but not egocentrically) upright. This is the explanation given by Harris (1965) and Rock (1966) for the occasional reports of apparent righting of the visual field for subjects wearing inverting spectacles (Chapter 5).

THE ISOLATION OF ADAPTIVE CHANGES IN EGOCENTRIC ORIENTATION

The effects on apparent gravitational vertical induced by tilts of the body and/or the visual framework are interesting, but they should not be considered adaptation since they do not represent responses to the optical distortion per se. The present concern is whether or not a subject wearing goggles that optically tilt the visual world can undergo a genuine change in the apparent tilt of the visual field relative to himself. Tilting goggles disorient the visual field whether the observer's head or entire body is upright or at some degree of tilt relative to gravity, and, consequently, it is the perception of egocentric orientation that is in error. However, since subjects in experiments such as those by Brown (1928) and Ebenholtz (1966) have been allowed to view from an upright position a large, apparently tilted field composed of familiar objects, it is likely that such changes in apparent gravitational upright as the Wertheimer effect have occurred. Therefore, it is necessary to preclude or allow for such effects if it is to be demonstrated that genuine (i.e., egocentric) adaptation to optical tilt is possible.

Mack and Rock (1968) took such precautions in one of their experiments. Subjects wore monocular 25° tilt goggles while walking about for a total period of .5 hr. Throughout this exposure period a subject held his head in a bent-over position, looking down at the floor. Because the line of gravity was thus perpendicular to the visual field (the floor), the goggles affected only apparent egocentric orientation with respect to the head. The test of adaptation required the subject to place his head in a horizontal position and to indicate when a spot of light rotating around another spot in the horizontal plane appeared to be at "12 o'clock" in relation to his head. The exposure period led to an adaptive shift of over 4.5°. Thus, it appears that genuine visual adaptation to an optically tilted field is possible and, therefore, that the normal orientation of the retinal image is not necessary for veridical spatial orientation—the answer to Stratton's original question.

THE PROBLEM OF "CONFIGURATIONAL ADAPTATION"

Unfortunately, there are a few other effects that, although they involve egocentric orientation, cannot be considered to represent adaptation to optical tilt. The first of these is referred to as the *Gibson effect*. Not long after Brown's historic study, Gibson (1933) noted that the apparent curvature of objectively straight lines when viewed through a wedge prism decreases as exposure continues and that straight lines come to look curved in the opposite direction when the prism is removed. He later discovered that the same effects can be obtained from viewing *objectively* curved lines with normal vision. Next, Gibson and Radner (1937a,b) observed that lines physically tilted from the vertical (or horizontal) axis come to look less tilted after a while and lead to an aftereffect when a vertical (or horizontal) line is viewed. The effects of exposure to a physically or apparently curved or tilted contour are depicted in Figure 6.2. It was concluded that there is a perceptual tendency to "normalize" configurations. That is, for "oppositional scales," such as the orientation of an object in the frontal plane or the relative curvature of a line, "neutral points" or norms (i.e., vertical/horizontal and straight) exist, perhaps based on previous experience. If a stimulus object diverges by some degree from the neutral point on a particular dimension, the perceptual system will adapt such that the appearance of the stimulus, and possibly the entire scale, will shift toward the norm. This effect is rather small, as shown by Gibson and Radner (1937a), who reported that after 45–90 sec of exposure to 5° tilted lines the aftereffect reached a maximum of only 1.5°. Longer exposure periods apparently fail to lead to any further adaptation. The effect increases with increasing tilts, up to about 20°, and then declines; there is no effect at all for 45°, presumably because this tilt is equidistant between the two major axes. The effect has been found to transfer from exposed to unexposed eye (e.g., Ohwaki, 1961), probably implicating a central process, as Gibson and Radner had suggested. Finally, exposure to a line tilted away from one axis (e.g., vertical) produces a relatively small tilt aftereffect for a line on the other axis (e.g., horizontal), which is called the *indirect effect* (Gibson & Radner, 1937a).

Köhler and Wallach (1944) proposed that the Gibson effect is merely a special case of the so-called "figural aftereffect," which in turn they

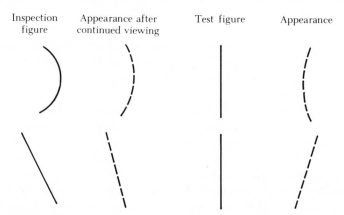

Figure 6.2. Perceptual effects and aftereffects from viewing a physically curved or tilted line.

presumed to be based on some sort of cortical satiation process that occurs when contours are fixated for a period of time. A variety of observations argue against this conclusion. For example, cortical satiation seems to require a stationary eye position during exposure, but the Gibson effect can be obtained when eye movement is allowed. Several studies (e.g., Morant & Harris, 1965; Morant & Mikaelian, 1960) have found both localized and generalizable components of the aftereffect from the fixation of a tilted line. Thus, the Gibson effect and figural aftereffects are probably independent perceptual events, which may combine their effects when the subject fixates one or more straight lines set at the optimal tilt for the Gibson effect (i.e., 5–20°). The part of the aftereffect attributable to satiation could presumably be distinguished from the Gibson effect by some test of generalizability or perhaps could be precluded by allowing the subject free eye and head movements during the exposure period.

GENUINE OPTICAL TILT ADAPTATION

It can be seen that even when exposure and test for optical tilt adaptation are designed so that only egocentric orientation is being assessed, certain changes in apparent tilt can occur that should not be viewed as evidence of adaptation. If a subject wearing optical tilt goggles is exposed to objectively vertical contours, the conditions are appropriate for producing the Gibson effect and possibly a satiation process of the type proposed by Köhler and Wallach (1944) for figural aftereffects. Because such *configurational adaptation* occurs with *objectively* tilted contours it does not conform to the present definition of perceptual adaptation as a change in perception that reduces an intersensory discordance. To isolate tilt adaptation from configurational effects, the extent of the latter must be measured and subtracted from the total measured change in apparent vertical or the exposure period must be designed to prevent the effects. Prevention was used by Mikaelian and Held (1964), who eliminated all vertical contours by furnishing a small room with a large number of randomly placed luminous styrofoam spheres. Subjects who actively moved about in this room while wearing 20° optical tilt goggles showed small but statistically significant tilt aftereffects. Presumably, this type of stimulus situation produces a "pure" measure of optical tilt adaptation because it eliminates the possibility of configurational adaptation and the Wertheimer effect. Another means of excluding configurational effects, suggested by Rock (1966, pp. 75–76), is to have the subject first view with normal vision and freely moving eyes a field of lines objectively tilted by an amount equal to the optical tilt to be used during the exposure period. If the preexposure measure of apparent visual vertical is taken after this "normalization period," the pre-post shift should be free of configurational adaptation.

Experiments that have included such precautions are quite rare; most have used exposure conditions and adaptation tests that confound configurational adaptation and changes in apparent gravitational vertical with genuine egocentric tilt adaptation. However, in many instances the concern has been with the necessary conditions or types of information required for tilt adaptation and less on the nature of the end product. If it can be assumed that at least some genuine optical tilt adaptation occurred, the results are probably relevant to the experimental question. The fact that configurational adaptation is typically on the order of 1-2°, whereas aftereffects of optical tilt exposure of 5-7° are reported in a variety of studies (e.g., Ebenholtz, 1966), clearly indicates that a certain amount of genuine tilt adaptation has been obtained. The following section presents the major findings of these tilt adaptation studies.

GENERAL FINDINGS AND THEORIES OF OPTICAL TILT ADAPTATION

Characteristics

Like other forms of adaptation to perceptual rearrangement, optical tilt adaptation typically increases as a negatively accelerated function of exposure time and reaches asymptote at a level below the maximum determined by the imposed distortion (e.g., Ebenholtz, 1966; Redding, 1973b; Rierdan & Wapner, 1967). The only report of complete tilt adaptation is by Mikaelian and Held (1964), who obtained a 20° aftereffect with three especially adaptable subjects after 2 hr of active exposure to 20° tilt. A second experiment, however, suggested that a portion of this adaptive shift might have been attributable to the Gibson effect. When the adaptive shifts of all subjects are combined, the result for most experiments is a mean aftereffect of between 20 and 30% of the theoretical maximum.

The magnitude of adaptation is positively related to the size of the imposed tilt, a function which turns out to be linear, at least for tilts of

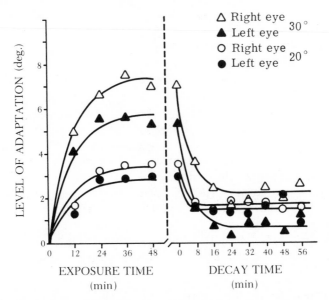

Figure 6.3. Mean level of adaptation to 30 and 20° of optical tilt in the exposed (right) and unexposed (left) eyes as a function of exposure time in acquisition and decay time in the dark. (From G. M. Redding. Decay of visual adaptation to tilt and displacement. *Perception & Psychophysics,* 1975, *17,* 203–208.)

up to 30° (Ebenholtz, 1966; Redding, 1973b).[1] Another well-established characteristic of optical tilt adaptation is the substantial transfer from exposed to unexposed eye (e.g., Ebenholtz, 1966).[2]

When tilt goggles are removed and the subject's eyes are closed, adaptation undergoes rapid spontaneous decay (e.g., Ebenholtz, 1967, 1969; Redding, 1975b), which is negatively decelerated but, surprisingly, reaches asymptote at a level significantly greater than zero. Figure 6.3 presents data obtained by Redding (1975b) that show the typical decay curves for tilt adaptation as well as the acquisition func-

---

[1] Although Morant and Beller (1965) reported a linear function for tilts as large as 75°, an experiment by Ebenholtz (1973), discussed later in this chapter, found that tilts of greater than 30° were associated with a negatively accelerated increase in adaptation.

[2] Actually, a number of experiments (e.g., Ebenholtz, 1966) have reported only about 50% interocular transfer. However, this may represent an underestimate, due to the fact that the unexposed eye was measured only after the exposed eye had been tested. Spontaneous decay of adaptation is likely to have occurred before the extent of transfer could be measured. When the order is counterbalanced, interocular transfer is complete, or nearly so (Mack & Chitayat, 1970; Quinlan, 1970; Redding, 1973b).

tion, the effect of different magnitudes of tilt, and degree of interocular transfer.

Redding (1973a,b, 1975a,b) directly compared adaptation to prismatic displacement with adaptation to optical tilt, and his evidence suggests that the two processes are qualitatively different. The acquisition curve for visual adaptation is more gradual but ascends to a higher level for displacement than for tilt. The decay curve also is more gradual for displacement and reaches zero, whereas the curve for tilt quickly levels off above the preexposure baseline. Redding (1973a,b, 1975a) also showed that the occurrence and magnitude of both visual and visuomotor adaptation to optical tilt are not affected by simultaneous exposure to prismatic displacement (and vice versa) and that there is no correlation between the magnitudes of the two types of adaptation. These results strike a blow at the widely held, often implicit belief that the findings from studies of one form of visual rearrangement can be generalized to other forms.

Active versus Passive Movement

Most studies of optical tilt adaptation have included exposure periods in which the subject is required to walk about and otherwise actively interact with the environment because it is assumed that stationary viewing or even passive movement will lead to little if any genuine adaptation. This assumption stems from Held's reafference hypothesis and the results of experiments on prism adaptation (e.g., Held & Hein, 1958). However, experiments have not always shown that passive exposure is an ineffectual condition for optical tilt adaptation.

In support of the importance of active movement, Mikaelian and Held (1964) found significantly greater tilt adaptation for subjects who walked up and down a hallway while wearing monocular 20° optical tilt goggles than for prism-wearing subjects who were moved in a wheelchair along the same route. Although the latter condition did produce a small amount of adaptation (about 2°, as compared to almost 7° for the active condition), it was suggested that this shift could be attributable to the Gibson effect. Indeed, when passive exposure occurred in a room devoid of vertical contours (the luminous spheres described in a preceding section), no tilt aftereffect was observed. Mikaelian and Held concluded that their results supported the reafference hypothesis. However, this model was designed to explain perceptual–motor, not perceptual, adaptation (Chapter 4), and it is unclear how the recorrelation of efference copies and reafferent input would affect the *appearance* of the visual field. Quinlan (1970) compared active and passive conditions in much the same manner as Mikaelian and Held (1964) and reported similar results.

Mack (1967) found small but equal tilt aftereffects after 30 min of active or passive exposure to 40° tilt. The two conditions each produced adaptive shifts of about 3.5°. Her conditions were similar to those of Mikaelian and Held (1964) and Quinlan (1970). However, the size of the visual field and the degree of tilt were greater and, in contrast to the previous experiments, her subjects were precluded from making head movements in both conditions by means of a bite-board attached to the cart that the subject either walked within or stood in as he was pushed around by the experimenter. It is not clear why Mack found so little adaptation (about half as much as Mikaelian and Held reported) and, more important, why she failed to replicate the active–passive difference. One possibility, suggested by Quinlan (1970), is that when head movement is precluded, as in the study by Mack (1967), passive movement of the body through a normal indoor environment provides information sufficient to produce as much adaptation as from active movement, which argues against reafference as a necessary condition for optical tilt adaptation. However, when head movements are allowed for subjects in both conditions, as in the studies by Mikaelian and Held (1964) and Quinlan (1970), a difference in magnitude of adaptation favoring the active condition occurs because the head movements induce even more adaptation for actively moving subjects and *suppress* adaptation for passively moving subjects. Suppression might occur because information (e.g., from vestibular cues) obtained from passive bodily movement is disrupted or made ambiguous by the reafference resulting from active head movements. An experiment is needed to examine this hypothesis.

Studies concerned with adaptation differences between active and passive movement have important implications for an understanding of the types of information that instigate the adaptive process. Whereas the reafference hypothesis states that the "adequate stimulus" for adaptation is the discrepancy between "expected" and actual reafferent input, Rock (1966) and others have argued that optical tilt adaptation should result when the observer is provided with any kind of information serving to indicate that what appears to be tilted actually is not. Rock (1966, p. 39) has suggested three situations where such information would be available to the subject: (a) looking at a familiar scene in which objects of known orientation are present; (b) looking at part or all of the body; and (c) observing the retinal "flow pattern" contingent upon movement of the head or entire body. Let us look at the evidence concerning the efficacy of each of these potential sources of information.

Types of Information Concerning the Optical Tilt

LOOKING AT A FAMILIAR SCENE

Morant and Beller (1965) found a small adaptive shift of apparent vertical for subjects who sat for 15 min looking at corridors through goggles that tilted the visual field by 15, 45, or 75°. Significant adaptation occurred for all three tilts, but it was only about one-half of the amount produced by walking through the corridors. The finding of adaptation for the 45° tilt indicates that the shift for the stationary viewing condition was not merely a Gibson effect, since this particular tilt is not subject to normalization. Mack (1967) and Mack and Chitayat (1970) reported similar results. Thus, it would appear that stationary viewing of an optically tilted familiar scene may be sufficient to produce a small amount of optical tilt adaptation. However, an alternate interpretation of these results is that when a subject is exposed to a well-structured visual field that has been tilted (optically or physically) and is required to indicate the apparent vertical of an object, his *concept* of vertical may be influenced by the framework (Harris, 1974). This concerns the subject's interpretation of "vertical" and is not a perceptual effect. According to this hypothesis, even if the instructions have explicitly required the subject to use his body as the standard of reference, he may "define" upright in terms of the framework, which leads to an almost immediate shift in the subject's setting of an object when viewing the tilted scene and possibly an aftereffect when the goggles are removed. This is the analog of the "straight-ahead shift" discussed in Chapter 3, (pp. 46–48). Since this artifact would occur only when viewing a well-structured field, it is difficult to see how the efficacy of exposure to a familiar scene as a source of optical tilt adaptation can be assessed independently of this proposed nonperceptual effect on the subject's response.

LOOKING AT THE BODY

Several experiments have examined the effect of allowing the subject to view part or all of his body through the optical tilt goggles. Mack and Rock (1968) provided the subject with a stationary view of his entire body by placing a large mirror on the floor and having him look down at it while wearing goggles that tilted the visual scene 30, 50, or 60°. Little or no adaptation resulted from this condition. In another experiment it was shown that even when an actively moving subject was allowed to see his legs, tilt adaptation was not increased over that achieved by a walking subject who was kept from seeing any part of his body. Mikaelian (1967) did not find any visual adaptation for his subjects after .5 hr of exposure to a 20° counterclockwise tilt during which only the actively moving hand was seen, but the same period spent walking in a hallway, without a view of the hands, led to significant adaptation. Redding (1975c) reported similar results.

Finally, Rierdan and Wapner (1966) and Quinlan (1970) found significant tilt adaptation for subjects allowed to view the mirror reflection of the optically tilted body. These observations do not necessarily conflict with those of Mack and Rock because the investigators required their subjects to make judgments of *gravitational* vertical and did not constrain them from moving while viewing the optically tilted reflection of the body. Thus, the sight of the body was confounded with active movement.

It may be concluded from the preceding studies that viewing part or all of the body is a rather ineffectual condition for eliciting optical tilt adaptation, except perhaps when it occurs together with active movement of the entire body.

THE RETINAL FLOW PATTERN AND EBENHOLTZ'S "INDEPENDENCE-COMPARATOR" MODEL

The third basic information source for optical tilt adaptation is the altered retinal flow pattern. When a person moves his head or entire body while viewing the environment a flow of retinal images occurs that could serve as an unambiguous cue for the direction in which he is moving (J. J. Gibson, 1968). With normal vision, a lateral head movement causes the field to move in the opposite direction along the same axis. When optical tilt goggles are worn, the same head movement leads to a diagonal flow pattern (i.e., perpendicular to the tilt). This potential informational source of optical tilt adaptation does not require that the environment contain familiar objects, that the body be visible, or even that the observer's movement be self-initiated. All that is required is that the subject have information as to how his head or body is moving.

In an impressive set of experiments, Ebenholtz (e.g., 1966, 1967) supported a model of optical tilt adaptation in which the primary informational source is presumed to be the retinal flow pattern. The exposure period used in these experiments involved active movement through corridors and up and down stairs, and the subject was often encouraged to move his head from side to side, since this activity leads to a very clear-cut retinal flow pattern effect. Adaptation was measured in terms of a pre–post shift in the setting of a luminous line to the upright (both gravitational and egocentric) with normal vision. According to Ebenholtz' model, when the tilt goggles are worn and the subject moves about, the memory for the preexperimental flow pattern is compared to the flow pattern produced by the prisms. The discrepancy between long- and short-term memory of the flow pattern contingent upon a particular movement of the head or body is the stimulus for the adaptive process. This *comparator model* is presented in schematic form in Figure 6.4. It is quite similar to the mechanism proposed by Holst (1954) to account for visual position constancy (see Chapter 7, p. 162) and by Held (e.g., 1961) for prism adaptation (see Chapter 2, pp. 21–23), but does not demand that body movement be self-initiated.

Ebenholtz's assumption that it is the flow pattern that provides the basic information for tilt adaptation is probably based on the fact that most studies have found other informational sources to be relatively ineffective. However, his use of an unrestricted exposure period leaves one uncertain which of the several types of available information about the optical tilt is (are) actually being used. Regardless of this ambiguity, Ebenholtz's model can be distinguished in an important way from an alternate hypothesis. Ebenholtz proposes that the crucial stimulus for optical tilt adaptation is the discrepancy between the previous and present *optical/retinal* situation. This may be contrasted with the equally plausible hypothesis that the necessary condition for adaptation is the discrepancy between the previous and

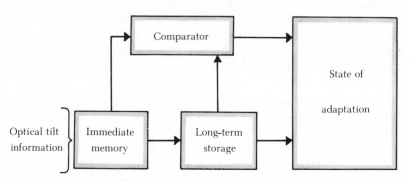

Figure 6.4. The flow of information in a memory–comparator model of optical tilt adaptation. (From S. M. Ebenholtz. Transfer and decay functions in adaptation to optical tilt. *Journal of Experimental Psychology*, 1969, *81*, 170–173. Copyright 1969 by the American Psychological Association. Reprinted by permission.)

present *appearance* of the visual field. According to Ebenholtz's model, tilt adaptation is *independent* of how the visual field appears to the subject and whether (or to what extent) he has adapted to the optical tilt (independence hypothesis). The alternate hypothesis is that the occurrence and extent of adaptation are *dependent* upon the current state of adaptation—how the world looks (dependence hypothesis).

The distinction between these hypotheses may be seen most clearly in the differing interpretations of the negatively accelerated acquisition function of tilt adaptation reported by many investigators (e.g., Ebenholtz, 1966). If a subject has adapted to the optical tilt, the magnitude of the perceived tilt has decreased. According to the dependence hypothesis, the rate of adaptation declines during the exposure period because the world is looking progressively less tilted, and the stimulus for adaptation is thereby decreasing in strength. The independence-comparator hypothesis, on the other hand, attributes the negatively accelerated acquisition curve to the fact that the long-term memory for the preexposure optical situation (perhaps the retinal flow pattern, in particular) gets weaker with time. The proposed comparator becomes increasingly less sensitive to the discrepancy between the current input and the remembered optical/ retinal state of affairs, given a particular bodily movement. When this memory reaches a critical degree of "deterioration," adaptation will be at asymptote. Based on the typical acquisition curve (see Figure 6.3), the pre-tilt memory no longer has an influence after about 30 min of unrestricted exposure activity.

The fact that tilt adaptation curves typically indicate that 100% adaptation will never be obtained, regardless of the length of the exposure period, can be taken as evidence against the dependence hypothesis (as Ebenholtz has stated it). That is, if adaptation is a constant proportion of the difference between perceived and optical tilt, the adaptation curve, though negatively accelerated, should eventually reach a level of complete compensation for the tilt, because there would continue to be a discrepancy until complete adaptation was achieved.

One questionable aspect of Ebenholtz's comparator model as it applies to the acquisition function of tilt adaptation is that if adaptation reaches asymptote at the point in time when the memory for the preadaptation optical input is so weak as to have no more impact, why is it that the observer continues to perceive any visual tilt at all? If the experience of tilt is ultimately the recognition that contours are not aligned with the body (or head) in the same way as before, then it seems that this memory must still be intact even when adaptation has reached asymptote, since subjects continue to report the experience of tilt. A reformulation of Ebenholtz's comparator model might state that the effective stimulus for tilt adaptation is the conflict between the current optical tilt and the "expected" tilt. After a while the subject comes to "expect" just as much tilt as he perceives and it is at this point that the adaptation process ceases. This hypothesis is elaborated upon and generalized to other forms of rearrangement in Chapter 13.

According to Ebenholtz, normal vision is not a unique visual condition, but rather a state of optical tilt whose value happens to be zero. Ebenholtz (1968b) supported this assumption in two experiments in which subjects in some conditions were first adapted for .5 hr to optical tilt (either 15 or 30°) and then were allowed to move about with normal vision. The rate of "unlearning" of the acquired tilt adaptation (or of "relearning" to the 0° tilt) during the second half-hour period was no more rapid than the rate of initial acquisition, which argues against attributing any special status to the 0° tilt. Thus, for example, a switch from a 0° tilt to a 30° tilt will induce as much adaptation as a shift from 10 to 40°. In each case, "the change in magnitude of adaptation . . . is a linear function of the angular difference between successively exposed optical rotations [Ebenholtz, 1967, p. 266]." On the other hand, Ebenholtz (e.g., 1968b, 1969) and others have reported significant (although incomplete) decay of adaptation after a postexposure period during which the subject is blindfolded. Since this represents a return of vision toward "normal," it would seem to contradict the conclusion that normal vision is merely another state of adaptation. A possible resolution suggested by Ebenholtz (1969) is that 0° tilt is indeed unique, but only in the sense that it is the average of all possible tilts and that when vision is precluded the comparator generates random "noise," causing a regression toward the mean.

In a critical test of the independence-comparator model by Ebenholtz (1967), subjects were adapted for .5 hr to a 10° tilt in one direction and then immediately switched to a 10° tilt in the opposite direction. In accordance with the independence hypothesis, the magnitude of adaptation to the second tilt was equal (although in the opposite direction) to the adaptation to the first tilt. Thus, the total shift in apparent vertical during the second exposure period was the same as would be predicted from a switch from 0 to 20° tilt. This is contrary to the dependence hypothesis, which predicts that if a subject has adapted to some extent to one tilt, the optical discrepancy imposed by an opposite tilt will be reduced perceptually by the adaptation already achieved. For example, if a subject demonstrates 5°

of adaptation to a 10° clockwise tilt (+10°), subsequent exposure to a 10° counterclockwise tilt (−10°) would represent an effective discrepancy of 10° − (−10°) − 5° = 20° − 5° = 15°. Since the adaptation obtained in Ebenholtz's experiment was that predicted for a 20° discrepancy, the dependence hypothesis was disconfirmed. These results also represent a negative case for the learning interpretation of adaptation discussed in Chapter 4, since that position would presumably predict "negative transfer" of adaptation as a result of switching to the opposite tilt.

In another study, Ebenholtz (1968a, Experiment 1) supported the dependence hypothesis by finding that tilt adaptation declined rapidly when, after adapting partially to a particular optical tilt, the subject was exposed to a tilt equal to the amount by which he had adapted. According to the dependence hypothesis, no decline (except, perhaps, that due to spontaneous decay) should have occurred, since a tilt equal to the level of adaptation will appear vertical and therefore no *perceptual* discrepancy exists.

Since the proposed comparator becomes less sensitive to the discrepancy between "old" and "new" retinal events as exposure to a given optical tilt continues, it should be possible to keep the adaptive process active by periodically increasing the tilt. Ebenholtz and Mayer (1968) exposed subjects in one group (Group V) to an increase in optical tilt in steps of 5° at 5-min intervals for a total period of 30 min, reaching a maximum tilt of 30°. As seen in Figure 6.5, the adaptation increased in nearly linear fashion throughout the exposure period. This is in sharp contrast to the typical negatively accelerated acquisition curve, which the investigators replicated in a second condition (Group C) in which tilt was set at a constant 30°. A similar finding was reported by Ebenholtz (1969) in an experiment in which 8° increments were used, terminating at a 40° tilt. With larger increments (10 or 12°) Ebenholtz (1973) found that the rate of increase of adaptation over a 25-min period was reduced. The acquisition function was negatively accelerated and asymptotic, rather than linearly increasing. In fact, tilt increments of 12° appeared to *suppress* the adaptive mechanism, as seen by the generally low level of adaptation achieved throughout the incremental period. It seems that the comparator cannot efficiently handle such large discrepancies, at least for the relatively short periods of exposure allowed at each step of increasing tilt. Therefore, the original assumption that the magnitude of adaptation is linearly related to the angle of the difference between the pre-tilt and tilt values must be qualified. Either this function holds only for relatively small tilts (10–30°) or the exposure time for a given tilt must be

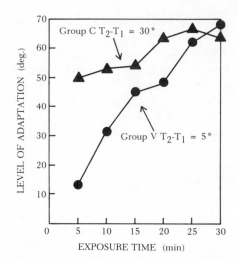

Figure 6.5. Magnitude of adaptation as a function of exposure time for the constant (30°) tilt condition (Group C) and the 5° tilt increment condition (Group V). (Reprinted with permission of author and publisher from: Ebenholtz, S. M. & Mayer, D. Rate of adaptation under constant and varied optical tilt. *Perceptual and Motor Skills,* 1968, *26,* 507–509.)

increased proportionally for larger tilts before the linear function can again be obtained.

The evidence provided by Ebenholtz and his colleagues is quite convincing in its support of the hypothesis that the stimulus for optical tilt adaptation is independent of the current level of adaptation.[3] Determining if this stimulus involves only the retinal flow pattern, as Ebenholtz believes, cannot be done until this cue is examined apart from the other types of available information. If Ebenholtz is correct, it should be possible to produce quite significant adaptation to optical tilt for a subject whose sole activity during the exposure period is moving his head back and forth while viewing a structured visual scene.

Before leaving Ebenholtz' theory, it should be pointed out that although it seems likely that tilt adaptation is independent of the level of adaptation already achieved, it does not necessarily follow that the comparator model holds. It might be possible to obtain Ebenholtz's results even if the stimulus for adaptation is the current flow pattern

---

[3] Perhaps related to and corroborative of this is the finding by Held (1966) that directional optokinetic nystagmus is determined by retinal tilt independently of any adaptive change in *perceived* tilt.

(or tilt), independent of any previously existing retinal events. As Ebenholtz (1968a) has suggested, the vertical meridians of the eyes might serve as standards of comparison by which flow pattern and tilt are evaluated.[4]

What Is It That Adapts?

EYE TORSION

The preceding evidence has demonstrated that active exposure to an optically tilted environment leads to adaptive changes in perceived vertical. It may now be asked what it is that has adapted. One possibility is that an unnoticed rotation of the eyes in the direction of the tilt might have occurred. However, although Howard and Templeton (1964) showed that the eyes will rotate a little (about 1°) in response to a rotation of the visual field (optokinetic torsion), this has not been observed for subjects who have adapted to optical tilt (Howard & Templeton, 1964; Mack & Chitayat, 1970). Thus, we may dismiss eye torsion as a locus of tilt adaptation.

CHANGE IN FELT HEAD ORIENTATION

Another possibility is that a change has occurred in the felt orientation of the head relative to the torso. If after exposure to a 10° clockwise optical tilt, the subject felt his head to be tilted by 10° counterclockwise when it was actually upright, the perceived orientation of a line objectively coincident to the vertical axis of the head should be perceived as tilted by 10° counterclockwise relative to the torso (and to gravity if the subject is standing or sitting in an upright position). There would be no perceived tilt with respect to the head (Figure 6.6). Thus, it is crucial to know what part of the body the observer is using as his standard of egocentric orientation. If he is instructed to orient a luminous line to the vertical in terms of his trunk, then it is possible that tilt adaptation could be accounted for, at least in part, by a misperception of head orientation.

Redding (1975c) exposed subjects to a 20° clockwise tilt, before and after which he required them to reach out in the dark and make three marks on the frontoparallel surface, corresponding to points projected from (a) the forehead; (b) between the eyes; and (c) the nose. Any pre–post shift in the subject's placement of these marks was

---

[4] Indeed, if the stimulus for tilt adaptation must involve a long-term memory component, then it ought to be impossible for a newborn organism to adapt to such a distortion, which seems unlikely.

Felt orientation of an objectively upright head

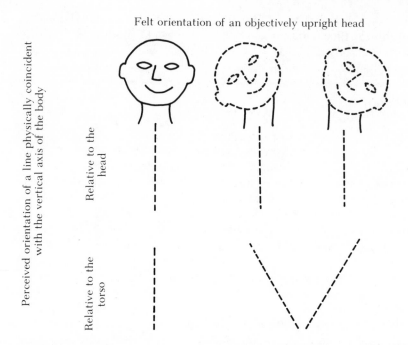

Figure 6.6. Perceived orientation of a line as a result of a shift in felt orientation of the head relative to the torso. When the head is used as the standard of reference, the objectively vertical line appears vertical, regardless of the felt orientation of the head. When the torso is used as the standard of reference, the objectively vertical line appears to be vertical when the upright head is felt to be upright, but appears tilted if the upright head is felt to be tilted.

assumed to indicate a change in the felt relationship between the head and the rest of the body. An adaptive shift was obtained, but it is impossible to tell if the change in position sense was between head and trunk or limited merely to the arm's relation to the rest of the body. That the latter was the case is suggested by the finding of a large proprioceptive shift when exposure consisted of viewing the actively moving hand.

The most straightforward way of measuring change in the felt relation of head to trunk is to have a blindfolded subject attempt to align his head with the rest of his body. This task was used by Lotto, Kern, and Morant (1967) and Shulman and Morant (1968), in a series of unpublished experiments. Lotto et al. found that 30 min of unrestricted exposure to a 40° optical tilt resulted in feeling that the upright head was tilted. When the subject felt that his head was aligned with his trunk, it was actually turned in the same direction as the optical tilt. However, the extent of visual tilt adaptation exceeded the observed change in felt head orientation. This suggests that egocentric tilt adaptation, when measured with the torso as referent, is composed of two components: (a) the felt relation of head to trunk and (b) an aspect specific to the eye–head relationship, which therefore is independent of the orientation of the head. This latter event concerns egocentric orientation with reference to the head.

ALTERED MEMORY TRACES

Mack and Rock (1968) demonstrated that when a subject's judgments of vertical are to be made specifically in terms of the axis of the head, measurable adaptation to optical tilt can be obtained. Because any changes in felt relation of head to trunk in this situation are irrelevant, it was argued that the basis of egocentric tilt adaptation is a change in the egocentric tilt adaptation is a change in the egocentric significance of the tilted retinal image. That is, after a period of exposure to the visual field or the body, the tilted image elicits a memory trace of egocentric verticality. In further support of this theory, Mack and Chitayat (1970) induced tilt adaptation in opposite directions for subjects whose left eye was exposed to one optical tilt (5°) and the right eye to the opposite tilt.[5] The failure of a stationary viewing condition to lead to any change in apparent tilt rules out the possibility that the effects experienced in the experimental condition were due to configurational adaptation or a Wertheimer aftereffect. Since no evidence of eye torsion was found and changes in head orientation are irrelevant in this situation, this finding represents good support for Mack and Rock's explanation of tilt adaptation when the head is used as the standard of reference.

CHANGE IN FELT EYE MOVEMENTS

Not ruled out by the preceding experiments is the possibility, first suggested by Harris (1965) with respect to adaptation to prismatic curvature, that the subject will misperceive the direction of his eye movements as he scans the tilted visual field. If a subject moving his eyes along an optically tilted line (while keeping its image directly on the fovea) feels as if he is moving his eyes vertically, than he would perceive the line as vertical. From this it follows that, with the eyes *sta-*

---

[5] However, Ebenholtz (personal communication, 1975) reports that he was unable to obtain eye-specific adaptation of this sort with larger optical tilts (20–30°).

tionary, the field would have to appear just as tilted as when the goggles were 'first worn. However, no one has reported that visual tilt adaptation is measurable only when the eyes are scanning the test stimulus, so a simple eye movement theory of tilt adaptation is not viable. A related possibility is that the subject acquires a *readiness* to make oblique eye movements. This is the "efferent readiness theory" (Kohler, 1964; Taylor, 1962; Festinger *et al.,* 1967), discussed in Chapter 9 and for which there is little or no conclusive evidence.

It may be concluded that, when the head serves as the standard of reference, egocentric tilt adaptation is a truly visual phenomenon, not based on the felt position or motion of the eyes. This appears to represent the first instance that we have seen of adaptation based on a change in the values of retinal loci.

SUMMARY AND CONCLUSIONS

When a subject is exposed to optically induced tilt, and after ruling out (a) changes in apparent gravitational vertical and (b) configurational adaptation, it is possible to measure a "genuine" adaptive change in apparent egocentric orientation.

If the entire body is used as the standard of egocentric orientation, tilt adaptation is probably based on a change in the felt relation of head to trunk, together with a recalibration of retinal values. The existence of the latter component argues against the necessity that the retinal image be oriented in a particular, innately determined manner for the veridical perception of egocentric orientation in adult subjects. However, it should be kept in mind that *complete* optical tilt adaptation has never been obtained, except perhaps for especially selected subjects; the adaptation curve typically reaches asymptote at less than one-third of the theoretical maximum. Such a poor showing suggests that egocentric adaptation to inverted or reversed vision would never occur, regardless of the length of the exposure period. The possible significance of the subjects' inability to adapt fully to these and other forms of visual rearrangement is discussed in Chapter 13.

The best condition for producing tilt adaptation appears to be whole-body movement in a structured, although not necessarily familiar, environment. If this movement is self-initiated, head motion probably facilitates adaptation, whereas if the subject is moved through the environment by the experimenter, it may be a source of interference.

Based on the research of Ebenholtz, it appears that the "adequate stimulus" for tilt adaptation does not involve the *perceived* orientation or flow pattern, but rather a comparison of the optical/retinal conditions before optical tilt to the conditions during optical tilt or, perhaps, the retinal events in comparison with the vertical meridians of the eyes.

7

Adaptation to
the Loss of Visual Stability

When Stratton (1897a,b) first donned his inverting goggles he was confronted not only with an upside down world but one that turned in the same direction as his head movement and at twice its velocity (see Chapter 5). Happily for Stratton, this visual instability subsided after several days, although it reappeared as a visual aftereffect when the goggles were removed. Thus, although it is unlikely that Stratton ever came to see the world consistently as right side up during his 8-day experiment, he did succeed at least in overcoming one drastic visual disturbance—the loss of *visual position constancy*. The aim of the present chapter is to examine adaptation to this form of visual rearrangement. However, before doing so, it is necessary to clarify the nature of visual stability during normal vision.

THE CONSTANCY OF VISUAL DIRECTION
AND VISUAL POSITION

Active movements of the eyes, head, or entire body cause visual contours to sweep across the retina or the eyes or head to compensate as if tracking a moving object. However, the observer generally experiences little or no apparent visual movement or displacement.[1] Somehow, as with the other perceptual constancies, the

---

[1] It appears that visual *motion* and visual *displacement* (i.e., change in direction) are separable processes, based on different physiological mechanisms (e.g., MacKay, 1973). Similarly, the perception of bodily motion may be distinguished from the perception of the position of that body part (relative to other parts).

observer is able to extract from the wildly fluctuating proximal stimulus a stable perception that closely matches the distal stimulus. It
should be noted that why the visual world remains apparently stable
during eye or bodily movement is independent of where the world
appears to be located during this movement. The first of these questions concerns the presence or absence of visual motion or of a
change in visual direction, while the second concerns visual direction
itself. Only the first of these perceptual capacities is discussed here.

It is useful to differentiate the situation in which only the eyes are in
motion from that in which head and/or torso are moving. In the
former case, despite changes in retinal locus, apparent direction relative to the head (i.e., egocentric direction) remains constant. This is
visual direction constancy (VDC). In the second case, changes in the
position of the head and/or trunk may lead to shifts in egocentric
direction, but do not produce a change in the apparent *position* of
the object or entire visual field. For example, turning the head to the
right while in the presence of a visual target ojectively located in the
median plane of the trunk will cause the apparent direction of the
target (relative to the head) to shift to the left, but will leave its
apparent position in the environment unchanged. This is *visual position constancy* (VPC).[2]

For both VDC and VPC the crucial question concerns how the
organism is able to discriminate (a) retinal image motion/displace-
ment (or the visual tracking behavior arising from the organism's own
bodily movements) from (b) that elicited by physical displacements of
the environment (i.e., "true" visual motion). There appear to be two
(not necessarily mutually exclusive) general answers to this question.
First, the two situations differ with respect to the characteristics of the
retinal image or its movement. Second, there is some form of
extraretinal information, such as kinesthetic–proprioceptive input
from the eye or neck muscles, that allows the organism to detect if
and to what extent its own movements have led to the retinal effects.
Shebilske (in press) has reviewed the arguments and data in favor of
the "retinal information hypothesis" of VDC and VPC and concluded
that "higher-order" (i.e., relational) retinal cues, such as the optical
flow pattern (J. J. Gibson, 1968) or the relationship between the retinal
projection of the nose and that of other visual objects (Bower, 1974,
Chapter 3), may play an important role in these constancies. However,
the latter have also been manifested when higher-order retinal

---

[2] I became aware of the distinction between VDC and VPC after reading a paper by
Shebilske (1977).

information is not available (e.g., when viewing a small luminous spot in the dark). Thus, extraretinal cues are also important, and have received a great deal of experimental attention, particularly as they apply to eye movements (i.e., VDC).

MECHANISMS OF VISUAL DIRECTION CONSTANCY (VDC)

Theories

It is beyond the scope of this chapter to engage in a detailed discussion and comparison of the proposed mechanisms of VDC in which extraretinal cues play a role. (The interested reader may refer to a review by MacKay, 1973.) There are three general theories. The first of these, the *suppression theory,* was suggested by a number of investigators (Holt, 1903; Howard, 1973; Wallach & Lewis, 1965) and proposes that the absence of apparent motion when the eyes are engaged in saccadic movement results from a suppression of or lack of attention to retinal input during the saccade; that is, we are essentially blind for the brief duration of each saccadic eye movement. However, while sensitivity to light and visual motion is attenuated during saccadic eye movements, these perceptual capacities are not entirely absent, at least when the target is the only thing visible (e.g., Latour, 1962; Mack, 1970). In the latter situation it is often reported that an actually stationary point of light appears to move ("smear") during saccadic eye movement. On the other hand, if the eye movements take place in a fully lighted environment, it is possible that such factors as "masking" do serve to eliminate retinal input, thereby abolishing the experience of visual motion. Thus, the suppression theory could account for the absence of visual motion in a lighted field.

The second explanation of VDC was proposed by MacKay (1958, 1973) and termed the *expectation–confirmation theory.* MacKay argued that visual stability should be considered the *norm* and that the real question concerns how it is possible to perceive *true* motion or displacement. The observer "expects" (not necessarily consciously) that a movement of the eyes will lead to an equal but opposite visual displacement. As long as this expectation, or "conditional readiness," is confirmed, the visual field will appear stable. Any mismatch between expected and actual retinal motion results in illusory visual motion or displacement, but this mismatch must be fairly large before the "null hypothesis" of visual stability will be "rejected" by the perceptual system.

The final and certainly the most widely accepted theory was proposed by Holst and Mittelstädt (1950). It is the primary example of a *cancellation theory* and is often referred to as the "reafference model." This model proposes that a neural copy of the efferent command to the eye muscles is "compared" to the resulting retinal motion (visual "reafference") and, as long as the two neural events represent equal (but opposite) movements, they will cancel each other out, thereby causing the visual field to appear stable. This model served as the starting point for Held's (1961) influential theory of prism adaptation (see Chapters 2 and 3).

The Nature of the Extraretinal Cues:
Inflow, Outflow, or Both?

In principle, the mechanism of VDC is independent of the nature of the extraretinal cues upon which this mechanism is based. Traditionally, two possibilities have been entertained. The first is that the information used to "discount" the retinal image motion comes solely from the neural *inflow* (or "feedback") emanating from the eye muscles. The second argues that it is neural *outflow* that serves this purpose. The reafference model makes the latter assumption.

The original proponent of the inflow model was Sherrington (1918), who argued, on the basis of his previous discovery of stretch receptors (i.e., muscle spindles) in the extraocular muscles, that kinesthetic impulses serve to "account for" the retinal motion caused by eye movements. Contrary to this is the theory, first proposed by Helmholtz (1925), that the felt position of the eyes is based entirely on the "effort of will" (i.e., neural outflow). The outflow theory of VDC has generally been accepted as fact. Evidence commonly cited in favor of this theory is Brindley and Merton's (1960) experiment in which a subject who was deprived of all visual clues failed to detect passively induced eye movements of up to 40°, the latter effected by the experimenter, who pulled the subject's eye muscles by means of forceps. This observation, which had actually been made previously by Irvine and Ludvigh (1936), strongly suggests that the stretch receptors of the extraocular muscles are nonfunctional.

However, these studies of "forced" eye movements can be criticized on the grounds that the response measures used were insensitive and the procedure for rotating the eye so distracting that it caused the subject to be inattentive to his proprioceptive input.

Indeed, when these problems are rectified it can be shown that subjects are capable of consciously perceiving the direction of passively induced rotations of the eye solely on the basis of inflow signals from the eye muscles. Skavenski (1972) demonstrated this in an experiment in which a tight-fitting contact lens was placed on the right eye of each of two subjects, attached to which was a 3-cm stalk that could be gently turned, to cause a passive rotation of the eye. Using a forced-choice procedure, he found that his subjects were able to detect fairly large rotations of the eye. Local anesthesia was used to rule out tactile or pressure signals from the eyes (as they moved in their sockets) as possible sources of information about eye position.

In spite of this evidence, there are reasons for believing that the *precise* registration of eye position requires both inflow and outflow. If you close one eye and then gently jiggle the other with your finger (this is not suggested for contact-lens wearers!), the visual field will appear to jump around. Since it appears that VDC is lost with such passive movements, it is reasonable to conclude that inflow alone is not sufficient to "discount" the retinal motion. Another interesting observation (e.g., Gregory, 1973, pp. 97–98) is that when a positive afterimage is placed on the retina, with the subject in the dark, jiggling the eye does not produce an experience of visual motion. Active eye movement, on the other hand, leads to apparent motion of the afterimage that follows precisely the movement of the eyes (Mack & Bachant, 1969).[3]

The most commonly cited *positive* evidence for the importance of neural outflow to VDC is the fact that if the eyes are immobilized or impeded (e.g., by means of a neuromuscular blocking agent such are curare), the *attempt* to move the eyes leads to the experience of illusory visual motion or to a jump in apparent visual direction (Brindley & Merton, 1960; Mach, 1959; Skavenski, Haddad, & Steinman, 1972; Stevens et al., 1976). Thus, it is the intent, not the actual eye movements (and concomitant neural inflow), that determines the perceptual outcome.

There is now evidence for an alternative to both the inflow and outflow theories of VDC. These data, which have been reviewed by Shebilske (1977), support the usefulness of neural inflow from the eye muscles as a basis of VDC. However, it is proposed that this feedback is dependent on or facilitated by outflow. According to this

---

[3] With *rapid* eye movements, however, there may be a suppression of the visual input such that the afterimage is not seen, or seen very poorly, *during* the saccade. Nevertheless, when the eye has stopped moving, the afterimage will appear to have shifted to this new position.

"hybrid" theory, motor commands to the eye muscles induce neural inflow via the gamma efferents, even before the eye muscles have had a chance to contract or perhaps in the complete absence of muscular movement (Matin, 1972). Thus, efference is necessary, but only as a "catalyst" for kinesthetic–proprioceptive afference. This interesting suggestion is congruent with some of the observations previously used to support the outflow theory. For example, it could be argued that the loss of VDC when the eyes are moved passively results from the absence or significant reduction of the inflow normally produced by the efferent commands. In fact, spindle afference is markedly reduced in the absence of gamma efference (Bach-y-Rita, 1972). Likewise, the experience of illusory visual motion or displacement when attempting to move an immobilized eye may occur because there is a certain amount of efferently induced inflow from the eye muscles, even though the latter have failed to contract.[4] Evidence that feedback from some source is both available and used has been provided by Shebilske (1977), who found that saccadic eye movements to predetermined visual targets that disappeared at the initiation of the eye movement were often in error, but could be corrected quite accurately after a short delay. This replicated the results of other investigators (Barnes & Gresty, 1973; Becker, 1972; Becker & Fuchs, 1969; Weber & Daroff, 1972) and supported a servocontrol model of eye movements proposed by Weber and Daroff (1972), in which there are two kinds of extraretinal signals: one that represents the intended eye position (the command or reference input signal) and another that represents the actual eye position (the feedback signal). After a main saccade that ends off target, these two signals differ, causing an actuating or error signal that results in a corrective movement. Shebilske addressed a second experiment to whether the space perception system monitors the command signal or the feedback signal. It was suggested that, during the time when the command and feedback signals differ according to the model, apparent visual direction is consistent with the feedback signal and contrary to the command signal. However, Shebilske warned that the actual source of the feedback signal may not be inflow from muscle spindles; it could instead

[4] Stevens et al. (1976) found that, with "partial" paralysis (i.e., a low dose of curare), attempts to move the eyes led to a strong illusory visual displacement; with "complete" muscular immobilization (high dose), however, the unsuccessful attempts to move the eyes did not produce a clear-cut impression of retinal displacement. Similar results were obtained by Brindley, Goodwin, Kulikowski, and Leighton (1976). The outflow hypothesis would not have predicted these results and they suggest the possibility that some inflow emanates from the eye muscles when paralysis is only partial.

be feedback from an internal monitor that "looks at" the innervation pattern before it reaches the muscles. Thus, the possibilities appear to be much more complex than the original inflow–outflow dichotomy suggested.

It may be concluded that both neural inflow and outflow provide extraretinal cues for VDC, and it is likely that each of the three major theories concerning how these cues are used—suppression, expectation–confirmation, and cancellation—explains certain aspects of VDC that the others cannot. For example, it is possible that the absence of apparent visual motion during saccadic eye movements is handled, at least in part, by some variety of the suppression theory, while constancy of visual direction before and after the saccade may be explained by either cancellation or expectation–confirmation.

MECHANISMS OF VISUAL POSITION CONSTANCY (VPC)

When the head or entire body is free to move, the visual field is experienced as stable, a phenomenon referred to here as visual position constancy (VPC). For simplicity, the present discussion will be limited to head movement. When the head is turned, the eyes typically do not move with it, but undergo an involuntary rotation in the opposite direction, which allows them to remain on their initial fixation point. This is the *vestibulo-ocular reflex* and can be demonstrated in complete darkness; this response is not to be confused with "optokinetic nystagmus," which serves to prolong fixation on a moving visual stimulus or background. If the vestibulo-ocular reflex occurs when a visual stimulus is present, it precludes retinal image displacement, but this does not eliminate the need for a VPC mechanism. That is, one may still ask how the observer experiences a stable visual field during the vestibulo-ocular reflex when his eyes are now engaged in an activity essentially the same as that required to track an objectively moving object.

The neck and other muscles involved in head movements provide kinesthetic–proprioceptive afference and vestibular cues are available as well, so it has generally been assumed that motor outflow is not necessary for VPC. However, this is not to say that outflow is not used. A number of experiments have demonstrated that bilateral deafferentation of the limbs does not interfere greatly with visuomotor coordination, at least in monkeys (Taub & Berman, 1968; Taub & Goldberg, 1974), suggesting that outflow may normally be used to monitor this activity. Probably both inflow and outflow are involved in the VPC process.

A suppression theory does not seem to explain VPC since, as the reader can easily verify, vision is not attenuated during head movement, even when the vestibulo-ocular reflex is precluded. Thus it may tentatively be proposed that VPC is based on a process where outflow in combination with a variety of types of inflow is compared to the retinal effects and stability is achieved by either cancellation or expectation–confirmation.

The theories of VDC and VPC are essentially neutral with respect to the nature–nurture question and to the potential for modifiability, both of which are empirical questions. The remainder of this chapter is devoted to the issues of whether and in what manner observers can adapt to an induced loss of VDC or VPC.

ADAPTATION TO THE LOSS OF VISUAL DIRECTION AND POSITION CONSTANCY

Visual Direction Constancy (VDC)

When distorting goggles or spectacles are worn there is a loss of VPC. However, there is no change in VDC, since the device is attached to the subject's head. Thus, for example, when looking through inverting goggles, an eye movement to a position that appears to be in the upper part of the visual field will, from the very beginning, lead to foveation, with little or no error. (The apparent position of the target does not coincide with its actual position, but this has no effect on *oculomotor* coordination.) Head movement, however, is initially inaccurate and leads to a severe disruption of VPC. Thus, to disrupt VDC it is necessary to cause eye *movements* to lead to a new form of retinal image displacement, and a variety of procedures have been devised to do this (Mack, 1970; Mack & Bachant, 1969; McLaughlin, 1967; Pola, 1976; Wallach & Lewis, 1965; Yarbus, 1967). With rare exceptions (Wallach & Lewis, 1965), atypical displacement of the retinal image during active eye movements has produced the experience of external motion or at least a change in apparent egocentric direction. For example, Mack (1970) found that when a cathode ray oscilloscope trace moved (relative to the *environment*) by at least 20–40% of the extent of the concurrent eye movement, subjects consistently reported apparent external motion. Displacements of 5% were almost never detected. That fairly large discrepancies between eye movement and retinal image displacement are not experienced as external motion is contrary to the reafference model but in line with MacKay's expectation–confirmation theory, which does not require a precise match to produce visual stability.

Only a few experiments have attempted to assess the ability of human subjects to adapt to altered VDC. McLaughlin (1967) created a situation in which a point of light located 10° off to one side at the initiation of a saccadic fixation eye movement was caused to shift 1° toward the initial point of fixation. Eventually, the 10°-displaced target elicited a 9° eye movement, thereby eliminating the initial fixation errors. Although it is not clear from McLaughlin's report, it seems that this change in oculomotor coordination was accompanied by the experience that the visual target was no longer changing its position. Assuming that this is true, McLaughlin's study was the first to demonstrate adaptation to altered VDC. Pola (1976) has also reported the occurrence of this form of adaptation.

Visual Position Constancy (VPC)

VARIETIES OF ALTERED VPC

Stratton was the first to report an experimentally induced loss of VPC. It might not at first be clear to the reader why he initially saw the visual field move with his head and at a faster rate of speed. This visual experience may be understood by considering what happens when the head is moved in a particular direction while an image remains in a *fixed* position on the retina, as when tracking a moving object. Here the experience will be one of an object moving in the same direction and at the same velocity as the head. When up/down- and right/left-reversing spectacles are worn, a movement of the head to the right causes objects that are incorrectly seen as being to the left to come into central view, which is the opposite of what occurs with normal vision. It follows that, if head movement while viewing a fixed retinal image produces the experience of a visual field moving along with the head, actual retinal displacement in the direction opposite normal should lead to apparent motion in the same direction the head is turning and by twice the angle.

Stratton (1897b) experienced an aftereffect of visual motion after he removed the goggles:

> When I turned my body or my head, objects seemed to sweep before me as if they themselves were suddenly in motion. The "swinging of the scene," observed so

continuously during the first days of the experiment, had thus returned with great vividness [p. 470].

Unfortunately, this statement does not indicate the *direction* of the perceived motion. As Taylor (1962, p. 186) first deduced, the direction of the aftereffect is crucial to the issue of whether or not the visual field ever came to look right side up. If it did appear normally oriented, then after removing the spectacles it should have looked, at least momentarily, upside down and a movement of the head would have led to the same experience as when the spectacles were first worn. It would have appeared to move rapidly in the *same* direction as the head movement. If egocentric reorientation had not occurred and a shift in the visual field in the same direction as head movement had come to signify a stationary field, then after removing the prisms the world should have appeared to move rapidly in the *opposite* direction. It is likely that this was Stratton's experience since he apparently failed to undergo a stable righting of visual egocentric orientation.

A loss of VPC can also be induced by size-altering lenses, which can be demonstrated by looking through binoculars while turning the head. The visual field appears to move too rapidly in the direction opposite the head turn, since the apparent displacement of the visual field is magnified along with the image. If looking through the "wrong" end, the reduced image appears to move in the same direction as the head turn, but at a slower speed, because the retinal image is displacing in the opposite direction by a smaller amount than the head is rotating. Size distortion-induced illusory motion when engaging in head movement is also experienced with eye glasses that have a strong spherical correction and when an underwater scene is viewed through a diving mask (see Chapter 12). Illusory visual motion results when head movements are made while wearing goggles that tilt the field (Chapter 6), and adaptation to this distortion has been measured by several investigators (Brown, 1928; Taylor & Papert, 1956).

Lateral head movements while wearing base-left or base-right wedge prisms lead to an alternating compression and expansion of the visual field, while up and down movements produce a "see-saw" rocking effect (see Chapter 2, pp. 14–15). Pick and Hay (1964, 1966a) found that after 21 days of exposure subjects showed partial compensation for these visual effects. Wallach and Flaherty (1976) demonstrated that, after only 10 min of head nodding while wearing a wedge prism and viewing a striped pattern, a compensatory shift of VPC representing 9% of full adaptation occurred, which is close to the

11% reported by Pick and Hay after many days of unsupervised activities. Wallach and Flaherty also showed that this adaptation failed to occur when the visual deformations of the field were viewed with a stationary head. Thus, it appears that adaptation to this disruption of VPC requires a linkage between atypical visual motion and the bodily movements upon which this motion is contingent.

DIRECT TESTS OF VPC ADAPTATION

The first experiments designed specifically to test adaptation to VPC loss were by Wallach and Kravitz (1965a,b) and, independently, by Posin and Rock (described by Rock, 1966, pp. 87–91). Before and after the exposure period, Wallach and Kravitz showed the subject a single luminous spot in a dark room, thereby preventing him from experiencing any higher-order retinal cues or motion of the object in relation to other objects. The target was projected onto a curved screen by means of headgear worn by the subject, and its position relative to his head could be changed during lateral head rotation. This device made it possible to effect a displacement of the target in any ratio to the rotation of the head and in either direction. For example, if a 10° rightward turn of the head were arranged to cause a 10° leftward shift of the light (relative to the head), a target to head "displacement ratio" of 100% would exist and, because of VPC, the subject would experience no motion. This would be a veridical perception since the light did not move relative to the environment. By this means it is possible to measure both the precision of VPC with normal vision and the magnitude of adaptation to the loss of VPC. Before this device was developed, only qualitative, "all-or-none" reports of adaptation and aftereffect to distortions of VPC had been possible (e.g., Kohler, 1951; Stratton, 1897a,b).[5]

In one experiment, Wallach and Kravitz (1965a) had their subjects wear reducing goggles (x.66), which cause the visual field to appear to

---

[5] In a number of later experiments (Wallach & Floor, 1970; Wallach & Frey, 1969, 1972a; Wallach, Frey & Romney, 1969), a more rapidly administered adaptation test was used. In the case of exposure to altered VPC in the horizontal dimension the test involved viewing a spot of light oscillating in a *vertical* path as the subject turned his head from side to side. If adaptation has resulted from a preceding exposure period, then the illusory horizontal motion component representing the aftereffect will add vectorally to the objective vertical motion component to produce an apparent *diagonal* direction of motion for the spot. The subject's task was to view the moving spot of light and then to attempt to match its apparent slant by means of a rotatable rod; the greater the slant, the more the adaptation. The advantage of this procedure is that it requires only one trial, thereby allowing adaptation to be measured before it has had a chance to decay significantly.

move initially in the same direction as the head, although more slowly. In this case, the displacement ratio was 34%. Using the testing procedure described in the preceding paragraph, the investigators found that after 6 hr of wearing the goggles and engaging in everyday activities outside the laboratory, subjects showed (without the goggles) an average adaptive shift of the "no-motion" head–target displacement ratio of 17.5%, which is 50% of full adaptation. While before the exposure period a displacement ratio of 100% (plus or minus a few degrees) was required to experience the luminous spot as stationary, it was now necessary for the target to move significantly in the same direction as the head. Alternatively, if the target were stationary relative to the environment, a turn of the head would lead to a perception of motion in the opposite direction. In a second experiment, Wallach and Kravitz (1965b) demonstrated that significant adaptation of altered VPC could be produced merely by turning the head back and forth for 10 min while viewing a relatively large patterned field that was caused to move in the direction opposite that of the head turn and at a greater rate (displacement ratio = 150%). After the exposure period the experience of no motion was produced when the spot was actually moving against the head turn by an amount significantly greater than 100% of the rotation. More important, it was found that *passive* rotation of the head did not lead to an appreciable reduction of adaptation, suggesting that outflow (or efferently induced inflow) is not necessary for adaptation of this sort. This result was independently replicated by Posin (see Rock, 1966, pp. 87–91).

Wallach and Kravitz (1968) also found that adaptation to the loss of VPC by means of optical reduction does not result in a concomitant shift in *auditory* position constancy. This result appears to rule out the possibility that adaptation of altered VPC is based on a change in the felt position or motion of the head, since such a recalibration would be expected to affect auditory localization.

Additional experiments by Wallach and his coworkers have demonstrated that adaptation to altered VPC increases in magnitude as a function of exposure time (e.g., Wallach & Floor, 1970) and extent of distortion (e.g., Wallach & Frey, 1969). Still other adaptation experiments from Wallach's laboratory have led to the conclusion that the normal experience of VPC is based on or is at least maintained by everyday experience. Specifically, they showed that:

1. VPC adaptation is subject to rapid spontaneous decay (Wallach & Floor, 1970; Wallach & Frey, 1969, 1972a).
2. Concentrated prior exposure to the normal relationship between

head movements and optical motion retards subsequent adaptation (Wallach & Floor, 1970).

3. Exposure to optical motion in the same direction as the head's rotation produces greater, more decay-resistant adaptation than does exposure involving optical motion against head rotation, the latter being the normal state of affairs (Wallach et al., 1969).

4. Adaptation to altered VPC when the optical motion is in the same dimension as the head movement is subject to much greater decay than adaptation to optical motion in the orthogonal direction (Wallach & Frey, 1972a).

These results suggest that normal visual experience establishes and/or maintains a "long-term memory" that proactively interferes with adaptation to experimentally induced distortions (particularly those involving optical motion of the sort encountered normally) and that reasserts itself soon after the termination of the exposure period. That it is possible to compensate (partially) for optical motion at a right angle to the head's line of rotation indicates that the VPC adaptation mechanism is functional even when the movement-induced optical inputs are of a sort never encountered in normal experience.

Working independently of Wallach's laboratory, Hay and his colleagues (Hay, 1968, 1971; Hay & Goldsmith, 1973) also examined the ability of human subjects to adapt to atypical optical motion contingent on head movement. They caused up and down head movements to produce a right to left oscillation of an oscilloscope trace, which the subject was required to fixate, and measured the pre- and post-exposure "no-motion" point, using the same apparatus. During the exposure period, the subject's eyes were forced to move along a diagonal path to maintain fixation of the spot of light as the head moved up and down. Hay (1968) found that after as little as 1 min of this experience subjects revealed a measurable adaptive shift, confirming the work of Wallach et al. Other results from Hay's laboratory are directly concerned with the process by which adaptation to altered VPC takes place and the nature of its end product(s).

THE MECHANISM AND END PRODUCT(S)
OF VPC ADAPTATION

What is the nature of the process by which human observers adapt to altered VPC when only extraretinal cues are present, and what is it that adapts? The necessary and sufficient condition for the occurrence of this form of adaptation is exposure to a new and consistent relationship between head movement and optical motion. The presence of one or the other of these constituents alone produces little or no change in perception (Hay, 1968; Posin, 1966, described by Rock, 1966, pp. 87–91; Wallach & Flaherty, 1976). We have already seen that the adaptive process operates as well with passive head movements as with active movements (Wallach & Kravitz, 1965b; Posin, 1966), indicating that kinesthetic and/or vestibular inflow is a usable source of information for this type of adaptation. Since adaptation has occurred even in situations where the atypical optical motion is a physical reality, rather than an illusion induced by distorting goggles (e.g., Wallach & Kravitz, 1965a), it can be seen that activating the adaptive process does not require any information that the field is stationary.

With respect to the end products of adaptation to altered VPC there are, as Wallach and Kravitz (1968) have indicated, three logical possibilities: (a) a change in visual motion perception; (b) a change in felt head rotation; and (c) a change in the *relationship* between these two elements. Luckily, there is evidence to rule out the first two of these alternatives. Disconfirming the first suggestion is Hay's (1971) finding that the adaptation produced by the exposure condition described in the previous section was not accompanied by a change in apparent motion of the moving spot of light when viewed with a stationary head. Several forms of evidence also rule out the second possibility— that the subject comes to reinterpret his kinesthetic (or vestibular) sensations. Rock (1966, p. 95) pointed out that if Stratton had come to feel as if his head were turning in the direction opposite its actual rotation, the visual motion aftereffect he reported would have been one of seeing the field move *with* the head (a *positive* aftereffect). For example, if an observer, with inverting goggles removed, turns his head to the left but (mis)perceives that he is turning it to the right, then an object that is seen to move to the right as the head turns will be experienced as moving in the same direction as the head is felt to be rotating. However, it is likely that Stratton's experience and those of other subjects were of visual motion *against* the head's rotation. Another fact that is at odds with a recalibration of kinesthetic and/or vestibular sensations is Wallach and Kravitz's (1968) failure to find a change in auditory position constancy as a concomitant of the VPC adaptation they had obtained.

Thus, it appears that VPC adaptation involves a recorrelation between head movements and the optical motions to which they lead. Hay has proposed a model for this process, which is depicted in Figure 7.1. This represents a modification of Held's (1961) "reafference model" of prism adaptation, which, in turn, had been slightly modified from the mechanism proposed by Holst and Mittelstädt

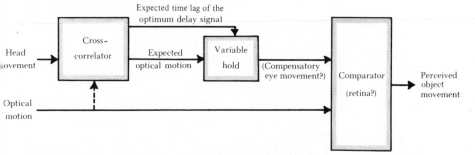

Figure 7.1. A cross-correlator model of adaptation to the loss of visual position constancy. (From J. C. Hay & W. M. Goldsmith. Space–time adaptation of visual position constancy. *Journal of Experimental Psychology*, 1973, *99*, 1–9. Copyright 1973 by the American Psychological Association. Reprinted by permission.)

(1950). This general model explains VPC and its adaptability far better than it does visuomotor prism adaptation. According to Hay's model, as long as head movements lead to the "expected" optical motion, visual stability will be experienced. That is, on the basis of "cross-correlation" (i.e., finding the best of several possible correlations), in flow and/or outflow information about head motion come to elicit an "expectation" of a particular type of optical motion, which is compared to the optical motion that actually occurs. A match leads to VPC; a mismatch leads to the experience of external visual motion (i.e., a loss of VPC). The details of this model derive from the results of several experiments from Hay's laboratory. Hay and Goldsmith (1973) demonstrated that if the vertical motion of the luminous spot, which was contingent on horizontal head turning, was *delayed* by 150 or 225 msec, adaptation was undiminished over that occurring with essentially no delay, as long as the test of adaptation involved the same time lag as the exposure period. Delays of 300 or 600 msec failed to produce adaptation; they apparently exceed the limits of the adaptive mechanism. It was concluded from these results that adaptation to the loss of VPC involves a "cross-correlator" that measures both the time lag and the space vector of the optical motion and, after a period of training, produces an expected time lag and an expected optical motion for a given head movement that are then compared with the actual optical motion. Thus, the expected optical motion is sent to the comparator only after a time lag corresponding to that of the training experience. In other experiments, Hay (1968, 1971) found that even when random visual *exafference* ("real" visual motion) is combined with the head movement-contingent optical motion (reafference), the àdaptive mechanism is capable of extracting that aspect of the visual input that represents an invariant relationship between head movement and optical motion. Interestingly, subjects in these studies were unaware during training that any of the visual motion was causally related to their head movements.

Hay has gone further with his model and suggested that the expected optical motion may take the form of compensatory eye movements (the vestibulo-ocular reflex) and that the retina serves as the comparator. He has also argued that the up/down and right/left eye movement mechanisms are *independently* adaptable. Thus, the end product of adaptation to altered VPC is a change in the relationship between head and eye movements. This conclusion is supported by the results of several experiments by Melvill Jones and Gonshor (1975), whose subjects wore right/left-reversing goggles for up to 2 weeks and underwent a *complete* reversal of the vestibulo-ocular reflex, as tested in the dark.

It is possible that the compensatory eye movements acquired during exposure to optically altered VPC are merely a "symptom" of adaptation, rather than the adaptation itself. Perhaps the subject acquires an expectancy for the visual motion that is now produced by a given movement of the head and then engages in the appropriate compensatory eye movement to maintain visual stability. Hay (1968) provided evidence that, at first glance, would appear to rule out this interpretation. He showed that no adaptation resulted if the subject fixated a stationary point as he nodded his head up and down in the presence of a laterally oscillating spot of light, and eye movements alone also failed to produce an adaptive shift. Adaptation was produced only when the subject followed the atypically moving stimulus object with his eyes while he moved his head. However, perhaps this was not the most appropriate test of the notion that VPC adaptation is merely a new head–eye movement relationship. It could be argued that when an observer who is moving his head is confronted with a "choice" between maintaining an "old" correlation (with respect to the stationary spot) and acquiring a "new" one (the vertically moving spot) he naturally opts for the former. In any event, several experiments by Wallach and Canal (1976) and Wallach and Bacon (1976) have apparently failed to confirm Hay's results. Wallach and Canal found that adaptation occurred when the subject fixated a stationary dot as he turned his head and observed a larger visual field that moved in the same direction as the head (displacement ratio = 40%). An adaptive shift of the no-motion point also occurred when head movements led to atypical motion of a spot of light that was ocularly tracked as it moved upon a stationary background.

It is possible, as Wallach and Canal concluded, that exposure to altered VPC induces *two* forms of adaptation: (a) a new relationship between head motion and compensatory eye rotation and (b) a "pure" expectancy for a new form of optical motion. The latter is similar to the end product of VPC adaptation suggested by Rock (1966, p. 86), namely, a change in the memory trace of the retinal motion that is now produced by a given head movement. Perhaps the most direct test of the latter form of adaptation has yet to be done. This would be to look for adaptation as a result of exposure to altered VPC when the test for the adaptation entails pre- and postexposure measures in which the subject's eyes are fixated straight ahead of the nose as he turns his head back and forth. In this fashion the adaptation period would not involve a "choice" between a stable and an unstable visual field, and the adaptation measured would represent a test of whether the subject is able to adapt to the new head movement–optical motion relation even when prevented from engaging in compensatory eye movements.

SUMMARY AND CONCLUSIONS

Human beings perceive a stable visual field when they actively move either their eyes or the remainder of their body, capacities referred to as visual direction constancy (VDC) and visual position constancy (VPC), respectively. Numerous experiments have demonstrated that subjects are capable of overcoming the initial loss of visual stability resulting from the optical alteration of either of these perceptual capacities. The majority of these experiments have been concerned with the loss of VPC.

On the basis of the research by Wallach and his colleagues, it appears that "normal" VPC, if not originally acquired from experience, is certainly maintained by it. Although exposure to a new head movement–optical motion relationship quickly produces adaptation, thereby overcoming years of previous normal experience, this compensation is subject to "proactive inhibition," as manifested, for example, by rapid spontaneous decay.

That we should be in possession of such a flexible perceptual mechanism is not surprising if one considers the fact that the human infant must be able to maintain VPC despite the fact that his rapidly growing head is continuously changing the relationship between head movements and the resulting optical motion. However, the existence of perceptual plasticity does not guarantee that the capacity in question was originally acquired through experience. An examination of such organisms as fish, monkeys, and human beings strongly suggests that VPC is present innately (see Ganz, 1975, for a review of this literature). This conclusion is drawn from the fact that, from the very beginning, these organisms (and others) manifest optokinetic nystagmus and/or the optokinetic reflex, which is the tendency to turn the eyes or entire body in the same direction and at the same speed as a physically moving visual field. These reflexes maintain orientation with respect to the field while the organism is moving. Since the organism does not engage in optokinetic responses when the visual field is stationary and it is instead the organism that turns, this organism must possess VPC.

The model suggested by Hay (see Figure 7.1) seems to represent a good general explanation of adaptation to altered VPC. However, this is not to imply that Hay's *implementation* of the model is necessarily correct. It remains to be seen if the adaptive changes in the vestibulo-ocular reflex demonstrated by Hay (and others) represent one end product of VPC adaptation or merely the reflexive response elicited by a change in expected optical motion. In any event, it seems unlikely that recalibration of the vestibulo-ocular reflex will be found to be a complete explanation for adaptation to altered VPC since, as Shebilske (1977) has pointed out, the eye movements that compensate for head motion vary as a function of the apparent distance of the object fixated.

Adaptation to altered VPC gives indications of being the most complete of any type of adaptation so far examined in this book. Stratton's report that he no longer saw any illusory motion toward the end of the exposure period suggests that adaptation had actually reached completion. In addition, Melvill Jones and Gonshor (1975) obtained complete reversal of the vestibulo-ocular reflex in a subject who wore right/left-reversing spectacles for 14 days. Why adaptation to the loss of VPC should be so extensive is not clear. It may have something to do with the fact that adaptation to the loss of VPC requires only that a *concomitance* exist between bodily motion and retinal image displacement. For adaptation to other forms of perceptual rearrangement, some kind of information about *actual* object location, orientation, and so forth is required. Another potentially important distinction is that adaptation to altered VPC involves a recalibration of a reflexive eye movement (although perhaps only as a "by-product"), which does not occur with the other distortions.

Although it is possible that the only limit to the magnitude of VPC adaptation is that set by the extent of the rearrangement itself, there certainly must be constraints on the *type* of concomitant optical motion that can be expected eventually to lead to visual stability. As we have seen, there is an upper limit on the delay between head movement and resulting optical motion that the adaptive mechanism will tolerate (Hay & Goldsmith, 1973). But other possibilities remain untested. It would be interesting to see if VPC could be regained after extended exposure to a spot of light that moved in a curved or even a zig-zag path as the subject rotated his head back and forth in the lateral dimension. In fact, one might ask the more general question of what happens to perception whenever motor movements lead to consistent sensory effects. Hay (1974) has mentioned some preliminary experiments in which head movements were tied to a variation of auditory pitch or of brightness. Although Hay found no change in head movement-contingent perception, Kohler (personal communication, cited by Hay, 1974) has reported some success with the brightness contingency. This topic merits further investigation.

8

Adaptation to Distortions of Depth, Distance, and Size

The ability of human beings to adapt to visual distortions of the third dimension and of size perception is examined in this chapter. Visual perception of the in-out dimension involves two closely related but distinguishable components: *depth* and *distance.* Depth perception refers to apparent *solidity* or to the experience that several objects are at different distances *relative to each other.* The most extensively investigated visual depth cue is binocular disparity, which is the noncorrespondence of the retinal projections of the eyes that occurs with binocular viewing. It results because the eyes are separated from each other (by about 6.5 cm, on the average) and therefore view a solid object from slightly different directions. That binocular disparity is a powerful cue is clear from the realistic experience of depth one has when looking into a stereoscope or at so-called "three-dimensional movies," both of which are based on the use of slightly offset retinal images, each available to only one eye. Another important cue for solidity, which was introduced in Chapter 1, is the "kinetic depth effect" (KDE). This monocular cue derives from the dynamic change in the shape of the retinal image that occurs when a solid object is rotated (or when the object is stationary and viewed by the observer as he moves around it). Wallach and O'Connell (1953) showed that, in the absence of any other depth cues, this deformation of the retinal projection produces the experience of solidity, as long as it involves a simultaneous change in both the length and orientation of the edges of the image. Other monocular depth cues are linear perspective, texture gradient, and attached shadow (see Rock, 1975, Chapter 3, for a detailed discussion of these and other cues of depth and distance).

Distance perception involves the assessment of how far away an object is *from the observer.* In contrast to depth perception, it involves a "judgment" of absolute location along the third dimension. Several cues for the perception of distance have been suggested, some of which involve the eyes, whereas others pertain to the visual array. One example of the former is *accommodation,* which is the reflexive modification of the shape of the lens so that the focus of objects within the range of "near" distance is maintained. A second is *convergence,* the degree to which the eyes are rotated toward each other to allow for as close a correspondence in retinal projections as possible and thereby facilitate their fusion into a single image. Thus, when looking at a nearby object, the lenses will be bulged out and the eyes highly converged, events that (via the concomitant neural inflow or outflow) can presumably serve as cues that the object is a short distance away. One example of distance cues involving the visual array is familiar size. If one is accustomed to the "true" size of an object, then decreases in its retinal size with increasing physical distance can, in principle, be "compared" to its remembered size and its absolute distance from the observer can thereby be deduced.

Depth and distance perception are closely related. Furthermore, varying the distance between a solid object and the observer does not lead to a significant change in apparent solidity, despite the fact that binocular disparity decreases as the square of the distance. Registered distance is apparently taken into account in the assessment of a given degree of disparity. This "stereoscopic depth constancy" has been shown to operate according to a formula known as *Zuckerman's Law* (Wallach & Zuckerman, 1963):

Apparent depth = retinal disparity × registered distance^2.

One prediction from this formula is that a change in registered distance, with binocular disparity remaining constant, will lead to a change in apparent depth, which appears to be what occurs with optical magnification. For example, if one looks through binoculars, the convergence of the eyes is appropriate for an object nearer than is actually the case, resulting in a decrease in registered distance. However, the retinal disparity, while increased to some extent by the magnification, is not changed enough to offset the decreased apparent distance. According to Zuckerman's Law, this optical situation should result in a reduction in apparent depth, and such a "flat-tening" of the visual field is a common experience when looking through binoculars.[1] Wallach and Zuckerman (1963) supported this prediction more directly by using an arrangement of mirrors and lenses that left binocular disparity unchanged but caused accommo-dation and convergence to be that normally required for an object at half of the actual distance of the three-dimensional form used in the experiment. As expected, subjects experienced a marked reduction in the apparent depth of the object.

Perceived distance is integrally related to perceived size; this can best be seen in the capacity of "size constancy," which refers to the fact that an object whose distance from an observer is changing (thereby producing a diminishing or expanding retinal image) continues to appear roughly the same size. This fact of perception has received several explanations, one of which is that retinal image size is "interpreted" in terms of registered distance. This relationship is referred to as the *size–distance invariance principle* and is formulated as follows.

Apparent size = retinal image size × registered distance.

This is analogous to Zuckerman's Law, except that in the latter case registered distance is *squared*. Here, too, certain misperceptions may be predicted, a good example of which is the "moon illusion." It seems that the primary reason that the moon appears unusually large when it first rises above the horizon is that it appears to be at a greater distance when on the horizon than when at the zenith (Kaufman & Rock, 1962). The moon produces a retinal image of the same size at the two locations, but because registered distance is greater when the moon is on the horizon apparent size must also increase.

Now that the necessary groundwork has been laid, let us turn to the question of primary concern: the degree to which human observers can adapt to optical distortions of the third dimension and of size.

ADAPTATION TO DISTORTIONS OF DEPTH

Early Experiments

The first experiments relevant to adaptation to depth distortion were actually designed to examine the response of human subjects to visual

---

[1] Although depth constancy is partially lost in this situation, size contancy may remain. That is, the decrease in apparent distance *is* offset by an increase in retinal image size, causing may observers to experience objects as closer but unchanged in size.

inversion (Chapter 5). In those experiments in which *binocular* rearrangements were used, the right/left reversal included a transposition of the binocular disparity cue and therefore a reversal of apparent depth. Actually, a depth reversal was first produced by Wheatstone (1852), one of the inventors of the stereoscope. He showed that when the patterns that were presented to the eyes were reversed, in what he referred to as a "pseudoscope," depth was also reversed. In addition, he observed that if veridical monocular depth and distance cues were also present, they would occasionally "dominate," leading to a fluctuation between reversed and normal depth experience.

Ewert (1930) and Peterson and Peterson (1938) were apparently unaware of the depth distortion produced by their binocular inverting spectacles. It is likely that their subjects failed to consistently experience this distortion due to the many veridical distance and depth cues that were available. In any event, the presence of depth reversal has been suggested as one reason why Ewert and Peterson and Peterson were unable to obtain even the partial visual adaptation reported by Stratton and Kohler, who used devices that did not invert the third dimension.

Brown (1928) was the first to deliberately investigate the possibility of adaptation to distorted visual depth. Capitalizing on the fact that large *binocular* optical tilts cause isolated visual objects to appear flat, he placed before each eye of his subjects two right-angle prisms, which were rotated to effect a 75° tilt (see Figure 6.1, p. 136). After daily half-hour exposure periods, Brown's subjects revealed little or no recovery of depth perception, although visuomotor coordination became accurate. This result lends futher support to the conclusion drawn in Chapter 5 that human beings are incapable of undergoing consistent visual adaptation to "drastic" optical distortions, at least within the time limits that have been provided. Consequently, subsequent research on the question of depth adaptation has involved the use of relatively minor rearrangements.

Telestereoscopic Distortion

The *telestereoscope* may be used to effect a small distortion of apparent depth. It is a mirror arrangement (see Figure 8.1) that functionally increases or decreases the interocular distance, thereby altering the magnitude of binocular disparity. If a solid object is viewed with this device, its in–out dimension will appear to be greater (or less) than it actually is.

Wallach, Moore, and Davidson (1963) were the first to determine if continued exposure to telestereoscopic distortion would result in an adaptive shift in depth perception (see Chapter 1, p. 3). Their subjects viewed a rotating three-dimensional wire form through the telestereoscope, which was arranged to add 7.6 cm to the subject's normal interocular distance (thereby increasing it more than twofold). Because the cube was rotating (at 12 rpm), the most salient cue concerning its true shape was the KDE. Thus, while the KDE continued to provide a veridical description of the object's three-dimensional shape, binocular disparity was now signaling the presence of an object with greater depth than was actually the case. Since the distortion occurred only for that part of the wire form that was pointing away from the observer at a given moment, the initial experience was of an object whose shape was constantly changing as it rotated. After 1, 4, or 10 min of exposure, during which the subject passively viewed the turning wire form, measures of his experience of the now-stationary object, viewed through the telestereoscope, revealed a reduction in apparent depth. The longest exposure period resulted in an adaptive shift equal to 20% of the theoretical maximum. Adaptation was found to increase as a negatively accelerated function of exposure time and to generalize, with some decrement, to wire forms that differed somewhat from that used during exposure. The subjects showed no change in the apparent size of the object or in the experience of depth produced by the KDE when only one eye was used, confirming that the adaptation represented a recalibration between binocular disparity and perceived depth. In another experiment, the telestereoscope was arranged to produce *diminished* disparities (see Figure 8.1, B). Adaptation of apparent depth again occurred, but this time in the

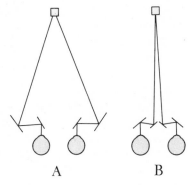

Figure 8.1. Schematic representation of the light paths from the target (square) through the telestereoscope as set to produce enhancement (A) and reduction (B) of binocular disparity. (From H. Wallach, M. E. Moore, & L. Davidson. Modification of stereoscopic depth perception. *American Journal of Psychology*, 1963, *76*, 191–204.© 1963 by the University of Illinois Press.)

A   B

form of enhancement. Finally, adaptation was found to decline quite rapidly as a result of viewing a rotating wire form with normal vision ("unlearning") and somewhat less rapidly after sitting quietly with eyes closed ("decay").

A later experiment by Epstein (1968) demonstrated that telestereo-scopic adaptation could be obtained by means of an *aftereffect* measure, using test objects and a procedure quite unlike those of the exposure period. These results rule out the possibility that the effects observed by Wallach *et al.* were indicative of a "rule" or "conscious correction," which is a potential hazard when using reduction of effect as a measure. Epstein also found that the most effective rate of form rotation is 8–18 rpm.

Wallach and Karsh (1963a) demonstrated, as Wallach and his colleagues had for adaptation to visual position constancy (Chapter 7, pp. 170–171), that adaptation to altered binocular disparity is retarded if normal visual experience precedes it. When subjects were required to look at the rotating wire form for 10 min with *normal* vision, subsequent exposure to the form through the telestereoscope produced significantly less adaptation than occurred in the absence of "pretraining." This result, coupled with the fact that adaptation is subject to rather significant spontaneous decay in a short period of time, suggests that stereoscopic vision is a very modifiable perceptual capacity.

Optically Induced Slant

Mack and Chitayat (1970) exposed subjects to a binocular arrangement of right-angle prisms that tilted the retinal image of each eye by 5° in opposite directions. This procedure causes an objectively upright line, viewed binocularly, to appear inclined away from or toward the observer, depending on the direction of the rotation. In one group, free exploration in an indoor environment for 20 min or more resulted in adaptation to this form of depth distortion. A line that had appeared to be inclined by about 12.5° at the outset of the exposure period eventually came to look upright. The investigators concluded that a recalibration between the binocular disparity cue and apparent depth had occurred.

The same conclusion was reached by Epstein and his colleagues on the basis of an extensive series of experiments involving optically induced rotation of the frontoparallel plane. This depth distortion was effected by means of a procedure, apparently first used by Burian (1943), in which a 4–8% "meridional-size lens" (MSL) is placed before one of the subject's eyes while the other remains uncovered. An MSL magnifies the visual image along the meridian perpendicular to its axis. With the lens in a vertical orientation and the other eye uncovered, the magnification of the horizontal dimension alters the disparities between the images of the two eyes. This in turn causes the visual frontoparallel plane to appear slanted, the side in front of the lens-covered eye appearing farther away. For example, if the horizontal meridian of the right eye is magnified, a wall objectively at a right angle to the observer's line of vision will appear to be slanted away to the subject's right,[2] because binocular disparity is placed in conflict with the available veridical monocular depth cues.

In the first experiment of this series (Epstein & Morgan, 1970), subjects were exposed to the MSL-induced slant for a 1-hr period, during which they engaged in unrestricted activity in an indoor environment. Periodic tests of depth discrimination, with and without the lens present, revealed adaptation that reached asymptote at approximately 38% of the theoretical maximum by the end of the first 20 min of exposure. The perceptual test entailed depth matching of two vertical electroluminescent targets when the only usable cue was binocular disparity. The authors argued that the locus of MSL adaptation is a recalibration of the relationship betweeen binocular disparity and perceived depth, based on the many veridical monocular cues present during the exposure period. Epstein (1971) provided support for this hypothesis by showing that the adaptive shift was greatly enhanced by the use of a preadaptation period during which binocular visual experience was precluded, either by allowing only one-eyed, normal vision or by blindfolding the subject. Apparently the disuse of disparity provided the monocular depth cues that were present during the adaptation period with a greater capacity to suppress and recalibrate the nonveridical disparity information produced by the MSL.

Based on the logic of the preceding experiment, Epstein (1972a) adapted subjects to the MSL and then provided different groups with various activities during the postadaptation retention period. As predicted, 5 min of undistorted binocular vision, subsequent to a 20-min MSL-exposure period, led to a more rapid reduction of the aftereffect (setting a luminous line to the frontoparallel plane) than did either monocular experience or no vision (with no difference between the two). Veridical perception of the frontoparallel plane was regained most rapidly when the subject was exposed to the normal relationship between disparity and monocular depth cues. That there

---

[2] For a more detailed description of this and other perceptual effects of "uniocular magnification" see Ames (1946) and Ogle (1964, Chapter 15).

was some decline of adaptation even without binocular experience was explained by proposing that the recalibration of disparity requires constant visual support; if this is lacking, the "old," overlearned value will reemerge (i.e., proactive inhibition).

An alternative to Epstein's hypothesis, proposed by Ebenholtz (1970), is that MSL adaptation is merely a change in the registered direction of gaze. According to this, a subject looking straight ahead while wearing an MSL over the right eye would eventually come to feel that his head is rotated to the left and his eyes turned to the right. Such a misperception of the eye–head relationship would result in veridical perception of the frontoparallel plane with the lens on. If an observer with *normal* vision were to view the frontoparallel plane from this posture, the result would be essentially the same difference in the views of the two eyes that the MSL produces.[3] Such a potential end product of MSL exposure does not represent a recalibration of disparity and perceived depth, and therefore does not qualify as adaptation. Epstein (1972b) tested this "gaze-shift" hypothesis by exposing subjects to an "overall-size lens" (OSL). An OSL magnifies the image in all meridians and, when worn over one eye with the other eye uncovered, it produces the binocular input that occurs with normal vision when the eyes are asymmetrically converged, as described in Footnote 3. Contrary to the MSL, an OSL does not lead to a conflict between disparity and the monocular depth cues, because the slant of the frontoparallel plane caused by the distorted horizontal disparities is canceled by the opposing rotation produced by the distorted vertical disparities. Viewing a frontoparallel plane while wearing an OSL over the right eye is exactly like looking with normal vision at this plane with the head turned to the left and the eyes turned to the right. This represents an ideal situation in which to pit the gaze-shift and recalibration hypotheses, since the former predicts adaptation, whereas the latter does not. Epstein found that after 20 min of free exploration while wearing the OSL, subjects did not show adaptation, in terms of depth discrimination, thus providing indirect support for Epstein's cue discrepancy → cue recalibration hypothesis.

Epstein and Daviess (1972) directly tested the gaze-shift hypothesis by measuring MSL-adapted subjects on a task sensitive to changes in felt direction of gaze. They found that although their subjects showed

---

[3] As Ebenholtz (1970) points out, however, there is actually no eye–head relationship that would produce exactly the experience of wearing an MSL, since the latter causes magnification of only one meridian. Rather, the posture described would produce an *overall* magnification of the right-eye image when vision is normal.

adaptive shifts in the apparent frontoparallel plane after a 10-min active exposure period, there were no accompanying changes in felt direction of gaze, as measured by setting a visual target to the apparent straight-ahead position. In a second experiment, they examined the hypothesis that the shift in perceived depth as a result of MSL exposure is merely a "side effect" of a change in apparent *distance*. The reduction in depth might have been the result of objects coming to look closer to the observer, in accordance with Zuckerman's Law. That is, a given degree of retinal disparity will be perceived as signifying decreasing depth (i.e., solidity) as the apparent distance of the object from the observer decreases. However, the investigators failed to obtain a shift in a visuomotor indicator of distance perception with MSL-adapted subjects, thereby ruling out this alternative and bolstering the hypothesis that the effects of MSL exposure are limited to depth perception, specifically the binocular disparity cue. In another study, Epstein and Morgan-Paap (1974) found that adaptation increased as a function of the degree of imposed discrepancy between the MSL-induced slant and the slant signified by perspective cues. They also found that adaptation was significantly greater when the subject was forced to *use* his depth cues to accomplish a task. Both of these findings support a general informational-discrepancy theory of adaptation.

ADAPTATION TO DISTORTIONS OF DISTANCE

Wallach and his colleagues have assessed the ability of human subjects to adapt to distortions of distance. A reduction in apparent distance was produced by placing before each eye a "meniscus lens," which entailed a 1.5-diopter spherical lens together with a 5-diopter base-out wedge prism. The lenses led to increased accommodation and the prisms to increased convergence, the two changes combining to signify distances shorter than true object distances by an amount equivalent to 1.5 lens diopters. In order to increase apparent distance, a combination of 1.5-diopter lenses and 5-diopter base-in wedge prisms was used. These optical arrangements also have an immediate effect on apparent size; that is, in the absence of distance cues other than accommodation and convergence, objects viewed through the "near" glasses look smaller than they are, whereas with the "far" glasses they look larger. These illusions follow from the size–distance invariance principle. The glasses have an even greater effect on the peceived *depth* of a solid object, as is predicted from Zuckerman's Law.

In the first experiment, Wallach and Frey (1972a) found that subjects who wore the glasses for as little as 15 min, while engaging in eye-hand activities or free locomotion in an indoor environment, revealed significant adaptation, as measured by an aftereffect of altered visual size. The aftereffect was assumed to be indirect evidence that an adaptive shift in apparent distance had occurred, an assumption that was subsequently tested and confirmed by Wallach, Frey, and Bode (1972, Experiments 1 and 3). In another experiment, Wallach et al. also ruled out the possibility that exposure to the distance distortion had produced a change in stereoscopic depth perception. Finally, a small adaptive shift was obtained from an exposure period in which the subject was allowed to move only his eyes, demonstrating that the veridical distance cues of perspective (Experiment 4) or familiar size (Experiment 5) were sufficient to trigger the adaptive process.

In the preceding experiments on distance distortion the assumption had been that the adaptation obtained was limited to changes in vision. Although visuomotor estimates of apparent distance were sometimes used to measure this adaptation, eye–hand coordination was not thought to have been modified, and precautions had been taken to preclude subjects from viewing or using their limbs during the exposure period. However, Wallach and Smith (1972) found that if the subject were allowed to move a stimulus object toward and away from him with his unseen hand while wearing the distance lenses, and thus was placed in a situation in which accommodation/convergence cues of distance were in conflict with (veridical) kinesthetic/proprioceptive input, an adaptive change occurred that was limited almost entirely to eye–hand coordination. That is, the subject manifested an adaptive pre–post shift in pointing to a specified distance with the unseen hand. If both kinesthetic/proprioceptive and monocular distance cues were available and the subject was allowed to see his visually distorted hand as it moved, the resulting adaptation comprised changes in both kinesthesis/proprioception and visual distance perception. Thus, in this latter situation, a two-component model of adaptation was suggested.

It appears from the experiments by Wallach et al. that exposure to distance distortion leads to a genuine modification of vision, in the form of a recalibration between accommodation/convergence cues and the distance they signify. However, an alternative hypothesis has been offered by Ebenholtz (1970, 1974), who proposed that the maintained convergence of the eyes at a "near" or a "far" point will lead to "eye muscle potentiation" (EMP), which in turn may require that an abnormal amount of voluntary efferent output be emitted when subsequently fixating an object at some other distance. This expenditure of efference is presumed to lead to an alteration in apparent visual distance. This theory was introduced in Chapter 3 in the context of visual adaptation to prismatic displacement. Evidence in support of the EMP hypothesis, as it refers to distance perception, is found in experiments by Craske and Crawshaw (1974), Ebenholtz (1974), Ebenholtz and Wolfson (1975), and Paap and Ebenholtz (1977). Ebenholtz and Wolfson showed that if the subject fixated a target at a particular distance for 6–8 min, he would subsequently underestimate the distance of a target located nearer than the "exposure" target and overestimate the distance of a test target located at a greater distance. Even when the convergence point was allowed to vary during the "exposure" period, a shift in apparent distance of the test target was obtained. These results have serious implications because they suggest that the changes in apparent distance reported by Wallach et al. were manifestations merely of the visual effects of maintained convergence and not of *recalibration*. In other words, the presence of the visual distortion may be necessary not as a means of creating a discrepancy between distance cues but to cause a specific chronic state of convergence. To rule out this interpretation, it will be necessary to obtain changes in apparent distance when the test targets require the same degree of convergence as occurred (at least on the average) during the exposure period. In such a situation, there would be no necessity to overcome an EMP effect.

ADAPTATION TO DISTORTIONS OF SIZE

Only a very few experiments have tested for adaptation to optically induced changes in apparent size and, interestingly, the majority of these have occurred *underwater*! When a submerged observer peers through his diving mask, objects look larger than they actually are, apparently as the result of a simultaneous overestimation of distance. A number of investigators have sought to determine if it is possible for divers to adapt to these size (as well as distance) distortions. Chapter 12 is devoted to a detailed discussion of these experiments and their results. Briefly, it has been demonstrated that some subjects eventually come to see underwater objects as more nearly their true size, whereas others adapt in terms of apparent distance. In fact, the two types of adaptation seem to be negatively correlated. In the extreme case, adaptation to one of the distortions produces an *increase* in the other, the latter being an example of "counteradaptation" (Luria, McKay, & Ferris, 1973; Ross & Lennie, 1972), a response that serves to maintain size–distance invariance. On the other hand, several investigators (Franklin, Ross, & Weltman, 1970; Luria *et al.* 1973) found subjects who simultaneously adapted to both distortions, although the magnitudes of the shifts were negatively correlated. This may be referred to as "relative counteradaptation."

Several experiments of adaptation to size distortions in the air have used various magnifying lens systems. Unfortunately, as mentioned previously (see footnote 1), such devices often lead to a change in apparent distance but not in size, which presumably results from the size-constancy mechanism. Giannitrapani (1958), in an unpublished dissertation, provided children with 10 min of exposure to visual magnification and obtained evidence of adaptation in the form of a reduction of effect. However, because there was little or no aftereffect it is doubtful that genuine adaptation occurred. Foley (1965), in a unpublished experiment that has been cited and briefly described by Rock (1966, pp. 158–159) and by E. J. Gibson (1969, p. 205), apparently found only slight adaptation to magnification or reduction for observers who, over a 3-week period, wore binoculars for 6 hr a day. Moreover, these minor effects were primarily in terms of apparent distance, since the subjects generally failed to experience a distortion of size. Rock (1966, pp. 164–165) also reported initial failure to produce consistent adaptation to reduction effected by a reverse Gallilean telescope. He found, as Foley had, that many subjects failed to experience objects as reduced in size, but merely saw them as farther away than they were.

Clearly, it is desirable to create an optical situation in which only apparent size is altered. A device for doing this is the *convex mirror*, which Rock (1965, 1966, pp. 164–175) used in a series of experiments on adaptation to optical reduction. Subjects looked through a large cardboard tube at a 12-in. mirror that reduced by a factor of 2 the apparent size of a number of familiar objects that could be seen in it. The results of a control condition demonstrated that the apparent distance of these objects remained unaltered. In a series of experiments, 10–30 min of exposure to the reduction produced adaptation of as much as 23% of the theoretical maximum. Adaptation was measured in terms of a pre–post shift of the apparent size of a luminous line with respect to a remembered length. After exposure to the reduction (and without the mirror), a line that had appeared to be 12 in. long now looked to be greater than 12 in. and so had to be made physically shorter to match the memory standard. Exposure typically involved viewing the head, arms, part of the trunk, and hands as the latter manipulated the objects. However, adaptation occurred even when the stationary subject was not allowed to see any part of his body. It was also shown that the mere viewing of an array of actually miniature familiar objects leads to a small, but statistically significant, increase in apparent size. In several control experiments Rock ruled out the possibilities that the altered size perception was the result of a change in apparent distance or of successive contrast.

In an experiment by Rock, Mack, Adams, and Hill (1965), it was found that when the only form of veridical information about the visually reduced objects was their felt size, a half-hour exposure period produced no change in apparent visual size. Instead, the objects were almost immediately felt to be as small as they appeared, and this "visual capture" of the haptic sense persisted beyond the exposure period as a change in the felt size of unseen objects.

Rock has apparently demonstrated that human observers are capable of genuine adaptation to size distortion, which, except in the condition examined by Rock et al. (1965), entails a change in apparent visual size. He suggested that visual adaptation to this form of distortion derives most importantly from the observer's experience that the *relationship* between the apparent size of objects and the apparent size of the visible body (e.g., the hands) does not change during exposure to the distortion. Also presumed to be involved are the facts that (a) the size of objects relative to each other is unaltered; (b) a movement of the head or entire body by a certain amount now leads to atypical visual motion (cf. Chapter 7), which is indicative of the nature of the distortion; and (c) familiar objects appear to be of an abnormal size. According to Rock, the result of these experiences is a change in the memory trace for phenomenal size elicited by an image of a particular retinal size (for a given distance).

Rock's theory of the conditions and end state of adaptation to size distortion is essentially the same as the theory that he applied to adaptation to visual inversion (Chapter 5, pp. 125–127). Although this theory appears quite reasonable, it is perhaps best, given the scarcity of research in this area, to consider it a working hypothesis for future investigators.

SUMMARY AND CONCLUSIONS

Human observers have proven to be capable of partial adaptation to distortions of apparent depth, effected by a variety of optical arrangements. It seems clear that the locus of this adaptation is a recalibration of the binocular disparity cue. Exposure to distorted depth produces a state in which noncorresponding retinal points may be associated with the experience of equidistance and corresponding points with apparent depth. Thus, it may be concluded from these results that there exists no immutable relation between the physical correspondence or noncorrespondence of retinal points and stereoscopic depth.

Optical distortions of distance can also be overcome, as seen in the experiments by Wallach and his colleagues. Here, the end state of adaptation appears to be a recalibration of accommodation, convergence, or both, although it is not yet possible to rule out the "eye muscle potentiation" hypothesis of Ebenholtz (e.g., 1970).

The fact that the human perceptual system is able to adjust to distortions of the in–out dimension, providing that they are not too large, might well have been anticipated from a consideration of the rapid head growth that infants and young children undergo. The increase in interocular distance with age obviously necessitates a recalibration of both the binocular disparity and convergence cues, or else depth and distance perception (in the absence of other cues) would come to be increasingly in error. However, whether or not the newborn human infant must learn initially how to use the cues of binocular disparity and convergence is a different question.

It is reasonable to conclude that the normal perceptions of depth and of distance—insofar as they are based on the cues of binocular disparity, accommodation, and convergence—are modified and maintained by a process of calibration and recalibration. The basis for this process is probably the monocular depth and distance cues, since their efficacy is relatively unaffected by developmental changes in head size. Indirect evidence for this hypothesis was provided when it was found that if exposure to the depth or distance distortion was preceded by concentrated practice in the use of the to-be-changed cues, adaptation was attenuated, whereas preclusion of such experience facilitated adaptation (Epstein, 1971; Wallach & Karsh, 1963a). It was also demonstrated that the abolishment of adaptation could be accelerated by providing postexposure practice with the altered cue (Epstein, 1972a; Wallach, Moore, & Davidson, 1963).

The research by Wallach and by Epstein (and their collaborators) on depth and distance distortions has led both of them to postulate what Wallach (1968) has referred to as the "process-assimilation" theory of perceptual adaptation. According to this notion, when two or more cues (e.g., accommodation and interposition) that normally represent the same perceptual parameter are caused, by optical means, to signify different parameters, an intersensory discrepancy exists, which immediately sets into action a process of perceptual change. This discrepancy is eventually reduced when the discrepant cues come to signify the same or nearly the same perceptual event. One way in which this state may be achieved is when one of the cues is "assimilated" by or recalibrated in terms of the other. However, according to this theory, there is no inherent advantage of veridical over nonveridical cues. Thus, it is an empirical question if the resolution of a given discrepancy between cues will be in the direction of more accurate perception or of increased perceptual error. In a distance-distortion experiment not discussed previously, Wallach and Frey (1972c) demonstrated that "adaptation" could lead to increased misperception. In this experiment, a luminous figure was caused to physically expand as it moved toward the observer and contract as it receded. Thus, the change in retinal size was greater than would be the case if the moving object were of a fixed size, producing a discrepancy between convergence and accommodation, on the one hand, and the fluctuation in retinal image size on the other. Twenty minutes of this experience led to adaptation, as measured by several different indexes of apparent distance. Since this adaptive shift represented a departure from initially accurate perception, Wallach and Frey referred to it as "counteradaptation." Although the investigators considered this to be the first observation of such a phenomenon, evidence for an induced change toward increasing perceptual error had been made at least as early as Harris's (1963) demonstration that exposure to prismatic displacement can result in a shift in felt limb position.

Which cue will "dominate" in a given state of intersensory discrepancy has not been answered. However, when the distorted cue is clearly outnumbered by veridical cues, as in the experiments on adaptation to optically induced slant (e.g., Epstein & Morgan, 1970), it is likely that veridical cues will prevail, resulting in more accurate perception. On the other hand, it is difficult to predict the result in a situation involving a "one-on-one" confrontation between cues. A few experiments have involved such a condition and have led to conclusions about the relative importance of the various spatial cues. As we have seen, when accommodation and/or convergence cues of distance are at odds with changes in the retinal image size of an object moving toward or away from the observer, the perceptual shift is in the direction of a recalibration of the distance cues. This is true whether it is the distance cues that have been distorted (Wallach et al., 1972, Experiment 2) or the retinal image size (Wallach & Frey, 1972b). For some reason, the nervous system appears to consider changes in retinal size to be a more important distance cue than accommodation/convergence. One is tempted to conclude from this that, during normal vision, the size change in the retinal image is a more heavily weighted cue than the oculomotor adjustments of accommodation and convergence. Another instance of a confrontation between two spatial cues is seen in the experiment by Wallach and Smith (1972), where it was found that when accommodation/convergence was at odds with proprioception/kinesthesis, the latter underwent the change—another example of "counteradaptation." Likewise, Rock et al. (1965) found that when subjects grasped an object that was caused to look half its true size, it was the initially veridical haptic sence that became altered. These examples of the "dominance" of vision over body sense are analogous to the "visual capture" and more persistent shifts in felt body position sense that occur with prismatic displacement (Chapter 3, pp. 43–45).

The process-assimilation theory of adaptation to distortion in the in-out dimension of visual space appears to be a highly tenable account, which figures importantly in a general model of adaptation proposed in the concluding chapter of this book.

Finally, the few experiments to deal with distortion of apparent size (e.g., Rock, 1965) have demonstrated limited adaptability. It is to be hoped that the paucity of research on this variety of visual rearrangement will soon be overcome.

9

Adaptation to
Distortions of Form

Not only does the visual system provide for the accurate and precise localization of objects in three-dimensional space but it also helps to identify what it is that is located. Of particular importance for the latter achievement is the capacity of form (or pattern) perception, which, at a very basic level, is the ability to detect brightness gradients. These gradients, or visual contours, may be either closed or open. It is also possible for form perception to occur when there are no visual contours present, as with "subjective contours" Kanizsa (1955), or with figures constructed out of unconnected dots.[1] We have seen that egocentric localization is subject to significant changes as the result of exposure to prismatic displacement (Chapters 2, 3, and 4); the aim of this chapter is to consider the evidence pertaining to the plasticity of form perception.

It might be misleading to distinguish the locus-analysis from the form-analysis function of vision, since this implies a qualitative difference between these capacities that may not actually exist. It is possible that the perception of form is merely a manifestation of spatial localization. By this way of thinking, form perception involves the detection of the relationship between a set of points emanating from different directions relative to the observer. If this analysis is correct, then one might be justified in concluding that the results from

[1] For a comprehensive review of the literature and current thinking about form perception, the reader is referred to Rock (1975, Chapters 6–8).

studies of rearranged visual direction, such as the research on prism adaptation, may validly generalize to the question of adaptation to the optical distortion of form. However, there are good reasons for believing that the capacities of egocentric localization and form perception are at least partially independent of each other. Held (1968a) pointed out that, while neonatal deprivation has very detrimental consequences for visuomotor localization (e.g., Held & Bauer, 1967; Held & Hein, 1963), it has little or no effect on pattern perception provided that the testing procedure does not require localizing or orienting responses (e.g., Meyers & McCleary, 1964). Schneider (1967, 1969) has demonstrated, in the golden hamster, that ablation of the superior colliculi destroys visual localization but not pattern discrimination, whereas destruction of the striate areas of the cortex has the opposite effects.

Thus, the initial distinction between egocentric localization and form perception appears to be justified. However, the two perceptual capacities are not entirely independent of one another. That is, while egocentric localization exists as an isolable perceptual capacity, the perception of a form probably involves both an "assessment" of the relations of its contours to one another and the localization of its parts relative to the observer. Rock (1966, p. 180) has referred to these as the "object-relative" and "subject-relative" aspects of form perception. A good example of a form whose perception relies strongly on both of these capacities is a curved line. By Rock's two-component analysis, the perception of curvature is based on the detection that (a) segments of the contour are not parallel to one another and (b) various points are located in particular directions relative to the observer. The first of these refers to the internal geometry of the form. The second, which involves egocentric localization, may be understood by considering Figure 9.1. The line may be perceived as curved, in part, because its center is seen as straight ahead of the observer, whereas the ends both appear to be off to one side. For a straight line, regardless of its location or orientation, points along it alter their position relative to the observer at a constant rate (Rock, 1966, p. 178). For example, all points of a vertical line located off to one side of the observer are seen as being to the left of the sagittal plane by the same amount and vary in their direction relative to the horizontal plane by a constant rate. Rock (1966, Chapter 6) has pointed out that for a *moving* observer there are additional localization cues defining curvature and straightness.

It may be concluded that the perception of visual forms involves the analysis of both egocentric loci and geometric relationships. Further-

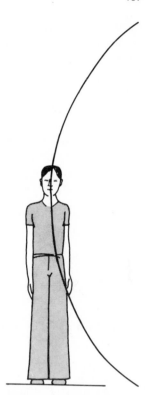

Figure 9.1. A vertically oriented curved line as viewed in the sagittal plane. (After Figure 6-2, p. 179, in *The Nature of Perceptual Adaptation*, by Irvin Rock, © 1966 by Irvin Rock, Basic Books, Inc., Publishers, New York.)

more, it is likely that the relative importance of these two components varies with the nature of the form. For example, object-relative characteristics are probably a more dominant factor in the perception of a closed figure than of an unclosed form. Rock and others have proposed that the perception of the geometry of a form, and of the *difference* between several forms, is directly tied to the retinotopic projection onto the cortex and therefore this capacity is both innately determined and relatively resistant to modification.[2] Egocentric localization, on the other hand, may be inherently modifiable, since it is

[2] Although it is likely that oculocentric values are fixed, or nearly so, for adult organisms, it is not certain that they are innately given. Mitchell (in press), for example, has recently reviewed an array of experiments and found that the rearing of neonatal cats, monkeys, and perhaps human beings in environments comprised primarily of contours of a specific orientation causes cortical neurons to become selectively tuned to these contours. Differential perceptual sensitivity parallels this physiological modification. It would appear that there is an early "critical period" for these physiological and perceptual changes, a fact that accounts for the relative unmodifiability of contour analysis in the mature organism.

necessary for organisms to be able to adjust to the changes in apparent direction that result from normal bodily growth. If these contentions about the relative plasticity of the two aspects of form perception are correct, then magnitude of adaptation should be positively related to the degree to which the analysis of egocentric localization is involved in the perception of the form that has been optically distorted. It is likely that the subject-relative aspect of form perception is importantly involved in the experience of curvature. Therefore, it should be possible for observers to adapt, at least partially, to optically induced curvature. This, as seen in the next section, is indeed the case.

ADAPTATION TO PRISMATICALLY INDUCED CURVATURE

The Early Experiments

Nearly all of the research concerning adaptability to optical distortions of form has involved prismatically induced curvature. It will be recalled that when looking through a wedge prism, straight contours perpendicular to the direction of displacement appear curved (see Figure 1.1, p. 5). The possibility that human observers might adapt to such a distortion was first tested by Wundt (1898; cited by Rock, 1966). He reported that after wearing prism goggles for several days, the apparent curvature of straight contours diminished significantly and, after removing the prism, objectively straight lines appeared curved in the opposite direction of the prism-induced curvature. This sequence of perceptual events, presented in Figure 9.2, appears to show that human observers are capable of adapting to prismatic curvature. More than three decades later, the phenomenon of prismatically induced changes in the perception of curvature was rediscovered by J. J. Gibson (1933) in a series of experiments that serve as a prototype for the subsequent investigations of this type of adaptation. In his first study, which has typically received only passing mention in the literature, a subject engaged in everyday activities for 4 consecutive days (45 waking hours) while wearing goggles containing in each eyepiece a base–left prism that displaced the visual field by 14–15°. Toward the latter part of the exposure period the subject reported a decrease in the apparent curvature of vertical contours and, without the goggles, a curvature aftereffect in the opposite direction. This aftereffect continued to be noticed until well into the second postexposure day. In other experiments it was demonstrated that measurable adaptation

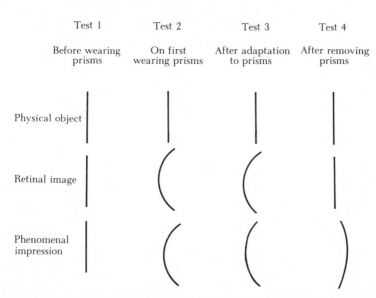

Figure 9.2. Sequence of perceptual events indicative of adaptation (difference in phenomenal impression between 'Test 2 and Test 3) and aftereffect (difference in phenomenal impression between Test 1 and Test 4) to a base-left prism. (After J. J. Gibson. Adaptation, after-effect, and contrast in the perception of curved lines. *Journal of Experimental Psychology*, 1933, *16*, 1–31. Copyright 1933 by the American Psychological Association. Reprinted by permission.)

and aftereffect could be obtained after an active exposure period as short as 1 hr. One of Gibson's tests for adaptation has been used in virtually all of the subsequent experiments in this area. It required that the subject cause a visual contour to appear straight, the latter representing a convenient memory standard. This measure was obtained before and after the exposure period and, as usual, the difference between the two tests served as the measure of adaptation.

Gibson proposed two explanations regarding the nature of the alteration in perceived curvature. The "recalibration hypothesis" held that it represented a partial resolution of the conflict between the initial visual experience of curvature and input from other sensory modalities indicating the objective nature of the contour; this is "genuine" adaptation. The second possibility, the "normalization hypothesis," said that there was something about merely viewing a number of apparently curved edges that led to a modification of perceived curvature. Thus, the prism was irrelevant, merely serving as a convenient means of presenting the subject with an array of curved lines. Unfortunately, Gibson considered his two hypotheses to be mutually exclusive and believed that the way to decide between them was to determine if subjects would undergo a lessening of apparent curvature when exposed to curved contours in the absence of intersensory conflict. He created this situation either by having subjects wear prisms while holding the head motionless or by exposing them to objectively curved lines without prisms. Both of these conditions were found to produce a reduction in apparent curvature and an aftereffect. For example, mere visual inspection of prismatically curved lines led to an apparent straightening of 3–4 diopters (out of a possible 26), reaching asymptote after only about 2 min of exposure. Gibson was forced by his own logic to reject the recalibration hypothesis. This phenomenon of adaptation without intersensory conflict is referred to as the *Gibson effect* (see Chapter 6, pp. 139–141). Its discovery led Gibson to suggest that when a human observer is exposed to one or more curved lines, whether real or apparent, there is initiated a process of "normalization" (toward straightness). As noted in Chapter 6, Gibson later showed that exposure to objectively tilted lines also leads to a perceptual shift, in this case toward verticality.[3]

In retrospect, it is clear that Gibson made a mistake by failing to compare the conflict and no-conflict conditions in terms of the *magnitude* of change in apparent curvature. If he had done so, he would have found that while both conditions lead to a reduction in apparent curvature, the change is significantly greater when the subject has been provided with the information contingent upon active interaction with the distorted environment. The evidence for this statement comes from experiments that have involved active visuomotor behavior, sometimes for quite extended periods of time, and have produced shifts in apparent curvature that gradually increase to a magnitude significantly exceeding that of the Gibson effect, indicating the presence of true adaptation to prismatic curvature.

It is now generally accepted that active exposure to prismatic curvature in an environment containing objectively straight contours will initiate two independent processes of perceptual change—quick-acting normalization and more gradual recalibration. The latter process results in genuine adaptation and it is important to be able to obtain a "pure" measure of this end state. One way to do this is to eliminate all

---

[3] It will also be recalled from Chapter 6 that Köhler and Wallach (1944) attempted to explain both curvature and tilt normalization in terms of the cortical satiation process that they had applied to "figural aftereffects." However, the demonstration by Gibson (and later by Held, 1962) that the effect occurs when eye movements are allowed effectively rules out this explanation.

straight contours from the subject's visual field. Another is to allow the stationary subject to view a set of contours for a period of time sufficient for the Gibson effect to reach its maximal level before beginning the active exposure period. The subtraction of the postexposure measure of apparent curvature from the preexposure measure (taken after the initial stationary viewing period) represents a measure of adaptation uncontaminated by the Gibson effect. It is also possible to expose the subject to contours that are objectively curved in the opposite direction of the prismatic curvature and therefore appear straight.

Evidence of Genuine Adaptation to Prismatically Induced Curvature

The first of the "modern era" investigations of prismatic curvature in which exposure was that presumably required to produce genuine adaptation was by Erismann and Kohler (e.g., Kohler, 1964, pp. 34–42). In a series of experiments, subjects wore either full or "split-field" prisms while engaging in strenuous, "real-life" activities over a period of days, weeks, and occasionally months. Although quantitative measures were rarely taken, the verbal reports of the subjects suggest that the shift in apparent curvature and aftereffect exceeded in magnitude the changes one could expect from the Gibson effect alone. The results with the split-field prisms are especially interesting because they bear upon the distinction between the subject-relative and object-relative components of form perception. It will be recalled from Chapter 4 (p. 91) that the Erismann–Kohler split-field prism spectacles involve the placement of a 10-diopter prism in the upper half of each frame, while the lower half remains uncovered. After wearing this device for a number of days, the apparent curvature of straight contours seen in the upper visual field was reduced by approximately one half (although quantitive measures were not obtained). More interesting is the fact that the initial experience that the top half of a vertical contour was displaced relative to the lower half all but disappeared. However, this was true only when the subject avoided directly examining the line of transition between the upper and lower halves of the visual field. If he fixated the midpoint, the spatial discrepancy was quite apparent, even after many weeks of exposure. These results were replicated by Pick et al. (1969a), who used a larger number of subjects and several quantitative measures. Thus it appears that the *localization* of the upper and lower segments of a vertical contour eventually came to be congruent, whereas the apparent *geometry* of the line remained unmodified. These results fit nicely with the hypothesis that the subject-relative aspect of form perception is adaptable, whereas the object-relative aspect is not.

In the 42-day prism-exposure study of Hay and Pick (1966a) (see Chapter 3), the postexposure tests showed that objectively straight lines appeared straight to subjects only when the variable prism through which they looked was set to 6 diopters in the same direction as the prismatic curvature used during the exposure period, which is approximately a 30% reduction of the prism effect. Although no precautions were taken to assess or eliminate the Gibson effect, the measured shift in apparent curvature clearly exceeded the change expected if only the normalization process had occurred. Furthermore, its acquisition was not almost immediate, as is the Gibson effect, but gradual, requiring days to reach asymptote. Later experiments by Hajos and Ritter (1965) and Pick *et al.* (1966) have generally confirmed these findings. Thus it may be concluded that human beings are capable of genuine, albeit partial, adaptation to prismatic curvature.

The Necessary and Sufficient Conditions
for Curvature Adaptation

It was suggested in the previous section that the necessary condition for the production of the Gibson effect of curvature is mere exposure to curved lines, whether prismatically induced or actual, whereas some sort of information about the presence and nature of the prismatic distortion must be available if genuine adaptation is to occur. Assuming that it is primarily the subject-relative aspect of form perception that is modifiable, the conditions necessary to activate the adaptive process are probably those that indicate that what appears to be a curved contour actually obeys the "rules" of a straight line with reference to the observer. Rock (1966, pp. 178–179) has clearly delineated some of these rules or properties of straight (versus curved) lines. One of them is that a straight line remains in the same orientation and position on the retina when an observer moves parallel with it, whereas a curved line veers away. If a subject were to view a prismatically curved line on the floor as he began to walk in a straight line (starting at one end of the line), he would find that, rather than veering away, the line appeared to remain directly in front of him, indicating that it was actually straight. If the subject walked in a curved path in an attempt to remain directly on the apparently curved line, he would quickly find that he had strayed away from it. Head or hand movements would also lead to this kind of error and, therefore, should inform the subject of the nature of the prismatic distortion.

M. M. Cohen (1965) compared the conditions necessary to produce the Gibson effect of curvature with those required for genuine prism adaptation and obtained results in line with the preceding analysis. He found that when an objectively curved line was caused to look straight, by means of the prism, adaptation occurred if the subject was allowed freedom of head movement, but not if the head was held stationary. The former condition presumably led only to genuine curvature adaptation, since it involved intersensory conflict in the absence of apparent curvature. When looking at objectively straight contours, which appeared curved, a small reduction in the effect occurred with a stationary head and a larger one when head movement was allowed. The latter presumably represented a combination of Gibson effect and genuine adaptation. If objectively curved lines were viewed with normal vision, a small reduction in perceived curvature occurred, whether or not head movements were made, further supporting the hypothesis that the necessary and sufficient condition for the Gibson effect is exposure to curvature. Finally, Cohen found that if the prism-wearing subject's visual field was restricted to a dot of light, curvature adaptation occurred only if head movement was allowed. Since a dot presumably activates only the subject-relative, or locus-analyzing, system of vision, it must be this system that adapted, and this is probably also the case for the genuine adaptation that Cohen observed with prismatically distorted contours.

It has been argued that genuine adaptation to prismatic curvature will occur if the observer is confronted with information that a contour initially appearing to be curved (straight) is actually straight (curved). A more precise formulation of this informational hypothesis is that the primary condition for curvature adaptation is a discrepancy between expected and actual perceptual results when moving the body or part of the body relative to one or more contours. For head movements, this resolves to a discrepancy between expected and actual optical motion and thus represents a situation where visual position constancy has been lost (Chapter 7). For example, an up and down head movement while facing a prismatically curved vertical line will result in a continuously changing shape, although the specific segment of the line located directly ahead of the prism will always appear straight. Unexpected optical motion due to movement of the entire body, as when walking and viewing a contour on the floor, has already been mentioned. With movements of other parts of the body, information relating to the prismatic distortion is provided by the mismatch between the apparent visual locus of the body part (relative to the contour) and its expected locus.

The informational hypothesis is by now familiar, having been applied in its general form to several types of adaptation. As usual, it follows that the better (i.e., more precise) the information about bodily movement, the greater the resulting adaptation should be. Therefore it is likely that prismatic curvature adaptation will be enhanced when movement is actively initiated by the subject, since the perceived position and motion of the body are more precise (and more salient) in this condition than when the observer is moved about by some external force. Held and Rekosh (1963) carried out an ingenious experiment to compare the efficacy of these two types of bodily motion for adaptation to 20-diopter prismatic curvature. Subjects were required to move around for 30 min inside a large drum, the walls of which were covered with randomly positioned spots, similar to the setting used by Mikaelian and Held (1964) in their study of adaptation to optical tilt (Chapter 6, p. 144). The purpose of eliminating all vertical contours was to preclude the Gibson effect. In the active-movement condition of the experiment by Held and Rekosh, the subject walked about in the random-spot environment, whereas in the passive-movement condition he was pulled in a cart over the same path. Head movements were not allowed in either condition. In line with Held's reafference hypothesis (Chapter 2, pp. 21–23), only the active condition produced adaptation of apparent curvature, as measured by a pre-post shift in setting a grating of bars to apparent straightness. However, the reason for this active–passive difference in adaptation was probably the difference in available information about the optical distortion, rather than in the type of movement per se. That is, the subjects may have been so poorly informed about the nature of their bodily motion when it was effected by the cart that no clear expectation of optical motion was induced and therefore no discrepancy with the actual transformation of the visual field. According to the informational hypothesis, it should be possible for a passively exposed subject to adapt to prismatic curvature if he could somehow be provided with salient cues about the nature of his bodily motion. Victor (1968) apparently succeeded in this goal by comparing active and passive movement and several different directions of bodily motion, the latter designed to provide contour information of the type proposed by Rock (1966, Chapter 6). Victor found that passively and actively moved subjects adapted by the same amount when moved in the same direction as

the prismatically curved lines. As discussed previously, bodily movement along a line leads to retinal motion that is different for straight
than for curved lines, and therefore a prism-wearing observer will be
provided with information that the line is actually straight. Victor also
noted significant adaptation when the subject moved toward the
curved stimulus, but not when he moved at right angles to the direction of the contour. In a final condition the subject was told to move
around a solid horizontal line while looking through base-up prisms
(producing convex-upward apparent curvature). When observed
head-on, the line projected to a single point, thereby obeying one of
the rules of a straight line. As predicted, this condition led to very significant curvature adaptation, with either active or passive movement.

Although it has been shown that externally induced bodily motion
can lead to curvature adaptation, it is likely that self-initiated movement is an especially effective condition toward this end, particularly
when there are no visual contours present. It is possible that Held and
Rekosh's failure to obtain adaptation with passive exposure resulted
from the absence of visual contours during the exposure period.
Perhaps being able to view contours, as in Victor's experiment, makes
it possible for passive movement to provide the necessary information
for adaptation, whereas the connection between passive bodily
motion and the sweep of a "random-spot" field across the retina is
not sufficiently salient to activate the adaptive process.

Another possibility, which was raised with respect to the effect of
active versus passive movement on adaptation to optical tilt (Chapter
6, p. 145), has to do with the presence of head movements. The
argument is that passive bodily motion will produce adaptation (if
relevant information has been provided), but only if the subject is not
allowed to move his head while he is being carted about. Victor used
head constraint, whereas the head was free to move about in both the
passive and active conditions of Held and Rekosh's experiment. As
argued in Chapter 6, such movement may have served to inhibit the
adaptation that would otherwise have resulted from the passive
exposure condition.

In general, the most effective condition for adaptation to prismatic
curvature is one where the subject has very good information about
the discrepancy between the initial appearance of a contour and its
physical properties. Therefore, if the observer is required to perform
bodily movements that conform to the *objective* characteristics of the
prismatically distorted visual contour, the nature of the distortion will
be made quite clear, thereby vigorously activating the adaptive
process. In support of this conclusion, several investigators (Burnham,

1968; Festinger *et al.*, 1967; Gyr & Willey, 1970) have demonstrated that adaptation is enhanced when active movement involves "efferent instructions" appropriate to the objective contour. In Experiment II of the study by Festinger *et al.* (1967), the subject viewed through a 25-diopter prism two parallel and vertically oriented rods that were either objectively straight and apparently curved or vice versa. In the "nonlearning" condition, the subject was instructed to place a hand-held stylus between and at the top of the two rods, which were .5 in. apart, and then to rapidly slide the stylus down, maintaining pressure against one of the rods. In the "learning" condition, he was specifically told to avoid touching either of the rods as he made the rapid downward swing of the hand and thus was forced to instruct his hand to move in a straight line for rods that appeared curved or in a curved line for rods that appeared straight. As predicted, 40 min of prism exposure resulted in significantly greater curvature adaptation for this condition. Several variations of this paradigm were carried out by Festinger *et al.*, with essentially the same results. The finding of less adaptation when the subject moved his stylus along the rods might be explained more simply by noting that when the hand is moved along an optically curved surface there is an immediate "visual capture" of the felt direction of the hand's movement such that it feels as if it is moving in a curved manner when it is moving straight. Thus, the absence of a consciously experienced discrepancy between felt and seen motion of the hand would be expected to retard the adaptive process, whereas moving the hand in such a manner as to avoid contact with the optically curved surface should represent a source of discordance, thereby eliciting adaptation.

In experiments on adaptation to prismatic curvature the wedge prisms are usually attached to goggles worn by the subject and as a result there is one type of visuomotor behavior that is *not* in confict with the apparent curvature—eye movements. The subject at no time will experience difficulty in keeping his eyes on a prismatically curved contour as he scans it. Consequently, if only this form of bodily movement is allowed (as in the original observations of the curvature Gibson effect), there is no reason to expect any adaptation to occur. The only way that eye movements can be caused, by means of errors, to reveal the existence of the prismatic distortion is to attach the prism to a contact lens. With the prism moved about by the eye the observer quickly learns that the only way that he can keep the image of a prismatically curved contour centered on the fovea is to make his eye movements conform to the objective contour. Several investigators have found that the curvature adaptation resulting from eye movement while wearing this device is substantially greater than that achieved by means of prism goggles. Taylor (1962, pp. 222–231) and Festinger et al. (1967) demonstrated that, by using the prism–contact lens, relatively short exposure periods, devoted primarily to moving the eyes along visual contours, were sufficient to produce adaptive shifts ranging from 40% to complete (the Gibson effect included) to rather small prismatic curvature (2–8 diopters). (The *measurement* of this adaptation did not require moving eyes.) In contrast to these results, Pick and Hay (1964), using 20-diopter prism goggles, reported only 30% adaptation after a 42-day wearing period. Since the prism strength was much greater in the latter case than with the prism–contact lens arrangement, a direct comparison of their respective percentages of adaptation is suspect. Festinger et al. also found that nearly all of the curvature adaptation measured with the exposed eye transferred to the unexposed eye.[4] Slotnick (1969) replicated this finding and, more important, corroborated a tentative observation by Festinger et al. that adaptation is greater for saccadic than for tracking eye movements. The explanation given for this finding was that saccadic eye movements are the result of efferent instructions for movement of eyes to particular positions in space, whereas tracking movements are concerned only with velocity matching (e.g., Festinger & Canon, 1965). Since prismatic curvature represents, in part, a distortion of visual position, only the former type of eye movement should provide the basis for adaptation. According to the informational hypothesis, it is only with saccadic movements that an expected optical motion will be generated, thereby resulting in a registered discrepancy when the actual motion is perceived.[5]

It may be tentatively concluded that prismatic curvature adaptation is enhanced when eye movements are involved, although the reason is not entirely clear. Festinger et al. have suggested two possible explanations. First, the information resulting from visuomotor errors may be more heavily weighted when it arises from eye movements than

[4] Hajos and Ritter (1965) also observed 100% interocular transfer of curvature adaptation induced by 14-diopter prism goggles. However, Pick et al. (1966) obtained only 55% transfer to 20-diopter prismatic distortion after a comparable exposure period. The explanation for this discrepancy is not apparent, although perhaps it is related to the difference in prism strengths.

[5] In an unpublished experiment by Gyr, Willey, and Gourlay, it was found, using a computer-simulated prism–contact lens exposure condition, that adaptation was significantly retarded when the subject was led to believe that the changes in the shape of the line being scanned had no relation to his eye movements. This is further evidence of the importance for adaptation that a *registered* discrepancy exist between expected and actual visual input.

from other forms of bodily motion. This is not unreasonable, given the normally invariant correspondence between eye movements and resulting optical motion, together with the great deal of experience an adult subject has had with this relationship. Second, when prism goggles are worn, the information from head, arm, and entire body movements signaling the presence and nature of the prismatic curvature is at odds with the information from the eye movements, since these are perfectly accurate in their attempts to locate or trace the prismatically distorted contours. No such contradiction exists when the contact lens arrangement is worn. This second hypothesis could be tested if subjects wearing prism goggles were prevented from making gross eye movements while moving the head and/or entire body; if the hypothesis is correct, significantly greater adaptation will be found.

The End Product

Let us now consider what it is that has been modified when genuine curvature adaptation is obtained. One possibility that may be ruled out immediately is a change in felt direction of gaze or of eye scanning. As we have seen, it is unnecessary for the eyes to move during the postexposure test of curvature adaptation, which precludes the possibility that curvature adaptation results from coming to feel that a curved eye movement is straight. This misperceived eye movement theory, however, does seem to apply for visual adaptation to split-field prisms, since here an unconscious eye movement, in the form of a lateral jump at the midline, *is* necessary if upper and lower halves of a vertical line are to appear connected.

In contrast to adaptation to prismatic displacement, curvature adaptation may be based on a genuine alteration of retinal values. Two hypotheses have been offered concerning the nature of this proposed visual recalibration. One of these is the "efferent readiness theory," formulated by Festinger *et al.* (1967), although actually originating with the work and theorizing of Taylor (1962) and Erismann and Kohler (e.g., Kohler, 1964). This theory, which was introduced in Chapter 5 (pp. 123–125) as a potential account of adaptation to visual transposition, proposes that adaptation to prismatic curvature (and the perception of visual contours, in general) is based on and equivalent to the *readiness* to make the appropriate motor movements to sensory input. It is maintained that adaptation to prismatic distortion entails a learned tendency to make objectively accurate motor responses, even though these responses need not be carried out. Festinger *et al.* (1967)

maintained that this theory was supported by the results of their experiments, which showed that adaptation is enhanced by a condition in which new efferent instructions are acquired. However, the fact that a condition involving the use of new visuomotor instructions facilitates adaptation does not necessitate the conclusion that the end product of adaptation is composed of these instructions or the readiness to make them. It may simply be that in such a condition the presence and nature of the distortion are made most salient, thereby producing a maximal shift in apparent curvature, whatever the nature of this visual adaptation. The primary problem with the efferent readiness theory, as it applies to adaptation to visual rearrangement, is the difficulty or impossibility of equating the informational content of the "learning" and "nonlearning" conditions, to provide an unconfounded test of the importance of the acquisition of new efferent readinesses. While it must be true that an adapted subject has a readiness to move his eyes in a more objectively correct manner than he did before adaptation, it is quite possible that this is merely a "symptom" of adaptation, rather than its cause.[6]

The second hypothesis concerning curvature adaptation was proposed by Rock (1966, Chapter 6) and is the same theory that he has applied to other forms of adaptation—that as a result of information concerning the objective nature of the visual field, the proximal stimulus comes to elicit a memory trace of the observer's egocentric relation to the stimulus. Thus, the sensory input from a prismatically curved contour comes to elicit the memory that this stimulus obeys the rules of straightness, and it is this memory that represents the phenomenal impression of straightness (i.e., adaptation). In other words, a particular curved image becomes the "sign" of phenomenal straightness via memories acquired during the exposure period.

ADAPTATION TO DISTORTIONS OF CLOSED FIGURES

One of the many "side effects" of prismatic displacement is a change in the apparent shape of closed forms, as shown in Figure 9.3. An objectively square figure when viewed straight-on through a base-left wedge prism will appear to be a trapezoid with curved vertical

[6] In an experiment by Miller and Festinger (1977), adaptive changes in eye movements during exposure to computer-simulated optical curvature were found to have little or no relation to the concomitant curvature adaptation. Thus, the efferent readiness theory was not supported. On the other hand, the presence of good information about the nature of the distortion did positively correlate with level of adaptation.

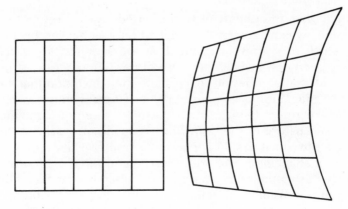

Figure 9.3.   Distortion of a square by means of a base-left prism.

edges. If the observer is allowed to move his head about, these distortions cause the visual field to alternately expand and contract (with lateral movements) or to rock in a see-saw fashion (with up and down movements). This represents a loss of visual position constancy, which is at least partially overcome after a period of head or entire body movement (Chapter 7). If it could be shown that prism exposure ultimately causes a form to look closer to its true shape when using a test of adaptation in which the subject's head is *stationary,* then it could be concluded that adaptation to distortion of a closed figure has occurred, unconfounded by potential adaptation to the loss of visual position constancy.

Pick and Hay (1966a) obtained just such an effect. One of their many tests involved restraining the subject's head movements by means of a biteboard while having him direct the experimenter in adjusting the spatial positions of four dots so that they constructed an apparent square. Pick and Hay reported a substantial adaptive shift in the placement of the dots, particularly when measured without the prisms. This aftereffect reached 51% of the theoretical maximum by the end of the 42-day wearing period, although most of it had been achieved after about 6 days. This is much greater than the 30% curvature adaptation found in the same experiment, a difference that contradicts the hypothesis alluded to earlier that the perception of closed figures, being particularly dependent on object-relative parameters, will be less modifiable when subjected to optical distortion than will the perception of unclosed forms. However, perhaps the comparison in Pick and Hay's experiment is unfair, because curvature adaptation was measured by means of a *contour,* whereas adaptation to the distortion of rectilinear objects was tested by means of *dots*. Single points of light are likely to be "assessed" primarily, if not entirely, by the locus-analyzing aspect of vision. Therefore, Pick and Hay may have unwittingly enhanced the adaptation of this aspect of form perception by avoiding the potential constraint imposed when contours are present.[7] Perhaps if the test had involved viewing through a variable prism a square composed of straight lines and changing the prism power until the object actually appeared square, adaptation would have been significantly less than that achieved in Pick and Hay's test.

A similar test was employed in an unpublished experiment by Mack and Quartin (1974), in which a "meridional-size lens" (MSL) was used to produce a distortion of closed forms. As will be recalled from the preceding chapter, the MSL produces a magnification of the visual dimension perpendicular to its axis. In Mack and Quartin's experiment, the MSL, with axis vertical, was worn over one eye while the other eye was closed. The result was a monocular view of a visual field whose horizontal dimension was magnified,[8] and a square and a circle would initially appear as a rectangle and ellipse. Using either a 10% or a 25% MSL and an exposure period entailing either 1 or 8 hr of walking through corridors, the investigators obtained quite significant adaptation, as measured by a test in which the subject adjusted a luminous rectangle until it appeared to be a square. In the 1-hr exposure experiment the aftereffect equaled 34% of the initially experienced distortion for the 10% magnification and 15% for the 25% magnification, a difference that was not statistically significant. In the 8-hr experiment the two figures were 49.5 and 38%, respectively, again a nonsignificant difference.

Mack and Quartin's experiment indicated that rather substantial adaptation to optically distorted closed forms is possible. Rock (1966, p. 209) had speculated earlier that such adaptation might occur, assuming that *size* adaptation in only one dimension is possible. Perhaps such a mechanism accounts for the adaptation observed in Mack and Quartin's experiments.

Malatesta and Mikaelian (1975) proposed that if it is assumed that *large* figures are perceptually encoded primarily in terms of their

---

[7] The fact that adaptation to the expansion–contraction of a *contoured* field when tested with lateral head movements was only about 10% and adaptation to the rocking motion contingent on head nodding was about 15% suggests that this constraint was operating here. If these dynamic tests of adaptation had used dots of light, it is likely that measured adaptation would have been greater.

[8] If the other eye had been unobstructed, the experience would have been of the visual field slanting away on one side, as in the experiments by Epstein *et al.* (Chapter 8).

spatial (subject-relative) components, whereas *small* figures are encoded in terms of their geometric relations, then adaptation to optical *tilt* should be manifested more strongly with the large than with the small figure. The basis of this argument is that optical tilt, like displacement, induces a change in the localizing system and that such a change is most free to express itself when the adaptation *test* figure is relatively unconstrained by object-relative aspects. As predicted, 1 hr of unconstrained exposure to 30° optical tilt led to an obtained pre–post shift in apparent verticality that was much greater when the square, which was used as the test stimulus, was large.

SUMMARY AND CONCLUSIONS

It has been repeatedly demonstrated that human observers are capable of adapting partially to optical distortions of form, in most cases prismatically induced curvature. Of the two aspects of form perception—object relative and subject relative—the latter is presumed to be more susceptible to modification during prismatic distortion. A necessary condition for genuine curvature adaptation (in contrast to the so-called "Gibson effect") is bodily motion, because such motion inevitably leads to a discrepancy between expected and actual visuomotor performance, which is the adequate stimulus for curvature adaptation. The magnitude of this adaptation is likely to be positively related to the precision with which the movement of the body is registered, since the greater the precision, the more salient the discrepancy information. It follows from this that adaptation will be greater when bodily movement is initiated by the subject than when it is controlled externally, unless the latter condition is accompanied by salient and useful information about the nature of the distortion (e.g., Victor, 1968). Both active and passive movement will be effective in producing adaptation if forced to conform to the objective nature of the visual contour, since this leads to what is perhaps the most unambiguous information possible concerning the nature of the distortion.

It is important to note that even after extended exposure periods, the magnitude of prismatic curvature adaptation is rather small, rarely exceeding 30% of the theoretical maximum, with the Gibson effect usually included in this figure. One explanation is that, because the perception of the internal geometry of the contour (i.e., the object-relative aspect) is relatively unmodifiable, it constrains the (subject-relative) adaptation produced. A second possibility concerns the fact that most curvature adaptation experiments use prism–*goggles* and therefore fail to involve the eyes in the distortion. It has been suggested that the undiminished accuracy of oculomotor behavior serves to counteract the adaptation induced by the initial inaccuracy of other visuomotor responses. In the few experiments in which the prism was attached to the eye, by means of a contact lens, adaptation was found to be unusually large after relatively short periods of exposure. In fact, Taylor (1962, pp. 222–231) reported *total* adaptation after only a few minutes of scanning contours. However, since he served as his only subject and relied entirely on introspective report, more confidence should be placed on the results of Festinger et al. (1967) and Slotnick (1969), who quantified the perception of several subjects and obtained adaptive shifts of around 40%. Thus, when the eyes join the rest of the body in leading to error input, adaptation is enhanced, but still fails to approach its theoretical maximum. It appears likely that adaptation to prismatic curvature is retarded by the relatively unmodifiable object-relative component of form perception. If so, it may be surmised that if the form that is used to *test* prismatic curvature adaptation were designed to minimize the object-relative aspect, the magnitude of obtained adaptation would be increased. This might be achieved by replacing with a column of widely separated dots the contour (or grating) with which the subject is typically confronted in the pre- and postexposure tests.

It was proposed that closed figures would be particularly resistant to adaptation when optically distorted because they are presumed to entail a strong object-relative component. Nevertheless, adaptation has been reported for this type of rearrangement. This adaptation probably involved the alteration of the subject-relative aspect, which was perhaps measured in relatively "pure" form by Pick and Hay (1966), who used a test involving points of light. In the case of adaptation to shape distortion induced by magnification of one dimension (Mack & Quartin, 1974), it is possible that the compensation involved a unidimensional adaptation to *size*, which, according to Rock (1966, p. 209), can be understood in subject-relative terms.

10

Adaptation to Auditory Rearrangement

THE EARLY STUDIES

When distorting spectacles are placed before the eyes not only is spatial vision made discrepant with respect to the body position sense but with audition as well. At the outset, a sound-emitting object is both felt and heard to be where it really is, but it is seen elsewhere.[1] The original question in studies of visual rearrangement was whether or not vision would ever return to normal. However, as we have seen, it is usually the initially veridical felt body position that shifts in the direction of the altered visual sense. It appears that the auditory modality is also "dominated" by vision, even though here again the result is one of misperception. Stratton (1897b) described in passing the fact that sound sources viewed through his inverting spectacles occasionally seemed to emanate from their visual locations:

> The sound of my footsteps conformed to the tactual and visual localization of my feet, and . . . in general the sight of the sound's place of origin carried with it the localization of the sound [p. 478].

[1] Actually, this is true only for the "drastic" distortions such as inversion and right/left reversal. With prismatic displacement or other means of creating a moderate lateral discrepancy between visual and auditory inputs, an immediate "visual capture" of auditory location occurs and little or no intersensory conflict is perceived. This phenomenon is referred to as the *ventriloquism effect* (Howard & Templeton, 1966, p. 361) and has been the subject of numerous experiments (e.g., Jackson, 1953; Pick et al., 1969b; Radeau & Bertelson, 1974; Thomas, 1941; Witkin, Wapner, & Leventhal, 1952).

Wooster (1923) and Ewert (1930), using 21° prismatic displacement and inversion, respectively, examined in a more systematic manner the effect of visual rearrangement on auditory localization and reported that, at least for some subjects, the object's visible locus had a powerful influence on its apparent auditory position.

To examine directly adaptability to auditory rearrangement it is necessary to place some device on the subject's head that alters auditory space and then to note the extent (if any) to which he is capable of regaining his preexposure accuracy in auditory localization. Such a device is the reversing "pseudophone," apparently first designed and used by Hornbostel and Wertheimer (1920; cited by Young, 1928),[2] which functionally reverses the right/left position of the two ears by placing a sound-collecting device on each side of the head and connecting it to the ear on the opposite side. Naturally, precautions are taken to prevent direct access of sounds into the ears. Since differences in auditory input (arrival time, intensity) between the ears represent important cues for auditory localization in the lateral dimension, the pseudophone serves to produce a right/left reversal of apparent auditory location.

Young (1928) was the first investigator to test the possibility of adaptation to pseudophonic rearrangement. His pseudophone was crude, bulky, and quite uncomfortable. It consisted of two ear trumpets of the sort worn in those days by the hard-of-hearing. A trumpet was placed adjacent to each ear and connected via a soundproof tube to the other ear. The earpiece, which was attached to the end of each tube, fit snugly into the ear canal. Too snugly, in fact, since Young's subjects complained of headaches and soreness. Although there was a certain amount of sound leakage, a very definite right/left reversal of the heard location of sounds was reported with the eyes shut, along with an increase in loudness and change in timbre, both due, presumably, to the large ear trumpets. The transposition involved not only right/left reversal for sounds on the interaural axis but a front/back reversal for sounds located less than 90° from the midline. For example, a sound objectively located ahead and 20° to the right of the median plane might be heard coming from a point behind and 20° to the left. The explanation for this is not obvious. In fact, one may ask, how it is that the front and back of auditory space are distinguished with *normal* hearing. Head movements are probably an important fac-

---

[2] The term *pseudophone* was coined by Thompson (1879; cited by Young, 1928) to describe a pair of flaps that could be attached to the ears and adjusted in various ways to effect changes in auditory localization.

tor. For example, with a motionless head a sound located straight ahead of the observer would be indistinguishable from a sound directly behind him.[3] As soon as the head begins to turn, the inter-aural differences in intensity and arrival time will clearly indicate the sound's front/back locus (and, for that matter, its *distance* from the observer). For example, with a sound source located straight ahead, a rightward turn of the head will cause the left ear to be favored, whereas with the sound behind the observer the same head turn causes the right ear to be favored. This relationship is reversed when a pseudophone is worn. Thus, it seems likely that the front/back reversals of auditory localization occasionally noted by Young were largely due to head movements.

The nine subjects in Young's experiments wore the pseudophone for short periods of time, both in and out of doors. However, Young devoted most of his report to his own observations during more extended exposure periods, the longest of which lasted 3 days (58 waking hours). Like Stratton's papers, Young's is written in great detail, includes a wealth of anecdotal report, and involves few statistics. In short, it makes much more enjoyable reading than most contemporary journal articles.

From the very beginning, Young noted that sounds often seemed to emanate from their visible locations. This was especially likely if the sound was the human voice, with the speaker in view. Young (1928) writes:

> The assistant who stood in front of the window spoke and his voice was normally localized but at the same time the rain pattering on the window was heard on the opposite side [p. 402].

Paying close attention to the visible source appeared to facilitate its "capture" of the sound's location, but it is possible that at least some of the instances in which the sound was correctly localized occurred simply because the sound happened to be located directly on the median plane of the head. In this case, the pseudophonic reversal would have no effect on auditory localization, as long as the head

---

[3] This disregards the possibility that differences in the intensity and timbre of a sound due to the "sound shadows" cast by the pinnea might serve as a cue for back/front discrimination. However, this cue would seem to be useful only for familiar sounds. Another alternative has been proposed by Batteau (1967), who argued that the folds within the pinnae cause sounds to enter the ear as a series of "echoes," the timing of which varies as a function of the front/back position (as well as azimuth and distance) of the second source.

remained motionless. If the source of a sound could not be seen, it was almost always incorrectly localized, even by the end of the longest exposure period. Nevertheless, Young learned to correct deliberately his motor behavior with respect to these sounds:

> I have learned that when I hear a sound on the left it is necessary to look to the right in order to see the source, and vice versa. Consequently I sometimes look deliberately in the *wrong* direction and this generally brings the expected source into view [p. 409].

One interesting observation was that of "double localizations." A visible sound source was sometimes heard to be coming from both the left and the right, a phenomenon termed *diplophonia*.

When the pseudophone was removed, there was no aftereffect of auditory localization, whether the eyes were open or shut. This, coupled with the general failure to localize correctly unseen sounds during the exposure period, clearly indicates that Young (and his subjects) had failed to adapt to the auditory reversal. Only when an object could be seen and heard simultaneously was auditory localization likely to be veridical. This "ventriloquism effect" (see footnote 1) is not considered to be adaptation, because it does not represent a change in perception persisting beyond the exposure period. Young concluded that even with unlimited exposure to the auditory rearrangement, normalization of purely auditory localization would fail to develop.

Willey, Inglis, and Pearce (1937) repeated Young's experiment, using three observers who wore the reversing pseudophone for 3, 7, and 8 days, respectively. Except that it lacked the large receiving trumpets, their device was comparable to that used by Young. During the wearing period the subjects moved about indoors and out, noting the apparent auditory loci of sound-emitting objects. Periodic tests of auditory localization without vision were taken in a sound-attenuating room.

The results of this experiment agreed with several of Young's observations. Most important, purely auditory localization of unseen sound sources remained right/left reversed throughout the exposure period and there were no auditory aftereffects when the pseudophone was removed. In contrast to Young, Willey *et al.* reported very few cases of the visual dominance of audition during exposure. They concluded that a sound seeming to come from the visible source could be attributed to disattention to or suppression of auditory cues, rather than to their reinterpretation. They suggested that when the observer was paying close attention to the visual source and "empathizing" with it, the discrepancy between its visual and auditory locus was simply not noticed. A change of attitude or attention could lead to an immediate awareness of the discrepancy:

> When a person talking to an observer laughed, or coughed, or changed his tone of voice from that which he customarily used, a clear reversal was immediately perceived, even though the localization just previously had seemed normal [Willey et al., 1937, p. 125].

Young's experience of complete normalization of auditory localization by the end of his longest exposure period may have been due to an unusual ability to attend and "empathize" with the visible sources. The subjects in the Willey et al. study were perhaps more analytic in their auditory localization. Such individual differences in the degree to which vision dominates audition were noted by both Wooster (1923) and Ewert (1930).

It may be concluded from the pioneering experiments by Young and Willey et al. that when auditory space is pseudophonically reversed subjects are incapable of reacquiring normal auditory localization of unseen sound sources, at least for exposure periods of up to 8 days. Although the visual and auditory loci of objects may occasionally appear identical when the sound source is visible, this is only true if the observer's attention is directed strongly to the visual object; a "critical" attitude will emphasize the visual–auditory discrepancy.

LATER STUDIES

Necessary and Sufficient Conditions for Auditory Adaptation

As with vision, the human auditory localizing system may not be able to completely adapt to reversal in a relatively short period of time. However, it might be possible to partially adapt to a less drastic auditory rearrangement. This reasoning has underlain the later investigations of adaptation to auditory rearrangement, most of which have involved the lateral displacement of auditory space by 20 to 30°. This auditory analog to prismatic displacement is effected by a pseudophone whose interaural axis is turned by a relatively small amount. For example, if the right "ear" is rotated 10° forward from the normal axis and the left "ear" 10° back, the result is a 10° counterclockwise auditory displacement.

Held (1955b) was the first to examine human adaptability to auditory displacement. His pseudophone was much more sophisticated than that used by Young and Willey et al. It had two small electronic hearing aids for receivers, one placed directly above each ear on the ends of a rotatable horizontal rod. The input was fed into a battery-powered amplifier that drove miniature earphones inserted into the auditory canals. A cushion placed over each ear markedly attenuated external sounds entering the ear directly. Measurements of auditory localization were taken in an anechoic chamber and required that the blindfolded subject turn himself in a rotating chair until an unseen sound source seemed to be centered in his median plane. During this test, the microphones were set parallel to the normal interaural axis. Precautions were taken to eliminate interaural differences in intensity as a localizing cue. Consequently, time of arrival was presumed to be the primary cue in localizing the auditory stimuli (repetitive tone pips with a carrier frequency of 2000 Hz).

Held's first experiment was a semireplication of the experiments by Young and Willey et al., but used 22° clockwise or counterclockwise auditory displacement and involved 7 hr of everday activities, preceded and followed by measures of the auditory midline. None of the three subjects reported an apparent discrepancy between the auditory and visual positions of objects at any time during this exposure period, indicating that this relatively minor auditory rearrangement was subject to an immediate and continuous vertriloquism effect. Without vision, however, auditory localization was initially in error by the full amount of the pseudophonic displacement. These results generally agree with those of Young and Willey et al. However, the dominance of visual over auditory localization appears not to have been merely an attention phenomenon, as seen by the fact that even when critically evaluating their perceptions, subjects failed to detect the visual–auditory discrepancy. The most important finding of all was that the measures taken at the end of the exposure period revealed an average adaptive shift in auditory midline of 10°—evidence of genuine auditory adaptation.[4] There were also several instances in which an unseen test stimulus seemed to have two points of origin: a strong source at its true location, and a weak source off in the direction opposite the auditory displacement. This is similar to Young's observation of dipliphonia except that in his case double localizations, when

[4] Held reported that in a preliminary study stable adaptation to 45° rotation could not be obtained—suggesting the limits of auditory adaptability.

they occurred, were observed only while the pseudophone was being worn and the sound source was visible.

Held's second experiment was aimed at specifying the conditions required for auditory adaptation and was by far the most carefully controlled and thorough study of auditory rearrangement ever implemented. Six subjects were measured before, during, and after 1 hr of exposure to 22° displacement. Held reasoned that since with normal vision the unambiguous localization of a fixed sound source requires head and/or body movement (to discriminate the third dimension of auditory space), movement of some sort would be necessary for auditory adaptation. Consequently, he examined a number of different conditions of bodily movement relative to fixed sound sources heard through the 22°-rotated pseudophone. Exposure involved walking a triangular path at a paced rate of speed while listening to a sound source that was located in front, behind, or lateral to the subject's head. Adaptation occurred only when the subject moved directly toward or away from the sound source; the visibility of the source turned out to be irrelevant. Furthermore, a control condition where the subject rotated himself through a 120° angle while listening to the displaced sound source did not produce adaptation. These results indicate that a sufficient stimulus for auditory adaptation is the presence of an atypical relation between bodily (head) translation and the resulting change in interaural arrival-time differences. For example, a sound positioned directly ahead of an observer wearing the pseudophone will produce an arrival-time difference indicative of a locus 22° to one side of the median plane. However, as the subject walks toward the sound the time difference diminishes (because the auditory displacement is *angular*), thereby reducing the apparent displacement of the sound until it is localized near its objective straight-ahead position. The reverse occurs when the observer is walking away from a sound.

Held concluded that adaptation to auditory displacement results from the acquisition of an association between a given interaural arrival-time difference and the particular translation of the body (or head) required to move toward the sound source. Error-corrective feedback is unnecessary. He further suggested that such a process might underlie the *origin* of normal auditory localization and the ability to adapt to changes in localization resulting from the developmental increase in head size. Although it seems clear that a certain amount of "natural" adaptation must take place during the head-growth period and may well be based on the type of process suggested by Held, there is evidence to suggest that the auditory-localizing capacity is innate. For example, Wertheimer (1961) observed that an infant of less than 10 min of age turned its head correctly to localize a sound presented in a number of different positions.

Two of Held's colleagues, Freedman and Mikaelian, have carried out a number of studies in an attempt to delineate both the sources and characteristics of adaptation to auditory displacement. These experiments have typically entailed an electronic pseudophone similar to that used by Held but, interestingly, have used artificial pinnea, cast from human ears. This pseudophone was designed and described by Batteau (1963). Placing the microphones within replicas of the outer ears causes sound sources to be more definitely *externalized* than is otherwise the case (Batteau, 1967).

Using this device, Freedman and Stampfer (1964) reported that walking about during exposure to 20° clockwise or counterclockwise rotation of the auditory axis, for periods ranging from 8 to 16 min, led to small but statistically significant adaptive changes in auditory localization, as measured by the apparent alignment of an unseen auditory stimulus and a visual target. Freedman and Gardos (1965) exposed subjects to 20° left or right auditory displacement by having them sit in the dark and listen to a hand-held sound source (pulsed white noise) as they moved it from side to side in front of the body for 5 min. This is a direct analog of the exposure activity used by Held and Gottlieb (1958) in their pioneering study of prism adaptation. Subjects were measured on accuracy in pointing at an unseen auditory target before and after the exposure period. Adaptation, as assessed by this ear–hand task, was obtained, the average pre–post shift for tests taken with and without the pseudophonic rotation being about 8°. These results were later replicated by Freedman, Wilson, and Rekosh (1967) and Mikaelian (1969).

As seen in previous chapters, an important issue in adaptation to visual rearrangement concerns the role of active movement. Surprisingly, a direct comparison between passive and active exposure to auditory displacement has yet to be made, but several experiments have been carried out in which exposure involved either no bodily movement or active movement without sensory feedback (reafference).

In experiments described in Chapter 3 (p. 75), Canon (1970, 1971) exposed subjects to a sound source (a speaker) that was visually displaced in one direction by a prism and simultaneously shifted in the opposite direction by a pseudophone. The exposure condition involved using an unseen pointer to track either the visual source or the repetitive sound, depending on the instructions. Since the subject was not allowed to move his head and never saw his pointing hand, this condition was devoid of the ingredients originally considered by proponents of the reafference model to be necessary for adaptation. Nevertheless, significant and adaptive pre–post shifts in pointing at unseen auditory targets were observed for both tracking conditions— evidence of genuine adaptation to the auditory displacement. Radeau and Bertelson (1969, 1974) carried out similar experiments and reported essentially the same results.

Although it appears that adaptation to displaced auditory space can occur in the absence of movement or of reafference, it may be that active movement, in conjunction with sensory feedback, serves to *facilitate* the adaptive process. The only relevant experiments in which active and passive exposure have been compared involved auditory "*dis*arrangement." This, as will be recalled from Chapter 2 (p. 17), is a condition in which movement and the resulting sensory changes have been decorrelated. According to the reafference hypothesis, active movement in the presence of disarrangement should lead to the *deterioration* of perceptual or perceptual–motor behavior, as shown by an increase in localizing variability. This prediction was examined in a series of experiments by Freedman and his colleagues (Freedman & Pfaff, 1961, 1962a,b; Freedman & Secunda, 1962; Freedman & Zacks, 1964). Subjects were exposed to white noise presented separately to each ear whose inputs were not quite synchronous; therefore, the experience was of a series of fused sounds whose apparent position along the right/left dimension varied in a random manner. Over a period of time, a given movement of the head or entire body would be paired with a variety of interaural arrival-time differences, in contrast to the normally occurring one-to-one relationship.

In line with the reafference hypothesis, exposure to the dichotic noise led to an increase in variability in localizing an unseen sound source when the exposure activity involved walking, active rotation of the head, or active rotation of the entire body; no change in the precision of localization occurred when the subject was recumbent, passively rotated, or moved about in a wheelchair.

Although these results show that auditory disarrangement leads to the degradation of auditory localization only when movement is active, it is unclear how to interpret this finding. It would seem that for the lack of relationship between interaural arrival-time differences and movement to be realized by the nervous system, it would be necessary that there be information to indicate the presence of a *fixed* sound source. How can the adaptive mechanism "know" if the randomly changing interaural arrival-time difference is indicative of a fixed sound source whose apparent auditory locus is changing unpredictably or is merely a number of different fixed sources located at various positions along the right/left dimension? If the latter is the case, there is no auditory distortion present and hence no "reason" for any change in the auditory localizing mechanism. If one wishes to study disarrangement of auditory space in the same fashion that it has been investigated in the visual modality (e.g., Cohen & Held, 1960), several alternatives may be suggested. The subject can hold the auditory source in his hand, swinging it from side to side and listening to it as his pseudophones oscillate back and forth by differing amounts, randomly changing direction from moment to moment. The efferent and afferent indicators of limb position would specify the existence of a fixed sound source (at a given moment in time), whereas the moving pseudophone would serve to disarrange the subject's auditory space. The subject can also walk about in the presence of visible sound sources while wearing the oscillating pseudophone. Vision would indicate that a given sound source is fixed, even though its apparent auditory location is fluctuating.

What Is It That Adapts?

THE LOGICAL POSSIBILITIES

The evidence has clearly established that human subjects are capable of partial adaptation to relatively small pseudophonic displacements of auditory space. It may now be asked what the nature of this adaptation is.

One of the most commonly used measures of adaptation to displaced hearing is the pre-post shift in the accuracy of pointing at unseen auditory targets (e.g., Freedman et al., 1967). However, as with prism adaptation, a change in perceptual-motor behavior is ambiguous with respect to the locus of the adaptation. Let us examine the logical possibilities and how they may be tested.

First, exposure to auditory displacement might lead to a change in purely auditory localization, such that the cues for right/left directionalization come to be reinterpreted so as to compensate for the rearrangement. This was what Held (1955b) assumed had occurred in his experiments. This sort of adaptation may be detected by a task in which the subject is required to set a hidden sound source to the apparent straight ahead with respect to the *head*. A second means of

testing for changes in the "ear–head articulation" is to have the subject attempt to align a visual stimulus and an unseen auditory target
(Freedman & Stampfer, 1964), which assumes that visual localization
has remained unaltered. Finally, a change in "pure" auditory localization will be manifested in any task requiring the subject to move part
or all of his body with respect to a fixed sound source or vice versa;
no changes involving visual or other targets should occur.

A second possibility is that the pseudophonic displacement induces
a change in the felt relation of head to torso that would presumably
have no effect upon judgments relative to the head (i.e., recalibration
of the interaural cues), but would be manifested when the torso is
used as the standard of reference. If, for example, a subject who is
exposed to rightward auditory displacement comes to feel his right-
turned head to be oriented in the same direction as the rest of his
body, then a sound objectively in the median plane of the head would
seem to be straight ahead of the trunk. If the task is to set a sound to
the median plane and the subject is either told or assumes that the
trunk is to be used as the standard, a change in felt head orientation
will lead to an adaptive auditory shift and will also influence ear–hand
coordination, with either hand, as well as locomotory behavior. Visual
and visuomotor localization with respect to the trunk will also be
affected.

A third potential end state of auditory adaptation, specific perhaps
to exposure conditions involving a hand-held auditory source (e.g.,
Mikaelian, 1974c), is a change in the felt relation of the exposed hand
to the remainder of the body. Such a shift might be limited to the
exposed limb and would be manifested in pointing at both auditory
and nonauditory targets, such as a visual stimulus or the "straight-
ahead" position.

Finally, it could be that pseudophonic changes in ear–hand coordination are just that—changes in the relationship between apparent
auditory location and reaching responses. Such a consequence of
auditory displacement would be likely to occur only in the hand-held
sound exposure condition. Evidence for this highly specific form of
adaptation would be seen when the only demonstrable adaptive pre–
post shift is in reaching for auditory targets.

Nothing in this analysis precludes the possibility that exposure to
auditory rearrangement leads to several adaptive end states or that
different conditions of exposure induce different varieties of auditory
adaptation. Furthermore, the various components might be additive,
as is the case for prism adaptation (Chapter 3, pp. 71–72).

THE EVIDENCE

Freedman and Stampfer's (1964) finding of adaptive auditory shifts when the subject attempted to align visual and unseen auditory targets suggests that "genuine" (ear–head) auditory adaptation is possible. However, this study should be replicated, since it involved only five subjects and two failed to adapt.

There is as yet no direct evidence that exposure to auditory displacement can lead to a change in the felt position of the head. In those experiments in which the task involved setting a sound to the median plane (e.g., Held, 1955b), the instructions apparently failed to make explicit the part of the body with which the alignment was to be made. If the subject had been required to set the sound "straight ahead of the nose," the interpretation of the adaptive shifts obtained would be less ambiguous. Thus, it is not clear if the results of those investigators (e.g., Held, 1955b) who have found adaptive changes in auditory midline are indicative of a change in ear–head or head–torso relationships.

Studies of auditory rearrangement using exposure to a hand-held auditory source have, understandably, looked for changes in auditory target-pointing behavior. Mikaelian (1970b, 1972, 1974c) examined the hypothesis that adaptation from this sort of exposure activity is limited to the exposed hand and in two experiments (1970b, 1972) found no evidence of intermanual transfer of adaptive ear–hand shifts resulting from exposure to the hand-held auditory source, which was pseudophonically displaced by 30°. This finding rules out the possibility of changes in either the ear–head or head–torso relationship. Mikaelian (1974c) also found evidence that this change in ear–hand coordination was not based on an alteration of felt limb position because no error was measured in pointing at visual targets. In the same experiment subjects in a second condition were exposed to 20-diopter prismatic displacement and revealed shifts in pointing at both auditory and visual targets, confirming the fact that changes in felt limb position underlie prism adaptation, at least when exposure is limited to the hand.

Mikaelian's results appear to be contradicted by those obtained in two other experiments. Craske (1966b) found that exposure to a simulated 12° auditory displacement in which error-corrective feedback was provided for the subject's auditory target-pointing responses led to equal pre–post shifts for both visual and auditory target pointing. It is possible, however, that the error-corrective exposure led to a conscious correction tendency on the part of the subject, which persisted into the postexposure period and was not limited to auditory targets.

Freedman and Gardos (1965, Experiment 2) used the same type of exposure condition as Mikaelian (1974c) and found a small, statistically significant shift in eye–hand coordination for leftward, but not rightward, auditory displacement. Clearly, there is a need to replicate Mikaelian's experiment.

It is reasonable to conclude from the rather sparse data that there are several varieties of adaptation to auditory displacement and that the type obtained is determined by the nature of the exposure condition. Changes in auditory midline (with respect to the head or to the trunk) have been found as the result of whole-body movement (e.g., Held, 1955b) or stationary viewing (e.g., Radeau & Bertelson, 1974), whereas adaptive changes specific to the exposed limb result from exposure to a hand-held auditory source. These findings are quite similar to those of prism adaptation (Chapter 3), where changes in apparent visual location occur when the subject moves about in his environment or looks at his stationary body, whereas it is primarily visuomotor adaptation that results from exposure to the hand alone, especially under concurrent, no-target conditions.

THE RELATIONSHIP BETWEEN VISUAL AND AUDITORY ADAPTATION

It should be quite obvious by now that the different spatial modalities are interdependent. Exposure to auditory rearrangement has potential implications for visual localization and visual rearrangement may affect auditory localization.

A number of investigators have looked for possible visual and visuomotor effects of auditory rearrangement. Although Mikaelian (1974c) failed to observe a shift in eye–hand coordination from pseudophonic displacement, Craske (1966b) and Freedman and Gardos (1965) apparently succeeded. As we saw earlier, Canon (1970, 1971) found changes in the apparent location of a visual target after stationary viewing of a pseudophonically and prismatically induced auditory–visual discrepancy.

Even more apparent is the effect of visual rearrangement on auditory localization. First, vision has a strong dominating influence on apparent auditory location, even for severe rearrangements such as inversion (Stratton, 1897b).[5] Second, this ventriloquism effect can lead

[5] Lackner (1973a,b, 1974b) has reported that when subjects first look through 13° leftward-displacing prisms at the experimental room there is an immediate 13° *rightward* shift in auditory midline as measured by the "phantom sound" produced by dichotically presented clicks. It is not apparent how this result should be interpreted.

to auditory aftereffects, as demonstrated by Canon (1970, 1971) and Radeau & Bertelson (1974). Third, if exposure to visual rearrangement leads to a change in felt head or arm position sense, auditory localization may be affected. Harris (1965), Freedman and Gardos (1965), and Mikaelian (1974c, Experiment 2) have all shown that prismatic exposure leads to a change in ear–hand (as well as eye–hand) coordination, clearly implicating a change in felt limb position. A change in the felt relation of head to torso should affect both auditory and visual localization relative to the trunk, as well as auditory and visual target-reaching responses. Several investigators (e.g., Kohler, 1964, p. 38) have reported changes in felt head position as a result of prismatic exposure. Furthermore, M. M. Cohen (1974) found that terminal exposure to prismatic displacement caused the pre–post shifts in pointing at auditory and visual targets to transfer in part to the unexposed hand. It has usually been assumed that the presence of intermanual transfer of prism-adaptive eye–hand coordination is based on a change in apparent visual location. The fact that auditory target pointing was also affected in Cohen's study suggests that a change in felt head position might have occurred, causing a shift in both auditory and visual judgments of egocentric direction relative to the torso.

Changes in auditory localization resulting from exposure to visual rearrangement are in the direction of nonveridicality. However, continued exposure to visual rearrangement might lead eventually to recovery of the normal auditory-localizing capacity. Rekosh and Freedman (1967) examined this possibility by measuring subjects on both visual and auditory straight ahead before, during, and after walking about outdoors while wearing 30-diopter prisms. In the second of two experiments subjects in one condition wore ear muffs that attenuated sound, whereas in another condition hearing was unimpeded. In each case (but more so in the first) both auditory and visual localization shifted in the same direction during the initial part of the exposure period. This shift was, of course, maladaptive for the auditory modality. With further exposure, auditory errors decreased to near zero, whereas visual adaptation continued to increase. One possible interpretation of these results is that exposure to prismatic displacement leads initially to a change in the felt relation of head to torso, which in turn affects both visual and auditory localization (relative to the torso). With continued exposure this shift diminishes, whereas the felt direction of gaze (eye–head relationship) remains altered, thereby influencing visual but not auditory localization. A similar analysis may apply to the results of the 42-day experiment by

Hay and Pick (1966a), who found that visual adaptation increased during the exposure period, whereas the initially manifested position sense change eventually declined toward its veridical baseline level.[6] The investigators also measured auditory localization, but since the test involved directing the *head* toward a hidden sound, it is not surprising that changes in auditory localization did not occur, even during the early stages of prismatic exposure. As argued previously, a shift in felt head position should have no effect on auditory localization when the head is serving as the egocentric referent.

SUMMARY AND CONCLUSIONS

When human observers are exposed for a period of time to a lateral displacement of auditory direction, effected by means of a pseudophone, they undergo partial recovery of their normal auditory-localizing capacity. On the other hand, they do not appear to be capable of adapting to a right/left reversal of auditory space. It is only during exposure to visible sound sources that this severe form of auditory–visual discordance may be resolved, in the form of the ventriloquism effect, and then only when the subject is not critically evaluating his perception.

Adaptation to pseudophonic displacement, like prism adaptation, is facilitated by active bodily movement but can also occur in its absence, as long as some source of information about the auditory–visual discrepancy is provided.

Although the evidence is sparse and somewhat unclear, it appears that adaptation to auditory displacement is composed of as many as three different components: (a) a recalibration of interaural difference cues (e.g., time of arrival); (b) a shift in the felt position of the head relative to the torso; and (c) an alteration specific to ear–hand coordination. It is likely that the nature of the end products of auditory adaptation is determined by the characteristics of the exposure period. Whole-body movement has been found to lead to a change in apparent auditory direction (presumably based on a reinterpretation of interaural difference cues or a shift in felt head position), whereas exposure to a hand-held sound source, as it swings back and forth, leads to adaptation specific to the subject's accuracy in reaching for auditory targets with that hand.

---

[6] Mikaelian (1974c) has also reported an early, but short-lived, shift in proprioception as a result of 2 hr of exposure to 20° counterclockwise optical tilt.

With extended exposure to prismatically displaced vision, there is an initial maladaptive shift in auditory localization (measured in the absence of vision), which eventually disappears, leaving only an adaptive shift in visual direction. It was suggested that this might be the result of a transitory recalibration of felt head position, having effects on both apparent visual and auditory direction, which is then replaced by a change in the felt direction of gaze.

The study of adaptation to auditory rearrangement represents relatively "virgin" research territory. In general, experiments are needed to delineate more carefully the various components of auditory adaptation and, more important, the conditions of exposure necessary and/or sufficient to produce them. Relatively little is known about the role of active (versus passive or stationary) exposure to auditory rearrangement. The effects of error-corrective feedback have not been systematically investigated and studies of auditory disarrangement along the lines suggested previously are needed.

Research on adaptation to auditory rearrangement has a number of important implications. First, the results of these experiments will undoubtedly shed light on the nature and modifiability of auditory localization. Second, the very fact that auditory localization has proven to be adaptable suggests the relevance of auditory rearrangement research for mobility training of the blind and for the presumed

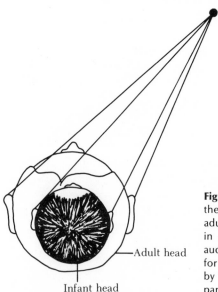

Infant head — Adult head

Figure 10.1. A schematic representation of the increase in head size from infancy to adulthood. The change causes the difference in arrival time at the two ears for a given auditory source to be less for the infant than for the adult. (From *Development in Infancy* by T. G. R. Bower. W. H. Freeman and Company. Copyright © 1974.)

changes in localizing capacity of individuals suffering from the sudden loss of hearing in one ear. Finally, it is clear that adaptation to imposed changes in auditory space is a fact of life for the growing child. Head growth must certainly lead to changes in interaural differences in auditory input, as shown in Figure 10.1. Failure to adapt in some way to these changes would lead to increasing errors of localization. Obviously, such "natural adaptation" does occur and not on the basis of a maladaptive shift in any other perceptual system (e.g., felt relation of head to torso). This fact suggests an interesting possibility. Perhaps the limits to which an adult subject is capable of adapting to pseudo-phonic displacement are set, at least approximately, by the amount by which human beings must be capable of adapting to handle the total change in auditory localization that results from the full developmental increase in head size. If so, it should be possible for an adult to adapt *completely* only to an auditory displacement of this magnitude or less.

It may be concluded that the present area of research is relevant to both developmental changes in and the maintenance of the human capacity of auditory localization.

11

Interspecies and Individual
Differences in Adaptability

Traditionally, research in psychology has attempted to establish general laws applicable to all or most human beings, and possibly to other organisms as well, but there has always been a certain amount of interest in the psychological differences that exist both within and between species. Research on adaptation to perceptual rearrangement has mirrored psychology's preoccupation with the nomothetic method. However, here, too, there exists a literature pertaining to interspecies and individual differences. The aim of this chapter is to review this literature and to assess its contribution to our understanding of adaptation and perception.

ADAPTATION IN NONHUMAN ORGANISMS

A surprisingly large variety of so-called "lower" organisms have been confronted with visual or visuomotor rearrangement, induced either optically or by means of anatomical alteration.[1] Although it is often implied that the perceptual results of these two procedures are identical, the validity of this assumption has yet to be tested. Nevertheless, for the purposes of the present review optical and anatomical rearrangements will be dealt with together. We will begin with

[1] For reviews of much of this literature, see Smith and Smith (1962, Chapter 5) and Taub (1968).

233

the lowest organisms on the phylogenetic scale and work our way up to the nonhuman primates.

Submammals

The simplest animal to be confronted with perceptual rearrangement is the fly *Eristalis*. Holst (1954) reported experiments, in collaboration with Mittelstädt, in which the head of this organism was turned by 180°. As we saw in Chapter 7, optical right/left reversal or inversion causes the visual field to appear to move in the same direction as the head or body is turning, and at twice the velocity. Furthermore, the fly and many other animals are subject to the *optomotor reflex*, which operates to maintain the organism's orientation with respect to a moving visual field. If Holst and Mittelstädt's head-rotated fly happened to move, the resulting illusory visual field motion induced the optomotor reflex, which maintained the apparent motion. Consequently, the animal would continue to circle as it attempted, unsuccessfully, to regain its visual stability, until finally collapsing from exhaustion. No fly was ever observed to overcome this self-defeating behavior. Holst and Mittelstädt (1950) reported a similar experiment in which inverting prisms were placed on fish. These animals also engaged in circling behavior that failed to diminish, even after long periods of time.

Sperry (1943a,b, 1944, 1948), Stone (1944, cited by Taub, 1968; 1953), and Weiss (1937a,b) rearranged the limbs of amphibia and fish and demonstrated the inability of these organisms to adapt to the resulting visual and visuomotor disruption. Frogs with 180°-rotated eyes would continue to strike for prey at their apparent visual locations and thus miss them, even to the point of starvation. Stone (1953) observed that an adult salamander with rotated eyes persisted in its abnormal perceptual–motor behavior (e.g., swimming) for over 4.5 years. Even amphibia whose eyes are rotated during embryonic development (during or after the "optic-cup stage") suffer life-long visuomotor disruption (Stone, 1953).

The ability of the chicken to adapt to visual rearrangement has been tested in several experiments. Pfister (1955) failed to obtain adaptation in two adult chickens who wore monocular right/left-reversing goggles for 3 months and were tested on pecking accuracy and adequacy of escape responses to threat. Rossi (1967), however, has pointed out that the animals in this experiment were probably confronted not only with right/left reversal, but with a 90° lateral displacement as well as apparent motion of the visual field with lateral head movements. If true, it is not at all surprising that the chickens failed to adapt, since it is unlikely that even human subjects would be capable of this feat. In an often-cited study by Hess (1956), newborn Leghorn chicks were forced to wear 7° wedge prisms during the first 4 days of life. They were unable to overcome their prism-induced pecking errors during this period, although a decrease in the variability of a given chick's errors around the misperceived location of the target occurred. Hess also reported the failure of both newborn and 6 to 8-week-old chickens to adapt to the foreshortening of visual distance, effected by the wearing of a base-out prism before each eye. The fact that such an optical arrangement induced a visual displacement in the third dimension indicates that chickens are capable (innately) of distance perception based on the cues provided by binocular vision.

On the basis of these experiments, it was concluded that chickens, and probably birds in general, are too behaviorally "inflexible" to modify an innately given visuomotor response (e.g., Hess, 1956; Gregory, 1973, p. 209). However, a number of authors have offered alternative interpretations of these failures to adapt. For example, it has been suggested that a prism-wearing chicken is probably unable to see its beak when pecking at a food target and, in any event, would probably fail to note the prism-induced error since the target would be out of view (or at least quite out of focus) at the termination of each pecking response (e.g., Arlinsky, 1967; Howard & Templeton, 1966, p. 390). Thus it might be possible to induce adaptation to visual rearrangement in this animal by redesigning the conditions of exposure.

Rossi (1967, 1968, 1969, 1971, 1972) attained this goal in a series of experiments that seems to have gone largely unnoticed. He found that White Leghorn chicks that wore 8–8.5° binocular wedge prisms for 6 posthatch days or more revealed a certain amount of adaptation, often in terms of both a reduction in pecking error while wearing the prisms and a negative aftereffect. A test at the fourth posthatch day, however, revealed no adaptation, confirming Hess's results. Apparently, the reason Hess had been forced to end his experiment after only 4 days was that his chicks were starving to death. Rossi, on the other hand, was able to prevent this by the ingenious procedure of including an older, non–prism-wearing chick in the same cage with the prism-exposed animals. The successful pecking behavior of this "starter chick" apparently motivated the other animals to continue working for their food, thereby decreasing the mortality rate. In one experiment (Rossi, 1969), the chicks were tested on adaptation to 8° prisms at 4, 8, 12, and 16 days of exposure. Pecking errors did not decrease during this period but a large negative aftereffect occurred when the prisms were removed on Day 16. In an attempt to explain this paradoxical result Rossi suggested that the chicks were acquiring a correcting tendency for their pecking behavior during the exposure period but that this correction was being nullified by the increasing *linear* displacement resulting from the animals' rapid growth. This growth served to increase the distance between prism and target and consequently the prism-corrective response could be revealed only when the prisms were removed. In a later experiment, Rossi (1972) found that 7 days of exposure to the prismatic displacement was much more likely to produce a pecking aftereffect if the chicks were reared in large groups. It was proposed that this effect resulted from the increased rate of rapid pecking responses observed with high population density.

Rossi's research has not only indicated that chickens are capable of adapting to optical rearrangement, but provides hope that even less complicated animals might also prove to be adaptable if special procedures were implemented, in conjunction with relatively mild forms of rearrangement, such as prismatic displacement.

"Lower" Mammals

The simplest mammal that has proven to be capable of adapting to rearrangement is the rat. Albert (1966) surgically rotated by 90 or 180° both eyes of male, hooded rats (age not specified). He found that these animals, when first tested 2-3 months after the operation, performed nearly indistinguishably from normal rats on several tasks of visuomotor coordination. Taub (1968) has suggested that the rat may represent a *transitional* stage of phylogenetic development, because Sperry had found no adaptation to the disruption of coordination caused by tendon or nerve crossings involving the animal's hind limbs (Sperry, 1940, 1941), but had reported some degree of adaptation for the forelimbs (Sperry, 1942).

Bishop (1959) replicated Hess's 1956 experiment, using the cat as his subject and optical inversion as the form of rearrangement. He reared two groups of kittens in the dark for the first 8 weeks of life before testing them. Bishop used a series of measures, including the ability (time and/or accuracy) to negotiate obstacle courses, climb up and down stairs of unequal heights, walk a straight line, traverse a maze, and learn an eye–paw response leading to a food reward. To keep the animals from learning a specific sequence of motor responses on the obstacle courses and maze, the arrangement of barriers was changed from day to day. Bishop found that kittens whose first view of the world was through monocular inverting (but not right/left-reversing) goggles were rather uncoordinated but apparently no more so than a group whose first experience entailed the wearing of nondistorting goggles. Both groups made rapid gains in task performance. Nevertheless, the normal-vision control group may have improved a little more rapidly. After 4 weeks the optical conditions were reversed and the group going from inversion to normal vision appeared to experience less initial disruption, and to overcome it more quickly, than did subjects in the reserve condition. Bishop's results suggest that cats are quite capable of adapting to visual rearrangement, but that they have an innate *bias* for normal, upright vision. Unfortunately, a serious flaw in his experiment makes this conclusion tentative. The Dove prisms used not only inverted the visual field but also caused a loss of visual position constancy (VPC) when the head was tilted or moved vertically. It is possible that it was the illusory movement of the visual field, rather than the inversion, that retarded the rate of adaptation in the prism-wearing conditions.

Ito, Shiida, Yagi, and Yamamoto (1974) assessed the capacity of the rabbit to adapt to the loss of VPC. The animal was passively oscillated around the vertical axis for several hours in the presence of a luminous slit that was moved in the same direction the animal was being turned and at twice the speed, thereby simulating the effect of optical right/left reversal. This experience led to adaptive shifts in the vestibulo-ocular reflex, which is the involuntary eye movement that serves to maintain visual fixation when the head is turned by either an external force or the organism itself (Chapter 7). In the experiment by Ito et al., exposure to the moving slit led to a reduction in the gain of the vestibulo-ocular reflex such that, when tested in total darkness, these animals came to turn their eyes by a smaller amount in one direction than their heads had turned in the opposite direction. It is reasonable to conclude that this change signals the presence of partial adaptation to the loss of VPC. Recovery from this adaptive shift in eye movements occurred after 24 hr in the dark.

Robinson (1975a,b) put right/left-reversing prisms on cats for extended periods of time and he, too, found adaptation of the vestibulo-ocular reflex. After about 1 week of exposure, during which the animals were treated as pets in the laboratory, the gain of the reflex dropped from a preadaptation average of .85 to about .40. Two hours a day of forced turning for one cat further reduced the gain to about .10. Thus, although the reflex failed to reverse itself, it was at least nearly extinguished by these exposure activities. Surgical removal of

the cerebella from four cats eliminated the ability to modify the vestibulo-ocular reflex. Robinson (1975b) concluded, on the basis of the
latter result and the results of other investigators, that the areas of the
brain responsible for adaptation of this sort in both animals and
human beings are the floccular–nodular lobes of the vestibulocerebellum.[2]

Monkeys

Monkeys appear to adapt to both optical and anatomical rearrangement in much the same manner and to the same extent as human subjects. The first study of adaptation in this animal was by Foley (1940).
He reported significant adaptation for a 9-year-old female rhesus
monkey after 1 week of exposure to binocular inversion, with
behavioral negative aftereffects for several days after the removal of
the goggles. Unfortunately, quantitative measures of this adaptation
were not taken. A number of investigators (Bossom, 1964, 1965;
Bossom & Hamilton, 1963; Hamilton, 1967; Healy, Symmes, &
Ommaya, 1973; Lund, 1970) have obtained adaptation for both "split-
brain"[3] and normal monkeys as a result of exposure to 11–13° prismatic displacement under a variety of exposure conditions. For
example, Healy et al. (1973) placed four 16- to 20-month-old rhesus
monkeys in a restraining chair and required them to reach under an
occluding shelf for a banana pellet reward placed at the far edge of
the apparatus. Exposure to the effects of the 20-diopter prism was provided by allowing the animal to see its hand when it appeared at the
terminus of each of 60 reaching responses. The result of this terminal
display condition was a significant visuomotor negative aftereffect.

Of theoretical interest is the fact that both Bossom and Hamilton
(1963) and Hamilton (1967) obtained interocular transfer of visuomotor
prism adaptation for split-brain monkeys, whereas Hamilton (1967) and
Lund (1970) found no intermanual transfer. This combination of results
supports the view that, under these circumstances, prism adaptation
involves the position sense of the exposed limb and not the visual or
oculomotor system. That is, since it is clear that visual learning does
not transfer interocularly in split-brain monkeys (e.g., Hamilton &
Gazzaniga, 1964), the fact that interocular transfer of prism adaptation

---

[2] Further support for the importance of the cerebellum for adaptation was provided
by Baizer and Glickstein (1973), who found that cerebellar lesions impaired prism
adaptation in monkeys.
[3] This operation involves the sectioning of one or more of the major neural tracts that
connect one half of the brain with the other.

occurred suggests that the adaptive shift was in the exposed limb (or, more precisely, in the cortical and/or subcortical areas subserving the proprioceptive-kinesthetic sense of this limb). The failure to observe intermanual transfer is convincing evidence that adaptation is non-visual, since a change in visual localization should affect both limbs equally.

Taub et al. (1966) and Bossom and Ommaya (1968) found that fore-limb-deafferented rhesus monkeys can adapt quite significantly to prismatic displacement when allowed only free head movement, but Healy et al. (1973) argued that sources of information about the rear-rangement other than those contingent on movements of the head might have been present. Nevertheless, the finding that eye-hand coordination can be modified in the absence of kinesthetic-proprioceptive feedback suggests that one component of visuomotor prism adaptation is an alteration in motor commands. It is possible that this outflow control mechanism is located in the caudate nucleus since lesions there have been found to markedly reduce visuomotor prism adaptation in monkeys (Bossom, 1965). Therefore, the combina-tion of forelimb deafferentation and destruction of the caudate nuclei should leave an animal unable to adapt to visual rearrangement or, for that matter, to coordinate eye and limb when vision is normal, assum-ing that visual monitoring of the hand is precluded. These predictions were borne out by Bossom and Ommaya (1968), who subjected a monkey to both of these operations.

Miles and Fuller (1974) demonstrated that the rhesus monkey is cap-able of adapting its vestibulo-ocular reflex to the disruption of VPC induced by head movements while exposed to telescopic reduction or magnification. Each of three animals was fitted with the telescopic spectacles and situated in a primate chair that precluded viewing the limbs and body. Exposure lasted for several days and was limited to ad lib movements. In one condition, x.5 reducing spectacles were worn and after 3 days all three monkeys revealed a reduction in vestibulo-ocular reflex gain from preexposure values of .90–1.00 to postexposure values of .60–.70. The results were essentially the same whether the head was rotated during the adaptation test by the experimenter (passive movement) or by the monkey (active movement). No further change in gain occurred beyond the third day of exposure, even when the period was extended to 18 days. Recovery from the change was rather slow, requiring 2–5 days of normal experience in the home cage. Interestingly, one animal whose head was immobilized for 2 weeks following the exposure period revealed little or no recovery of the normal vestibulo-ocular reflex. When wearing x2.0 magnifying spectacles, the reflex *increased* to as much as 1.80 by about the third day of exposure. Recovery took 2–3 days of normal experience and, again, immobilization (for 14 days) preserved the adaptive shift.

Conclusions[4]

The research on nonhuman organisms strongly suggests that, as with learning, the ability to adapt to optical or anatomical rearrangement is positively related to phylogenetic level. Animals less complex than the chicken have yet to demonstrate adaptation, whereas "higher" organisms manifest increased adaptability, the monkey being nearly identical in this respect to human subjects. This fact represents one of the strongest arguments in support of the position that adaptability and learning are closely linked (Chapter 4). Nevertheless, it should not be concluded that it is *impossible* for lower animals, such as amphibia, to adapt to visual rearrangements. Even these organisms might be capable of adaptation if less drastic rearrangements and the institution of special training procedures, such as behavior shaping or the selective administration of rewards and punishments, were used.

Most of the remaining theoretical contributions from the animal research have come from experiments that would not have been ethically or practically possible with human subjects. One example is the research in which visuomotor coordination with rearranged vision has been examined in newborn or very young organisms. These experiments have demonstrated that visual localization and visuomotor coordination are innate for amphibia, chickens, and perhaps cats. Research with the chicken suggests the existence of an adaptive "critical period." Both Hess (1956) and Rossi (e.g., 1968) obtained no adaptation in chicks during the first 4 posthatch days and Pfister (1955) failed to observe adaptation for the adult animal. However, Rossi found that chicks older than 4 posthatch days are able to adapt to a relatively small prismatic displacement, suggesting the beginning of a critical period. On the other hand, it is possible that chicks merely require more than 4 days of prism exposure to adapt and that the reason for the nonadaptability of adults of this species is that they have yet to be provided with the appropriate conditions. The existence of a critical period for adaptation has important theoretical implications, and this issue merits further, direct investigation.

---

[4] Because this chapter is devoted to two major topics that do not share much common ground, the format will depart from that of the other chapters by omitting the "Summary and Conclusions" section normally found at the end. Instead, the overall conclusions will be drawn for each of the two topics separately.

A second instance where animal subjects have advanced our knowledge of adaptation to perceptual rearrangement and "normal" perception is in testing questions about physiological mechanisms. Taub et al. (1966), Bossom and Ommaya (1968), and Taub, Goldberg, and Taub (1975) have demonstrated that monkeys can coordinate movements rather well when all kinesthetic–proprioceptive feedback from the forelimbs has been abolished. Furthermore, prism adaptation may occur with and be demonstrated by these deafferented limbs. This suggests that exposure to the visual effects of head movements can lead to new motor outflow instructions, although one cannot rule out the possibility of a shift in felt head (or eye) position.

With regard to the loci of the brain involved in adaptation, the results of several animal experiments have suggested that the caudate nuclei and cerebella are crucial for visuomotor prism adaptation and the vestibulocerebellum for adaptation to the loss of VPC.

Experiments with "split-brain" and normal monkeys have demonstrated (a) that the locus of adaptation for exposure conditions of the type used in these experiments is in the exposed limb and (b) that direct communication between the hemispheres is not necessary for normal eye–hand coordination.

In studying the adaptability of nonhuman subjects, there is still the problem of specifying the adaptive end product. When compensatory changes in visuomotor coordination are obtained for animals, it is usually unclear if this modification represents a change in vision, body position sense, or visuomotor behavior. Only the experiments (e.g., Hamilton, 1967) in which the presence of intermanual transfer was assessed (and found lacking) have provided evidence, albeit indirect, relevant to the nature of the adaptive end state. Rock (1975, p. 474) has suggested that, for animals less advanced than human beings and the lower primates, adaptive changes in visuomotor coordination may be taken as evidence that visual adaptation has occurred. He finds it difficult to believe that a "lower" animal could ever come to coordinate its vision and motor behavior during optical (or anatomical) rearrangement and yet continue to misperceive the location of objects. Thus, it is possible that the motor behavior of animals less advanced than the monkey may be completely dominated by apparent visual locus. If true, this would mean that the visuomotor adaptation demonstrated by chicks (e.g., Rossi, 1968) and kittens (Bishop, 1959) is indicative of visual change. It is necessary to obtain *direct* measures of visual adaptation before this conclusion can be confirmed, but such measures are not easily implemented with animals. While human subjects who have been exposed to prismatic displacement can simply be instructed on the task of setting a luminous target to apparent straight ahead, animals would first require extensive training. Even then, one would have to determine that the animals did not forget the task over the course of the experiment, thereby invalidating the pre–post measures of adaptation.

Assuming that nonhuman subjects can be assessed unambiguously for visual adaptation, a potentially informative experiment may be suggested. As was seen in Chapter 5, the evidence that human beings can adapt visually to inverted vision is rather scanty and equivocal. One explanation for this finding may be that, for practical or ethical reasons, the inverting spectacles have not been worn for a sufficiently long period of time. However, this limitation would not pertain for an animal subject. For example, if inverting spectacles were attached securely to the head of a monkey and the animal were allowed unrestricted activity for an indefinitely long period of time (years, if necessary), it might be possible eventually to demonstrate the occurrence of apparent reinversion of the field by means of a direct measure of visual orientation. One way of doing this would be first to use rewards and punishments to rigorously train the animal to distinguish visually between upright and inverted objects. The same discrimination could then be tested at the outset of the inverted vision exposure period and periodically thereafter. Naturally, the reward and punishment contingencies would no longer obtain. At the outset of the exposure period, the animal would be expected to make an objectively incorrect choice between the upright and inverted test objects, reaching for the one that had been associated with punishment during the discrimination training period. However, if the animal eventually came to choose consistently the appropriately oriented object, it might be concluded that the visual field had once again come to look upright. One could also test for a visual aftereffect after removing the inverting spectacles. Perhaps an adventuresome investigator will someday attempt such an experiment.

INDIVIDUAL DIFFERENCES IN HUMAN SUBJECTS

The bane of perceptual researchers seeking statistically significant main effects is the large within-group variance associated with most perceptual tasks. This is a serious problem for research on adaptation to perceptual rearrangement, and it is rare to find an experiment that has not attempted to deal with it by means of some form of screening or training procedure. For example, subjects have often been dropped from experiments for demonstrating excessive variability or inaccuracy on the preexposure measures (e.g., Kennedy, 1969; Wallach & Floor, 1970; Wallach & Karsh, 1963b). There are also cases where subjects have been eliminated from the final sample for failing to experience the distortion initially (e.g., Epstein, 1968) or for showing little or no adaptation (e.g., Redding, 1975b). The result of these procedures is the creation of artificially homogeneous groups, leading to a lowered within-group variance and therefore an increased chance of detecting differences between group means.

An alternative to labeling within-group variance in adaptation studies a nuisance is to entertain the possibility that this variability may provide us with a better understanding of adaptation and of perception in general. It may prove theoretically fruitful to determine the proportion of the within-group variance that is truly random (i.e., "error") and the proportion that is lawfully related to specifiable subject characteristics (i.e., "between-subjects variance"). An examination of the latter form of variability may provide some important insights. First, however, it should be determined if there is, in fact, a "trait" of adaptability.

Evidence for Intrasubject Reliability in Adaptation

Do subjects show consistent individual differences in adaptation? There is little published evidence directly relevant to this question. However, the results of one experiment suggest that a *general* trait of adaptability does not exist. Redding (1973b) found a correlation of essentially zero between visual adaptation to prismatic displacement and visual adaptation to optical tilt. Thus, it appears that the issue should be whether or not there exists a long-term trait of adaptability to a particular type of perceptual rearrangement. A few experiments have reported the test–retest correlation for subjects exposed to the same optical rearrangement in separate sessions. Redding (1973a) found that two tests of visual adaptation to prismatic displacement, taken 2 days apart, produced a reliability coefficient of .74, whereas the test–retest correlation for adaptation to optical tilt was .76. Mack (1967) also found a high intrasubject correlation (.78) for tilt adaptation when comparing subjects' performances in active- and passive-movement conditions, occurring 2 days apart. Thus, Redding's and Mack's results support the existence of a relatively stable trait of adaptability for both lateral displacement and optical tilt. Welch et al. (1974) measured subjects on prism adaptation in two different sessions, separated by a 1-week interval. Adaptation—as measured by the

visuomotor negative aftereffect, proprioceptive shift, and visual shift—
produced test–retest correlations of .68, .77, and .75, respectively.
Finally, in an experiment to be described shortly, Kottenhoff (1957)
calculated a split-half reliability coefficient of .83 for adaptation to the
loss of VPC during head movement while wearing right/left-reversing
spectacles.

Personality Traits and Adaptation

The preceding observations suggest that adult human subjects are
reasonably consistent over time in their adaptability to a given form of
perceptual rearrangement, so it is legitimate to ask if the magnitude of
a person's adaptation is correlated with other subject characteristics.
However, a distinction should be made between (a) traits related to
the behavior in which the subject engages during the exposure period
and/or the tests of adaptation and (b) traits related to his "inherent"
adaptability. An example of the first of these is the way that subjects
respond to the instruction to point at a target during exposure to prismatic displacement. Welch (unpublished data) and Warren and Platt
(1974) reported that some of their subjects chose to point at the
apparent position of the target, even after discovering that this led to
errors, whereas others would make a very deliberate correction after
the first few errors had revealed the nature of the rearrangement.
Welch (unpublished data) also found that "image pointers" adapted
significantly less than "object pointers." Another example of this type
of subject characteristic was observed by Warren and Platt (1975). They
found that, when confronted with a condition of continuous prismatic
exposure, some subjects would visually track the hand as it moved
toward the target, whereas others kept their eyes on the target
throughout the response, which placed them in what was functionally
a condition of terminal display. Furthermore, Warren and Platt found
that the number of saccadic eye movements made by the subject during exposure was negatively correlated with the amount of visual
adaptation.

Thus, one of the general sources of the observed variability of
adaptation scores may be the manner in which the subject performs
the exposure and/or test tasks, rather than actual differences in
adaptability. This general source of between-subjects variability is
likely to be amenable to experimental control. For example, instead of
letting subjects decide for themselves how to go about the job of
pointing at a target during exposure, the experimenter could require
that they all conform to a particular strategy.

The second category of subject characteristic consists of those traits that are *directly* related to adaptability. For example, it might be discovered that subjects who adapt especially quickly or fully also tend to be particularly "flexible," according to some written test. This type of trait is less likely to be experimentally manipulable, but it is useful to see if such correlates exist. Not only will this knowledge help to explain a certain proportion of the within-group variance, but it may lead to a better understanding of the nature of adaptation.

Several experiments have searched for correlations between personality traits and perceptual adaptation. Kottenhoff (1957) exposed 12 subjects for 3 hr to right/left-reversing spectacles and measured adaptation to the resulting loss of VPC. He found a highly significant correlation (.72) between level of adaptation and degree of introversion–extroversion, as measured by the R ("rhathymia") scale of Guilford's (1940) test. Introverted subjects experienced an *increase* in the illusory motion of the visual field, whereas the more extroverted subjects showed either no change or a decrease.

Melamed, Wallace, Cohen, and Oakes (1972) found an r of −.70 between field dependence–independence, as measured by the rod and frame test, and magnitude of the "immediate correction effect," which is the tendency, when exposed to a prismatically displaced, visually structured field, to perceive from the outset much less of an optical shift than would be predicted from the prism strength (see Chapter 3, pp. 45–46). The negative correlation obtained by Melamed *et al.* signifies that the greater the field dependence, the less the correction effect. This result seems counterintuitive, however. One would expect that since the correction effect results from the presence of a structured visual surround, field-dependent subjects would be more, rather than less, susceptible to it.

In our laboratory, Heinrich (1975) exposed subjects to prismatic displacement involving terminal exposure with targets and measured the resulting adaptation in terms of the visuomotor negative aftereffect, proprioceptive shift, visual shift, and reduction in target-pointing error during exposure. Subjects were also given a battery of personality tests: the California Psychological Inventory (CPI; Gough, 1957), the Trait Anxiety Scale (Spielberger, Gorsuch, & Lushene, 1968), the Achievement Anxiety Test (Alpert & Haber, 1960), the Tennessee Self-Concept Scale (Fitts, 1965), the Internal–External Locus of Control of Reinforcement Test (I–E Scale; Rotter, 1966); and the Extroversion Scale (Eysenck, 1965). The results of this experiment were quite complex and do not summarize well. In general, very few of the many personality dimensions measured appeared to be related to prism adaptability, and those relationships obtained were never very strong.

Wallace, Melamed, Cohen, and Oakes, in an unpublished experiment, measured both the immediate correction effect to 11° prismatic displacement and the visuomotor adaptation resulting from active arm movement in a Held-type exposure situation. Subjects were also given the I–E scale and McDonald's (1970) scale of ambiguity tolerance. The immediate correction effect measures were taken on one day and the adaptation and personality measures on the next. Subjects showed both an immediate correction effect and a visuomotor negative aftereffect, but neither of these effects correlated significantly with either of the personality measures and the latter were not correlated with each other.

An unpublished experiment[5] from our laboratory measured prism adaptation to 20-diopter displacement for field-independent, "intermediate," and field-dependent groups, as defined by performance on the rod and frame test. The mean constant errors (out of a possible 28°) in rod setting for the three groups were 1.8, 10.7, and 18.9°. Adaptation was measured in terms of reduction in target-pointing errors during exposure, visuomotor negative aftereffect, and shift in felt limb position. No difference between the groups was observed on any of the measures, although there was a nonsignificant tendency for magnitude of the errors on the first few prism-exposure trials to be positively related to degree of field dependence.

With a few exceptions (e.g., Kottenhoff, 1957), the evidence does not show a relationship between adaptation and personality traits. However, the experiment by Melamed et al. (1972), which found a high correlation between performance on the rod and frame test and the immediate correction effect, suggests that it may be fruitful to look for correlates of adaptation among the subject's "perceptual traits," rather than his "gross" personality characteristics.

"Perceptual Traits" and Adaptation

In two rather extensive experiments by Warren and Platt (1974, 1975), subjects were administered a battery of perceptual and perceptual–motor pretests that included the abilities to (a) engage in accurate and smooth eye placement or tracking (eye measures); (b) point accurately at fixed or moving targets with each of the unseen hands (pointing measures); and (c) assess accurately and smoothly the position of the unseen limbs on the basis of their felt position (hand measures). In the same testing period, subjects were exposed to 10°

[5] With the assistance of Michael Nardie, of the University of Kansas.

prismatic displacement. Exposure involved terminal display in one study and concurrent display in the other; a target was provided in both cases. The primary measure of adaptation was the pre-post shift in target-pointing accuracy with the prism in place (i.e., the reduction of effect). Although only the right hand was exposed, both limbs were measured for signs of adaptation.

In the terminal exposure experiment large and significant adaptation was found for the right hand, 50% of which transferred to the left hand. More important, it was found that a significant proportion of the variance of the right and left hand adaptation scores could be attributed to the pretest measures. For right-hand adaptation, the better the subject's felt limb position sense (hand measures), the less adaptation occurred, whereas the better the visual sense (eye measures), the more the adaptation. When intermanual transfer (proportion of left- to right-hand shift) was the dependent variable, these correlations were found to be just the reverse. Warren and Platt explained their results by assuming that the terminal prism exposure had led to both a change in felt position of the exposed limb and a change in vision, the latter serving as the basis for the observed intermanual transfer. They argued that if a subject has good control over his eyes, he will resist changes in vision and consequently reveal little intermanual transfer. Instead, his adaptation will be primarily in the form of a shift in felt limb position sense and therefore occur as a large right-hand shift. On the other hand, if a subject possesses an especially accurate and precise felt limb position sense, he will reveal relatively little right-hand adaptation, but most of it will transfer to the other limb, indicating that it is based primarily on a change in vision. Unfortunately, the investigators failed to obtain direct measures of the presumed felt position and visual shifts.

Warren and Platt's strategy of taking measures of various perceptual and perceptual–motor capacities as potential subject correlates of prism adaptation appears promising. One such "trait," suggested by Cegalis (1971), is the magnitude of experienced distortion when the rearranging device is first worn. That is, an important source of intersubject variability in adaptation may be the variability in extent of *perceived* distortion.[6]

Further experiments involving a "microanalysis" of the relevant behaviors, such as Warren and Platt have performed, would be useful, not only with respect to adaptation to perceptual rearrangement but possibly for other perceptual capacities as well. It should be

---

[6] Wallach et al. (1963) found just such a relationship with telestereoscopic distortion.

emphasized again that the goal of this undertaking is not merely to document the existence of individual differences but, more important, to gain a better understanding of the nature of perception and adaptation. For example, Warren and Platt's experiments have provided further evidence in support of the two-component model of prism adaptation (see Chapter 3, pp. 71–72) and of Canon and Uhlarik's directed attention hypothesis of the adaptive end product (Canon, 1966, 1970, 1971; Uhlarik & Canon, 1971). The latter, as will be recalled from Chapter 3 (pp. 75–77), proposes that whether adaptation will be in the form of a change of vision or of felt limb position depends upon the individual subject's relative dependence on the two modalities. Finally, the delineation of perceptual correlates to adaptability may ultimately lead to attempts to *manipulate* these capacities. For example, it might be feasible to train subjects to be more precise in their limb positioning. Given that there is a *causal* relation between this capacity and adaptation, subjects trained in this manner should reveal a reduced level of adaptation in the hand and an increase in the eye.

Other Subject Characteristics

SEX AND AGE

A number of investigators of adaptation to perceptual rearrangement (e.g., Hay, 1971; Lotto et al., 1967) have used subject's sex as one factor in the design. However, this factor has rarely been found to be the basis of a significant main effect.

Relatively few studies have compared the effect of different age groups on adaptability. Smith and Greene (1963), using a television monitor to provide normal, reversed, inverted, or reversed and inverted visual feedback from the subject's hand, found evidence for a "critical period" in the ability to perform adequately. They reported that only 1 out of 15 subjects aged 9, 10, and 11 years was able to perform all of the various tasks (e.g., drawing a triangle) under the four exposure conditions, whereas only 10 of 21 of the 12- and 13-year-olds failed on one or more of the tasks. However, as Howard and Templeton (1966, p. 375) point out, it is not clear if the children in the younger age groups were capable of drawing upside down or reversed (or both) figures *without* visual distortion. Consequently, these data represent equivocal support for a developmental trend in adaptability.

A series of experiments by Smothergill et al. (1971) also used closed-circuit video feedback as the source of visual rearrangement. In one experiment, groups of 7-, 9-, and 11-year-olds and adults were compared on pattern-tracing tasks under conditions of 0, 30, 60, 90, 120, 150, and 180° visual rotation. The dependent variables were errors and elapsed time to complete a pattern. All groups experienced difficulty with rotations of 90° or greater. However, beyond 120°, performance began to improve, especially for the adults. In fact, the adults were almost as good with the 180° as with the 0° rotation. The investigators suggested that this reversal in performance signaled the presence of a strategy, such as attempting to do just the opposite of what vision indicated. It is reasonable to suppose that older subjects would be more capable of this insight and better able to act on it. This general result was replicated in a second experiment, which found greater improvement at the 180° rotation for a group with an average age of 15.5 years than for a group of 12.5 years. In a third experiment, using adult subjects only, rotation was gradually and continuously increased during the exposure period and no improvement with the larger rotations occurred, suggesting that reversals in performance were manifestations of a strategy and that only with abrupt, obvious distortions could such a strategy be elicited.

The results from video feedback experiments are probably not directly relevant to adaptation, for the reasons given in Chapter 5 (pp. 112–113). To reiterate, it is not likely that subjects confronted with this form of rearrangement acquire a semipermanent change in visuomotor behavior or of perception that is measurable in other situations or as an aftereffect.

Thus, the meager data on age trends and adaptation to visual rearrangement presented thus far have been limited to situations in which it is unclear that genuine adaptation has taken place. It seems more likely that what these experiments measured was the ability to correct consciously for the distortion. Thus, the results lead to the not too surprising conclusion that there is an improvement with age in the ability to "figure out" how to compensate for rearranged vision.

Only a handful of experiments have examined the relation between age and performance using a paradigm and measures designed to induce and reveal *genuine* adaptation. The first systematic attempt to discern age trends in adaptation to perceptual rearrangement appears to have been by Giannitrapani (1958). He reported a decline with increasing age (6 to 21 years) in adaptation to size distortions (cf. Chapter 8) for both males and females and a decline in adaptation to optical tilt (cf. Chapter 6) for males only.

There appears to be no relationship between age and adaptation to prismatic displacement. Howard and Templeton (1966, p. 376) mentioned observing prism adaptation in a group of 4-year-olds, but no other details were provided. The implication was that the adaptability of this young group was no different than that of adult subjects. Pick and Hay (1966b) measured both proprioceptive and visual adaptive shifts after 15 min of very active prism exposure in children aged 9, 13, or 16 years and found no differences among the three groups. Finally, Wallace and Anstadt (1974), using 6-, 11-, and 18-year-olds, also failed to obtain an age trend for prism adaptation.

It appears that the ability to adapt to visual rearrangement is present in human beings at least as early as 4 years of age and, with the possible exception of the experiment by Giannitrapani, this capacity is not subject to developmental change. However, it is possible that clearcut age trends in adaptability may yet be discovered, particularly if very young (or, for that matter, very old) subjects are examined.

MENTAL ILLNESS

Several experiments have examined the adaptability associated with different categories of mental illness. Jaensch and Mandowsky (1932) found that normal ("integrated") subjects adapted to prism-induced curvature more quickly and revealed greater aftereffects than did mentally disturbed ("disintegrated") subjects. Eysenck, Granger, and Brengelmann (1957) reported a study in which visual adaptation to 15 min of exposure to binocular prismatic curvature was found to be greater for "normals" than for neurotics, with psychotics the least adaptable of all, although no tests were reported to indicate if these group differences were statistically significant. Eysenck et al. did not find a difference among the groups in terms of initially experienced curvature. A second test measured eye–hand coordination and entailed the rather unusual task of dropping darts on a target. Although Kranz (cited by Eysenck et al., 1957) had reported a positive correlation between ability on this task and degree of "personality integration," Eysenck et al. found no difference in adaptation among their three groups. However, normals did demonstrate significantly less initial error than did the other two groups, a finding that makes the failure to find a difference in pre–post shifts ambiguous.

There is evidence to suggest that schizophrenics are deficient in the integration of vision and felt limb position, but not in either of these modalities alone (e.g., McGhie, Chapman, & Lawson, 1965). On this basis, Ebner, Broekema, and Ritzler (1971) predicted less adaptation after 2 min of prism exposure in a Held-type condition for a group of nonorganic schizophrenics than for a nonschizophrenic group. The results supported the investigators' hypothesis: The normals adapted significantly, whereas the schizophrenics did not. It seems unlikely, on the basis of other observations in this study, that the failure of the latter group to adapt was due to inattention, confusion, or an inability to understand the instructions.

BRAIN DAMAGE

Several experiments have involved an examination of the potential relationship between brain damage in human patients and adaptability to rearrangement. Meier and French (1966) compared patients with right versus left temporal lobectomies on a drawing accuracy task while looking through Dove prisms that were set to produce optical rotation in either direction and by varying amounts. In general, no differences in the performance of the two groups were observed. However, when subjects were divided into two groups in terms of the presence or absence of extratemporal spike activity (indicating involvement outside the excised area), differences were found. Irrespective of ablation laterality, the presence of extratemporal spike foci was associated with poorer initial performance on the drawing task and less subsequent adaptation on some of the rotations.

Meier (1970) tested patients with left-hemisphere impairment, patients with right-hemisphere impairment, and non–brain-damaged controls on ability to place the 10 forms of the Seguin–Goddard Form Board. This task was performed either with direct vision or when looking at a television screen under conditions of (a) normal visual orientation; (b) right/left reversal; or (c) inversion. Performance for each hand was measured separately. Response time for the limb contralateral to the lesion was found to be retarded for both hemisphere groups with respect to the inverted and the reversed TV pictures. However, contralateral impairment was greater when it was the right (nondominant) hemisphere that was damaged. These data may or may not be indicative of genuine adaptation, due to the limitations of the video feedback technique.

Welch and Goldstein (1972) compared brain-damaged, psychiatric, and normal groups on prism adaptability, using an exposure condition entailing terminal display and a target. Adaptation was measured in terms of the visuomotor negative aftereffect and proprioceptive shift. The brain-damaged group included patients with damage in a variety of loci and from various causes, whereas the psychiatric group consisted of hospitalized patients suffering from a range of nonorganic mental disturbances. No difference was found among the groups in terms of proprioceptive shift. However, the brain-damaged group showed significantly less visuomotor negative aftereffect than either of the remaining two groups. For the latter groups, negative aftereffect was larger than proprioceptive shift, whereas for the brain-damaged group the two measures were equal. It was concluded from these results that brain-damaged individuals are, in general, unable to acquire the assimilated target-pointing corrective response that, if it occurred, would add with proprioceptive shift to produce a large visuomotor negative aftereffect.[7] In a supplementary analysis it was found that patients with frontal damage adapted, on both measures, as much as non-brain-damaged subjects. This finding raises some questions about Teuber's (1961, 1964) suggestion, and the conclusion drawn from a number of previously cited animal studies (e.g., Baizer & Glickstein, 1973), that the frontal lobes are involved in adaptation.

Conclusions

The ease with which a subject adapts to perceptual rearrangement is not generally related to sex, age, or performance on written or other tests of personality. With a few exceptions, only such basic subject characteristics as mental illness and certain kinds of brain damage appear to be related to adaptability. For the researcher, these results mean that the control of "gross" subject characteristics will have little or no effect on the error term of his statistical analysis of the data. From a theoretical orientation, the adaptive process has been shown to be a relatively noncognitive event, essentially unrelated to the "higher" brain processes presumably associated with personality characteristics. On the other hand, it is clear from the work by Warren and Platt that adaptability *is* closely linked to subjects' capabilities on tasks that tap the basic perceptual and perceptual–motor components upon which adaptation is based. It is to be hoped that this fact will spur further research of this type, leading both to the ability to reduce within-group variance and to a better understanding of adaptation and perception.

---

[7] No measures of visual shift were taken, since previous experiments in our laboratory using this particular form of exposure had failed to obtain this component of prism adaptation.

12

Adaptation to
Underwater Distortions

The recent entry of man into outer space has brought to public awareness the fact that human perception is subject to disruption and error when confronted with an environment for which it has not been prepared by evolution. However, it is the perceptual consequences of another exotic environment—the "inner space" beneath the oceans— that has received much greater experimental attention (cf. Adolfson & Berghage, 1974; Ross, 1971; Woods & Lythgoe, 1971). It is probably safe to say that every one of the underwater observer's sensory modalities is altered in some way. Sounds reach his ears much more quickly than in air, whereas his ability to localize them is attenuated, although by no means destroyed (e.g., Feinstein, 1966). Gravitational and kinesthetic–proprioceptive cues are also greatly affected (Ross, Crickmar, Sills, & Owen, 1969; Ross & Rejman, 1972; Ross, Rejman, & Lennie, 1972). However, vision is distorted the most and has been the subject of the majority of experiments on underwater perception.

The aim of this chapter is to review the growing body of knowledge on the diver's initial and subsequent visual experiences under water. As we shall see, he is confronted with a multitude of visual distortions, many of which are similar or identical to those that have been experimentally induced in the laboratory by means of prisms and lenses. The questions of primary interest to us are whether and to what extent the diver is capable of adapting to these effects. First, let us determine precisely what these distortions are.

VARIETIES OF UNDERWATER OPTICAL DISTORTION

The optical effects of an underwater environment are quite complex and involve many variables, including the type of diving equipment worn, relative clarity of the water, and direction of view. The naked eye when submerged in water is quite far-sighted, because the refractive index of water is very nearly the same as that of the aqueous humor behind the cornea. Thus, only the lens remains to focus the light rays, but since it has a relatively low refractive power, it causes the image to be focused at a theoretical point well behind the retina. Consequently, underwater visual acuity for the naked eye is poor, even in very clear water (e.g., Baddeley, 1971; Luria & Kinney, 1969). Wearing goggles or a diving mask solves this problem by reinstating the interface of air and cornea. Contact lenses especially designed for underwater use are a third alternative (e.g., Faust & Beckman, 1966), but they are expensive, require individual fitting, and have proven rather uncomfortable.

Thus, protective devices may be used to reestablish the normal point of focus on the retina. However, the abutment of water and the air trapped within the goggles or face mask has the unfortunate consequence of introducing a new set of optical distortions. Since the refractive index of water is about four thirds that of air, visual objects become located optically at about three quarters of their physical distance and produce a retinal image about four thirds the size of the image that would occur in air.[1] This situation is shown in Figure 12.1. Furthermore, the degree of refraction of light rays increases as a function of the angle of incidence. This causes objects on a given side of the visual field to be displaced optically farther in that direction, thereby increasing the magnification of an object whose edges extend into the visual periphery. For example, a large square when viewed head-on through the face mask produces an especially enlarged image, the sides of which are bowed inward, whereas the center is displaced away from the observer, much like an inverted pincushion (see Figure 12.2).

Perhaps a more troublesome consequence of the diving mask or goggles is the reduction in the size of the visual field—sometimes by

[1] This assumes that the glass of the diving mask is relatively thin and that the eyes are placed directly against it. Since in practice the eyes are usually about 2 in. back, the optical distortion is somewhat less. Here the magnification factor is about 1.27 for nearby objects, compared to 1.33 at the glass–air interface or for distant objects. A more detailed discussion of these optical considerations has been provided by Southall (1933, Chapter 4).

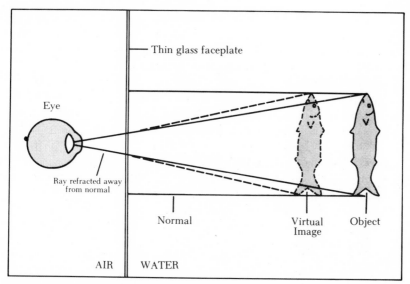

Figure 12.1. The optical effect of viewing an object under water through a face mask. (From H. E. Ross. Water, fog and the size–distance invariance hypothesis. *British Journal of Psychology,* 1967, *58,* 301–313. Reprinted by permission of Cambridge University Press.)

as much as 50% (Workman & Prickett, 1957). A large field is not necessarily an advantage, however, because of the increased optical curvature and displacement in the periphery.

Another effect, which occurs whether or not a diving mask is worn, is the attenuation or elimination of certain light frequencies due to the absorptive characteristics of the water. As one descends into the

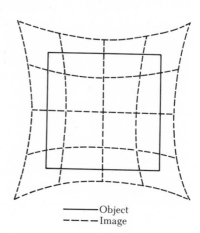

Figure 12.2. The "pincushion effect" of increased optical distortion in the periphery of the visual field when viewed under water through a face mask.

very clear water of some oceans and lakes, selective absorption of light occurs, progressing from the relatively low-energy long wavelengths (e.g., red) toward the shorter ones. Such waters appear blue or blue-green, since this portion of the spectrum is least subject to absorption. In murky water, the wavelengths that are most absorbed depend largely upon the nature of the contaminant. For example, in coastal water, plankton and the yellow substances from decaying vegetable matter combine with the water itself to absorb both red and blue wavelengths and to reflect green. The wavelengths of light that are least absorbed give a body of water its characteristic hue. Whether water is clear or murky, the overall illumination is reduced with increasing depth.

A final, but very important, underwater optical effect is the attenuation of figure–ground contrast, due to the reduced illumination and the scatter of light by suspended particles. The magnitude of this effect is a direct function of the turbidity of the water and viewing distance.

These are the major optical effects to which the underwater observer wearing goggles or a diving mask is exposed. Let us now see how these distortions and deprivations actually affect perception.

VISUAL EXPERIENCE UNDER WATER

Color Distortions

Controlled observations indicate that the selective filtering of light frequencies by water of varying degrees of clarity and depth has the predictable effects on color vision. Kinney, Luria, and Weitzman (1967, 1969) reported that under normal illumination well-saturated blue and green test objects are difficult to perceive as such in a water background of high turbidity, whereas oranges and reds are quite noticeable. On the other hand, these latter hues are difficult to see in the depths of very clear water, whereas blue becomes visible. When it is said that a hue is no longer visible it means either that the test object appears black or that it has taken on the color of the background light.

These effects on color vision are precisely those that are expected, since if the wavelengths normally reflected by an object have been absorbed, no light will be left for the object to reflect. Only objects that reflect at least some frequencies of visible radiation not absorbed by the water will be seen as colored.[2] This is not to say that they will necessarily be seen in their normal (air) color. For example, blood, which in air reflects a little green light and a great deal of red, will appear red in very clear water only when near the surface; at lower depths it will change to green and finally to black.

A number of steps have been taken to minimize these underwater color distortions. For example, it is useful to apply fluorescent paints to submerged man-made objects. These pigments absorb high-energy short-wave light in water and reemit it as long-wave light, thereby producing bright, highly saturated greens, oranges, and reds that remain perceptually "true" under many different water conditions, particularly at short viewing distances (e.g., Kinney, Luria, & Weitzman, 1967, 1969).

It is clear that in many situations the diver's color vision is distorted or disrupted. Although color constancy and a certain amount of rapid adaptation may occur (e.g., Ross, 1975a, p. 53), serious difficulties in spectral sensitivity and discrimination remain even for the experienced diver.

Distortion of Size and Distance

One of the most commonly reported underwater visual distortions is an increase in the apparent size of objects. Divers often bring to the surface what they believe to be a prize fish or lobster only to discover that their catch is of quite ordinary dimensions. The perception of underwater distance is also distorted but this effect is probably less salient to the diver. A great deal of research has been directed to underwater size–distance distortions and the results reveal that this problem is very complicated.

First, it is necessary to differentiate between "near" and "far" distances, a distinction involving the clarity of the water. On the basis of evidence to be discussed below, "near" may be defined as 2 to 6 ft. in murky water and up to 50 ft. in very clear water. It has been suggested by Woodley and Ross (1969) that the "crossover point" between "near" and "far" in a given body of water is in the region of half its total range of visibility.

---

[2] Actually, it is only if sufficient light is being reflected from the area of the spectrum in which a given object's *transition* from almost complete light absorption to high reflectance occurs that the object will appear in its characteristic hue. Otherwise, it will look white or pale gray (Lythgoe, 1971).

Controlled observations of size and distance perception in the range of near distance indicate that objects appear to the diver to be both larger and closer than they actually are (Ross, 1967b). Even when near objects are grasped, while they are being viewed, their true size may not be detected (Kinney & Luria, 1970), an example of underwater "visual capture." Naturally, visuomotor behavior with respect to such objects is often in error. Attempts to reach for objects tend to fall short initially and, for objects in the periphery, to err to one side (e.g., Ono & O'Reilly, 1971; Ross & Lennie, 1972). This disruption of eye–hand coordination is an important factor contributing to the reported performance losses on tests of underwater dexterity (e.g., Bowen, Andersen, & Promisel, 1966).

Although it is commonly supposed that the enlarged appearance of underwater objects is due to the magnification of the image by the face mask, this explanation is insufficient. As Ross (1967a) noted, the four-thirds increase in the retinal image is accompanied by a one-quarter decrease in optical distance.[3] If the observer perceives the magnified image as located at its optically foreshortened distance, and assuming that the size–distance invariance principle (apparent size = retinal size × apparent distance) holds under water, size constancy will be in effect. The object should appear to be closer but not larger than it is, since the increase in optical size is exactly offset by the decrease in optical distance. However, as was just noted, an object at a "near" distance tends to appear somewhat magnified under water and Ross (1967a) has demonstrated that this is due to the fact that the observer perceives the object as located at greater than its *optical* distance, although still less than its *physical* distance. In one of Ross's experiments, subjects who were submerged in a swimming bath were required to adjust the distance of a disk until it appeared to be 4 ft. from the nose, after having previously been trained to make such a judgment on land. If the subjects' underwater perception had been

---

[3] Ross assumed that this decrease in optical distance follows automatically from the fact that if an object of fixed size were caused to produce a four-thirds increase in retinal size, it would have to have been brought closer to the observer by one-quarter of the original distance. However, it has been argued by Ono, O'Reilly, and Herman (1970) that it would be necessary for the observer to be aware of the true size of an object for its retinal size to serve as a cue to absolute distance. They suggested instead that the underestimation of the object's physical distance when seen through a face mask is due to the cues of increased convergence and accommodation required by the greater divergence of the light rays caused by the water–glass–air interface. Despite this difference in interpretation, the concept of optical distance will be retained in this discussion.

veridical, they would have set the disk at 4 ft., whereas if they had correctly perceived the optical foreshortening produced by the face mask, they would have set the disk at about 5 ft., to make it appear to be 4 ft. away. The subjects' mean setting was found to be 4 ft. 5 in., part way between the optical and physical distances. On the basis of the size–distance invariance principle, such an overestimation of an object's optical (or physical) distance will lead to an increase in its apparent size, which, as mentioned in Chapter 8 (p. 181), appears to be the basis for the well-known "moon illusion" (Kaufman & Rock, 1962). In another experiment, Ross found that although relatively experienced divers overestimated both the size and the optical distance of various objects under water, the ratios of each of these to the corresponding estimate for objects on land were not the same. Underwater size was not overestimated by quite as much as would have been expected from the observed overestimation of distance. Thus, for reasons that are not clear, a precise adherence to size–distance invariance was not found to hold under water.

There are several reasons why optical distance is overestimated under water, the most important being the reduction in brightness contrast. Even in very clear water the reduced illumination and diffusion of light cause an attenuation of brightness or color contrast, in the same way that mist or haze produces "aerial perspective" on land. In either case, the poor contrast of objects with their background (or, perhaps more important, the unusually steep *gradient* of decreasing brightness contrast with distance) causes them to appear more distant than they are.[4] Compounding this source of misperceived distance is the fact that stereopsis is poor when brightness contrast is attenuated (e.g., Fry, Bridgman, & Ellerbrock, 1949). In addition, Luria (1969) found evidence that suggested that the marked reduction of stereoscopic acuity found even in very clear water is due, at least in part, to the relative absence of peripheral visual stimulation. Finally, Luria and Kinney (1968) showed that another possible reason that underwater objects are generally seen at greater than their optical distance is that they are often being viewed in a rather empty, visually homogeneous field—much like a *Ganzfeld*. In a control study in air they demonstrated that, as the number of objects in the field of view was

[4] This may not be the case for very short distances (e.g., 1–2 ft.) in very clear water. Here, in fact, optical and perceived distances are nearly identical (e.g., Ferris, 1972b; Ono et al., 1970). However, it is still true that one's hands or other body parts may appear enlarged. Ross (1975a, p. 57) has suggested that this may be due to feeling them to be at greater than their optical distance and/or seeing them to be larger than they feel.

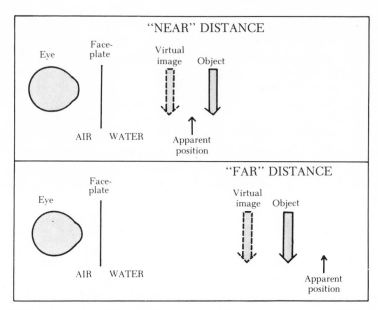

Figure 12.3. A comparison of the apparent position (distance) of an object viewed under water through a face mask when the object is located at "near" or "far" distance.

reduced, a test stimulus at a fixed distance was seen as progressively farther away.

When objects are located at a far distance, as defined by the clarity of the water, they continue to appear magnified to the diver, but now they look farther away than they really are (Ross, 1967a).[5] This may seem contradictory to the case with near objects, but actually it is not. What seems to be happening is that the various factors that lead to overestimation of the optical distance of near objects become so powerful at greater distances that the error extends beyond even the physical distance of the object. Figure 12.3 attempts to clarify this situation by comparing the perceived location (denoted by the thin arrow) of an object in clear water at a near versus a far distance.

Much of the research on size and distance perception in water has used unfamiliar objects as test stimuli. Woodley and Ross (1969)

---

[5] Apparently, many training manuals for skin divers inform the reader, quite incorrectly, that underwater objects always appear *closer* than they are (Kinney, personal communication, 1975). Perhaps this error stems from the assumption that if an object looks unusually large it must be closer, as is true when an object is brought physically nearer to the observer.

demonstrated, for moderately experienced divers, that the perceived distance of familiar objects (beer bottles) was nearly as accurate underwater as in the air, whereas the distance of unfamiliar objects (white squares) was underestimated (relative to the *physical* distance) when at a near distance and overestimated when at a far distance, in line with the preceding analysis. Thus, it appears that remembered size can override the underwater size illusion that would otherwise occur.

Interestingly, underwater distance perception in the vertical dimension appears to differ from that in the horizontal. Ross, King, and Snowden (1970) found that downward distances were estimated fairly accurately, whereas upward distances were significantly *underesti*-mated, and increasingly so the farther away the test object. Clearly, the latter effect has serious implications for the diver. These results may be due to the relative lack of depth cues in the vertical dimension, as compared to the number present in the horizontal direction, as well as to better figure–ground contrast in the former situation. Anecdotal reports indicate that such underestimation is accompanied by a *reduction* in the apparent size of objects (Ross, King, & Snowden, 1970), as the size–distance invariance principle would predict.

Illusory Visual Motion

The misperception of size and distance has an effect on perceived motion. Underwater objects, seen as farther away than they are, appear to move unusually rapidly (Ross & Rejman, 1972). Related to this is that, when the diver moves his head, objects appear to move; there is a loss of visual position constancy (Chapter 7). A third instance where illusory visual motion can occur is when the diver's body is subtly moved about by currents in such a manner that he is unaware that *he* is moving. He may attribute the resulting retinal motion to external objects in much the same fashion that a person sitting in a train may experience the train next to him as moving when actually his own vehicle is slowly accelerating. Similarly, the diver who is passively sinking or rising may experience false apparent motion (Ross & Lennie, 1968).

It is clear that the optical effects of viewing an underwater world through a diving mask lead to corresponding perceptual distortions. Let us now determine what capacity, if any, the diver has for adapting to these effects.

"IMMEDIATE" ADAPTATION TO
UNDERWATER DISTORTIONS

It has been observed casually that experienced divers report less visual distortion or disruption of visuomotor behavior than do novices, even at the outset of the dive. Furthermore, several investigators have found a significant difference in initial underwater perception among subjects with differing degrees of diving experience. Luria and Kinney (1970) compared the results of a number of experiments and found that the magnitude of the initial error (under-reaching) in localizing (in the distance dimension) nearby objects in clear water declined as a regular function of the amount of prior experience under water. This comparison is seen in Table 12.1. In addition, a correlation coefficient of .85 was obtained for the relationship between degree of immediate compensation and diving proficiency ratings for the group of Navy divers. Another example of "instantaneous adaptation" comes from Luria, Kinney, and Weissman (1967), who found significant perceptual overestimation of underwater far distances for novices but no difference between air and water judgments for experienced divers. Nichols (1967) made a similar observation. Kinney et al. (1970a) reported further evidence that experienced divers perceive less distance distortion than do novices, but they found essentially no relation between diving experience and either visuomotor errors to lateral displacement or accuracy in perceptual judgments of the size of coins or magazines viewed under water. Other reports

Table 12.1

Amounts of Underwater Experience and Initial Distortion (Error in Target Pointing)[a]

Subjects	N	Amount of distortion experienced[b] (cm)
Never used snorkel, mask	42	5.59
Occasionally used snorkel, mask	69	5.00
Frequently used snorkel, mask	20	3.30
Scuba class		
No scuba experience	14	3.23
Some scuba experience	12	2.64
Navy divers	8	2.03

[a] From S. M. Luria and J. A. S. Kinney, Underwater vision, Science, 1970, 167, 1454–1461. Copyright 1970 by the American Association for the Advancement of Science.

[b] The theoretical optical displacement in the test situation was calculated to be 5.60 cm.

of the immediate reduction in optically predicted errors for experienced divers have been made with respect to apparent size–distance relationships (Ross, 1967a; Ross, Franklin, Weltman, & Lennie, 1970) and curvature (Ross, 1970).

Thus, with repeated experience, cues such as the feel of the water, the pressure of the diving gear, or perhaps merely the knowledge that one is looking into water might come to elicit a partial adaptation response. On the other hand, one cannot rule out the possibility that at least some of these instances of apparent reduction in perceptual error at the outset of a dive are the result of a "cognitive correction." Some anecdotal evidence exists that with continued diving experience subjects can acquire the ability to correct deliberately for some of the underwater distortions (e.g., Ross et al., 1970b).

As argued in previous chapters, to assess visual or visuomotor adaptation it is necessary to obtain unequivocal evidence of how the world *appears* to the subject and/or of aftereffects after the removal of the distorting medium. In the next section, we will examine the results of underwater experiments that have clearly met these criteria.

"LONG-TERM" ADAPTATION TO UNDERWATER DISTORTIONS

Visual and Visuomotor Adaptation to Distance and Size Distortions

A number of experiments have demonstrated that genuine adaptation to underwater distortions can be induced by providing the diver with specific visuomotor tasks. In many of these studies the testing procedure has followed the sequence: (a) air pretest; (b) underwater pretest; (c) underwater adaptation period; (d) underwater posttest; and (e) air posttest. Any decline in perceptual error when comparing the two underwater tests is considered evidence of adaptation, in the form of a reduction of effect; an increase in error in the adaptive direction when comparing the pre- and posttests in the air is the negative aftereffect. Adaptation has been measured in absolute amount or as a percentage of the total possible shift. Percentage adaptation may be calculated by using either the theoretical maximum as determined by the optical situation or the *perceived* distortion of the subject upon first entering the water. However, the underwater distortion initially experienced by subjects is almost always less than the optics would predict, so using the underwater pretest measure as the basis for calculating percentage adaptation will lead to a lower figure than when the optical maximum is used. To clarify this point, assume that according to the optics of an underwater viewing condition an object 4 ft. away from the observer should appear to be 3 ft. away (three quarters of the physical distance, or a reduction of 12 in.), but that the subject's initial measures under water average 3 ft. 4 in. The *perceived* distance is 4 in. more than it "should" have been. If after a period of underwater activity the subject's underwater posttest measures average 3 ft. 7 in. (a pre–post shift of 3 in.), adaptation calculated as a percentage of the optical distortion is $7/12 = 58\%$. If the percentage is calculated on the basis of the perceived distortion, it comes to $3/12 = 25\%$. Unfortunately, in some of the experiments described in the following sections it is unclear from the information provided by the author(s) how to calculate the percentage adaptation obtained.

Kinney, McKay, Luria, and Gratto (1970) carried out a series of experiments designed to discover the optimal underwater training procedure for producing visuomotor adaptation to the optical foreshortening of near distance in clear water. In one of their studies they found that after a 15-min exposure period the adaptation of eye–hand coordination was greatest for subjects required to play underwater games (e.g., checkers) when compared to subjects who were allowed to swim freely or were given a lecture on underwater distortions and then required to practice a target-pointing task under water. Spaced practice of the game-playing activities tended to produce more adaptation than did massed exposure. Surprisingly, specific training, in the form of distributed game playing, led to a larger aftereffect (approximately 70% of the optical distortion) over a 15-min period than resulted from 4 weeks of scuba-diving lessons.

Ono and O'Reilly (1971) examined the efficacy of three half-hour-long underwater activities for producing adaptation to the reduced apparent distance of nearby objects, using experienced divers. Adaptation was tested by reaching with the unseen hand to the apparent position of a target located 7 or 14 in. away. No visuomotor negative aftereffect was found for an exposure task involving the continuous visual monitoring of reaching responses. A small amount of adaptation was produced by the second task, which required a certain amount of visually predirected movement. Finally, a large adaptive shift resulted when the subject was required to reach for a target and was provided with feedback only at the termination of each response. This, of course, is the underwater analog of the terminal display–target present condition used in many prism-adaptation experiments (Chapter 2). The investigators suggested that the crucial difference among the three conditions was the degree to which "new efferent instructions" were acquired. A more parsimonious explanation for their results is that the measured adaptation was maximized by using an exposure activity quite similar to the test of adaptation. Alternatively, it could be argued that the large adaptive shift for the terminal feedback condition resulted from the great deal of informational discrepancy provided.

O'Reilly (1975a,b), using generally the same exposure conditions and adaptation tests as Ono and O'Reilly, found that although both novices (0–10 hr of diving experience) and experts (40–1200 hr) could adapt their eye–hand coordination to the apparent reduction in distance of near objects in ultraclear water, only the experts underwent significant intermanual transfer. Based on the assumption that intermanual transfer signifies the presence of visual adaptation, it was concluded that extensive experience under water leads to a readiness to adapt visually, whereas a paucity of diving experience is associated with a shift in the felt position of the exposed limb.

Ross and Lennie (1972) examined visuomotor adaptation to both distance and lateral (expansion) distortions of the visual field in relatively inexperienced divers. Adaptation occurred in terms of both a 39% reduction in eye–hand errors under water and an aftereffect out of water.[6] Not only did some overall adaptation occur, but adaptation to one aspect of the distortion led to a certain amount of "counteradaptation" to complementary aspects. That is, adaptation to distance produced an increased apparent distortion in the lateral dimension and adaptation to one side led to increased apparent displacement on the other. The level of adaptation achieved as a result of free swimming during the exposure period was no different than that from practice on the visuomotor task with terminal display.

In an experiment by Franklin et al. (1970), experienced scuba divers were required to make visual size and distance estimates before and after a 20-min period under water, during which they explored the bottom of a swimming pool and stacked soft-drink cans. The water was very clear and the distances to be estimated were close by; therefore, the objects initially appeared larger and closer than they actually were. As a result of the underwater swimming period, the experimental group experienced a small adaptive shift in apparent

[6] Ross (personal communication, 1975) reported that the size of the aftereffect actually *increased* during the six measurement trials, an apparent case of "aftereffect reminiscence" (see Chapter 4, pp. 87–88). Furthermore, this aftereffect was about twice as large as the reduction of effect.

size, but not distance. On closer analysis, it was found that subjects who demonstrated a large amount of adaptation to size revealed only little adaptation (and even counteradaptation for a few subjects) to distance, and vice versa. The correlation between the two forms of adaptation was −.71. This result may be referred to as *relative counteradaptation* and has also been reported by Luria et al. (1973).

Finally, Ross, Franklin, Weltman, and Lennie (1970) found that, upon first entering the water, experienced divers perceived less size enlargement than did novices.[7] Both novices and experts revealed adaptation, in terms of size estimates, after 20- to 40-min underwater periods, during which they played pegboard games and stacked soft-drink cans. Adaptation measured in terms of a reduction of effect on the underwater pre- and posttest was quite small, reaching only 11% of the initial underwater error. Interestingly, the obtained aftereffect was greater than the reduction of effect (see footnote 6), but the aftereffect decayed completely within only four trials. This decay was particularly rapid for the practiced divers, a reasonable finding if it is assumed that their extensive experience had provided the existing situational cues with the power to induce both immediate adaptation under water and recovery out of water. In a second experiment, the investigators found that the greater initial accuracy of experienced divers was demonstrable even when they merely looked into a tank of water through a porthole. This suggests that the situational adaptation of the experienced divers is not necessarily the result of actually being in the water, wearing a face mask, etc., but may be signaled by certain nonadapted air–water distortions or merely by the knowledge that one is looking into water.

Adaptation to Apparent Curvature

A second underwater distortion is that of the apparent curvature (in all three dimensions) of contours that extend to the periphery of the visual field (see Figure 12.2). Ross (1970) tested for visual adaptation to the apparent bowing outward of a vertical line located on the frontoparallel plane, directly in front of the underwater observer. The measure of adaptation involved asking subjects to set a strip of flexible material so that it appeared just noticeably bent toward or away from

[7] This observation is in contrast to the failure of Kinney, Luria, Weitzman, and Markowitz (1970) to find a correlation between amount of diving experience and underwater size perception.

them, both before and after a 30-min free swimming period in the ocean. This exposure period resulted in adaptation equal to approximately 25% of the optical maximum under water and an equally large negative aftereffect in the air. In a second experiment, practiced divers showed some "instantaneous" visual adaptation to the curvature upon entering the water, whereas novices did not. Subjects were precluded from viewing any contours during the adaptation period and therefore were not likely to have become conscious of the distortion to which they ultimately adapted. It was suggested that the cues inducing this adaptation were those resulting from exposure to the "rubbery" appearance of the visual field caused by movements of the head.

Adaptation to Illusory Visual Motion

Ferris (1972b) examined adaptability to the loss of visual position constancy that occurs when the head is moved back and forth under water. He reported that a 15-min underwater period in which divers engaged in either head rotations or eye–hand responses produced a small, marginally significant reduction in the illusory motion of the visual field under water and a corresponding aftereffect in the air. Ferris found no relationship between reported past diving experience and the initially experienced distortion or level of adaptation achieved. The measure of apparent motion used in this experiment involved having the subject make a magnitude estimate, using as the referent the initially experienced head movement-contingent motion. Although this measure has the advantage of quick administration, it is relatively insensitive, which may account for the investigator's failure to obtain clear-cut evidence of adaptation. It is likely that this form of adaptation will occur for divers since it has been obtained in the air by numerous investigators (Chapter 7, pp. 169–175).

Due to the apparent expansion of the lateral dimension when looking through a diving mask, objects moving across the line of sight under water appear to move faster than in air. On the other hand, an object moving along the line of sight will seem to move more slowly if it is nearby and/or the water is clear, whereas at greater distances, or in turbid water, motion in this dimension should be perceived as greater than actual. Ross and Rejman (1972) demonstrated that after only 10 min of submersion, while swimming around and playing a pegboard game, relatively inexperienced divers revealed a very significant reduction of effect and aftereffect for both lateral and in–out visual speed distortions. The subject's perception of speed was indicated by magnitude estimation. The authors suggested that this adaptation was the result of compensation for the size and distance distortions, although this possibility was not specifically tested.

SUMMARY AND CONCLUSIONS

We have seen that many aspects of vision are affected when a person descends beneath the surface of the water. The underwater observer, wearing goggles or a diving mask, experiences deficits or distortions of color discrimination and of apparent distance, size, shape, and motion. Many of these underwater visual distortions are similar or identical to those examined in previous chapters; therefore, it is not surprising that divers have proven capable of adapting (partially) to them. It is unlikely that the processes and end states of underwater adaptation will prove to be fundamentally different from those that underlie the comparable forms of adaptation induced by prisms or lenses. Indeed, there is some evidence in support of this comparability. First, underwater adaptation appears to be facilitated by activities that provide a great deal of informational feedback (e.g., Ono & O'Reilly, 1971). Second, such adaptation appears to be subject to situational conditioning, assuming that this is the basis of the initial perceptual advantage that experienced divers have demonstrated over novices. Third, adaptive shifts in eye–hand coordination under water are much more extensive than are modifications of vision.

It has been argued (e.g., Luria & Kinney, 1970; Ross, personal communication, 1975) that there are certain *advantages* to using an underwater view through a diving mask to investigate adaptation to visual rearrangement. In the first place, it is easier to maintain the subject's preexposure naiveté concerning the fact that his vision is soon to be distorted because, contrary to the situation in which strange-looking goggles are being placed on the subject, divers are rarely suspicious that anything is about to happen to their vision. Second, underwater distortions are apparently not as obvious as those found in many of the experiments described in previous chapters. The significance of this fact is that a "conscious correction" is less likely to develop. Finally, because the underwater subject is generally allowed much freedom of movement, he is exposed at once to the full range of distortions, in contrast to the more narrowly defined experiences dictated by many of the "constrained exposure" experiments with prisms or lenses (Chapter 2).

There are certain disadvantages to underwater research as well, not the least of which is the fact that many investigators do not have handy a swimming pool or ocean or a willing group of subjects. Nevertheless, it is to be hoped that more research on underwater adaptation will be forthcoming.

For those investigators who wish to take advantage of this "natural" form of visual rearrangement, a number of suggestions may be offered. First, the ideal paradigm appears to be that used by Ross and her associates (e.g., Ross, Franklin, Weltman, & Lennie, 1970), in which pre- and posttest measures are taken both in the water and in the air. The subject should wear the face mask during the air pre- and posttests, since, given the fragile nature of the aftereffect, it is important that as much as possible the stimulus conditions associated with adaptation be maintained. The aftereffect is indeed transient, since it is usually found to decay completely in a matter of seconds, and therefore it is important to measure it as quickly as possible after the subject has emerged from the water. It may be necessary to limit the examination to only the first two or three postwater trials and/or to have the subject make magnitude estimates, because these are so quickly obtained. Subjects should also be carefully instructed to respond in terms of how the underwater world *looks*, rather than what they know (or think they know) about it. This form of instruction has been used in some experiments (e.g., Ono & O'Reilly, 1971), but the described procedures of others are often unclear on this point. This is particularly important if the subjects are experienced divers, who might otherwise tend to make "intellectual" judgments in response to the task. As with prism adaptation, the visuomotor response is most likely to be subject to conscious correction, after a certain amount of trial and error, and so the aftereffect represents a more convincing form of evidence for adaptation than does the reduction of effect measure taken during the water tests.

Research on underwater adaptation has led to several apparently unique findings. One of these is the occasional observation of an aftereffect whose magnitude is equal to or even greater than that of the reduction of effect (e.g., Kinney, McKay, Luria, & Gratto, 1970; Ross & Lennie, 1972; Ross, Franklin, Weltman, & Lennie, 1970). This is contrary to the usual finding in the above-water laboratory and it is not entirely clear what it means, especially since the aftereffect should have been subject to rapid decay. Probably the best explanation of this apparent anomaly is simply that during the underwater pretests a certain amount of very rapid adaptation occurs, thereby reducing the difference between this measure and the one taken under water at the end of the adaptation period (Ross, Franklin, Weltman, & Lennie, 1970). If it were possible to get an underwater pretest measure that was completely unaffected by adaptation, the reduction of effect would probably never be smaller than the aftereffect.

A second interesting observation from a number of the underwater experiments is the edge in perception that experienced divers enjoy over novices upon initial entry into the water. It is unlikely that the experienced diver has acquired a case of permanent partial adaptation, since this would lead to nonveridical perception and maladaptive behavior when out of the water. Consequently, this observation is perhaps best interpreted as evidence for conditioned adaptation (Chapter 4, pp. 96–101). The situation for the highly experienced diver is probably ideal for investigating the effect of situational cues on the adaptive process. Consider the fact that a person with many dives to his credit has repeatedly switched from one perceptual environment to another and that there are numerous salient cues (e.g., the feel of the water, the pressure of the diving gear, the reduced visual field) by which to discriminate these two situations.

Unfortunately, there are at least two other ways in which the "immediate" adaptation of experienced divers may be interpreted. First, it is possible that, at the very outset, the experienced diver actually perceives the distortion in full force but this signal is sufficient to elicit an extremely fast-acting adaptation process. In other words, a "learning set," rather than conditioning, may be involved in the so-called "instantaneous" adaptation effect for experienced divers. This fine distinction is difficult to test experimentally. Second, perhaps the experienced diver invokes a deliberate corrective tendency as soon as he finds himself looking into water and thus the reduced initial error is not a perceptual effect at all. If the latter is the case, a test for aftereffects at that point would prove fruitless. However, neither the conditioned adaptation nor learning set interpretations of the effect would predict aftereffects either, since the same process that operates to induce immediate or fast-acting adaptation would be expected to nullify it as soon as the diver emerges from the water. By instructing subjects to respond to the *appearance* of things and to avoid the use of strategies, the cognitive correction interpretation might be ruled out.

Another interesting observation, which was made in several studies of adaptation to underwater size and distance distortion, is that of *counteradaptation,* a phenomenon also reported by Wallach and Frey (1972c) (Chapter 8, p. 193). For example, when confronted with objects that look both nearer and larger than they are, underwater observers have sometimes responded by undergoing a reduction in one of the distortions and an increase in the other, thereby maintaining size–distance invariance (Luria et al., 1973; Ross & Lennie, 1972). Some subjects have evidenced adaptation to both distortions, although the magnitude of the two types of adaptation may be negatively correlated (Franklin et al., 1970; Luria et al., 1973). The latter observation is termed *relative counteradaptation*. The ideal solution to the observer's perceptual problem would be to come to see an object as closer to both its true size and its true distance. So far, few subjects have proven capable of this feat.

As we have seen, the investigation of underwater perception has led to several discoveries about "normal" perception. Experiments by Luria and Kinney (1968) demonstrated that distance was overestimated in fields relatively devoid of depth cues, and Luria (1969) found that stereoacuity is significantly retarded in a *Ganzfeld*-like situation. As a natural outgrowth of her underwater research, Ross (1967a, 1975b) has demonstrated that distance and size judgments are distorted in a fog or mist in the same manner as in the water: Objects look farther away and correspondingly larger than they actually are. She has also speculated plausibly that misperceptions of one's own speed or that of other vehicles when driving an automobile in a fog are based on these size–distance distortions as well as on the reduction in the visibility of objects in the periphery of the visual field. Such errors in perception are likely to be involved in some highway accidents. In general, Ross has defined the traditional distance cue of aerial perspective in terms of reduced brightness contrast and has expanded its applicability to both the underwater scene and fog. She has also suggested that the observation that objects of different hues at a given distance may be perceived as located at different distances is due not to their spectral characteristics but to the differential brightness contrast of the different hues as a result of the absorption characteristics of the viewing medium and/or the spectral sensitivity of the eye.

The investigations of underwater adaptation reviewed in this chapter are of both theoretical and practical interest. In terms of the former, we have acquired further information about some of the conditions that lead to adaptation and have obtained clear examples of conditioned or otherwise situationally induced adaptation. Since the underwater environment represents a naturally occurring situation where human beings are subject to a complex set of visual distortions, the results of the present research also have important and direct practical implications. By means of certain underwater training procedures, particularly those involving much eye–hand coordination, genuine visual and visuomotor adaptation can be significantly increased over that occurring as the result of a much longer period of unstructured swimming (e.g., Kinney, McKay, Luria, & Gratto, 1970). Unfortunately, underwater adaptation rarely exceeds 50% of the theoretical maximum and it is often much less than that. It seems that if the diver is to be made maximally effective, techniques must be devised to provide him with an understanding of the nature of the underwater distortions as well as the ability to allow for them intellectually. Ferris (1972a, 1973a,b) appears to be the only investigator who has attempted to do this. He showed that even relative novices can quickly be taught to overcome a large portion of the error in underwater distance judgments when they are provided with verbal feedback about their accuracy. It should also be possible to use this technique to train divers to make correct judgments of size. Thus, it would appear that the ideal procedure for equipping the novice diver to deal with underwater distortions is a combination of (a) activities conducive to genuine visual and visuomotor adaptation and (b) intellectual correction strategies to handle that portion of the distortion remaining after adaptation has reached its limit.

For the most part, research on adaptation to underwater distortions has not been designed with the methodological rigor and theoretical precision that characterize many of the above-water experiments described in previous chapters. While a number of experiments have dealt with the circumstances under which underwater adaptation occurs, most of these have involved the comparison of conditions that vary on a number of different dimensions. This state of affairs makes it impossible to specify with any exactness the necessary and sufficient conditions for this form of adaptation. A more serious problem is the paucity of research on the adaptive end product. In this regard, a number of unanswered questions remain:

1. What is the locus of the adaptive shifts in underwater eye–hand coordination reported by a number of investigators (e.g., Ross & Lennie, 1972)?

2. What proportion of the reduction in apparent curvature noted by Ross (1970) should be attributed to the Gibson effect, rather than to genuine adaptation?

3. Is the basis of the adaptive changes in underwater distance perception a recalibration of accommodation and convergence

cues, as appears to be the case in the above-water experiments on distance distortions (Chapter 8)?

The absence of answers to these and many other theoretical questions is symptomatic of the relative infancy of this area of research and points the way to further investigation.

13

Conclusions:
What Have We Learned?

At the outset of this book three motives underlying the vast array of studies on adaptation to perceptual rearrangement were delineated: (a) to examine the nature–nurture issue as it pertains to perception, particularly visual and auditory localization; (b) to acquire a better understanding of perceptual and perceptual–motor coordination; and (c) to elucidate the capacities of perceptual and perceptual–motor plasticity. Let us now determine to what extent these goals have been achieved. The last of these will be examined first by summarizing what we have learned from the preceding chapters about the nature of adaptation to perceptual rearrangement and then attempting to formulate a general model of this process.

THE NATURE OF PERCEPTUAL AND PERCEPTUAL-MOTOR PLASTICITY

General Findings

The use of perceptual rearrangement provides a unique opportunity to observe perceptual learning in action. The preceding chapters have revealed a great deal about certain forms of perceptual learning. The most obvious fact is that human beings are capable of modifying their behavior in response to almost every imaginable stable rearrangement of vision, as well as to the lateral displacement of auditory space.

We have seen several instances in which an immediate, but usually short-lived, modification of perception occurs merely from passively observing the visually distorted field (including the body) or an environment physically arranged to produce the effect of the distorting spectacles. Examples include *visual capture* of felt limb position for prismatic displacement, the *Wertheimer effect* for optical tilt, and a shift in apparent size as a result of stationary exposure to an array of miniature familiar objects. To produce significant and *persistent* changes in perception and perceptual–motor coordination (i.e., "true" adaptation), it is usually necessary that the observer receive much more salient and unambiguous information about the presence and nature of the rearrangement than is provided by passive or stationary exposure. This information can come from a variety of sources and is usually maximized if the observer is allowed to interact actively with his environment. Furthermore, it is likely that practice in making correct perceptual–motor responses during exposure to the distortion will transfer positively to those postexposure measures that demand the same sort of responses.

The adaptive process can be induced by many different informational sources and culminates in a variety of end states. The latter fact is quite apparent with prismatic displacement, by far the most thoroughly investigated form of visual rearrangement. The prism-induced change in eye–hand coordination, which is referred to as the *visuomotor negative aftereffect,* appears to be based, in some conditions, on a large shift in felt position of the arm and a lesser shift in apparent visual direction, whereas in other conditions the reverse is true.

There is some debate as to whether or not adaptation to prismatic displacement involves any visual component at all. This issue may be partly one of definition. It has been argued by Harris (1965) and others that the adaptive shift in apparent visual direction is the result of a change in the felt direction of gaze or of the head relative to the trunk. While there is now good evidence for the existence of these latter components, this does not mean that one must therefore abandon the notion of visual adaptation. The fact remains that after subjects are exposed to certain conditions of prismatic displacement, visual direction is experienced differently. It may be concluded that vision, by definition, has been altered. The *basis* of this change is another question, and it is likely that prism-induced visual shifts result entirely from a modification of felt eye or head position. This is certainly not the only instance of a visual experience based on a non-visual event. Other examples, noted by Rock (1966, pp. 133–134), are the perception of visual size, due (in part) to accommodation and convergence cues, and of visual vertical, as the result of the felt orientation of the head. It now appears certain that prism-adaptive shifts in visual direction are not based on changes in oculocentric values, although these "retinal events" are probably implicated in adaptation to optically induced curvature and perhaps tilt as well. The latter effects, however, are usually quite small.

Logically, a discrepancy between vision and position sense could be completely resolved by a recalibration either of felt limb position or of vision (based on felt direction of gaze). A third possibility is a partial shift in both of these modalities. The problem becomes one of predicting which form the resolution will take. In general, it appears that the modality that the observer attends, or accepts as veridical, will remain relatively unchanged, thereby serving as the basis for the recalibration of the other modality. There may be a natural tendency for vision to supersede felt position input from the limbs, based perhaps on its greater precision and dependability. Nevertheless, it has been proven possible to redirect observers' attention to felt limb position, and this has resulted in a predominantly visual adaptive shift (Kelso et al., 1975; Uhlarik & Canon, 1971), presumably in the form of recalibrated eye position.

Adaptation to perceptual rearrangement and learning are both positively correlated with phylogenetic level (e.g., Taub, 1968). There is also a great deal of within-species variability in adaptation. For human subjects, this variability has generally not been found to correlate with "gross" personality characteristics (e.g., internal–external locus of control, ambiguity tolerance). On the other hand, it does appear to be related to differences in the perceptual and perceptual–motor abilities involved in the production and measurement of adaptation (e.g., Warren & Platt, 1974). Individual subjects are relatively consistent in their ability to adapt to visual rearrangement from time to time, but there does not seem to be a "trait" of adaptability to distortions in general. Redding (e.g., 1973a) has demonstrated that the magnitude of adaptation to displacement is not correlated with the magnitude of tilt adaptation. This observation also indicates that the two perceptual capacities involved in these forms of adaptation—egocentric direction and egocentric orientation—are independent of one another.

A fact that, with a few exceptions (e.g. Smith & Smith, 1962, Chapter 6), has been ignored or glossed over is that there are *limits,* sometimes severe ones, on the ability to adapt to perceptual rearrangement. There are several aspects of this issue. First, it is clear that some varieties of perceptual rearrangement are more easily or fully adapted to than others. Exposure to small or moderate lateral shifts of the visual field, induced by wedge prisms, leads to greater *proportional* adaptation than is produced by particularly large displacements (e.g., Dewar, 1970b; Efstathiou, 1969). If optical tilt or curvature is too great, adaptation is depressed (Ebenholtz, 1973; Miller & Festinger, 1977), and visual transposition (e.g., right/left reversal) fails, in some instances, to produce any change in perception whatsoever (although perceptual–motor coordination is usually altered).

There are several ways in which these results can be interpreted. They may merely signify that the more drastic a distortion, the longer it takes to adapt. However, since even after extended exposure periods there is often a difference in proportional adaptation between small and large distortions, it seems more likely that there is something about the latter that *interferes* with the adaptive process. In the case of visual transposition, it may be an inability (perhaps innate) to make the complete "flip-flop" necessary for adaptation. Very large prismatic displacements may also exceed certain limits of adaptability. Alternatively, the crucial problem may be that when visual rearrangements become too severe the subject's "assumption" that his visual and proprioceptive inputs are emanating from one and the same object is violated, thereby eliminating the basis for a perceived, or registered, intersensory discordance.

Even if it is possible to adapt to a particular form of rearrangement, the magnitude of the adaptation almost always falls significantly short of the theoretical maximum. The typical acquisition curve rapidly rises, but negatively accelerates, and, depending on the type of distortion, variety of exposure, and other factors, reaches asymptote at 30–70% of the total possible adaptation. There have been several reports of complete or nearly complete adaptation, however. In the case of prismatic displacement, Hay and Pick (1966a) observed, after many days of exposure, a 90% reduction of effect, as measured by eye–hand coordination. Hein (1972) apparently succeeded in producing total adaptation to 20-diopter prisms by providing subjects with 3 min of continuous display, once every 40 min, for several hours, but his subjects were preselected on the basis of their high degree of adaptability. Held and Bossom (1961) and Mikaelian and Held (1964) also reported 100% adaptation for especially adaptable subjects. For many other types of distortion, there have been no reports of complete or even very large adaptive shifts for unselected samples. Group means for tilt adaptation, for example, rarely exceed 30%. On the other hand, there is one form of visual distortion for which complete or very substantial adaptation may actually be the rule, given a sufficiently extended exposure period: the loss of visual position constancy. Some reasons for this were suggested in Chapter 7 (pp. 176–177), although another possibility is presented later in this chapter.

The general failure of adaptation to reach completion might at first appear to pose problems for the "strong" empiricist position that spatial localization is entirely the result of learning. Specifically, since an "old" way of perceiving resists total recalibration, perhaps it did *not* originate from experience. However, it is argued in a later section that whether or not adult adaptation reaches completion or even occurs at all is irrelevant for the nature–nurture issue.

It is likely that each of the various perceptual rearrangements leads to a uniquely different mode of adaptation. Nevertheless, it is useful to look for common features in these varieties of adaptation, in the hope that a viable general model of adaptation will emerge. Such a model is proposed in the next section.

A General Model of Adaptation

AN OVERVIEW

In the next few pages I would like to propose and provide some empirical support for a model of the adaptive process, designed to apply to the gamut of perceptual rearrangements to which human observers have been exposed. By way of an overview, the model states that when an intersensory or sensorimotor discrepancy is encountered, an aversive drive is induced that, in turn, activates the adaptive process and results in the modification of a perceptual or perceptual–motor system, thereby reducing the discrepancy. This much of the model is entirely attributable to the thinking of other investigators, most notably Wallach (1968) and Taub (1968). However, a unique aspect, which I believe serves to make the present model superior to previous attempts, is that of *habituation*. It will be argued in the following sections that at the same time as the observer is adapting to the perceptual rearrangement, he is becoming accustomed to its presence. The effect of this increasing familiarity is to "short-circuit" the adaptive process by reducing and ultimately abolishing the aversive drive, bringing adaptation to a halt, usually well before it has been able to eliminate the discrepancy. Thus, the components of the model are a registered discrepancy, an aversive drive, an adaptive process, habituation, and, finally, an adaptive end product. Let us examine each of these in turn.

COMPONENTS OF THE MODEL

A registered discrepancy

All instances of adaptation begin with a registered discrepancy, of which there are three general categories. The first involves a discordance between two or more sensory modalities, as when viewing the hand through a wedge prism. A discrepancy exists here because a single distal object (the hand) is providing felt position and visual inputs that prior to exposure signified the presence of two spatially separated referents. With this form of discrepancy, the observer must assume that there is only one distal object. In the case of seeing the hand through a prism, this assumption is almost inevitable, except perhaps with very large displacements (Dewar, 1970b; Efstathiou, 1969; Warren & Cleaves, 1971). Even when the hand is represented by a "visual surrogate," such as a luminous spot (e.g., Hein, 1972; Mikaelian, 1974a), the assumption is likely to be maintained, as long as active movement of the limb is allowed. With a visual–auditory discrepancy it is perhaps not as immediately obvious or compelling to the observer that only one distal object is present, since in everyday circumstances these two modalities often do not have the one-to-one relationship enjoyed by vision and proprioception. Finally, the "assumption of identity" during prismatic exposure may be reduced or eliminated by instructing the subject that he is actually in the presence of two objects, as shown by Welch (1972) and discussed in Chapter 2 (pp. 18–19).

A second type of discrepancy arises when bodily motion, whether self-initiated (active) or the result of the experimenter moving the subject (passive), leads to visual consequences that do not match those normally produced by this movement. Situations in which this loss of visual position constancy is experienced include head and/or bodily motion while wearing displacing, tilting, or transposing spectacles.

Finally, a discrepancy arises when an attempt to reach for or move toward an object leads to an error. There is a mismatch between intended and actual placement of the limb or body relative to the visual environment.

The aversive drive

It may be postulated that when a discrepancy is registered in the nervous system an aversive drive state is induced, either as a result of previous punishing experiences or as an innate response to discrepancy. It will be argued here, in agreement with Taub (e.g., 1968), that this aversive state is necessary for the activation of the adaptive process. The more clear-cut the discrepancy, the more intense the aversive state and therefore the more substantial the resulting adaptation. The rate and extent of adaptation will be positively correlated with the number and magnitude of the currently registered discrepancies (i.e., amount of information).

The role of subject *awareness* in this formulation is unclear. Adaptation can occur when the subject is unaware that anything is wrong with his vision, as in the concurrent display, no-target procedure (e.g., Held & Gottlieb, 1958). Nevertheless, when there is a great deal of information (e.g., from target-pointing errors) concerning the rearrangement, subjects are usually able to describe the nature of the distortion, and adaptation is typically enhanced. Whether awareness is a cause of this facilitation or merely a correlate of the increased discrepancy that results from the additional information remains to be determined.

If and when the aversive state is eliminated, the adaptive process ceases. There are two ways in which this can occur: adaptation and habituation.

The adaptive process and reduction of the registered discrepancy

The details of the adaptive process vary as a function of the type of rearrangement, nature of the exposure period, assumptions and attentional biases of the observer, and other factors. In general, it represents (a) a recalibration of one or the other (or both) of the discrepant sensory inputs; (b) a modification of the central instructions for perceptual–motor coordination; or (c) a change in the expected visual outcome of a given head or eye movement. Whichever of these occurs in a given situation, the result is a reduction in the initially experienced discrepancy and therefore a diminution of the aversive drive. As long as this drive remains, adaptation should continue, which suggests that eventually adaptation must reach completion or at least a level so nearly complete that the discrepancy is below the observer's threshold. However, adaptation is rarely complete, usually falling far short of the theoretical maximum. This fact leads to the crucial aspect of the present model—the process of habituation.

Habituation

The second way in which the aversive drive may be reduced is for the subject to become *habituated* to the discrepancy. With repeated experience, memory traces for the subject's perceptual input while wearing the distorting spectacles are established, thereby reducing and eventually eliminating the difference between "expected" and actual sensory input. In short, the subject becomes accustomed to seeing a distorted world. It should be pointed out that the term "accustomed" is not intended to connote awareness. If the observer is not aware of the rearrangement in the first place, it would make no sense to argue that he is getting used to it in a conscious sense. All that is necessary for the concept of habituation, as it is used in the present model, is to assume that there exists a register that stores neural copies of recent experiences. It is further assumed that these traces are very quickly established and equally rapidly lost in the absence of further exposure. It is maintained here that familiarization with the discrepancy tends to nullify the aversive drive, thereby terminating adaptation. The fact that this habituation process occurs more rapidly than adaptation explains why adaptation is typically incomplete. That is, the aversive state is eliminated by habituation before adaptation has a chance to overcome the discrepancy. This explanation for the upper limit on adaptation is a modification of an aspect of Ebenholtz's (1969) comparator model of optical tilt adaptation, as described in Chapter 6 (pp. 147–153). The primary distinction is that in the present formulation the cessation of adaptation results not from the observer's inability to distinguish current perception from the preexposure state of affairs, but by reaching the point where he is no longer "surprised" by the discrepancy between these two events.

Figure 13.1 is a flow diagram of the present model. For the sake of simplicity, a number of details have been omitted. The proposed sequence of events is as follows. The presence of a registered discrepancy, as the result of the rearranging device, induces an aversive motivational state that leads to an adaptive process, resulting in the reduction of the registered discrepancy; simultaneously, rapid habituation to the discrepancy is taking place, leading to a lowering of the aversive state and therefore an attenuation of the adaptive process. At any point in this sequence of events it is possible to elicit a response (verbal or motor) from the organism to assess the current state of the registered discrepancy. This response is mediated by a "control process," involving various factors that may influence the response (such as biases and strategies). Since the outcome of this response is not fed back to the subject, it has no impact on any of the preceding or ongoing events of the model.

The end product(s)

Although not indicated in the flow diagram, it should be understood that the adaptive end product may take a variety of forms,

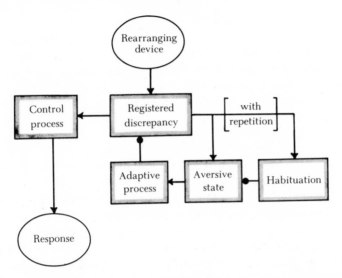

Figure 13.1. Flow chart of proposed general model of adaptation to perceptual rearrangement. Arrows indicate induction; knobs refer to attenuation (see the text for details).

depending upon the type of rearrangement, exposure condition, and so forth. The nature of the end product depends, in part, on the type of discrepancy encountered. If it involves an intersensory conflict (e.g., a prism-displaced view of the hand), adaptation will result in a recalibration of one or both of the modalities, depending on which is the more closely attended. It is likely that the effective variable is not attention per se, but rather which modality is accepted (rightly or wrongly) as veridical. Indeed, there cannot be a *total* failure to register one of the modalities, or else there would be no discrepancy and therefore nothing to adapt to.

When a discrepancy between actual and "expected" visual motion occurs, given a particular bodily movement (i.e., the loss of visual position constancy), the result will be a change in the "expected" input, and perhaps other visual effects as well. Finally, error feedback, as a result of target-reaching attempts or other types of localizing behavior, may produce a new set of efferent instructions as a consequence of punishment for incorrect responses and/or reward for correct ones. The magnitude of this efferent component of visuomotor adaptation is probably inversely correlated with the amount of *perceptual* adaptation that has occurred. This assimilated change in visuomotor instructions may represent a relatively minor aspect of visuomotor adaptation for prismatic displacement, since much of this

change in eye–hand coordination can be accounted for by a recalibration of felt limb or eye position. On the other hand, this may be a very
important component for adaptation to visual transposition since, at
least during the early stages of exposure, little if any perceptual
change takes place. As was seen in Chapter 3, usually more than one
adaptive component is produced by a given exposure condition, and
these changes sometimes combine in an additive fashion.

PREDICTIONS AND SUPPORTING DATA

The present hypothesis leads to the prediction that the rate and
extent of adaptation will be increased if the rearrangement is
presented in *increments*. With each increase in the distortion there
should be a disruption of the subject's short-term expectancy and
therefore an increase in the aversive drive, resulting in a reactivation
or facilitation of the adaptive process. It is possible for these increments to be too large, thereby exceeding the limits of the adaptive
mechanism or perhaps invalidating the "assumption of identity"
presumed here to be necessary for the registration of a discrepancy.
These expectations concerning the outcome of incremental exposure
conditions are in line with the results of several experiments that have
already been described. Ebenholtz and his associates (Ebenholtz, 1969;
Ebenholtz & Mayer, 1968) found a *linear* increase in optical tilt adaptation when the tilts increased by 5 or 8° steps, which contrasts with the
typical negatively accelerated acquisition curve for rearrangements of
constant value. When tilt increments were increased to 10 or 12°
(Ebenholtz, 1973), tilt adaptation was retarded, in agreement with the
present model.

Lackner and Lobovits (1977a) found that the magnitude of prism-
induced visuomotor negative aftereffect was only slightly greater for a
group exposed from the outset to a full 20-diopter displacement than
it was for a group exposed to a 1-diopter increase every 30 sec, until
receiving the 20-diopter maximum during the final 30 sec of the
exposure period. The investigators correctly noted that since the
average optical distortion experienced by the incremental displacement group over the length of the exposure period was half that of
the full displacement group, the former had actually been facilitated
substantially in their adaptation, which is consonant with the present
hypothesis. Presumably, continued exposure of the incremental group
to the 20-diopter displacement would ultimately have resulted in an
adaptive shift significantly exceeding that achieved by the full displacement group.

The notion that adaptation is determined by the presence of a discrepancy-induced aversive state may help to explain why distributed practice facilitates adaptation (Chapter 4, pp. 102–103). If the adaptation produced during exposure persists during a "rest period," while the memory traces for the discrepancy undergo rapid decay, then the onset of the next exposure interval should bring with it a "jolt" of aversive drive, which will strongly activate the adaptive process. In line with this suggestion, it may be noted that at least two of the very few instances of maximum adaptation to prismatic displacement (Hay & Pick, 1966a; Hein, 1972) involved quite substantial distribution of exposure. In Hay and Pick's (1966a) experiment, the 42-day exposure period was punctuated with daily 7- to 8-hr intervals of no exposure, while the subject slept. Each morning, the initial view through the distorting spectacles would be expected to reactivate the adaptive process.

As was seen in Chapter 3 (pp. 43–44), the observation of the hand through a prism induces an immediate effect of "visual capture." Since this serves to attenuate the registered discrepancy, it should, according to the present theory, reduce or eliminate the aversive drive and therefore retard adaptation. Because of this, prism adaptation is essentially nonexistent when the subject views his stationary hand. Movement, especially if actively initiated, will disrupt visual capture, keeping the intersensory discordance salient and thereby potentiating the aversive drive, resulting in further adaptation. Thus, contrary to some writers (e.g., Epstein & Morgan, 1970; Wallach, 1968), I am arguing that the occurrence of an immediate visual capture of felt limb position is *antithetical* to the process of adaptation, even though the end product of adaptation often turns out to be a change in felt limb position and therefore might reasonably be described as an instance of semipermanent visual capture. This conclusion was presented in Chapter 3 (pp. 44–45) and was supported by the results of an investigation from our laboratory (Welch et al., 1975), which demonstrated that active bodily movement facilitates prism adaptation but retards visual capture. Because visual capture requires continuous exposure, conditions in which the limb is constantly exposed should produce less adaptation than ones involving interrupted exposure. Such an effect occurs in the terminal display situation and with distributed exposure. Thus, perhaps there are two reasons why distributed practice facilitates adaptation: It allows for decay of recent memory traces of the distortion (thereby producing dishabituation) and it periodically interrupts visual capture.

A final observation that may be relevant to the proposed model is the fact that adaptation to the loss of visual position constancy appears eventually to reach completion, which does not occur for most other forms of rearrangement. According to the model, this can be explained by the fact that the registered discrepancy with a loss of visual position constancy is the mismatch between expected and observed visual input. Thus, in this case, the habituation to the discrepancy postulated in the model *is* the adaptive response and therefore becomes complete as soon as the observer has come to expect exactly the optical motion he receives.

Let us now turn to a second motive behind some of the adaptation research—the attempt to determine if and to what extent spatial localization is acquired by the neonate as the result of experience.

THE NATURE-NURTURE ISSUE

Some early investigators (e.g., Helmholtz, 1925; Kohler, 1964; Stratton, 1896; Weiss, 1941) believed that it would be possible to generalize from the behavior of an adult subject when exposed to perceptual rearrangement to that of the newly seeing neonate. It was argued that the observation of perceptual or perceptual–motor modifiability in adult organisms in response to rearrangement would represent clear evidence that the newborn must acquire these capacities from experience, presumably in the same fashion as adults. Evidence of unmodifiability was considered proof of the innateness of the capacities involved. Weiss (1941) unequivocally stated this position with reference to the failure of lower organisms to adapt to anatomical alterations of the eyes or limbs:

> If, on the other hand, corrective changes fail to occur and the nervous system continues to operate the part according to the old standard scheme of innervation now rendered inadequate, this would be incontestable proof of the *preformation* of coordination in form of definite central impulse patterns which do or do not produce appropriate effects, depending on whether the effector systems for whose operation they are predesigned is intact or disarranged [pp. 18–19].

Contrary to views such as this, there seems to be no logical reason why an innate perceptual or perceptual–motor capacity could not be modified or even completely reorganized in an adult. It is also possible to imagine a behavior that is acquired from experience but then becomes resistant to later attempts at modification. This latter notion is related to the "critical period" hypothesis (e.g., Scott, 1962), the classic example being "imprinting" in precocial birds. It is now obvious to many investigators that an adult is in so many important aspects dissimilar to an infant that it is foolhardy to generalize blindly from the former to the latter. It is generally accepted that the question of the heritability of a perceptual (or any other) capacity in human beings is most clearly answered by examining *infants*—the younger the better—despite the formidable methodological problems of test-ing these nonverbal and generally helpless subjects. This is not to say that one might not derive from the results of adult perceptual rear-rangement studies *hypotheses* about origin and development that could then be tested with human infants or other neonatal organisms. Indeed, Hein and Held, with their collaborators, have done just that. Based on their observations of the importance of active limb move-ment for prism adaptation (e.g., Held & Hein, 1958), some ingenious experiments were devised in which newborn kittens or monkeys were precluded from viewing their limbs and/or experiencing the visual results of their active bodily movement. Perhaps the best example of this paradigm is found in the now-classic "kitten carousel" experiment by Held and Hein (1963) where kittens were reared in the dark until they had reached a level of physical maturity that allowed them to be adequately tested—from 8 to 10 weeks of age. At that time, a pair of the animals was taken from the dark and placed in an open-ended drum, the inside wall of which contained vertical alternating black and white stripes. As shown in Figure 13.2, one of the two kittens was placed in a harness and the other in a gondola. As the first kitten walked parallel to the side of the drum, it pulled the other animal along the same path. For 3 hr a day, one of the kittens received visual experience (reafference) as a direct result of its active bodily move-ment, while the other was a passive recipient of much the same experience. In this situation (which is, perhaps, the first case of a yoked-control design involving a real yoke) even lateral or up and down movements of the active kitten's body were translated into identical motions for the passive animal. Each kitten was tested on three measures: (a) discrimination of the deep from the shallow side of the "visual cliff" (Walk & Gibson, 1961); (b) blink response to an object brought quickly toward the animal's eyes; and (c) ability to reach out the paws at the appropriate time to meet the edge of a table as the kitten was carried down past it ("visual placing"). As predicted by the investigators, at a time when the active kittens were able to demonstrate an appropriate response on each of the measures (after an average of 30 hr in the apparatus), the passive kittens failed. However, a 48-hr period of free locomotion in a lighted environment

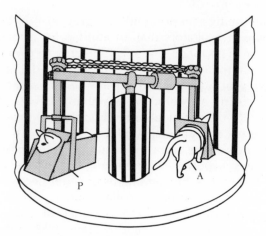

Figure 13.2. Apparatus for equating motion and consequent visual feedback for actively moving (A) and passively moving (P) subjects. (From R. Held & A. Hein. Movement-produced stimulation in the development of visually guided behavior. *Journal of Comparative and Physiological Psychology*, 1963, *56*, 872–876. Copyright 1963 by the American Psychological Association. Reprinted by permission.)

was sufficient to render the behavior of the two types of kittens indistinguishable.[1]

In later experiments it was demonstrated that dark-reared kittens whose subsequent visual experience occurred with active head and bodily movement but in the absence of a view of the limbs were deficient in reaching for discrete visual targets, but not in visually guided locomotion or in the ability to make localizing movements of the head and eyes (Hein & Diamond, 1971a,b; Hein & Held, 1967; Hein, Gower, & Diamond, 1970; Hein, Held, & Gower, 1970). Hein and Diamond (1972) also demonstrated that visually guided coordination of the limbs does not develop from active visuomotor experience unless the facility to locomote the entire body has already been, or is concurrently being, acquired by the animal. Interestingly, the various behaviors manifested as a result of active visuomotor experience have proven to be specific to the exposed eye (Hein, Held, & Gower, 1970; Held, 1964) or limb (Hein, 1970), and even for the particular visual system (day or night) being used at the time (Hein & Diamond, 1971a). An example of this specificity is the fact that the provision of active exposure for one eye and passive exposure for the other leads

[1] Hein (1972) has reported that subsequent to this experiment some kittens were provided with as much as 400 hr of passive movement and still proved unable to perform the tasks.

eventually to the demonstration of normal visually guided behavior only when looking through the "active eye" (Held, 1964).

Held and Bauer (1967) examined the nature–nurture issue by means of a species phylogenetically much closer to human beings than the cat. The investigators reared each of several infant monkeys from birth in a miniature primate chair that kept the animal from viewing its body. The monkey's reaching responses during this deprivation period, which were never rewarded, eventually became quite stereotyped and abbreviated. When, at the age of 35 days, the monkey was finally allowed to view one of its forelimbs, its reaching responses for objects were aborted as soon as the hand came into view. This behavior appeared to be the result of the fact that the animal, apparently quite fascinated by its hand, spent an inordinate amount of time watching this "novel" visual object, to the exclusion of other activities. When eye–hand coordination eventually began to approach normal, the other hand was exposed and this, too, resulted in an initial disruption of behavior, although recovery was more rapid than it had been for the first limb.

From these experiments, Hein, Held, and their colleagues have drawn two major conclusions:

1. Visual and visuomotor localizations in cats, monkeys, and presumably human beings *originate* from experience.
2. This experience consists specifically of the simultaneous registration of efferent outflow and reafference, which can occur only with active visuomotor behavior.

However, both of these conclusions may be questioned.

First, there are many data that suggest that visual localization—as measured by such tasks as visual placing, tracking and fixation, eye–hand coordination, optokinetic nystagmus, avoidance of looming objects, and visual cliff performance—is innate for most, if not all, "visual animals," including human beings. The evidence for this statement is too voluminous to describe here, but has been reviewed by Ganz (1975). This being the case, it may be asked why the kittens in the experiments described previously failed initially to demonstrate adequate localizing behavior. One answer to this question, as Ganz (1975) and others have suggested, is that the procedure of dark rearing, which is a necessity if this neonatally immature animal is to be adequately tested, may lead to a *suppression* of innate visual capacities. In short, the competence may be present but not the performance. There is much evidence of such suppression for a variety of species. Fantz (1965, 1967) found that visuomotor localization and depth discrimination were rather good for newborn monkeys reared in the dark for less than 1 month, but became increasingly worse as a result of longer periods of dark rearing. It has also been shown that the ability to perceive depth on the visual cliff is present for the rat on its first day of visual experience, but not if it has been reared in the dark for more than 5–6 months (Nealy & Riley, 1963). However, subsequent visual experience leads to eventual recovery from these losses. It might be concluded that in studies such as that by Held and Hein (1963) active visuomotor behavior facilitated the release of innate capacities from suppression, rather than providing the conditions for acquiring new capacities. This recovery could be based on the concurrence of bodily motion and sight of the limbs (or the visual effects of the movement), in line with the reafference model, or it might instead be due to the availability of greater or more salient *information* concerning the relation between bodily motion and its consequences, as has been suggested by Howard and Templeton (1966, p. 394).

Perhaps the difference in behavior between the reafferent and deprived conditions is produced not only by the facilitative influence of the former but by the *debilitating* effects of the latter. The demonstration by Held (1964) that the active–passive difference in visuomotor development could be produced in the same kitten when active exposure was limited to one eye and passive exposure to the other appears to rule out the hypothesis that the deficient visuomotor performance of the passive animal in the Held and Hein (1963) experiment was the result of a general lack of motivation or a disruptive emotional state. However, it does not preclude two other possibilities: selective extinction and selective decorrelation. First, it may be proposed that situations in which reafference is precluded are typically ones in which motor responses fail to lead to reinforcement and are therefore extinguished. For example, in the experiment by Held and Bauer (1967), reaching responses on the part of the neonatal monkeys during the deprivation period rarely, if ever, resulted in a successful grasp of a visual object and appeared to extinguish. Walk and Bond (1971) examined this response-extinction hypothesis by means of a modified replication of the Held/Bauer experiment in which infant monkeys were allowed to reach for and grasp a target, although they were never able to view their hands during the 35-day deprivation period. Contrary to Held and Bauer, these investigators found that when observation of the hand was finally provided, eye-hand coordination was relatively accurate and the animal did not engage in excessive hand watching. The second possible way in which a deprivation condition can lead to the degradation of behavior is seen clearly in the "kitten carousel" experiment. It can be argued that the passive exposure condition represented a situation of "disarrangement" (Chapter 2, p. 17) in which the movements or attempts to move on the part of the passive kitten were associated with *inconsistent* visual effects. That is, they became decorrelated with sensory input. For example, attempts by the passive kitten to turn to the left might on various occasions be followed by movement to the right, to the left, or to no movement at all, depending upon the concurrent behavior of the active kitten. Compounding this problem is the fact that the passive kittens in Held and Hein's experiment were allowed to move the head about. As was suggested with regard to adaptation to optical tilt (Chapter 6, p. 145) and curvature (Chapter 9, p. 205), it is possible that the coupling of passive transport of the body and active head movement leads to a degradation of perception. There are several observations that provide support for the hypothesis that conditions used to preclude visual reafference actually result in perceptual and perceptual–motor deterioration. Hein, Held, and Gower (1970) reported that passively moved kittens required a longer period of subsequent active movement in the "carousel" to attain adequate visuomotor performance than did animals reared in total darkness (41 versus 30 hr). Second, it has been shown that the visual placing response to a continuous surface is demonstrated by *totally immobilized* animals after patterned visual experience and by actively moving kittens provided with diffuse light only (Hein, Gower, & Diamond, 1970), whereas the original experiment by Held and Hein (1963) found no evidence of this ability for the passively moved kittens.

In general, it may be concluded that because Hein, Held, and their associates chose to use kittens as subjects for their studies and therefore were forced to institute dark-rearing procedures, it is possible to interpret many of their results, at least in part, in terms of the deleterious effects of neonatal deprivation. Perhaps a different picture would have emerged if they had chosen to use a more initially mature organism.

What, then, can be said about the origin and development of spatial localization? It seems likely that both visual and auditory localizability are present innately in many animals, including human beings, although these capacities may become more precise or otherwise altered as subsequent conditions require. Furthermore, continued normal perceptual and perceptual–motor experience may be necessary for the *maintenance* of these capacities. This notion, which Ganz (1975) termed the *weak empiristic hypothesis,* makes a great deal of sense. It would seem most reasonable for "visual organisms" to be born with at least a rudimentary capacity for the kind of perceptions which any member of that species, at any place in the world and at any time in history, will need to survive. However, there should also be some adjustability in the system, if for no other reason than to allow for adaptation to the perceptual effects of changes in body size. Two examples of such growth-induced forms of adaptation for human beings are (a) the recalibration of the felt position and length of the limbs and of the neural commands required for their coordination and (b) the recalibration of those cues of spatial location mediated by interocular and interaural distance. A variant of this general hypothesis was proposed by Bower (1974, p. 62). He argued that localization along the major axes (right/left and up/down) of the frontoparallel plane is innate, since the approximate doubling of head size with age will have no effect on these, whereas human beings may have to learn to perceive the angles in between since these *are* affected by head growth.

We may conclude that the pioneering studies of prism adaptation by Held and his colleagues have stimulated a great deal of research on the origin and development of perceptual and perceptual–motor coordination in neonatal organisms. Although the results of many of the latter experiments are subject to interpretations that differ from those espoused by the original investigators, they have led to a better understanding of the nature–nurture issue in perception, particularly as they have forced scholars to evaluate critically the likely detrimental effects of neonatal deprivation.

Even though the research on adaptation to perceptual rearrangement may have shed little *direct* light on the nature–nurture issue, it has certainly had an impact on our understanding of "normal" perception and perceptual–motor behavior. Let us now examine the nature of this impact.

CONTRIBUTIONS TO THE UNDERSTANDING OF PERCEPTION AND PERCEPTUAL-MOTOR COORDINATION

Research on adaptation to perceptual rearrangement has had both a direct and an indirect impact on our knowledge about human perception and perceptual–motor behavior. The direct contribution has been to elucidate those capacities affected by the various distortions. There are two aspects of this. First, the disruption of the perceptual or perceptual–motor capacities involved and the resulting adaptation have revealed many things previously unknown about these behaviors. Second, it has often been necessary to perform an unusually careful and critical analysis of the capacities as they operate under *normal* circumstances before the effects of their experimental alteration could be fully understood. This analysis has led to some important insights. The indirect contribution of the adaptation studies has been to generate a strong interest in other types of perceptual plasticity, which has inspired a number of important experiments.

Direct Contributions

ELUCIDATION OF VARIOUS PERCEPTUAL AND PERCEPTUAL–MOTOR CAPACITIES

Egocentric/radial localization

The studies of prismatic and pseudophonic displacement have substantially increased our understanding of perceptual and perceptual–motor localization in the lateral dimension. One of the most significant contributions in this regard has been to demonstrate the dominating role of vision in the resolution of intersensory discordance. This dominance has been seen in the immediate responses of *visual capture* and the *ventriloquism effect,* as well as the more slowly acquired but longer-lasting shift in the sense of felt bodily position (e.g., Harris, 1965). From these observations we may conclude that when several spatial cues are available, it is vision that serves as the primary determinant of localization. That is, it seems reasonable to assume that the spatial modality or cue found to remain relatively unchanged in the adaptive response to an imposed inter- or intrasensory discordance is the modality or cue that receives the greater "weight" or attention during everyday experience. The discovery that vision "educates" proprioception, touch, and the gravitational sense is in direct contradiction to the long-held belief in the primacy of the bodily senses (e.g., Berkeley, 1910). In retrospect, this belief is difficult to understand, since it is clear that these sensory modalities are much less precise than is spatial vision. Furthermore, it should be obvious that developmental changes in bodily size demand much greater plasticity in the felt position of body parts than they do of visual localization. The fact that vision will override auditory cues of location is also unsurprising, since it is now clear that hearing is a relatively poor spatial sense, although its ability to distinguish temporal intervals is unmatched by any other modality (e.g., Freides, 1974).

While the prism adaptation research has revealed the "normal" weighting of the various spatial modalities, it has also demonstrated that this weighting can be readjusted. Canon (1966, 1970, 1971) and others have found that the normal precedence of vision over the other spatial modalities may be largely reversed by instructing or forcing the observer to shift his attention from the former to the latter.

The research on prism adaptation has led to heightened interest in the body position sense and has clarified its role at the various joints. It has also suggested how these individual inputs may summate to produce accurate eye–hand coordination with normal vision (see Figure 3.1, p. 50). In addition, research attention has been focused on the role of felt eye position in visual and visuomotor localization. It is now clear that where the eyes are felt to be relative to the head will determine apparent visual location and visuomotor coordination. Furthermore, Ebenholtz and his colleagues (e.g., Paap & Ebenholtz, 1976) have provided convincing evidence that whenever the eyes are positioned asymmetrically for some period of time a change in their felt position is produced, leading to a misperception of visual direction.

An important contribution of the prism adaptation research has been to highlight the distinction between efferent and afferent determinants of body position sense and kinesthesis. For example, Taub and Goldberg (1974), using prismatic displacement and de-afferentation, have demonstrated that proprioceptive input is not necessary for adequate visuomotor coordination, although it does serve to make it more precise.

Finally, Harris (1974) has demonstrated that the act of locating the visual straight ahead is jointly determined by the perception of egocentric direction and by the influence of the visual framework upon the observer's concept of straight ahead.

Visual orientation

Perhaps the most important outcome of the research on adaptation to the disruption of visual orientation (i.e., transposition and optical tilt) has been to clarify the issues involved. First, it has become apparent that the question of why the world looks right side up when the retinal image is inverted is a pseudoproblem. As we have seen, the question that should be asked is whether or not it is necessary (for infant or adult) that the image be inverted if upright perception is to occur.

Second, on the basis of both logical analysis and the results of experiments on adaptation to transposed vision (Chapter 5), it has become clear that the experience of an upright visual environment and the ability to operate effectively in it involve three separable capacities: *environmental orientation, egocentric orientation,* and *egocentric direction.* This analysis has made it possible to interpret some apparently paradoxical results from previous studies (e.g., Kohler, 1964), but more important, it has led to a more differentiated view of the nature of spatial vision.

Another outcome of this research has been to demonstrate that a transposition or tilting of the visual field not only induces an initial change in apparent visual orientation but also causes familiar objects to look strange or perhaps unrecognizable. Rock (1973) has written a book devoted entirely to this phenomenon and its implications.

The research on adaptation to optical tilt, specifically that of Ebenholtz, has suggested that normal visual orientation is *maintained* by everyday experience. One form of evidence for this conclusion is the observation that "unlearning" of tilt adaptation is no more rapid than is its initial acquisition (Ebenholtz, 1968b). Thus, it appears that normal visual orientation is much like a state of adaptation to a 0° tilt.

Visual position constancy

Nearly all of the various types of visual rearrangements involve a disruption of visual position constancy, although only a few experiments have been designed as direct tests of adaptation to this distortion. From the latter studies has come a better understanding of the normal operation of this constancy as seen, for example, in Hay's model (Figure 7.1, p. 173). An integral aspect of this model is that the nervous system is continuously comparing expected with actual input. It follows from this that normal visual position constancy requires continuous maintenance and is easily modified. Evidence for these predictions has come from Wallach and his colleagues, in studies described in Chapter 7. This model also predicts and explains the recalibration of visual position constancy that must occur during the period of head growth. Furthermore, Robinson (1975a) has argued that the process of adaptation to induced loss of visual position constancy may reveal the mechanism by which the nervous system (perhaps the cerebellum) repairs itself from sudden peripheral vestibular lesions.

The perception of depth and distance

The study of adaptation to distortions of depth and distance has involved several instances in which normally redundant perceptual cues have been placed into conflict and their relative importance for "normal" vision thereby assessed. For example, when binocular disparity is made discrepant with the *kinetic depth effect* cue, it is the former that is recalibrated (Wallach *et al.,* 1963b). Similarly, when changes in retinal image size resulting from an approaching or receding object are discrepant with the concomitant changes in accommodation/convergence, the latter undergoes modification (Wallach & Frey, 1972c; Wallach *et al.,* 1972). On the other hand, a conflict between accommodation/convergence cues and proprioception/kinesthesis is resolved by a change in the body sense (Wallach & Smith, 1972). One conclusion from this series of experiments is that under everyday conditions depth perception relies more heavily on the *kinetic depth effect* than on accommodation/convergence cues, which, in turn, have priority over felt limb position sense.

As with visual orientation and visual position constancy, depth and distance perception appear to be maintained and strengthened by normal experience (Epstein, 1971; Wallach & Karsh, 1963a). It is reasonable to assume that head growth leads to a "natural" recalibration of those distance and depth cues that are mediated by interocular distance. As Epstein and Daviess (1972) suggested, the basis for this recalibration may be the monocular cues (e.g., interposition), since they are unaffected by head growth. Epstein (1968) has also speculated that the recalibration of some distance/depth cues in adults may result from a mechanism that operates during the neonatal period to impart to certain cues the ability to signal location in the in–out dimension. By repeated pairing with an innately effective cue (such as motion parallax) an initially ineffective cue (such as relative visual angle) may be made useful. Wallach (1968) proposed a similar mechanism when he argued that object-relative motion perception is acquired from repeated association with the innately present perception of subject-relative motion.

The research on underwater distortions (Chapter 12) has demonstrated that the distance cue of aerial perspective may be more important for both size and distance perception than has generally been thought and may operate to produce a variety of illusions, both under water and in fog or haze. This research has also led to some "dry" experiments in which it was demonstrated that distance is overestimated when depth cues are scarce (Luria & Kinney, 1968b) and that stereoacuity deteriorates in a *Ganzfeld* (Luria, 1969).

Form perception

The research on adaptation to distortions of form (Chapter 9) has led to still another theoretically important distinction. This is the difference between egocentric direction and internal geometry, or what has been termed the *subject-relative* and *object-relative* aspects of form perception (Rock, 1966, p. 180). This same sort of distinction has been made by Held (1968a) and Redding (1975a). As we have seen, these appear to be separate dimensions, differing in relative modifiability, physiological basis, and possibly developmental origin. It is likely that different forms vary with respect to the degree to which these two aspects contribute to the resulting perception.

IMPLICATIONS OF DIFFERENTIAL RATES OF ADAPTATION

The fact that different types of distortion generally induce different rates and extents of adaptation sheds light on the nature of the perceptual and perceptual–motor capacities involved. The distinctly different acquisition and decay curves for visual adaptation to optical tilt and prismatic displacement, as demonstrated by Redding (e.g., 1973b) and described briefly in Chapter 6 (p. 144), strongly suggest that visual orientation and egocentric direction are qualitatively distinct perceptual processes. The results of Hajos and Ritter (1965), Held (1955a), and Pick and Hay (1964), who obtained widely different adaptation curves for the various effects of prismatic distortion, also indicate independent mechanisms. In the study by Pick and Hay, the maximum adaptation after a 42-day wearing period ranged from 90% for eye–hand coordination to about 10% for the compression and expansion effects resulting from lateral head movements. Although this evidence that several perceptual capacities are qualitatively different does not explain how they operate, it does suggest the inadvisability of attempting to explain them as different manifestations of the same process or of seeking a common physiological basis.

SOME GENERAL THEORIES OF VISUAL PERCEPTION

The results of studies on adaptation to perceptual rearrangement and the logical analysis of the relevant capacities that has inevitably arisen from this research have had a strong impact on several general theories of visual perception.

The first of these was proposed by J. G. Taylor (1962), who spent some time at Kohler's laboratory at the University of Innsbruck. It is beyond the scope of this chapter to discuss in detail or critically evaluate Taylor's theory. In brief, he argues that perception is based on the acquisition of rather specific *readinesses* ("engrams") to emit motor or verbal responses to sensory input, based on a conditioning history of rewards and punishments. This is a strictly empiricistic theory, inspired in large part by the presumed perceptual plasticity obtained in the rearrangement studies by Kohler and by Taylor.

A modified version of Taylor's theory has been proposed by Festinger and his associates (e.g., Festinger et al., 1967), partly on the basis of studies of adaptation to prismatic curvature. This has been termed the *efferent readiness theory* and was discussed in some detail in Chapter 9 (pp. 208–209). Although Festinger et al. maintain that visual experience is the result of the readiness to respond motorically to the environment, they do not explicitly postulate the traditional learning concepts of reward, punishment, or a motivational system. Furthermore, their theory is limited to the perception of visual location and form.

Another theory of visual perception that emanated, in part, from the adaptation research is that proposed by Rock (1966) and discussed in various parts of this book. Rock has argued that normal visual perception (of size, shape, and orientation) is based on the registration of the *relationship* of retinal images to one another and to the visible or phenomenal body. Repeated experience with the everyday (or visually distorted) world leads to the establishment of *memory traces* of the retinal stimuli; these traces are in turn associated with memories of the relationship that these retinal images have with the visible body. For example, a retinal image of a particular size, in conjunction with cues for a particular distance, leads to the memory of the relationship between the visible object and the visible body. This memory represents the perception of *absolute* size and is responsible for the fact that a visually magnified or reduced environment will immediately be seen as large or small by the adult subject. In general, Rock's theory of adaptation gives strong emphasis to experience, although, contrary to Taylor's theory, it is not totally empiristic, nor does it involve reward and punishment.

Indirect Contributions:
The Stimulation of Other Varieties of Research

The adaptation research has inspired or reawakened interests in a number of related areas. The early work by Held and Hein (1958, 1963) on prism adaptation and its implications for neonatal development has contributed to a strong recent interest in the effects of various kinds of rearing conditions, such as deprivation and selective visual exposure, upon both behavioral and physiological development (Mitchell, in press). There have also been several neonatal enrichment experiments with human infants, and some of the results have been interpreted in terms of Held's reafference model (e.g., White & Castle, 1964; White, Castle, & Held, 1964; White & Held, 1966).

The interest in adaptation to perceptual rearrangement appears to have spread to other forms of perceptual plasticity. There has been a renewal of interest in *figural aftereffects* (Chapter 6, pp. 139–141; Chapter 9, pp. 199–201), as seen in the research of Ganz (1966). Another interesting example of visual modification which has attracted a great deal of attention is the so-called *McCollough effect* (McCollough, 1965a). This phenomenon, the discovery of which was apparently suggested to McCollough by Kohler's observation of eye position-contingent color aftereffects (Kohler, 1964, pp. 68–74), may be induced in the following manner. A grating of alternating *vertical* red and black bars is viewed for 5 sec, followed after a 1-sec interval by a *horizontal* grating of green and black bars. This sequence is repeated for several minutes, and it is found that vertical white bars in a black and white grating come to look distinctly tinged with green, whereas horizontal white bars appear pink. In the original experiment this orientation-specific color aftereffect was found to persist for several hours—much longer than any of the traditional color aftereffects.[2]

Although the McCollough effect has been examined in numerous experiments (see Skowbo, Timney, Gentry, & Morant, 1975, for a review), its explanation remains unclear. A number of investigators have concurred with McCollough's (1965a) conclusion that it represents the adaptation of edge detectors sensitive to both color and orientation, but there is a great deal of evidence (e.g., Murch, 1976) to suggest that it is actually an instance of very specific conditioning, in which the conditional stimulus is the retinal orientation of the contours and the conditioned response the color adaptation effect.

Numerous other examples of contingent aftereffects have been produced since Kohler's original reports. Examples are movement-contingent color aftereffects (Hepler, 1968; Stromeyer & Mansfield, 1970), color-contingent orientation aftereffects (Held & Shattuck, 1971; Shattuck & Held, 1974), color-contingent motion aftereffects (Favreau, Emerson, & Corballis, 1972), texture-contingent visual

---

[2] Jones and Holding (1975) reported that if the exposure period is extended and only one test of the aftereffect taken, McCollough effects could be detected *several months* later! Frome, Harris, and Levinson (1975) have also provided evidence of long-lasting "sensory" effects in the form of a size aftereffect that lasted for 24 hr after 15 min of inspecting a vertical or horizontal sinusoidal grating.

motion aftereffects (Mayhew & Anstis, 1972; Walker, 1972), and tactual size aftereffects contingent on hand position (Walker & Shea, 1974).

Directions for Future Research

In concluding this book I would like to suggest some areas relevant to the present topic where further research is likely to be especially fruitful.

PERCEPTUAL REARRANGEMENT STUDIES

Investigating adaptation to perceptual rearrangement will continue to produce useful information. Some of the more important goals of this future research are the following.

1. To devise new varieties of conflict between cues of distance perception, to add to our knowledge about the relative weighting of these cues during everyday vision.
2. To make further direct comparisons between different varieties of visual rearrangement, as Redding (e.g., 1973b) has done with prismatic displacement and tilt. By so doing it will be possible to look for common adaptive mechanisms and to examine the relationship between different perceptual capacities.
3. To examine the relationship between proprioceptive and visual adaptation to prismatic displacement. For example, it may prove informative to discover why it is that adaptation often begins as a shift in felt limb position but later becomes primarily a change in vision (i.e., oculomotor shift).
4. To determine the extent to which previous reports of visual *recalibration* should be reinterpreted as the visual effects of eye *muscle potentiation* (EMP), as proposed by Ebenholtz and his colleagues.
5. To expand greatly the relatively meager current knowledge about adaptation to auditory rearrangement, underwater distortions, and optically altered size.
6. To investigate further the conditions under which the normal "weighting" of various redundant cues or varieties of spatial input can be altered. More work is needed on the effects of selective attention, increasing the precision or saliency of various cues, and providing experience designed to strengthen or reduce reliance on particular cues prior to exposure to rearrangement involving these cues.
7. Finally, to attempt to formulate a viable model of adaptation,

perhaps along the lines of the one proposed in this chapter. Such a model must be capable of incorporating most or all of the adaptation findings and of successfully predicting novel observations.

RESEARCH ON OTHER PERCEPTUAL PHENOMENA

The adaptation studies have revealed a number of new things about "normal" perception and stimulated interest in a variety of questions that may be studied without recourse to perceptual rearrangement. A prime example is the EMP effect which, even if it is shown conclusively to be only one of the components of rearrangement-induced changes in vision, will remain an interesting phenomenon in its own right, since further investigation of its role in "normal" perception is likely to produce valuable information. Another area of research that is especially interesting is that of the so-called *contingent perceptions*. It is possible that the role of associative factors in perception is much greater than is generally believed. For example, Kohler (1974) has noted that the apparent velocity and acceleration of a falling object are quite different when the object is caused, by means of inverting spectacles, to fall in an apparently upward direction, and he argued that this is another example of conditioned perception. It might prove quite fruitful to embark on a systematic search for situations in which the perception of one event is typically associated (either naturally or experimentally) with some other event and then to assess the effect on this perception of removing or altering the associated event.

A final area where further research is likely to prove particularly valuable is the comparison between efferent and afferent determinants of felt body position. Recent examples of research on this issue are the investigations by Bossom (1974) and Taub, Goldberg, and Taub (1975) on the effects of deafferentation on visuomotor coordination, by Shebilske (1977) on the role of extraretinal factors on visual direction constancy, and by Stevens et al. (1976) on the perceptual effects of body and eye movements during muscular paralysis.

We have come a long way since the pioneering studies of Helmholtz and Stratton. As the reader can attest, the number of published experiments on adaptation to perceptual rearrangement to appear since those early days is staggering. An attempt has been made here to establish some order in this multitude and to assess the impact of this research on our understanding of perception and perceptual learning. If we have learned one thing, it is that human beings whose vision or hearing has been subjected to stable rearrangement are

capable of significantly modifying their perception and perceptual–
motor behavior. Contrary to the "hard empiricist" line, however, this
adaptability is not unlimited. Nevertheless, human beings have
repeatedly demonstrated the capacity to circumvent their perceptual
limitations intellectually when confronted with a disruptive sensory
environment, so that they may once again operate in it effectively.

References

Abplanalp, P., & Held, R. Effects of de-correlated visual feedback on adaptation to wedge prisms. Paper presented at meetings of Eastern Psychological Association, Atlantic City, April, 1965.

Adams, J. A., & Dijkstra, S. Short-term memory for motor responses. *Journal of Experimental Psychology,* 1966, *71,* 314–318.

Adolfson, J., & Berghage, T. *Perception and performance under water.* New York: Wiley, 1974.

Albert, D. J. Rotation of the visual field in the rat. Unpublished manuscript, Univ. of Michigan, 1966.

Alpert, R., & Haber, R. N. Anxiety in academic achievement situations. *Journal of Abnormal and Social Psychology,* 1960, *61,* 207–215.

Ames, A., Jr. Binocular vision as affected by relations between uniocular stimulus-patterns in commonplace environments. *American Journal of Psychology,* 1946, *59,* 333–357.

Ammons, R. B. Acquisition of motor skill. I. Quantitative analysis and theoretical formulation. *Psychological Review,* 1947, *54,* 263–281.

Ammons, R. B., Farr, R. G., Block, E., Neumann, E., Dey, M., Marion, R., & Ammons, C. H. Long-term retention of perceptual-motor skills. *Journal of Experimental Psychology,* 1958, *55,* 318–328.

Arlinsky, M. B. On the failure of fowl to adapt to prism induced displacement: Some theoretical analyses. *Psychonomic Science,* 1967, *7,* 237–238.

Asch, S. E., & Witkin, H. A. Studies in space orientation: I. Perception of the upright with displaced visual fields. *Journal of Experimental Psychology,* 1948, *38,* 325–337. (a)

Asch, S. E., & Witkin, H. A. Studies in space orientation. II. Perception of the upright with displaced visual fields and with body tilted. *Journal of Experimental Psychology,* 1948, *38,* 455–477. (b)

303

Aubert, H. Eine scheinbare bedeutende Drehung von Objekten bei Neigung des Kopfes nach rechts oder links. *Virchows Archives,* 1861, *20,* 381–393.

Bach-y-Rita, P. Extraocular proprioception and muscle function. *Bibliotheca Ophthalmologica,* 1972, *82,* 56–60.

Baddeley, A. D. Diver performance. In J. D. Woods and J. N. Lythgoe (Eds.), *Underwater science.* London: Oxford Univ. Press, 1971.

Baily, J. S. Adaptation to prisms: Do proprioceptive changes mediate adapted behavior with ballistic arm movements? *Quarterly Journal of Experimental Psychology,* 1972, *24,* 8–20. (a)

Baily, J. S. Arm-body adaptation with passive arm movements. *Perception and Psychophysics,* 1972, *12,* 39–44. (b)

Baizer, J. S., & Glickstein, M. Role of cerebellum in prism adaptation. *Journal of Physiology,* 1973, *236,* 34–35P.

Ballard, P. B. Oblivescence and reminiscence. *British Journal of Psychology Monograph,* 1913, No. 2.

Barnes, G. R., & Gresty, M. A. Characteristics of eye movements to targets of short duration. *Aerospace Medicine,* 1973, *44,* 1236–1240.

Batteau, D. W. Localization of sound: A new theory of human audition. Final Report, Contract N123-(60530) 302083A, U.S. Naval Ordinance Test Station, China Lake, Calif., Sept., 1963.

Batteau, D. W. The role of the pinna in human localization. *Proceedings of the Royal Society,* 1967, *168,* No. 1011, Series B, 158–180.

Bauer, J., & Efstathiou, A. Effects of adaptation to visual displacement on pointing "straight ahead." Paper presented at meetings of Eastern Psychological Association, Atlantic City, April, 1965.

Bauer, J. A., Jr., & Vandeventer, M. Changes in pointing straight ahead following displaced vision result from a process independent of that which produces adaptive shifts in eye-hand coordination. Paper presented at meetings of Eastern Psychological Association, Boston, April, 1967.

Becker, W. The control of eye movements in the saccadic system. *Bibliotheca Ophthalmologica,* 1972, *82,* 233–243.

Becker, W., & Fuchs, A. F. Further properties of the human saccadic system: Eye movements and corrective saccades with and without visual fixation points. *Vision Research,* 1969, *9,* 1247–1259.

Beckett, P. A., Melamed, L. E., & Halay, M. Prism awareness, exposure duration, and the linear model in prism adaptation. Paper presented at meetings of Midwestern Psychological Association, Chicago, May, 1975.

Berkeley, G. *An essay towards a new theory of vision.* New York: Dutton, 1910.

Bilodeau, I. McD. Information feedback. In E. A. Bilodeau (Ed.), *Acquisition of skill.* New York: Academic Press, 1966.

Bilodeau, E. A., & Levy, C. M. Long-term memory as a function of retention time and other conditions of training and recall. *Psychological Review,* 1964, *71,* 27–41.

Bishop, H. E. Innateness and learning in the visual perception of direction. Unpublished doctoral dissertation, Univ. of Chicago, 1959.

Black, A. H., Carlson, N. J., & Solomon, R. L. Exploratory studies of the conditioning of autonomic responses in curarized dogs. *Psychological Monographs,* 1962, *76,* (29, Whole No. 548).

Blough, D. S., & Lipsitt, L. P. The discriminative control of behavior. In J. W. Kling & L. A. Riggs (Eds.), *Woodworth & Schlosberg's experimental psychology* (3rd ed.). New York: Holt, 1971.

Bossom, J. Mechanisms of prism adaptation in normal monkeys. *Psychonomic Science,* 1964, *1,* 377–378.

Bossom, J. The effect of brain lesions on prism-adaptation in monkey. *Psychonomic Science,* 1965, *2,* 45–46.

Bossom, J. Movement without proprioception. *Brain Research,* 1974, *71,* 285–296.

Bossom, J., & Hamilton, C. R. Interocular transfer of prism-altered coordinations in split-brain monkeys. *Journal of Comparative and Physiological Psychology,* 1963, *56,* 769–774.

Bossom, J., & Held, R. Transfer of error-correction in adaptation to prisms. *American Psychologist,* 1959, *14,* 436.

Bossom, J., & Ommaya, A. K. Visuo-motor adaptation (to prismatic transformation of the retinal image) in monkeys with bilateral dorsal rhizotomy. *Brain,* 1968, *91,* 161–172.

Bowen, H. M., Andersen, B., & Promisel, D. Studies of divers' performance during the SEALAB II project. *Human Factors,* 1966, *6,* 183–199.

Bower, T. G. R. *Development in infancy.* San Francisco: Freeman, 1974.

Brindley, G. S., & Merton, P. A. The absence of position sense in the human eye. *Journal of Physiology,* 1960, *153,* 127–130.

Brindley, G. S., Goodwin, G. M., Kulikowski, J. J., & Leighton, D. Stability of vision with a paralyzed eye. *Journal of Physiology,* 1976, *258,* 65–66.

Brown, G. G. Perception of depth with disoriented vision. *British Journal of Psychology,* 1928, *19,* 117–146.

Burian, H. M. Influence of prolonged wearing of meridional size lenses on spatial localization. *Archives of Ophthalmology,* 1943, *30,* 645–666.

Burnham, C. A. Adaptation to prismatically induced curvature with nonvisible arm movements. *Psychonomic Science,* 1968, *10,* 273–274.

Burnham, C. A., & Aertker, D. R., Jr. Rotary motion and efferent readiness. *Perception & Psychophysics,* 1970, *7,* 311–314.

Canon, L. K. Adaptation to simultaneous displacement of the visual and auditory fields. *Proceedings of the 74th Annual Convention of the American Psychological Association,* 1966, *1,* 13–14.

Canon, L. K. Intermodality inconsistency of input and directed attention as determinants of the nature of adaptation. *Journal of Experimental Psychology,* 1970, *84,* 141–147.

Canon, L. K. Directed attention and maladaptive "adaptation" to displacement of the visual field. *Journal of Experimental Psychology,* 1971, *88,* 403–408.

Cegalis, J. A. Perceptual adaptation: An analysis of conflict. Unpublished doctoral dissertation, Pennsylvania State Univ., 1971.

Cegalis, J. A., & Murdza, S. Changes of auditory word discrimination induced by inversion of the visual field. Paper presented at meetings of Eastern Psychological Association, New York City, April, 1975.

Cegalis, J. A., & Young, R. Effect of inversion-induced conflict on field dependence. *Journal of Abnormal Psychology,* 1974, *83,* 373–379.

Choe, C. S., & Welch, R. B. Variables affecting the intermanual transfer and decay of prism adaptation. *Journal of Experimental Psychology,* 1974, *102,* 1076–1084.

Cohen, H. B. Some critical factors in prism adaptation. *American Journal of Psychology,* 1966, *79,* 285–290.

Cohen, M. M. Curvature after-effects following exposure under prismatic viewing conditions. Unpublished doctoral dissertation, Univ. of Pennsylvania, 1965.

Cohen, M. M. Continuous versus terminal visual feedback in prism aftereffects. *Perceptual and Motor Skills,* 1967, *24,* 1295–1302.

Cohen, M. M. Visual feedback, distribution of practice, and intermanual transfer of prism aftereffects. *Perceptual and Motor Skills,* 1973, *37,* 599–609.

Cohen, M. M. Changes in auditory localization following prismatic exposure under continuous and terminal visual feedback. *Perceptual and Motor Skills,* 1974, *38,* 1202.

Cohen, M. M., & Held, R. Degrading visual-motor coordination by exposure to disordered re-afferent stimulation. Paper presented at meetings of Eastern Psychological Association, New York City, April, 1960.

Cook, T. W. Studies in cross education. I. Mirror tracing the star-shaped maze. *Journal of Experimental Psychology,* 1933, *16,* 144–160.

Coren, S. Adaptation to prismatic displacement as a function of the amount of available information. *Psychonomic Science,* 1966, *4,* 407–408.

Coren, S., & Porac, C. The fading of stabilized images: Eye movements and information processing. *Perception & Psychophysics,* 1974, *16,* 529–534.

Craske, B. Change in transfer function of joint receptor output. *Nature,* 1966, *210,* 764–765. (a)

Craske, B. Intermodal transfer of adaptation to displacement. *Nature,* 1966, *210,* 765. (b)

Craske, B. Adaptation to prisms: Change in internally registered eye-position. *British Journal of Psychology,* 1967, *58,* 329–335.

Craske, B., & Crawshaw, M. Adaptive changes of opposite sign in the oculomotor systems of the two eyes. *Quarterly Journal of Experimental Psychology,* 1974, *26,* 106–113.

Craske, B., & Crawshaw, M. Spatial discordance is a sufficient condition for oculomotor adaption to prisms: Eye muscle potentiation need not be a factor. *Perception & Psychophysics,* 1978, *23,* 75–79.

Craske, B., & Gregg, S. J. Prism after-effects: Identical results for visual targets and unexposed limb. *Nature,* 1966, *212,* 104–105.

Craske, B., & Kenney, F. The shrinking arm: Adaptive plasticity in perceived arm length. Paper presented at meetings of Canadian Psychological Association, Vancouver, June, 1977.

Craske, B., & Templeton, W. B. Prolonged oscillation of the eyes induced by conficting position input. *Journal of Experimental Psychology,* 1968, *76,* 387–393.

Crawshaw, M., & Craske, B. No retinal component in prism adaptation. *Acta Psychologica,* 1974, *38,* 421–423.

Crawshaw, M., & Craske, B. Oculomotor adaptation to prisms: Complete transfer between eyes. *British Journal of Psychology,* 1976, *67,* 475–478.

Czermak, J. Physiologische Studien. III: Sitzungsberichte der kaiserlichen. Vienna: Akademie der Wissenschaften (Mathematische-Naturwissenschaftliche Klasse), 1885, *17,* 563–600.

Day, R. H., & Singer, G. Sensory adaptation and behavioral compensation with spatially transformed vision and hearing. *Psychological Bulletin,* 1967, *67,* 307–322.

Devane, J. R. Proaction in the recovery from practice under visual displacement. *Perceptual and Motor Skills,* 1968, *27,* 411–416.

Dewar, R. Adaptation to displaced vision: The influence of distribution of practice on retention. *Perception & Psychophysics,* 1970, *8,* 33–34. (a)

Dewar, R. Adaptation to displaced vision: Amount of optical displacement and practice. *Perception & Psychophysics,* 1970, *8,* 313–316. (b)

Dewar, R. Adaptation to displaced vision—type of information feedback. Paper presented at meetings of Canadian Psychological Association, Winnipeg, May, 1970. (c)

Dewar, R. Adaptation to displaced vision: Variations on the "prismatic shaping" technique. *Perception & Psychophysics,* 1971, *9,* 155–157.

Ebenholtz, S. M. Adaptation to a rotated visual field as a function of degree of optical tilt and exposure time. *Journal of Experimental Psychology,* 1966, *72,* 629–634.

Ebenholtz, S. M. Transfer of adaptation as a function of interpolated optical tilt to the ipsilateral and contralateral eye. *Journal of Experimental Psychology,* 1967, *73,* 263–267.

Ebenholtz, S. M. Some evidence for a comparator in adaptation to optical tilt. *Journal of Experimental Psychology,* 1968, *77,* 94–100. (a)

Ebenholtz, S. M. Readaptation and decay after exposure to optical tilt. *Journal of Experimental Psychology,* 1968, *78,* 350–351. (b)

Ebenholtz, S. M. Transfer and decay functions in adaptation to optical tilt. *Journal of Experimental Psychology,* 1969, *81,* 170–173.

Ebenholtz, S. M. On the relation between interocular transfer of adaptation and Hering's law of equal innervation. *Psychological Review,* 1970, *77,* 343–347.

Ebenholtz, S. M. Optimal input rates for tilt adaptation. *American Journal of Psychology,* 1973, *86,* 193–200.

Ebenholtz, S. M. The possible role of eye-muscle potentiation in several forms of prism adaptation. *Perception,* 1974, *3,* 477–485.

Ebenholtz, S. M. Additivity of aftereffects of maintained head and eye rotations: An alternative to recalibration. *Perception & Psychophysics,* 1976, *19,* 113–116.

Ebenholtz, S. M., & Mayer, D. Rate of adaptation under constant and varied optical tilt. *Perceptual and Motor Skills,* 1968, *26,* 507–509.

Ebenholtz, S. M., & Paap, K. R. Further evidence for an orientation constancy based upon registration of ocular position. *Psychological Research,* 1976, *38,* 395–409.

Ebenholtz, S. M., & Wolfson, D. M. Perceptual aftereffects of sustained convergence. *Perception & Psychophysics,* 1975, *17,* 485–491.

Ebner, E., Broekema, V., & Ritzler, B. Adaptation to altered visual-proprioceptive input in normals and schizophrenics. *Archives of General Psychiatry,* 1971, *24,* 367–371.

Efstathiou, E. Effects of exposure time and magnitude of prism transform on eye-hand coordination. *Journal of Experimental Psychology,* 1969, *81,* 235–240.

Efstathiou, A., Bauer, J., Greene, M., & Held, R. Altered reaching following adaptation to optical displacement of the hand. *Journal of Experimental Psychology,* 1967, *73,* 113–120.

Efstathiou, A. Correlated and de-correlated visual feedback in modifying eye-hand coordination. Paper presented at meetings of Eastern Psychological Association, New York, May, 1963.

Epstein, W. The influence of assumed size on apparent distance. *American Journal of Psychology,* 1963, *76,* 257–265.

Epstein, W. *Varieties of perceptual learning.* New York: McGraw-Hill, 1967.

Epstein, W. Modification of the disparity-depth relationship as a result of exposure to conflicting cues. *American Journal of Psychology,* 1968, *81,* 189–197.

Epstein, W. Adaptation to uniocular image magnification after varying preadaptation activities. *American Journal of Psychology,* 1971, *84,* 66–74.

Epstein, W. Retention of adaptation to uniocular image magnification: Effect of interpolated activity. *Journal of Experimental Psychology,* 1972, *92,* 319–324. (a)

Epstein, W. Adaptation to uniocular image magnification: Is the underlying shift proprioceptive? *Perception & Psychophysics,* 1972, *11,* 89–91. (b)

Epstein, W., & Daviess, N. Modification of depth judgment following exposures to magnification of uniocular image: Are changes in perceived absolute distance and

308   References

registered direction of gaze involved? *Perception & Psychophysics*, 1972, *12*, 315–317.

Epstein, W., & Morgan, C. L. Adaptation to uniocular image magnification: Modification of the disparity-depth relationship. *American Journal of Psychology*, 1970, *83*, 322–329.

Epstein, W., & Morgan-Paap, C. L. The effect of level of depth processing and degree of informational discrepancy on adaptation to uniocular image magnification. *Journal of Experimental Psychology*, 1974, *102*, 585–594.

Erismann, T. Das Werden der Wahrnehmung. *Tagungsbericht d. Berufsverbandes Deutscher Psychologen*, Bonn, 1947, 54–56.

Ewert, P. H. A study of the effect of inverted retinal stimulation upon spatially coordinated behavior. *Genetic Psychology Monographs*, 1930, *7*, 177–363.

Eysenck, H. J. The questionnaire measurement of neuroticism and extraversion. *Revista di Psicologia*, 1965, *50*, 113–140.

Eysenck, H. J., Granger, G. W., & Brengelmann, J. C. *Perceptual processes and mental illness*. New York: Basic Books, 1957.

Fantz, R. L. Ontogeny of perception. In A. M. Schrier, H. F. Harlow, & F. Stollnitz (Eds.), *Behavior of non-human primates*. New York: Academic Press, 1965.

Fantz, R. L. Visual perception and experience in early infancy: A look at the hidden side of behavior development. In H. W. Stevenson, E. H. Hess, & H. L. Rheingold (Eds.), *Early behavior*. New York: Wiley, 1967.

Faust, K. J., & Beckman, E. L. Evaluation of a swimmer's contact air-water lens system. *Military Medicine*, 1966, *131*, 779–788.

Favreau, O. E., Emerson, V. F., & Corballis, M. C. Motion perception: A color-contingent aftereffect. *Science*, 1972, *176*, 78–79.

Feinstein, S. H. Human hearing under water: Are things as bad as they seem? *The Journal of the Acoustical Society of America*, 1966, *40*, 1561–1562.

Ferris, S. H. Improvement of absolute distance estimation underwater. *Perceptual and Motor Skills*, 1972, *35*, 299–305. (a)

Ferris, S. H. Loss of position constancy underwater. *Psychonomic Science*, 1972, *27*, 337–338. (b)

Ferris, S. H. Improving absolute distance estimation in clear and in turbid water. *Perceptual and Motor Skills*, 1973, *36*, 771–776. (a)

Ferris, S. H. Improving distance estimation underwater: Long-term effectiveness of training. *Perceptual and Motor Skills*, 1973, *36*, 1089–1090. (b)

Festinger, L., Burnham, C. A., Ono, H., & Bamber, D. Efference and the conscious experience of perception. *Journal of Experimental Psychology Monograph*, 1967, *74*, (4, Whole No. 637).

Festinger, L., & Canon, L. K. Information about spatial location based on knowledge about efference. *Psychological Review*, 1965, *72*, 373–384.

Festinger, L., White, C. W., & Allyn, M. R. Eye movements and decrement in the Müller-Lyer illusion. *Perception & Psychophysics*, 1968, *3*, 376–382.

Fishkin, S. M. Passive vs. active exposure and other variables related to the occurrence of hand adaptation to lateral displacement. *Perceptual and Motor Skills*, 1969, *29*, 291–297.

Fitts, W. H. *Tennessee self concept scale*. Nashville, Tennessee: Counselor Recordings and Tests, 1965.

Foley, J. E. Adaptation to magnifying and minifying spectacles. Unpublished manuscript, Univ. of Toronto, 1965.

Foley, J. E. A further study of alternation of normal and distorted vision. *Psychonomic Science,* 1967, *9,* 483–484.

Foley, J. E. Prism adaptation with simultaneous receipt of normal input. *Perception & Psychophysics,* 1970, *8,* 393–395.

Foley, J. E. Factors governing interocular transfer of prism adaptation. *Psychological Review,* 1974, *81,* 183–186.

Foley, J. E., & Abel, S. M. A study of alternation of normal and distorted vision. *Canadian Journal of Psychology,* 1967, *21,* 220–230.

Foley, J. E., & Maynes, F. J. Comparison of training methods in the production of prism adaptation. *Journal of Experimental Psychology,* 1969, *81,* 151–155.

Foley, J. E., & McChesney, J. The selective utilization of information in the optical array. *Psychological Research,* 1976, *38,* 251–265.

Foley, J. E., & Miyanshi, K. Interocular effects in prism adaptation. *Science,* 1969, *165,* 311–312.

Foley, J. P. An experimental investigation of the effect of prolonged inversion of the visual field in the rhesus monkey (macaca mulatta). *Journal of Genetic Psychology,* 1940, *56,* 21–51.

Franklin, S. S., Ross, H. E., & Weltman, G. Size-distance invariance in perceptual adaptation. *Psychonomic Science,* 1970, *21,* 229–231.

Freedman, S. J. Perceptual changes in sensory deprivation: Suggestions for a conative theory. *Journal of Nervous Mental Disease,* 1961, *132,* 17–21.

Freedman, S. J. Perceptual compensation and learning. In S. J. Freedman (Ed.), *The neuropsychology of spatially oriented behavior.* Homewood, Illinois: Dorsey Press, 1968. (a)

Freedman, S. J. On the mechanisms of perceptual compensation. In S. J. Freedman (Ed.), *The neuropsychology of spatially oriented behavior.* Homewood, Illinois: Dorsey Press, 1968. (b)

Freedman, S. J., & Gardos, G. Compensation for auditory re-arrangement and transfer to hand-eye coordination. Paper presented at MIT Conference on Adaptation, Cambridge, Massachusetts, June, 1965.

Freedman, S. J., Hall, S. B., & Rekosh, J. H. Effects on hand-eye coordination of two different arm motions during adaptation to displaced vision. *Perceptual and Motor Skills,* 1965, *20,* 1054–1056.

Freedman, S. J., & Pfaff, D. W. The effect of exposure to dichotic noise on the discrimination of dichotic time differences. U.S. Air Force Office of Scientific Research, Technical Report AFOSR-503, April, 1961.

Freedman, S. J., & Pfaff, D. W. The effect of dichotic noise on auditory localization. *Journal of Auditory Research,* 1962, *2,* 305–310. (a)

Freedman, S. J., & Pfaff, D. W. Trading relations between dichotic time and intensity differences in auditory localization. *Journal of Auditory Research,* 1962, *2,* 311–318. (b)

Freedman, S. J., & Secunda, S. An analysis of the effects of motion upon auditory function during prolonged atypical stimulation. U.S. Air Force Office of Scientific Research, Technical Report AFOSR-2078, April, 1962.

Freedman, S. J., & Stampfer, K. Changes in auditory localization with displaced ears. Paper presented at meetings of Psychonomic Society, Niagara Falls, Ontario, October, 1964.

Freedman, S. J., Wilson, L., & Rekosh, J. H. Compensation for auditory re-arrangement in hand-ear coordination. *Perceptual and Motor Skills,* 1967, *24,* 1207–1210.

Freedman, S. J., & Zacks, J. L. Effects of active and passive movement upon auditory function during prolonged atypical stimulation. *Perceptual and Motor Skills,* 1964, *18,* 361–366.

Freides, D. Human information processing and sensory modality: Cross-modal functions, information complexity, memory, and deficit. *Psychological Bulletin,* 1974, *81,* 284–310.

Frome, F., Harris, C. S., & Levinson, J. Z. Extremely long-lasting shifts in perception of size after adaptation to gratings. Paper presented at meetings of Psychonomic Society, Denver, November, 1975.

Fry, G. A., Bridgman, C. S., & Ellerbrock, V. J. The effects of atmospheric scattering on binocular depth perception. *American Journal of Optometry,* 1949, *26,* 9–15.

Ganz, L. Mechanism of the figural after-effect. *Psychological Review,* 1966, *73,* 128–150.

Ganz, L. Orientation in visual space by neonates and its modification by visual deprivation. In A. H. Riesen (Ed.), *The developmental neuropsychology of sensory deprivation.* New York: Academic Press, 1975. Pp. 169–210.

Giannitrapani, D. Adaptation to a distorted visual field: An organismic approach. Paper presented at meetings of Eastern Psychological Association, New York City, April, 1957.

Giannitrapani, D. Changes in adaptation to prolonged perceptual distortion: A developmental study. Unpublished doctoral dissertation, Clark Univ., 1958.

Gibson, E. J. *Principles of perceptual learning and development.* New York: Appleton, 1969.

Gibson, J. J. Adaptation, after-effect, and contrast in the perception of curved lines. *Journal of Experimental Psychology,* 1933, *16,* 1–31.

Gibson, J. J. What gives rise to the perception of motion? *Psychological Review,* 1968, *75,* 335–346.

Gibson, J. J., & Mowrer, O. H. Determinants of the perceived vertical and horizontal. *Psychological Review,* 1938, *45,* 300–323.

Gibson, J. J., & Radner, M. Adaptation, after-effect, and contrast in the perception of tilted lines. I. Quantitative studies. *Journal of Experimental Psychology,* 1937, *20,* 453–467. (a)

Gibson, J. J., & Radner, M. Adaptation, after-effect, and contrast in the perception of tilted lines. II. Simultaneous contrast and the areal restriction of the after-effect. *Journal of Experimental Psychology,* 1937, *20,* 553–569. (b)

Goldberg, I. A., Taub, E., & Berman, A. J. Decay of prism after-effect and interlimb transfer of adaptation. Paper presented at meetings of Eastern Psychological Association, Boston, April, 1967.

Gough, G. H. *California psychological inventory.* Palo Alto, California: Consulting Psychological Press, 1957.

Graybiel, A. The oculogravic illusion. *Archives of Ophthalmology, New York,* 1952, *48,* 605–615.

Graybiel, A. M., & Held, R. Prismatic adaptation under scotopic and photopic conditions. *Journal of Experimental Psychology,* 1970, *85,* 16–22.

Greene, M. E. A further study of the proprioceptive change hypothesis of prism adaptation. Paper presented at meetings of Eastern Psychological Association, Boston, April, 1967.

Gregory, R. L. Eye movements and the stability of the visual world. *Nature,* 1958, *182,* 1214–1216.

Gregory, R. L. *Eye and brain.* New York: McGraw-Hill, 1973.

Grice, G. R. The relation of secondary reinforcement to delayed reward in visual discrimination learning. *Journal of Experimental Psychology,* 1948, *38,* 1–16.

Grice, G. R., & Reynolds, B. Effects of varying amounts of rest on conventional and bilateral transfer 'reminiscence.' *Journal of Experimental Psychology,* 1952, *44,* 247–252.

Guilford, J. P. *An inventory of factors S T D C R.* Manual and questionnaires. Beverly Hills, California: Sheridan, 1940.

Guttman, N., & Kalish, H. I. Discriminability and stimulus generalization. *Journal of Experimental Psychology,* 1956, *51,* 79–88.

Gyr, J. W., & Willey, R. The effect of efference to the arm on visual adaptation to curvature: A replication. *Psychonomic Science,* 1970, *21,* 89–91.

Gyr, J., Willey, R., & Gordon, D. G. Correlations between motor learning and visual and arm adaptation under conditions of computer-simulated visual distortion. *Perceptual and Motor Skills,* 1972, *35,* 551–561.

Gyr, J. W., Willey, R., & Gourlay, K. The importance of subject-relative parameters in the perception of straightness. Unpublished manuscript, Univ. of Michigan.

Hajos, A. Sensumotorische Koordinationsprozesse bei Richtungs lokalisation. *Zeitschrift fur Experimentelle und Angewandte Psychologie,* 1968, *15,* 435–461.

Hajos, A., & Ritter, M. Experiments to the problem of interocular transfer. *Acta Psychologica,* 1965, *24,* 81–90.

Hamilton, C. R. Studies on adaptation to deflection of the visual field in split-brain monkeys and man. Unpublished doctoral dissertation, California Institute of Technology, 1964. (a)

Hamilton, C. R. Intermanual transfer of adaptation to prisms. *American Journal of Psychology,* 1964, *77,* 457–462. (b)

Hamilton, C. R. Effects of brain bisection on eye-hand coordination in monkeys wearing prisms. *Journal of Comparative and Physiological Psychology,* 1967, *64,* 434–443.

Hamilton, C. R., & Bossom, J. Decay of prism aftereffects. *Journal of Experimental Psychology,* 1964, *67,* 148–150.

Hamilton, C. R., & Gazzaniga, M. S. Lateralization of learning of colour and brightness discriminations following brain bisection. *Nature,* 1964, *201,* 220.

Hamilton, C. R., Sullivan, M. V., & Hillyard, S. A. Effects of adaptation to displaced vision on reaching to remembered positions. Unpublished manuscript, Stanford Univ., 1971.

Hardt, M. E., Held, R., & Steinbach, M. J. Adaptation to displaced vision: A change in the central control of sensorimotor coordination. *Journal of Experimental Psychology,* 1971, *89,* 229–239.

Harlow, H. F. Learning set and error factor theory. In S. Koch (Ed.), *Psychology: A study of a science,* Vol. 2. New York: McGraw-Hill, 1959.

Harrington, T. Adaptation of humans to colored split-field glasses. *Psychonomic Science,* 1965, *3,* 71–72.

Harris, C. S. Adaptation to displaced vision: Visual, motor, or proprioceptive change? *Science,* 1963, *140,* 812–813.

Harris, C. S. Perceptual adaptation to inverted, reversed, and displaced vision. *Psychological Review,* 1965, *72,* 419–444.

Harris, C. S. Through the looking glass: Adapting to an optically reversed world. Paper presented at the Symposium on "Perceptual Change", American Association for the Advancement of Science, Washington, D.C., December, 1966.

Harris, C. S. Beware of the straight-ahead shift—a nonperceptual change in experiments on adaptation to displaced vision. *Perception,* 1974, *3,* 461–476.

Harris, C. S., & Gilchrist, A. Prism adaptation without prisms: A nonvisual change with implications about plasticity in the human visual system. Paper presented at

Association for Research in Vision and Ophthalmology, Sarasota, Florida, April, 1976.

Harris, C. S., Harris, J. R., & Karsch, C. W.Shifts in pointing "straight ahead" after adaptation to sideways-displacing prisms. Paper presented at meetings of Eastern Psychological Association, New York, April, 1966.

Hay, J. C. Visual Adaptation to an altered correlation between eye movements and head movement. *Science*, 1968, *160*, 429–430.

Hay, J. C. Does head-movement feedback calibrate the perceived direction of optical motions? *Perception & Psychophysics*, 1971, *10*, 286–288.

Hay, J. C. Motor transformation learning. *Perception*, 1974, *3*, 487–496.

Hay, J. C., & Goldsmith, W. M. Space–time adaptation of visual position constancy. *Journal of Experimental Psychology*, 1973, *99*, 1–9.

Hay, J. C., & Pick, H. L., Jr. Visual and proprioceptive adaptation to optical displacement of the visual stimulus. *Journal of Experimental Psychology*, 1966, *71*, 150–158. (a)

Hay, J. C., & Pick, H. L., Jr. Gaze-contingent prism adaptation: Optical and motor factors. *Journal of Experimental Psychology*, 1966, *72*, 640–648. (b)

Hay, J. C., Pick, H. L., Jr., & Ikeda, K. Visual capture produced by prism spectacles. *Psychonomic Science*, 1965, *2*, 215–216.

Healy, M. H., Symmes, D., & Ommaya, A. K. Visual discordance cues induce prism adaptation in normal monkeys. *Perceptual and Motor Skills*, 1973, *37*, 683–693.

Hein, A. Postural after-effects and visual-motor adaptation to prisms. Paper presented at meetings of Eastern Psychological Association. Atlantic City, April, 1965.

Hein, A. Visual-motor development of the kitten. *Optometric Weekly*, 1970, *61*, 890–892.

Hein, A. Acquiring components of visually guided behavior. In A. D. Pick (Ed.), *Minnesota symposia on child psychology*. Minneapolis: Univ. of Minneapolis Press, 1972.

Hein, A., & Diamond, R. M. Independence of the cat's scotopic and photopic systems in acquiring control of visually guided behavior. *Journal of Comparative and Physiological Psychology*, 1971, *76*, 31–38. (a)

Hein, A., & Diamond, R. M. Contrasting development of visually triggered and guided movements in kittens with respect to interocular and interlimb equivalence. *Journal of Comparative and Physiological Psychology*, 1971, *76*, 219–224. (b)

Hein, A., & Diamond, R. M. Locomotory space as a prerequisite for acquiring visually guided reaching in kittens. *Journal of Comparative and Physiological Psychology*, 1972, *81*, 394–398.

Hein, A., Gower, E. C., & Diamond, R. M. Exposure requirements for developing the triggered component of the visual-placing response. *Journal of Comparative and Physiological Psychology*, 1970, *73*, 188–192.

Hein, A., & Held, R. A neural model for labile sensorimotor coordinations. In E. E. Bernard & M. R. Kare (Eds.), *Biological prototypes and synthetic systems*. Vol. 1. New York: Plenum Press, 1962.

Hein, A., & Held, R. Dissociation of the visual placing response into elicited and guided components. *Science*, 1967, *158*, 390–392.

Hein, A., Held, R., & Gower, E. C. Development and segmentation of visually controlled movement by selective exposure during rearing. *Journal of Comparative and Physiological Psychology*, 1970, *73*, 181–187.

Heinrich, D. R. Personality correlates of prism adaptation. Unpublished master's thesis, Univ. of Kansas, 1975.

Held, R. Adaptation to chromatic dispersion. Paper presented at meetings of Eastern Psychological Association, Philadelphia, April, 1955. (a)

Held, R. Shifts in binaural localization after prolonged exposure to atypical combinations of stimuli. *American Journal of Psychology,* 1955, *68,* 526–548. (b)

Held, R. Exposure-history as a factor in maintaining stability of perception and co-ordination. *Journal of Nervous and Mental Disease,* 1961, *132,* 26–32.

Held, R. Adaptation to rearrangement and visual-spatial aftereffects. *Psychologische Beitrage,* 1962, *6,* 439–450.

Held, R. The role of movement in the origin and maintenance of visual perception. *Acta Psychologica,* 1964, *23,* 308–309.

Held, R. Maintaining stability in sensorimotor coordination. Paper presented at the Symposium on "Perceptual Change," American Association for the Advancement of Science, Washington, D.C., December, 1966.

Held, R. Dissociation of visual functions by deprivation and rearrangement. *Psychologische Forschung,* 1968, *31,* 338–348. (a)

Held, R. Action contingent development of vision in neonatal animals. In D. P. Kimble (Ed.), *Experience and capacity.* New York: New York Academy of Sciences, 1968. (b)

Held, R., & Bauer, J. A., Jr. Visually guided reaching in infant monkeys after restricted rearing. *Science,* 1967, *155,* 718–720.

Held, R., & Bossom, J. Neonatal deprivation and adult rearrangement: Complementary techniques for analyzing plastic sensory-motor coordinations. *Journal of Comparative and Physiological Psychology,* 1961, *54,* 33–37.

Held, R., Efstathiou, A., & Greene, M. Adaptation to displaced and delayed visual feedback from the hand. *Journal of Experimental Psychology,* 1966, *72,* 887–891.

Held, R., & Freedman, S. J. Plasticity in human sensorimotor control. *Science,* 1963, *142,* 455–462.

Held, R., & Gottlieb, N. Technique for studying adaptation to disarranged hand-eye coordination. *Perceptual and Motor Skills,* 1958, *8,* 83–86.

Held, R., & Hein, A. Adaptation to disarranged hand-eye coordination contingent upon reafferent stimulation. *Perceptual and Motor Skills,* 1958, *8,* 87–90.

Held, R., & Hein, A Movement-produced stimulation in the development of visually guided behavior. *Journal of Comparative and Physiological Psychology,* 1963, *56,* 872–876.

Held, R., & Mikaelian, H. Motor-sensory feedback versus need in adaptation to rearrangement. *Perceptual and Motor Skills,* 1964, *18,* 685–688.

Held, R., & Rekosh, J. Motor-sensory feedback and the geometry of space. *Science,* 1963, *141,* 722–723.

Held, R., & Schlank, M. Adaptation to disarranged eye-hand coordination in the distance-dimension. *American Journal of Psychology,* 1959, *72,* 603–605.

Held, R., & Shattuck, S. Color- and edge-sensitive channels in the human visual system: Tuning for orientation. *Science,* 1971, *174,* 314–316.

Helmholtz, H. V. *Treatise on physiological optics.* Vol. 3. Rochester, New York: Optical Society of America, 1925.

Hepler, N. Color: A motion-contingent aftereffect. *Science,* 1968, *162,* 376–377.

Hering, E. *Die Lehre vom Binocularen Sehen.* Leipzig: Engelman, 1868.

Hershberger, W. A., & Carpenter, D. L. Adaptation to inverted retinal polarity: What's up, Bishop Berkeley? *Journal of Experimental Psychology,* 1972, *94,* 261–268.

Hess, E. H. Space perception in the chick. *Scientific American,* 1956, *195,* 71–80.

Hillyard, S. A., & Hamilton, C. R. Mislocalization of the arm following adaptation to displaced vision. Unpublished manuscript, Univ. of California, San Diego, 1971.

Hochberg, J. Space and movement. In J. W. Kling & L. A. Riggs (Eds.), *Woodworth & Schlosberg's experimental psychology.* (3rd ed.) New York: Holt, 1971. Chap. 13.

Holst, E. von. Relations between the central nervous system and the peripheral organs. *British Journal of Animal Behavior,* 1954, *2,* 89–94.

Holst, E. von, & Mittelstädt, H. Das Reafferenzprinzip. *Naturwissenschaften,* 1950, *37,* 464–476.

Holt, E. B. Eye movement and central anesthesia. *Harvard Psychological Studies,* 1903, *1,* 3–45.

Hovland, C. I. The generalization of conditioned responses. I. The sensory generalization of conditioned responses with varying frequencies of tone. *Journal of General Psychology,* 1937, *17,* 125–148. (a)

Hovland, C. I. The generalization of conditioned responses. II. The sensory generalization of conditioned responses with varying intensities of tone. *Journal of Genetic Psychology,* 1937, *51,* 279–291. (b)

Howard, I. P. Response shaping to visual-motor discordance. Paper presented at meetings of Psychonomic Society, Chicago, November 1967.

Howard, I. P. Displacing the optical array. In S. J. Freedman (Ed.), *The neuropsychology of spatially oriented behavior.* Homewood, Illinois: Dorsey Press, 1968.

Howard, I. P. The adaptability of the visual-motor system. In K. J. Connolly (Ed.), *Mechanisms of motor skill development.* London: Academic Press, 1970.

Howard, I. P. Perceptual learning and adaptation. *British Medical Bulletin,* 1971, *27,* 248–252.

Howard, I. P. Seeing space. *Transactions of the Ophthalmological Societies of the United Kingdom,* 1973, *93,* 397–405.

Howard, I. P., Anstis, T., & Lucia, H. C. The relative lability of mobile and stationary components in a visual-motor adaptation task. *Quarterly Journal of Experimental Psychology,* 1974, *26,* 293–300.

Howard, I. P., & Templeton, W. B. Visually-induced eye torsion and tilt adaptation. *Vision Research,* 1964, *4,* 433–437.

Howard, I. P., & Templeton, W. B. *Human spatial orientation.* New York: Wiley, 1966.

Hughes, J. R. Post-tetanic potentiation. *Physiological Reviews,* 1958, *38,* 91–113.

Irvine, S. R., & Ludvigh, E. Is ocular proprioceptive sense concerned in vision? *Archives of Ophthalmology,* New York, 1936, *15,* 1037–1049.

Ito, M., Shiida, T., Yagi, N., & Yamamoto, M. The cerebellar modification of rabbit's horizontal vestibulo-ocular reflex induced by sustained head rotation combined with visual stimulation. *Proceedings of the Japanese Academy,* 1974, *50,* 85–89.

Jackson, C. V. Visual factors in auditory localization. *Quarterly Journal of Experimental Psychology,* 1953, *5,* 52–65.

Jaensch, W., & Mandowsky, C. Die klinische Bedeutung psychischer Labilität bei optischen Wahrnehmungsvorgängen, *Medizinische Welt,* 1932, *6,* 1162.

Jones, P. D., & Holding, D. H. Extremely long-term persistence of the McCollough effect. Paper presented at meetings of Association for Research in Vision and Ophthalmology, Sarasota, Florida, 1975.

Kalil, R. E., & Freedman, S. J. Intermanual transfer of compensation for displaced vision. *Perceptual and Motor Skills,* 1966, *22,* 123–126. (a)

Kalil, R. E., & Freedman, S. J. Persistance of ocular rotation following compensation for displaced vision. *Perceptual and Motor Skills,* 1966, *22,* 135–139. (b)

Kanizsa, G. Margini quasi-percettivi in campi con stimolazione omogenea. *Rivista di Psicologia,* 1955, *49,* 7–30.

Kaufman, L., & Rock, I. The moon illusion. I. *Science,* 1962, *136,* 953–961.

Kelso, J. A. S., Cook, E., Olson, M. E., & Epstein, W. Allocation of attention and the locus of adaptation to displaced vision. *Journal of Experimental Psychology: Human Perception and Performance*, 1975, *1*, 237–245.

Kennedy, J. M. Prismatic displacement and the remembered location of targets. *Perception & Psychophysics*, 1969, *5*, 218–220.

Kimble, G. A. Performance and reminiscence in motor learning as a function of the degree of distribution of practice. *Journal of Experimental Psychology*, 1949, *39*, 500–510.

Kimble, G. A. Transfer of work inhibition in motor learning. *Journal of Experimental Psychology*, 1952, *43*, 391–392.

Kimble, G. A., & Shattel, R. B. The relationship between two kinds of inhibition and the amount of practice. *Journal of Experimental Psychology*, 1952, *44*, 355–359.

Kinney, J. A. S., & Luria, S. M. Conflicting visual and tactual-kinesthetic stimulation. *Perception & Psychophysics*, 1970, *8*, 189–192.

Kinney, J. A. S., Luria, S. M., & Weitzman, D. O. Visibility of colors underwater. *Journal of the Optical Society of America*, 1967, *57*, 802–809.

Kinney, J. A. S., Luria, S. M., & Weitzman, D. O. Responses to the underwater distortion of visual stimuli. NSMRL Report No. 541, U.S. Naval Submarine Medical Center, Groton, Connecticut, 1968.

Kinney, J. A. S., Luria, S. M., & Weitzman, D. O. Visibility of colors underwater using artificial illumination. *Journal of the Optical Society of America*, 1969, *59*, 624–628.

Kinney, J. A. S., Luria, S. M., Weitzman, D. O., & Markowitz, H. Effects of diving experience on visual perception under water. NSMRL Report No. 612, U.S. Naval Submarine Medical Center, Groton, Connecticut, 1970.

Kinney, J. A. S., McKay, C. L., Luria, S. M., & Gratto, C. L. The improvement of divers' compensation for underwater distortions. NSMRL Report No. 633, U.S. Naval Submarine Medical Center, Groton, Connecticut, 1970.

Klapp, S. T., Nordell, S. A., Hoekenga, K. C., & Patton, C. B. Long-lasting aftereffect of brief prism exposure. *Perception & Psychophysics*, 1974, *15*, 399–400.

Kohler, I. Warum sehen wer aufrecht? *Die Pyramide*, 1951, *2*, 30–33.

Kohler, I. Experiments with prolonged optical distortions. *Acta Psychologica*, 1955, *11*, 176–178.

Kohler, I. Experiments with goggles. *Scientific American*, 1962, *206*, 62–86.

Kohler, I. The formation and transformation of the perceptual world. *Psychological Issues*, 1964, *3* (4), 1–173.

Kohler, I. Past, present, and future of the recombination procedure. *Perception*, 1974, *3*, 515–524.

Köhler, W., & Wallach, H. Figural after-effects: An investigation of visual processes. *Proceedings of the American Philosophical Society*, 1944, *88*, 269–357.

Kohnstamm, D. Demonstration einer katatonieartigen Erscheinung beim Gesunden. *Neurologie Zentralblatt*, 1915, *34*, 290–291.

Kolers, P. A. Memorial consequences of automatized encoding. *Journal of Experimental Psychology: Human Learning and Memory*, 1975, *1*, 689–701.

Kornheiser, A. S. Adaptation to laterally displaced vision: A review. *Psychological Bulletin*, 1976, *83*, 783–816.

Kottenhoff, H. Situational and personal influences on space perception with experimental spectacles. *Acta Psychologica*, 1957, *13*, 79–97, 151–161.

Kravitz, J. H. Conditioned adaptation to prismatic displacement. *Perception & Psychophysics*, 1972, *11*, 38–42.

Kravitz, J. H., & Wallach, H. Adaptation to displaced vision contingent upon vibrating stimulation. *Psychonomic Science,* 1966, *6,* 465–466.

Kravitz, J. H., & Yaffe, F. Conditioned adaptation to prismatic displacement with a tone as the conditional stimulus. *Perception & Psychophysics,* 1972, *12,* 305–308.

Krüger, U. Über die Art der Wahrnehmung eines künstlich verkehrt gemachten Gesichtsfeldes. Unpublished doctoral dissertation, Breslau Institute of Physiology, 1939.

Lackner, J. R. Visual rearrangement affects auditory localization. *Neuropsychologia,* 1973, *11,* 29–32. (a)

Lackner, J. R. The role of posture in adaptation to visual rearrangement. *Neuropsychologia,* 1973, *11,* 33–44. (b)

Lackner, J. R. Adaptation to displaced vision: Role of proprioception. *Perceptual and Motor Skills,* 1974, *38,* 1251–1256. (a)

Lackner, J. R. Influence of visual rearrangement and visual motion on sound localization. *Neuropsychologia,* 1974, *12,* 291–293. (b)

Lackner, J. R. Adaptation to visual and proprioceptive rearrangement: Origin of the differential effectiveness of active and passive movements. *Perception & Psychophysics,* 1977, *21,* 55–59.

Lackner, J. R., & Lobovits, D. Incremental exposure facilitates adaptation to visual rearrangement. *Aviation, Space and Environmental Medicine,* 1977, in press. (a)

Lackner, J. R., & Lobovits, D. Adaptation to displaced vision: Evidence for prolonged aftereffects. *Quarterly Journal of Experimental Psychology,* 1977, *29,* 65–69. (b)

Latour, P. L. Visual threshold during eye movements. *Vision Research,* 1962, *2,* 261–262.

Lazar, G., & Van Laer, J. Adaptation to displaced vision after experience with lesser displacements. *Perceptual and Motor Skills,* 1968, *26,* 579–582.

Lester, G. The case for efferent change during prism adaptation. *Journal of Psychology,* 1968, *68,* 9–13.

Lotto, D., Kern, A., & Morant, R. B. Prism induced tilt after-effects and changed felt head position. Paper presented at meetings of Eastern Psychological Association, Boston, April, 1967.

Lund, J. S. Adaptation to visual field displacement by monkeys with optic chiasm sectioned. *Experimental Neurology,* 1970, *27,* 334–343.

Luria, S. M. Stereoscopic and resolution acuity with various fields of view. *Science,* 1969, *164,* 452–453.

Luria, S. M., & Kinney, J. A. S. Judgments of distance under partially reduced cues. *Perceptual and Motor Skills,* 1968, *26,* 1019–1028.

Luria, S. M., & Kinney, J. A. S. Visual acuity underwater without a face mask. NSMRL Report No. 581, U.S. Naval Submarine Medical Center, Groton, Connecticut, 1969.

Luria, S. M., & Kinney, J. A. S. Underwater vision. *Science,* 1970, *167,* 1454–1461.

Luria, S. M., Kinney, J. A. S., & Weissman, S. Estimates of size and distance underwater. *American Journal of Psychology,* 1967, *80,* 282–286.

Luria, S. M., McKay, C. L., & Ferris, S. H. Handedness and adaptation to visual distortions of size and distance. *Journal of Experimental Psychology,* 1973, *100,* 263–269.

Lythgoe, J. N. Vision. In J. D. Woods & J. N. Lythgoe (Eds.), *Underwater science.* London: Oxford Univ. Press, 1971. Chap. 4.

Mach, E. *The analysis of sensations.* (5th ed.) New York: Dover, 1959.

Mack, A. The role of movement in perceptual adaptation to a tilted retinal image. *Perception & Psychophysics,* 1967, *2,* 65–68.

Mack, A. An investigation of the relationship between eye and retinal image movement in the perception of movement. *Perception & Psychophysics,* 1970, *8,* 291–298.

Mack, A., & Bachant, J. Perceived movement of the afterimage during eye movments. *Perception and Psychophysics,* 1969, *6,* 379–384.

Mack, A., & Chitayat, D. Eye-dependent and disparity adaptation to opposite visual-field rotations. *American Journal of Psychology,* 1970, *83,* 352–371.

Mack, A., & Quartin, T. A new kind of form adaptation: Adaptation to a unidimensional distortion of the image. Paper presented at meetings of Eastern Psychological Association, Philadelphia, April, 1974.

Mack, A., & Rock, I. A re-examination of the Stratton effect: Egocentric adaptation to a rotated visual image. *Perception & Psychophysics,* 1968, *4,* 57–62.

Malatesta, V., & Mikaelian, H. H. Dissociation of two modes of visually controlled behavior by prism adaptation. Paper presented at meetings of Eastern Psychological Association, New York, April, 1975.

Mather, J., & Lackner, J. Adaptation to visual rearranagement elicited by tonic vibration reflexes. *Experimental Brain Research,* 1975, *24,* 103–105.

Matin, L. Eye movements and perceived visual direction. In D. Jameson & L. M. Hurvich (Eds.), *Handbook of sensory physiology.* Vol. 7. New York: Springer-Verlag, 1972.

Matthaei, R. Nachbewegungen beim Menschen. (Untersuchungen über das sog. Kohnstammische Phänomen). *Pflügers Archiv für die Gesamte Physiologie des Menschen und der Tiere,* 1924, *202,* 88–111, 587–600.

Mayhew, J. E. W., & Anstis, S. M. Movement aftereffects contingent on color, intensity and pattern. *Perception & Psychophysics,* 1972, *12,* 77–85.

MacDougall, R. The subjective horizon. *Psychological Review Monographs,* 1903, *4,* 145–166.

MacKay, D. M. The stabilization of perception during voluntary activity. *Nature,* 1958, *181,* 284–285.

MacKay, D. M. Visual stability and voluntary eye movements. In R. Jung (Ed.), *Central processing of visual information.* New York: Springer-Verlag, 1973.

McCarter, A. Occluded and non-occluded arm movement reversal in prism adaptation. Paper presented at meetings of Eastern Psychological Association, New York, April, 1975.

McCollough, C. Color adaptation of edge-detectors in the human visual system. *Science,* 1965, *149,* 1115–1116. (a)

McCollough, C. The conditioning of color perception. *American Journal of Psychology,* 1965, *78,* 362–378. (b)

McDonald, A. P. Revised scale for ambiguity tolerance: Reliability and validity. *Psychological Reports,* 1970, *26,* 791–798.

McGhie, A., Chapman, J., & Lawson, J. S. The effect of distraction upon schizophrenic performance: I. Perception and immediate memory. *British Journal of Psychiatry,* 1965, *3,* 383–390.

McLaughlin, S. C. Parametric adjustment in saccadic eye movements. *Perception & Psychophysics,* 1967, *2,* 359–362.

McLaughlin, S. C., & Bower, J. L. Selective intermanual transfer of adaptive effects during adaptation to prism. *Psychonomic Science,* 1965, *3,* 69–70.

McLaughlin, S. C., Rifkin, K. I., & Webster, R. G. Oculomotor adaptation to wedge prisms with no part of the body seen. *Perception & Psychophysics,* 1966, *1,* 452–458.

McLaughlin, S. C., & Webster, R. G. Changes in straight-ahead eye position during adaptation to wedge prisms. *Perception & Psychophysics,* 1967, *2,* 37–44.

318

References

Meier, M. J. Effects of focal cerebral lesions on contralateral visuomotor adaptation to reversal and inversion of visual feedback. *Neuropsychologia,* 1970, *8,* 269–279.

Meier, M. J., & French, L. A. Readaptation to prismatic rotations of visual space as a function of lesion laterality and extratemporal EEG spike activity after temporal lobectomy. *Neuropsychologia,* 1966, *4,* 151–157.

Melamed, L. E., Haley, M., & Gildow, J. W. Effect of external target presence on visual adaptation with active and passive movement. *Journal of Experimental Psychology,* 1973, *98,* 125–130.

Melamed, L. E., & Wallace, B. An analysis of the role of the correction effect in visual adaptation. Paper presented at meetings of Eastern Psychological Association, New York City, April, 1971.

Melamed, L. E., Wallace, B., Cohen, R. R., & Oakes, S. Correction effect in visual adaptation as measure of field independence-dependence. *Perceptual and Motor Skills,* 1972, *34,* 554.

Melvill Jones, G., & Gonshor, A. Goal-directed flexibility in the vestibulo-ocular reflex arc. In G. Lennerstrand & P. Bach-y-Rita (Eds.), *Basic mechanisms of ocular motility and their clinical implications.* Oxford: Pergamon, 1975.

Mengelkoch, R. F., Adams, J. A., & Gainer, C. A. The forgetting of instrument flying skills as a function of the level of initial proficiency. U.S. Naval Training Device Center, *Human Engineering Technical Report* NAVTRADEVCEN 71-16-18, Sept., 1958.

Meyers, B., & McCleary, R. A. Interocular transfer of a pattern discrimination in pattern deprived cats. *Journal of Comparative and Physiological Psychology,* 1964, *57,* 16–21.

Mikaelian, H. H. Failure of bilateral transfer in modified eye-hand coordination. Paper presented at meetings of Eastern Psychological Association, New York City, April, 1963.

Mikaelian, H. H. Adaptation to rearranged eye-foot coordination. Paper presented at meetings of Eastern Psychological Association, New York City, April, 1966.

Mikaelian, H. H. Relation between adaptation to rearrangement and the source of motor-sensory feedback. *Psychonomic Science,* 1967, *9,* 485–486.

Mikaelian, H. H. Adaptation to rearranged ear-hand coordination. *Perceptual and Motor Skills,* 1969, *28,* 147–150.

Mikaelian, H. H. Adaptation to rearranged eye-foot coordination. *Perception & Psychophysics,* 1970, *8,* 222–224. (a)

Mikaelian, H. H. Failure of intermanual transfer of adaptation to rearranged ear-hand coordination. Paper presented at meetings of Eastern Psychological Association, Atlantic City, April, 1970. (b)

Mikaelian, H. H. Lack of bilateral generalization of adaptation to auditory rearrangement. *Perception & Psychophysics,* 1972, *11,* 222–224.

Mikaelian, H. H. Generalized sensorimotor adaptation with diminished feedback. *Psychologische Forschung,* 1974, *36,* 321–328. (a)

Mikaelian, H. H. Intersensory generalization and conditioning in adaptation to visual tilt. *American Journal of Psychology,* 1974, *87,* 197–202. (b)

Mikaelian, H. H. Adaptation to displaced hearing: A nonproprioceptive change. *Journal of Experimental Psychology,* 1974, *103,* 326–330. (c)

Mikaelian, H. H., & Held, R. Two types of adaptation to an optically-rotated field. *American Journal of Psychology,* 1964, *77,* 257–263.

Mikaelian, H. H., & Malatesta, V. Specialized adaptation to displaced vision. *Perception,* 1974, *3,* 135–139.

Miles, F. A., & Fuller, J. H. Adaptive plasticity in the vestibulo-ocular responses of the rhesus monkey. *Brain Research*, 1974, *80*, 512–516.

Miller, E. A. The interaction of vision and touch in form perception with a conflict task and a non-conflict task. Unpublished doctoral dissertation, George Washington Univ., 1971.

Miller, E. A. Interaction of vision and touch in conflict and nonconflict form perception tasks. *Journal of Experimental Psychology*, 1972, *96*, 114–123.

Miller, J., & Festinger, L. Impact of oculomotor retraining on the visual perception of curvature. *Journal of Experimental Psychology: Human Perception and Performance*, 1977, *3*, 187–200.

Mitchell, D. E. The influence of early visual experience on visual perception. In C. S. Harris (Ed.), *Visual coding and adaptability*. Hillsdale, New Jersey: Lawrence Erlbaum Associates, in press.

Mittelstädt, H. Telotaxis und Optomotorik von Eristalis bei Augeninversion. *Naturwissen*, 1944, *36*, 90–91.

Morant, R. B., & Beller, H. K. Adaptation to prismatically rotated visual fields. *Science*, 1965, *148*, 530–531.

Morant, R. B., & Harris, J. R. Two different after-effects of exposure to visual tilts. *American Journal of Psychology*, 1965, *78*, 218–226.

Morant, R. B., & Mikaelian, H. H. Inter-field tilt after-effects. *Perceptual and Motor Skills*, 1960, *10*, 95–98.

Moulden, B. Adaptation to displaced vision: Reafference is a special case of the cue-discrepancy hypothesis. *Quarterly Journal of Experimental Psychology*, 1971, *23*, 113–117.

Murch, G. M. Classical conditioning of the McCollough effect: Temporal parameters. *Vision Research*, 1976, *16*, 615–619.

Neal, E. Visual localization of the vertical. *American Journal of Psychology*, 1926, *37*, 287–291.

Nealy, S. M., & Riley, D. Loss and recovery of discrimination of visual depth in dark-reared rats. *American Journal of Psychology*, 1963, *76*, 329–332.

Nichols, A. K. A study of some aspects of perception in the underwater situation. Unpublished dissertation, Univ. of Leeds, 1967.

Nielsen, T. I. Volition: A New experimental approach. *Scandinavian Journal of Psychology*, 1963, *4*, 225–230.

Ogle, K. N. *Researches in binocular vision*. New York: Hafner, 1964.

Ogle, K. N. *Optics: An introduction for ophthalmologists*. (2nd ed.) Springfield, Illinois: Thomas, 1968.

Ohwaki, S. An investigation of figural adaptation: A study within the framework of sensory-tonic field theory. *American Journal of Psychology*, 1961, *74*, 3–16.

Ono, H., & O'Reilly, J. P. Adaptation to underwater distance distortion as function of different sensory-motor tasks. *Human Factors*, 1971, *13*, 133–140.

Ono, H., O'Reilly, J. P., & Herman, L. M. Underwater distance distortion within the manual work space. *Human Factors*, 1970, *12*, 473–480.

O'Reilly, J. P. Shifting adaptive systems with visually distorted input. Univ. of Hawaii, *Studies on Human Performance in the Sea*, 1975, *1*, 330–341. (a)

O'Reilly, J. P. Adaptation to underwater distance distortion. Univ. of Hawaii, *Studies on Human Performance in the Sea*, 1975, *1*, 342–348. (b)

Over, R. An experimentally induced conflict between vision and proprioception. *British Journal of Psychology*, 1966, *57*, 335–341.

Paap, K. R., & Ebenholtz, S. M. Perceptual consequences of potentiation in the extraocular muscles: An alternative explanation for adaptation to wedge prisms. *Journal of Experimental Psychology: Human Perception and Performance*, 1976, 2, 457–468.

Paap, K. R., & Ebenholtz, S. M. Concomitant direction and distance aftereffects of sustained convergence: A muscle potentiation explanation for eye-specific adaptation. *Perception & Psychophysics*, 1977, 21, 307–314.

Paillard, J., & Brouchon, M. Active and passive movements in the calibration of position sense. In S. J. Freedman (Ed.), *The neuropsychology of spatially oriented behavior.* Homewood, Illinois: Dorsey Press, 1968.

Park, J. N. Displacement of apparent straight ahead as an aftereffect of deviation of the eyes from normal position. *Perceptual and Motor Skills*, 1969, 28, 591–597.

Peterson, J., & Peterson, J. K. Does practice with inverting lenses make vision normal? *Psychological Monograph*, 1938, 50(5, Whole No. 225), 12–37.

Pfister, H. Über das verhalten der Hühner beim Tragen von Prismen. Unpublished doctoral dissertation, Univ. of Innsbruck, 1955.

Pick, H. L., Jr., & Hay, J. C. Adaptation to prismatic distortion. *Psychonomic Science*, 1964, 1, 199–200.

Pick, H. L., Jr., & Hay, J. C. A passive test of the Held reafference hypothesis. *Perceptual and Motor Skills*, 1965, 20, 1070–1072.

Pick, H. L., Jr., & Hay, J. C. Gaze-contingent adaptation to prismatic spectacles. *American Journal of Psychology*, 1966, 79, 443–450. (a)

Pick, H. L., Jr., & Hay, J. C. The distortion experiment as a tool for studying the development of perceptual-motor coordination. In N. Jenkin & R. H. Pollack (Eds.). *Perceptual development: Its relation to theories of intelligence and cognition.* Institute for Juvenile Research, Research Programs in Child Development, Chicago, Ill., 1966. (b)

Pick, H. L., Jr., Hay, J. C., & Martin, R. Adaptation to split-field wedge prism spectacles. *Journal of Experimental Psychology*, 1969, 80, 125–132.

Pick, H. L., Jr., Hay, J. C., & Pabst, J. Kinesthetic adaptation to visual distortion. Paper presented at meetings of Midwestern Psychological Association, Chicago, May, 1963.

Pick, H. L., Jr., Hay, J. C., & Willoughby, R. H. Interocular transfer of adaptation to prismatic distortion. *Perceptual and Motor Skills*, 1966, 23, 131–135.

Pick, H. L., Jr., Warren, D. H., & Hay, J. C. Sensory conflict in judgments of spatial direction. *Perception & Psychophysics*, 1969, 6, 203–205.

Pola, J. Voluntary saccades, eye position, and perceived visual direction. In R. A. Monty & J. W. Senders (Eds.), *Eye movements and psychological processes.* Hillsdale, New Jersey: Lawrence Erlbaum Associates, 1976.

Posin, R. L. Perceptual adaptation to contingent visual-field movement: An experimental investigation of position constancy. Unpublished doctoral dissertation, Yeshiva Univ., 1966.

Postman, L. Transfer, interference and forgetting. In J. W. Kling & L. A. Riggs (Eds.), *Woodworth and Schlosberg's experimental psychology.* (3rd ed.) New York: Holt, 1971.

Putterman, A. H., Robert, A. L., & Bregman, A. S. Adaptation of the wrist to displacing prisms. *Psychonomic Science*, 1969, 16, 79–80.

Quinlan, D. Effects of sight of the body and active locomotion in perceptual adaptation. *Journal of Experimental Psychology*, 1970, 86, 91–96.

Radeau, M., & Bertelson, P. Adaptation a un deplacement prismatique sur la base de stimulations exafferentes en conflit. *Psychologica Belgica,* 1969, *9,* 133–140.

Radeau, M., & Bertelson, P. The after-effects of ventriloquism. *Quarterly Journal of Experimental Psychology,* 1974, *25,* 63–71.

Redding, G. M. Simultaneous visual adaptation to tilt and displacement: A test of independent processes. *Bulletin of Psychonomic Society,* 1973, *2,* 41–42. (a)

Redding, G. M. Visual adaptation to tilt and displacement: Same or different processes? *Perception & Psychophysics,* 1973, *14,* 193–200. (b)

Redding, G. M. Simultaneous visuomotor adaptation to optical tilt and displacement. *Perception & Psychophysics,* 1975, *17,* 97–100. (a)

Redding, G. M. Decay of visual adaptation to tilt and displacement. *Perception & Psychophysics,* 1975, *17,* 203–208. (b)

Redding, G. M. Visual and proprioceptive adaptation to optical tilt. Paper presented at meetings of Midwestern Psychological Association, Chicago, May, 1975. (c)

Redding, G. M., & Wallace, B. Components of displacement adaptation in acquisition and decay as a function of hand and hall exposure. *Perception & Psychophysics,* 1976, *20,* 453–459.

Rekosh, J. H., & Freedman, S. J. Errors in auditory direction-finding after compensation for visual re-arrangement. *Perception & Psychophysics,* 1967, *2,* 466–468.

Reynolds, B., & Adams, J. A. Motor performance as a function of click reinforcement. *Journal of Experimental Psychology,* 1953, *45,* 315–320.

Rhoades, R. W. The effect of a visual feedback delay on adaptation to distorted vision. Unpublished manuscript, Univ. of California, Riverside, 1968.

Rierdan, J. E., & Wapner, S. Experimental study of adaptation to visual rearrangement deriving from an organismic-developmental approach to cognition. *Perceptual and Motor Skills,* 1966, *23,* 903–916.

Rierdan, J. E., & Wapner, S. Adaptive changes in the relationship between visual and tactual-kinesthetic perception. *Psychonomic Science,* 1967, *7,* 61–62.

Robinson, D. A. How the oculomotor system repairs itself. *Investigative Ophthalmology,* 1975, *14,* 413–415. (a)

Robinson, D. A. Oculomotor control signals. In P. Bach-y-Rita & G. Lennerstrand (Eds.), *Basic mechanisms of ocular motility and their clinical implications.* Oxford: Pergamon Press, 1975. (b)

Rock, I. Adaptation to a minified image. *Psychonomic Science,* 1965, *2,* 105–106.

Rock, I. *The nature of perceptual adaptation.* New York: Basic Books, 1966.

Rock, I. *Orientation and form.* New York: Academic Press, 1973.

Rock, I. *An introduction to perception.* New York: Macmillan, 1975.

Rock, I., Goldberg, J., & Mack, A. Immediate correction and adaptation based on viewing a prismatically displaced scene. *Perception & Psychophysics,* 1966, *1,* 351–354.

Rock, I., & Harris, C. S. Vision and touch. *Scientific American,* 1967, *216,* 96–104.

Rock, I., Mack, A., Adams, L., & Hill, A. L. Adaptation to contradictory information from vision and touch. *Psychonomic Science,* 1965, *3,* 435–436.

Rock, I., & Victor, J. Vision and touch: An experimentally created conflict between the two senses. *Science,* 1964, *143,* 594–596.

Ross, H. E. Water, fog and the size–distance invariance hypothesis. *British Journal of Psychology,* 1967, *58,* 301–313. (a)

Ross, H. E. Stereoscopic acuity underwater. *Underwater Association Report,* 1967, *2,* 61–64. (b)

Ross, H. E. Adaptation of divers to curvature distortion underwater. *Ergonomics,* 1970, *13,* 489–499.

Ross, H. E. Spatial perception underwater. In J. D. Woods & J. N. Lythgoe (Eds.), *Underwater science.* London: Oxford Univ. Press, 1971. Chap. 3.

Ross, H. E. *Behavior and perception in strange environments.* New York: Basic Books, 1975. (a)

Ross, H. E. Mist, murk and visual perception. *New Scientist,* 1975, *19,* 658–660. (b)

Ross, H. E., Crickmar, S. D., Sills, N. V., & Owen, E. P. Orientation to the vertical in free divers. *Aerospace Medicine,* 1969, *40,* 728–732.

Ross, H. E., Franklin, S. S., Weltman, G., & Lennie, P. Adaptation of divers to size distortion under water. *British Journal of Psychology,* 1970, *61,* 365–373.

Ross, H. E., King, S. R., & Snowden, H. Size and distance judgments in the vertical plane under water. *Psychologische Forschung,* 1970, *33,* 155–164.

Ross, H. E., & Lennie, P. Visual stability during bodily movement underwater. *Underwater Association Report,* 1968, *3,* 59–62.

Ross, H. E., & Lennie, P. Adaptation and counteradaptation to complex optical distortion. *Perception & Psychophysics,* 1972, *12,* 273–277.

Ross, H. E., & Rejman, M. H. Adaptation to speed distortions under water. *British Journal of Psychology,* 1972, *63,* 257–264.

Ross, H. E., Rejman, M. H., & Lennie, P. Adaptation to weight transformation in water. *Ergonomics,* 1972, *15,* 387–397.

Rossi, P. J. Prism adaptation in the chick. Unpublished doctoral dissertation, Univ. of California, Riverside, 1967.

Rossi, P. J. Adaptation and negative aftereffect to lateral optical displacement in newly hatched chicks. *Science,* 1968, *160,* 430–432.

Rossi, P. J. Primacy of the negative aftereffect over positive adaptation in prism adaptation with newly hatched chicks. *Developmental Psychobiology,* 1969, *2,* 43–53.

Rossi, P. J. Prism-induced negative aftereffects without food reinforced feedback in newly hatched chicks. *Psychonomic Science,* 1971, *24,* 141–142.

Rossi, P. J. Population density and food dispersion on the development of prism-induced aftereffects in newly hatched chicks. *Developmental Psychobiology,* 1972, *5,* 239–248.

Rotter, J. B. Generalized expectancies for internal versus external control of reinforcement. *Psychological Monographs,* 1966, *80* (1, Whole No. 287).

Schlodtmann, W. Ein Beitrag zur Lehre von der optischen Lokalisation bei Blindgeborenen. *Arch. f. Ophth.,* 1902, *54,* 256–267.

Schneider, G. E. Contrasting visuomotor functions of tectum and cortex in the golden hamster. *Psychologische Forschung,* 1967, *31,* 52–62.

Schneider, G. E. Two visual systems. *Science (Washington),* 1969, *163,* 895–902.

Scott, J. P. Critical periods in behavioral development. *Science,* 1962, *138,* 949–958.

Shattuck, S., & Held, R. Color and edge sensitive channels converge on stereo-depth analyzers. *Vision Research,* 1975, *15,* 309–311.

Shebilske, W. L. Visuomotor coordination in visual direction and position constancies. In W. Epstein (Ed.), *Stability and constancy in visual perception: Mechanisms and processes.* New York: Wiley, 1977.

Sherrington, C. S. Observations on the sensual role of the proprioceptive nerve supply of the extrinsic eye muscles. *Brain,* 1918, *41,* 332–343.

Shulman, S. M., & Morant, R. B. Equivalence of visual and head tilt after-effects in prism and non-prism conditions. Paper presented at meetings of Eastern Psychological Association, Washington, D.C., April, 1968.

Singer, G., & Day, R. H. Spatial adaptation and aftereffect with optically transformed vision: Effects of active and passive responding and the relationship between test and exposure responses. *Journal of Experimental Psychology,* 1966, *71,* 725-731.

Skavenski, A. A. Inflow as a source of extraretinal eye position information. *Vision Research,* 1972, *12,* 221-229.

Skavenski, A. A., Haddad, G., & Steinman, R. M. The extraretinal signal for the visual perception of direction. *Perception & Psychophysics,* 1972, *11,* 287-290.

Skowbo, D., Timney, B. N., Gentry, T. A., & Morant, R. B. McCollugh effects: Experimental findings and theoretical accounts. *Psychological Bulletin,* 1975, *82,* 497-510.

Slotnick, R. S. Adaptation to curvature distortion. *Journal of Experimental Psychology,* 1969, *81,* 441-448.

Smith, C. H. Oculomotor change in the compensation for prismatically displaced vision. Unpublished doctoral dissertation, Stanford Univ., 1973.

Smith, K. U. Cybernetic theory and analysis of learning. In E. A. Bilodeau (Ed.), *Acquisition of skill.* New York: Academic Press, 1966.

Smith, K. U., & Greene, P. A critical period in maturation of performance with space-displaced vision. *Perceptual and Motor Skills,* 1963, *17,* 627-639.

Smith, K. U., & Smith, W. K. *Perception and motion.* Philadelphia: Saunders, 1962.

Smothergill, D. W., Martin, R., & Pick, H. L., Jr. Perceptual-motor performance under rotation of the central field. *Journal of Experimental Psychology,* 1971, *87,* 64-70.

Snyder, F. W., & Pronko, N. H. *Vision with spatial inversion.* Wichita: Univ. of Wichita Press, 1952.

Snyder, F. W., & Snyder, C. W. Vision with spatial inversion: A follow-up study. *Psychological Record,* 1957, *7,* 20-30.

Southall, J. P. C. *Mirrors, prisms, and lenses.* (3rd ed.) New York: Macmillan, 1933.

Sperry, R. W. The functional results of muscle transposition in the hind limb of the rat. *Journal of Comparative Neurology,* 1940, *73,* 379-404.

Sperry, R. W. The effect of crossing nerves to antagonistic muscles in the hind limb of the rat. *Journal of Comparative Neurology,* 1941, *75,* 1-19.

Sperry, R. W. Transplantation of motor nerves and muscles in the forelimb of the rat. *Journal of Comparative Neurology,* 1942, *76,* 283-321.

Sperry, R. W. Visuomotor coordination in the newt (Triturus viridescens) after regeneration of the optic nerve. *Journal of Comparative Neurology,* 1943, *79,* 33-55. (a)

Sperry, R. W. Effect of 180 degree rotation of the retinal field on visuomotor coordination. *Journal of Experimental Zoology,* 1943, *92,* 263-279. (b)

Sperry, R. W. Optic nerve regeneration with return of vision in anurans. *Journal of Neurophysiology,* 1944, *7,* 57-70.

Sperry, R. W. Nature of functional recovery following regeneration of the oculomotor nerve in amphibians. *Anatomical Record,* 1947, *97,* 293-316. (a)

Sperry, R. W. Effect of crossing nerves to antagonistic limb muscles in the monkey. *Archives of Neurological Psychiatry, Chicago,* 1947, *58,* 452-473. (b)

Sperry, R. W. Patterning of central synapses in regeneration of the optic nerve in teleosts. *Physiological Zoology,* 1948, *21,* 351-361.

Spielberger, C. D., Gorsuch, R. L., & Lushene, R. E. The state-trait anxiety inventory. Palo Alto, California: Consulting Psychological Press, 1968.

Stevens, J. K., Emerson, R. C., Gerstein, G. L., Kallos, T., Neufeld, G. R., Nichols, C. W., & Rosenquist, A. C. Paralysis of the awake human: Visual perceptions. *Vision Research,* 1976, *16,* 93-98.

Stone, L. S. Normal and reversed vision in transplanted eyes. *Archives of Ophthalmology,* 1953, *49,* 28-35.

Stratton, G. M. Some preliminary experiments on vision without inversion of the retinal image. *Psychological Review,* 1896, *3,* 611–617.

Stratton, G. M. Upright vision and the retinal image. *Psychological Review,* 1897, *4,* 182–187. (a)

Stratton, G. M. Vision without inversion of the retinal image. *Psychological Review,* 1897, *4,* 341–360, 463–481. (b)

Stratton, G. M. The spatial harmony of touch and sight. *Mind,* 1899, *2,* 492–505.

Stromeyer, C. F., III, & Mansfield, R. J. W. Colored aftereffects produced with moving edges. *Perception & Psychophysics,* 1970, *7,* 108–114.

Tastevin, J. En partant de l'experience d'Aristote. *L'Encephale,* 1937, *1,* 57–84, 140–158.

Taub, E. Prism compensation as a learning phenomenon: A phylogenetic perspective. In S. J. Freedman (Ed.), *The neuropsychology of spatially oriented behavior,* Homewood, Illinois: Dorsey Press, 1968.

Taub, E., & Berman, A. J. Movement and learning in the absence of sensory feedback. In S. J. Freedman (Ed.), *The neuropsychology of spatially oriented behavior.* Homewood, Illinois: Dorsey Press, 1968.

Taub, E., & Goldberg, I. A. Prism adaptation: Control of intermanual transfer by distribution of practice. *Science,* 1973, *180,* 755–757.

Taub, E., & Goldberg, I. A. Use of sensory recombination and somato-sensory deafferentiation techniques in the investigation of sensory-motor integration. *Perception,* 1974, *3,* 393–408.

Taub, E., Goldberg, I. A., Bossom, J., & Berman, A. J. Deafferentation in monkeys: Adaptation to prismatic displacement of vision. Paper presented at meetings of Eastern Psychological Association, New York City, April, 1966.

Taub, E., Goldberg, I. A., & Taub, P. Deafferentation in monkeys: Pointing at a target without visual feedback. *Experimental Neurology,* 1975, *46,* 178–186.

Taylor, J. G. *The behavioral basis of perception.* New Haven, Connecticut: Yale Univ. Press, 1962.

Taylor, J. G., & Papert, S. A theory of perceptual constancy. *British Journal of Psychology,* 1956, *47,* 216–224.

Templeton, W. B., Howard, I. P., & Lowman, A. E. Passively generated adaptation to prismatic distortion. *Perceptual and Motor Skills,* 1966, *22,* 140–142.

Templeton, W. B., Howard, I. P., & Wilkinson, D. A. Additivity of components of prismatic adaptation. *Perception & Psychophysics,* 1974, *15,* 249–257.

Teuber, H.-L. Sensory deprivation, sensory suppression and agnosia: Notes for a neurologic theory. *Journal of Nervous and Mental Disease,* 1961, *132,* 32–40.

Teuber, H.-L. The riddle of frontal-lobe function in man. In J. M. Warren & G. Akert (Eds.), *The frontal granular cortex and behavior.* New York: McGraw-Hill, 1964.

Thomas, G. J. Experimental study of the influence of vision on sound localization. *Journal of Experimental Psychology,* 1941, *28,* 163–177.

Uhlarik, J. J. A device for presenting targets and recording positioning responses in one dimension. *Behavior Research Methods and Instrumentation,* 1972, *4,* 15–16.

Uhlarik, J. J. Role of cognitive factors on adaptation to prismatic displacement. *Journal of Experimental Psychology,* 1973, *98,* 223–232.

Uhlarik, J. J., & Canon, L. K. Effects of situational cues on prism-induced aftereffects. *Perception & Psychophysics,* 1970, *7,* 348–350.

Uhlarik, J. J., & Canon, L. K. Influence of concurrent and terminal exposure conditions on the nature of perceptual adaptation. *Journal of Experimental Psychology,* 1971, *91,* 233–239.

Underwood, B. J. Retroactive and proactive inhibition after 5 and 48 hours. *Journal of Experimental Psychology,* 1948, *38,* 29–38.

Van Laer, E. Transfer effects in adaptation to prismatic displacement. *Psychonomic Science,* 1968, *13,* 85–86.

Victor, J. The role of movement in perceptual adaptation to curvature. Unpublished doctoral dissertation, Yeshiva Univ., 1968.

Walk, R. D., & Bond, E. K. The development of visually guided reaching in monkeys reared without sight of the hands. *Psychonomic Science,* 1971, *23,* 115–116.

Walk, R. D., & Gibson, E. J. A comparative and analytical study of visual depth perception. *Psychological Monographs,* 1961, *75* (15, Whole No. 519).

Walker, J. T. A texture-contingent visual motion aftereffect. *Psychonomic Science,* 1972, *28,* 333–335.

Walker, J. T., & Shea, K. S. A tactual size aftereffect contingent on hand position. *Journal of Experimental Psychology,* 1974, *103,* 668–674.

Wallace, B. Prism adaptation to moving and stationary target exposures. *Perception,* 1975, *4,* 341–347.

Wallace, B., & Anstadt, S. P. Target location aftereffects for various age groups. *Journal of Experimental Psychology,* 1974, *103,* 175–177.

Wallace, B., & Garrett, J. B. Reduced felt arm sensation effects on visual adaptation. *Perception & Psychophysics,* 1973, *14,* 597–600.

Wallace, B., Melamed, L. E., & Cohen, R. R. An analysis of aftereffects in the measurement of the correction effect. *Perception & Psychophysics,* 1973, *14,* 21–23.

Wallace, B., Melamed, L. E., & Kaplan, C. Movement and illumination factors in adaptation to prismatic viewing. *Perception & Psychophysics,* 1973, *13,* 164–168.

Wallach, H. Informational discrepancy as a basis of perceptual adaptation. In S. J. Freedman (Ed.), *The neuropsychology of spatially oriented behavior.* Homewood, Illinois: Dorsey Press, 1968.

Wallach, H., & Bacon, J. The constancy of the orientation of the visual field, *Perception & Psychophysics,* 1976, *19,* 492–498.

Wallach, H., & Canal, T. Two kinds of adaptation in the constancy of visual direction. *Perception & Psychophysics,* 1976, *19,* 445–449.

Wallach, H., & Flaherty, E. W. Rapid adaptation to a prismatic distortion. *Perception & Psychophysics,* 1976, *19,* 261–266.

Wallach, H., & Floor, L. On the relation of adaptation to field displacement during head movements to the constancy of visual direction. *Perception & Psychophysics,* 1970, *8,* 95–98.

Wallach, H., & Frey, K. J. Adaptation in the constancy of visual direction measured by a one-trial method. *Perception & Psychophysics,* 1969, *5,* 249–252.

Wallach, H, & Frey, K. J. Differences in the dissipation of the effect of adaptation to two kinds of field displacement during head movements. *Perception & Psychophysics,* 1972, *11,* 31–34. (a)

Wallach, H., & Frey, K. J. Adaptation in distance perception based on oculomotor cues. *Perception & Psychophysics,* 1972, *11,* 77–83. (b)

Wallach, H., & Frey, K. J. On counteradaptation. *Perception & Psychophysics,* 1972, *11,* 161–165. (c)

Wallach, H., Frey, K. J., and Bode, K. A. The nature of adaptation in distance perception based on oculomotor cues. *Perception & Psychophysics,* 1972, *11,* 110–116.

Wallach, H., Frey, K. J., & Romney, G. Adaptation to field displacement during head movement unrelated to the constancy of visual direction. *Perception & Psychophysics,* 1969, *5,* 253–256.

Wallach, H., & Karsh, E. B. Why the modification of stereoscopic depth-perception is so rapid. *American Journal of Psychology*, 1963, *76*, 413–420. (a)

Wallach, H., & Karsh, E. B. The modification of stereoscopic depth perception and the kinetic depth effect. *American Journal of Psychology*, 1963, *76*, 429–435. (b)

Wallach, H., & Kravitz, J. H. The measurement of the constancy of visual direction and of its adaptation. *Psychonomic Science*, 1965, *2*, 217–218. (a)

Wallach, H., and Kravitz, J. H. Rapid adaptation in the constancy of visual direction with active and passive rotation. *Psychonomic Science*, 1965, *3*, 165–166. (b)

Wallach, H., & Kravitz, J. H. Adaptation in the constancy of visual direction tested by measuring the constancy of auditory direction. *Perception & Psychophysics*, 1968, *4*, 299–303.

Wallach, H., Kravitz, J. H., & Landauer, J. A passive condition for rapid adaptation to displaced visual direction. *American Journal of Psychology*, 1963, *76*, 568–578.

Wallach, H., & Lewis, C. The effect of abnormal displacement of the retinal image during eye movements. *Perception & Psychophysics*, 1965, *1*, 25–29.

Wallach, H., Moore, M. E., & Davidson, L. Modification of stereoscopic depth perception. *American Journal of Psychology*, 1963, *76*, 191–204.

Wallach, H., & O'Connell, D. N. The kinetic depth effect. *Journal of Experimental Psychology*, 1953, *45*, 205–217.

Wallach, H., & Smith, A. Visual and proprioceptive adaptation to altered oculomotor adjustments. *Perception & Psychophysics*, 1972, *11*, 413–416.

Wallach, H., & Zuckerman, C. The constancy of stereoscopic depth. *American Journal of Psychology*, 1963, *76*, 404–412.

Walls, G. L. The problem of visual direction. *American Journal of Optometry*, 1951, *28*, 55–83, 115–146, 173–212.

Warren, D. H., & Cleaves, W. T. Visual-proprioceptive interaction under large amounts of conflict. *Journal of Experimental Psychology*, 1971, *90*, 206–214.

Warren, D. H., & Platt, B. B. The subject: A neglected factor in recombination research. *Perception*, 1974, *3*, 421–438.

Warren, D. H., & Platt, B. B. Understanding prism adaptation: An individual differences approach. *Perception & Psychophysics*, 1975, *17*, 337–345.

Weber, R. B., & Daroff, R. B. Corrective movements following refixation saccades: Type and control system analysis. *Vision Research*, 1972, *12*, 467–475.

Webster, R. G. The relationship between cognitive, motor-kinesthetic, and oculomotor adaptation. *Perception & Psychophysics*, 1969, *6*, 33–38.

Weerts, T. C., & Thurlow, W. R. The effects of eye position and expectation on sound localization. *Perception & Psychophysics*, 1971, *9*, 35–39.

Weinstein, S., Sersen, E. A., Fisher, L., & Weisinger, M. Is reafference necessary for visual adaptation? *Perceptual and Motor Skills*, 1964, *18*, 641–648.

Weinstein, S., Sersen, E. A., & Weinstein, D. S. An attempt to replicate a study of disarranged eye-hand coordination. *Perceptual and Motor Skills*, 1964, *18*, 629–632.

Weinstein, S., Richlin, M., Weisinger, M., & Fisher, L. Adaptation to visual and nonvisual rearrangement. NASA Contractor Report No. 663, 1967.

Weiss, P. A. Further experimental investigation on the phenomenon of homologous response in transplanted amphibian limbs: I. Functional observations. *Journal of Comparative Neurology*, 1937, *66*, 181–209. (a)

Weiss, P. A. Further experimental investigation on the phenomenon of homologous response in transplanted amphibian limbs: IV. Reverse locomotion after the interchange of right and left limbs. *Journal of Comparative Neurology*, 1937, *7*, 269–315. (b)

Weiss, P. A. Self-differentiation of the basic patterns of coordination. *Comparative Psychology Monograph,* 1941, *17,* 1–96.

Welch, R. B. Adaptation to prism-displaced vision: The importance of target pointing. *Perception & Psychophysics,* 1969, *5,* 305–309.

Welch, R. B. Prism adaptation: The "target-pointing effect" as a function of exposure trials. *Perception & Psychophysics,* 1971, *9,* 102–104. (a)

Welch, R. B. Discriminative conditioning of prism adaptation. *Perception & Psychophysics,* 1971, *10,* 90–92. (b)

Welch, R. B. The effect of experienced limb identity upon adaptation to simulated displacement of the visual field. *Perception & Psychophysics,* 1972, *12,* 453–456.

Welch, R. B. Research on adaptation to rearranged vision: 1966–1974. *Perception,* 1974, *3,* 367–392. (a)

Welch, R. B. Speculations on a model of prism adaptation. *Perception,* 1974, *3,* 451–460. (b)

Welch, R. B., & Abel, M. R. The generality of the "target-pointing effect" in prism adaptation. *Psychonomic Science,* 1970, *20,* 226–227.

Welch, R. B., Bleam, R. J., & Needham, S. A. The postexposure decline of prism adaptation. Unpublished manuscript, Univ. of Kansas, 1970.

Welch, R. B., Choe, C. S., & Heinrich, D..R. Evidence for a three-component model of prism adaptation. *Journal of Experimental Psychology,* 1974, *103,* 700–705.

Welch, R. B., & Goldstein, G. Prism adaptation and brain damage. *Neuropsychologia,* 1972, *10,* 387–394.

Welch, R. B., & Rhoades, R. W. The manipulation of informational feedback and its effects upon prism adaptation. *Canadian Journal of Psychology,* 1969, *23,* 415–428.

Welch, R. B., Widawski, M. H., & Matthews, J. A test of the relationship between visual capture and prism adaptation. Paper presented at meetings of Psychonomic Society, Denver, November, 1975.

Wertheimer, M. Psychomotor co-ordination of auditory-visual space at birth. *Science,* 1961, *134,* 1692.

Wertheimer, M., & Arena, A. J. Effect of exposure time on adaptation to disarranged hand-eye coordination. *Perceptual and Motor Skills,* 1959, *9,* 159–164.

Wheatstone, C. On some remarkable and hitherto unobserved phenomena of binocular vision: Part 2. *Philosophical Magazine.* 1852, *4,* 504–523.

White, B. L., & Castle, P. Visual exploratory behavior following postnatal handling of human infants. *Perceptual and Motor Skills,* 1964, *18,* 497–502.

White, B. L., Castle, P., & Held, R. Observations on the development of visually-directed reaching. *Child Development,* 1964, *35,* 349–364.

White, B. L., & Held, R. Plasticity of sensorimotor development. In J. F. Rosenblith & W. Allinsmith (Eds.), *The causes of behavior: Readings on child development and educational psychology.* Boston: Allyn and Bacon, 1966.

Wilkinson, D. A. Visual-motor control loop: A linear system? *Journal of Experimental Psychology,* 1971, *89,* 250–257.

Willey, C. F., Inglis, E., & Pearce, C. H. Reversal of auditory localization. *Journal of Experimental Psychology,* 1937, *20,* 114–130.

Witkin, H. A., & Asch, S. E. Studies in space orientation: III. Perception of the upright in the absence of a visual field. *Journal of Experimental Psychology,* 1948, *38,* 603–614.

Witkin, H. A., Dyk, R., Faterson, H., Goodenough, D. R., & Karp, S. A. *Psychological differentiation: Studies of development.* New York: Wiley, 1962.

Witkin, H. A., Wapner, S., & Leventhal, T. Sound localization with conflicting visual and auditory cues. *Journal of Experimental Psychology,* 1952, *43,* 58–67.

Wohlwill, J. F. Perceptual learning. *Annual Review of Psychology,* 1966, *17,* 201–232.

Wolf, I. S., & Kellogg, W. N. Changes in general behavior during flexion conditioning and their importance for the learning process. *American Journal of Psychology,* 1940, *53,* 384–396.

Woodley, J. D., & Ross, H. E. Distance estimates of familiar objects underwater. *Underwater Association Report,* 1969, *4,* 58–61.

Woods, J. D., & Lythgoe, J. N. (Eds.), *Underwater science.* London: Oxford Univ. Press, 1971.

Wooster, M. Certain factors in the development of a new spatial coordination. *Psychological Monographs,* 1923, *32* (4, Whole No. 146).

Workman, R. D., & Prickett, C. M. Visual field perimeter and distortion in diving masks. Washington, D.C.: U.S. Navy Experimental Diving Unit, Rep. No. 4-57, 1957.

Yarbus, A. L. *Eye movements and vision.* New York: Plenum Press, 1967.

Young, P. T. Auditory localization with acoustical transposition of the ears. *Journal of Experimental Psychology,* 1928, *11,* 399–429.

Author Index

329

Subject Index

A

Accommodation, 180, 181, 187, 188, 192, 193, 194
Active versus passive movement, *see also* Reafference hypothesis
    auditory displacement adaptation and, 222–224
    neonatal development and, *see* Visuomotor coordination, neonatal development of
    prism adaptation and, 22–28, 44, 45, 73, 93
    tilt adaptation and, 125, 144–146, 156
Adaptation, *see also* names of specific varieties of adaptation
    acquisition functions of, 82–83, 278, 297
    age of subject and, 248–250, 252
    avoidance learning and, 106
    awareness of intersensory discordance and, 9, 281, 282
    body growth and, 292
    brain damage and, 251–252
    conditioning of, *see* Conditioned adaptation
    conscious corrective strategy in, 8–9, 249
    decay and decay functions of, 9, 83–86, 297, *see also* names of specific varieties of adaptation

definition of, 8–10, 48
delay of feedback and, 103–105, 107, *see also* Prism adaptation, delay of feedback and
egocentric localization and, 293–294
felt body position and, 294
felt eye position and, 294
form perception and, 296–297
future research in, 300–301
future research in perception and, 301
general model of, 279–286, *see also* Adaptation; and names of specific varieties of adaptation
    awareness of discordance and, 281, 282
    concurrent versus terminal exposure and, 285
    drive state and, 279, 280–281, 282, 285, *see also* Adaptation, motivation and
    end products and, 282–284
    flow chart of, 283
    habituation and, 279, 281–282
    incremental exposure and, 284
    massed versus distributed practice and, 285
    memory traces and, 281–282, 285
    predictions and support for, 284–286
    registered discrepancy and, 280
    terminal versus concurrent exposure and, 285